THE·RING·OF·THE·NIBELUNG

·VOLUME TWO·

BASED ON THE MUSIC DRAMAS OF RICHARD WAGNER

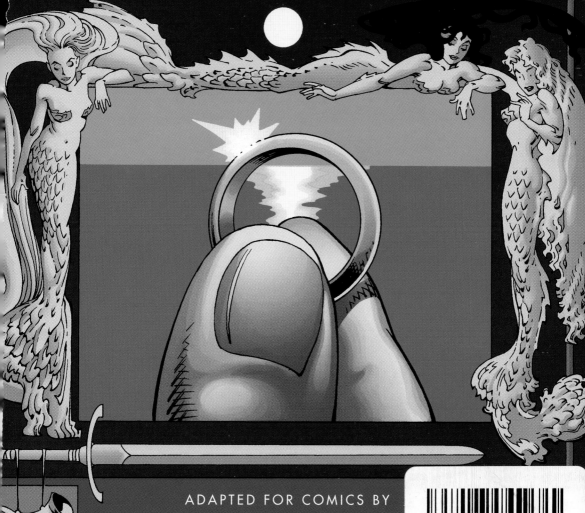

ADAPTED FOR COMICS BY
P. CRAIG RUSSELL

translated by
PATRICK
MASON

colored by
LOVERN
KINDZIERSKI

lettered by
GALEN
SHOWMAN

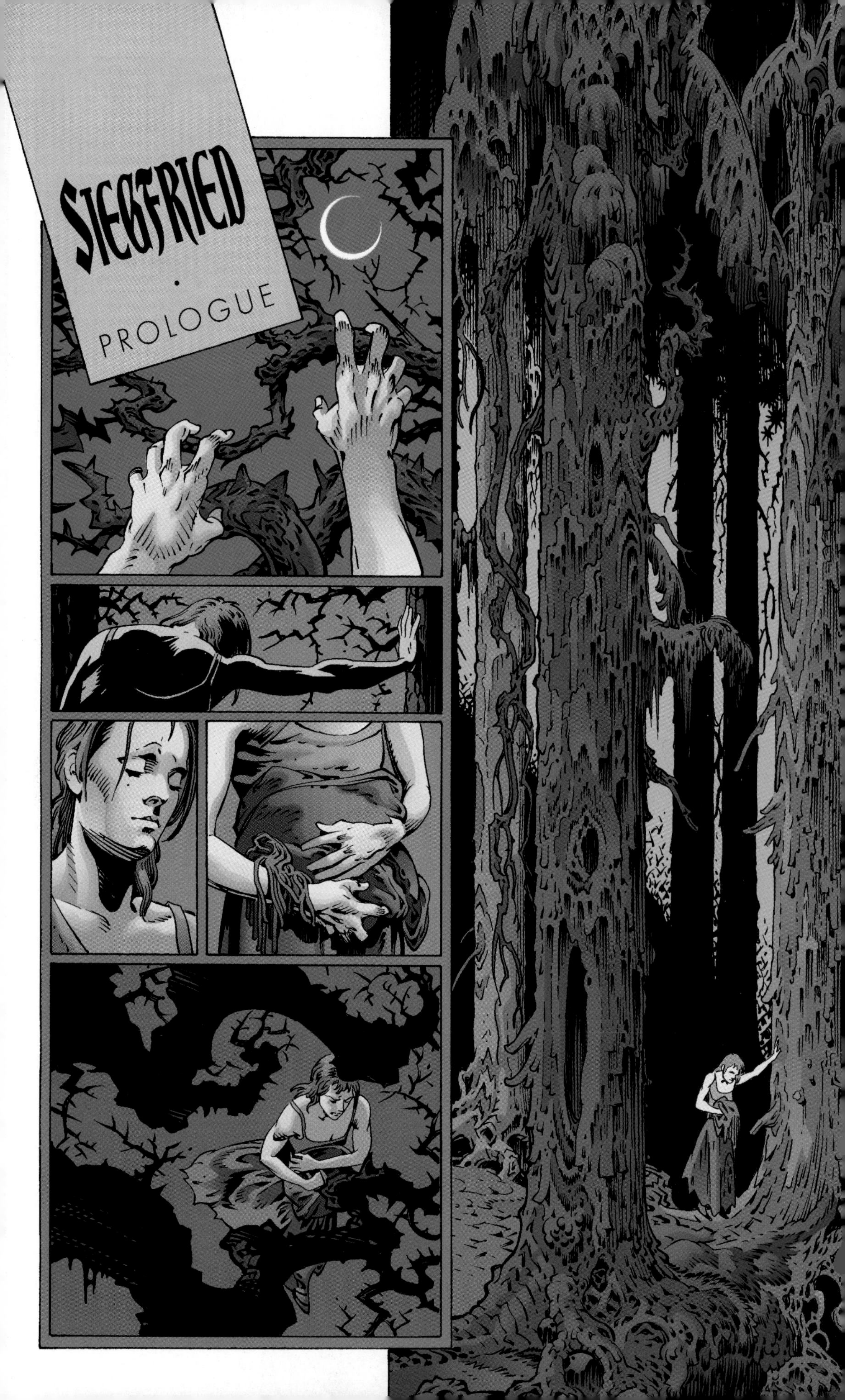
SIEGFRIED
•
PROLOGUE

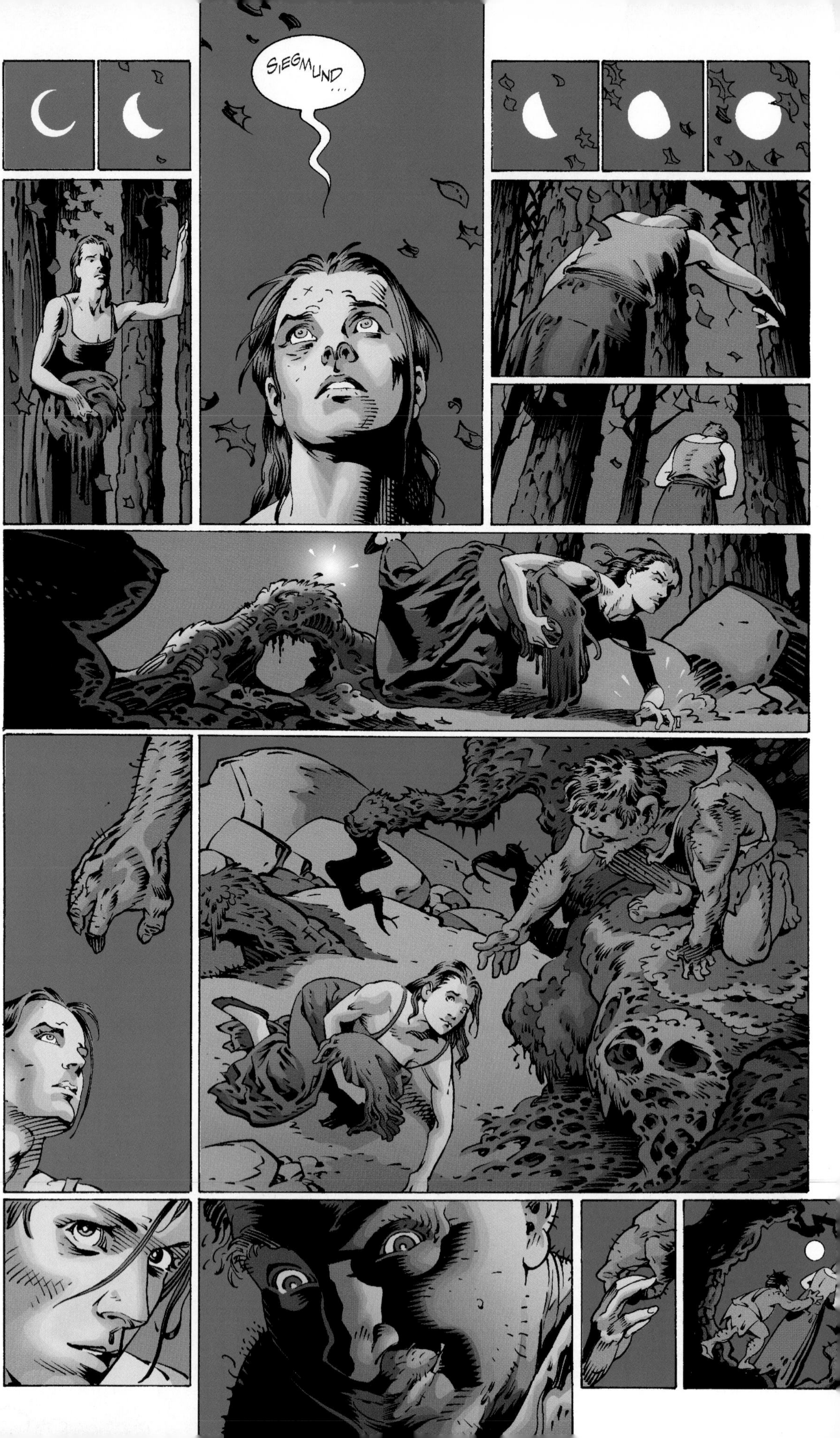
SIEGMUND ...

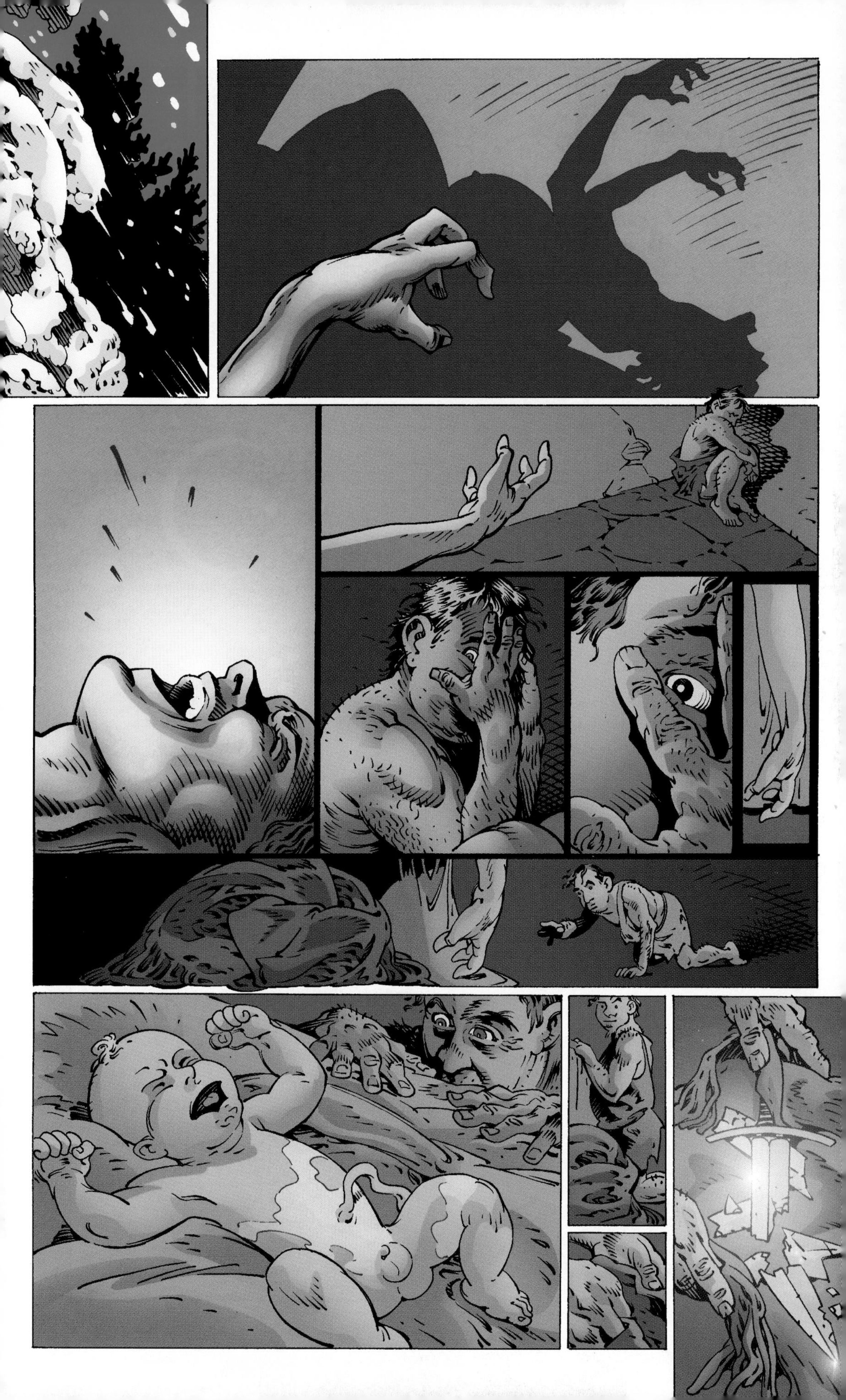

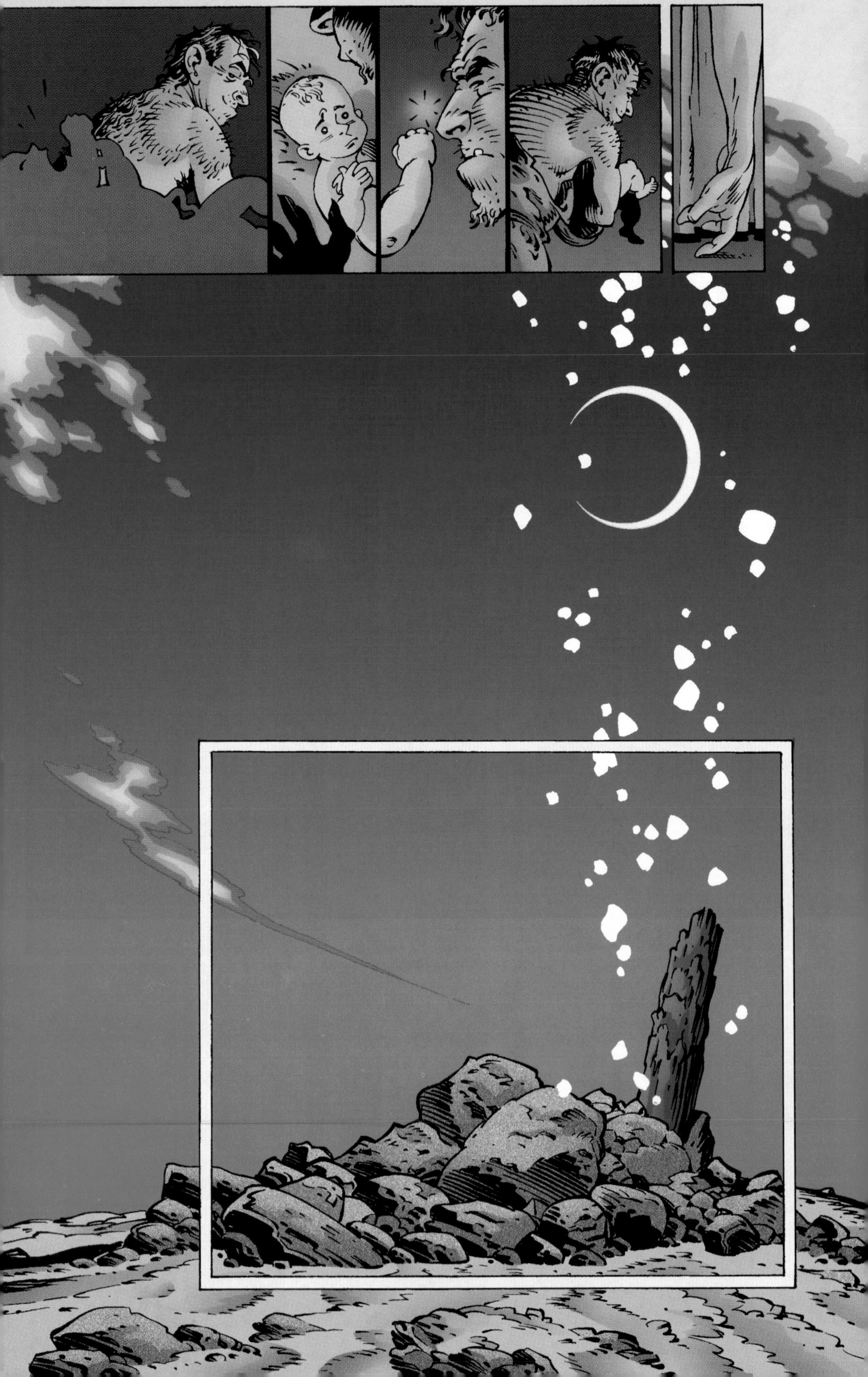

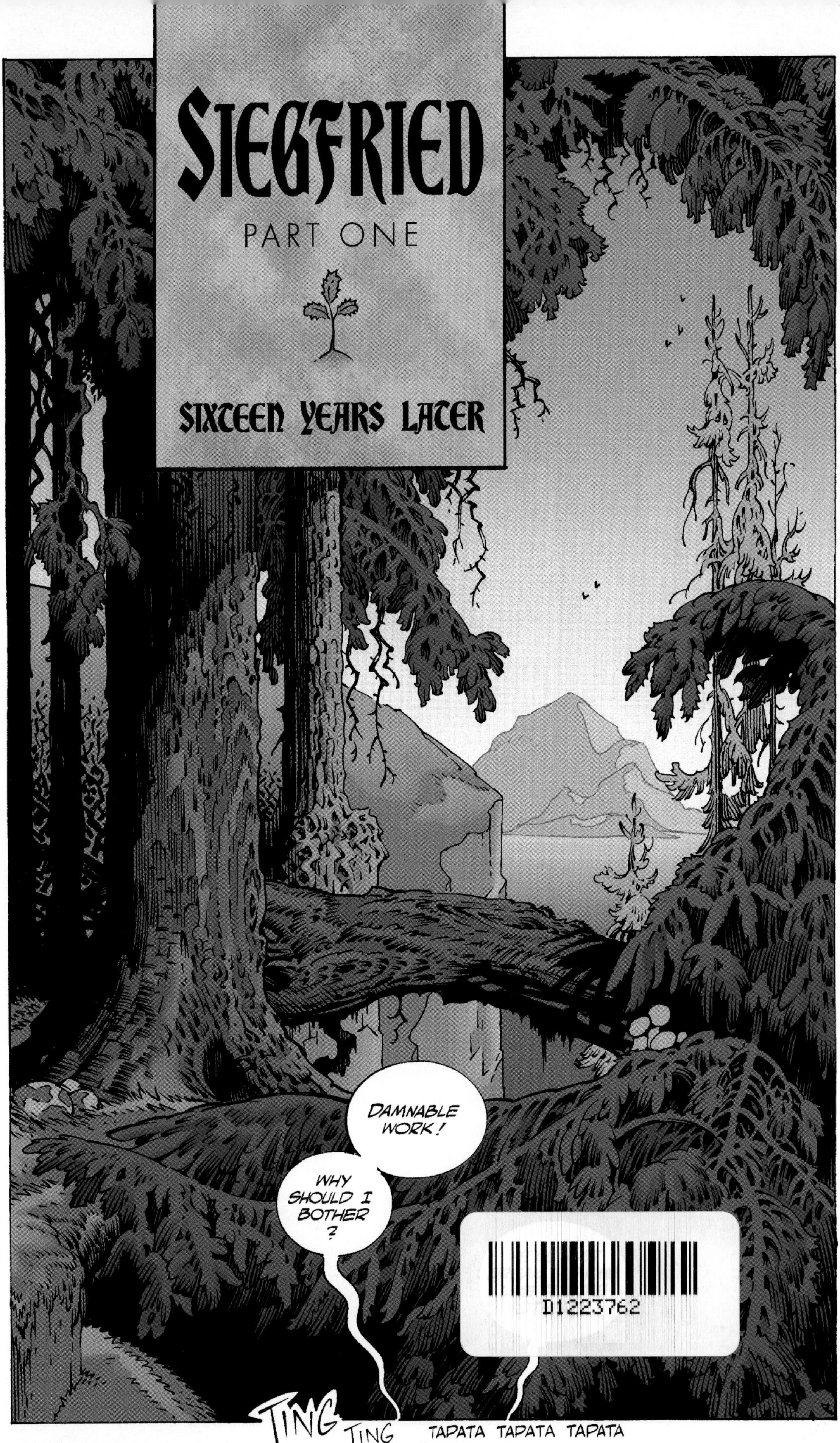
SIEGFRIED
PART ONE
SIXTEEN YEARS LATER
DAMNABLE WORK!
WHY SHOULD I BOTHER?
TING
TING
TING
TAPATA TAPATA TAPATA

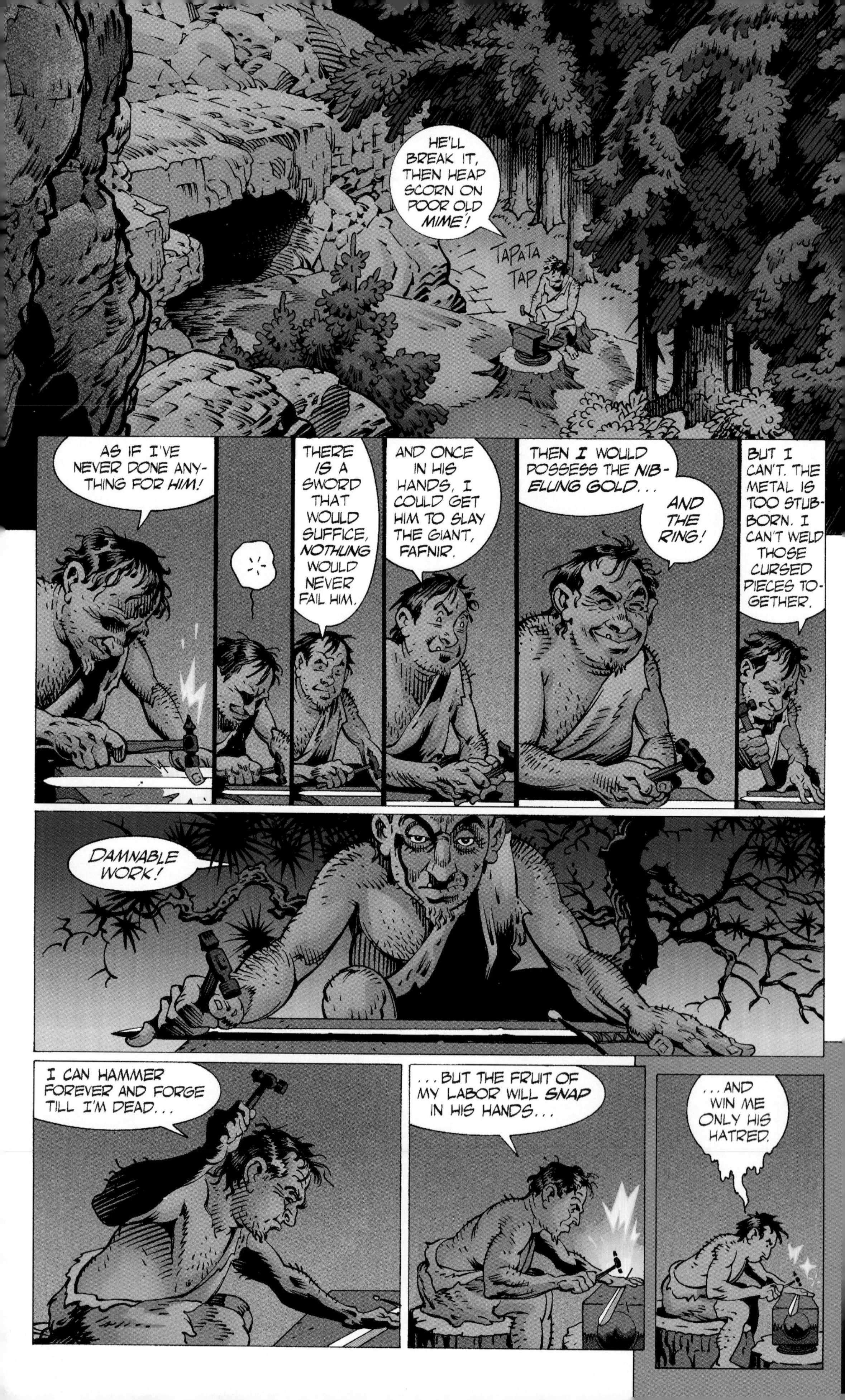
HE'LL BREAK IT, THEN HEAP SCORN ON POOR OLD MIME!
TAPATA TAP
AS IF I'VE NEVER DONE ANYTHING FOR HIM!
THERE IS A SWORD THAT WOULD SUFFICE, NOTHUNG WOULD NEVER FAIL HIM.
AND ONCE IN HIS HANDS, I COULD GET HIM TO SLAY THE GIANT, FAFNIR.
THEN I WOULD POSSESS THE NIBELUNG GOLD...
AND THE RING!
BUT I CAN'T. THE METAL IS TOO STUBBORN. I CAN'T WELD THOSE CURSED PIECES TOGETHER.
DAMNABLE WORK!
I CAN HAMMER FOREVER AND FORGE TILL I'M DEAD...
...BUT THE FRUIT OF MY LABOR WILL SNAP IN HIS HANDS...
...AND WIN ME ONLY HIS HATRED.

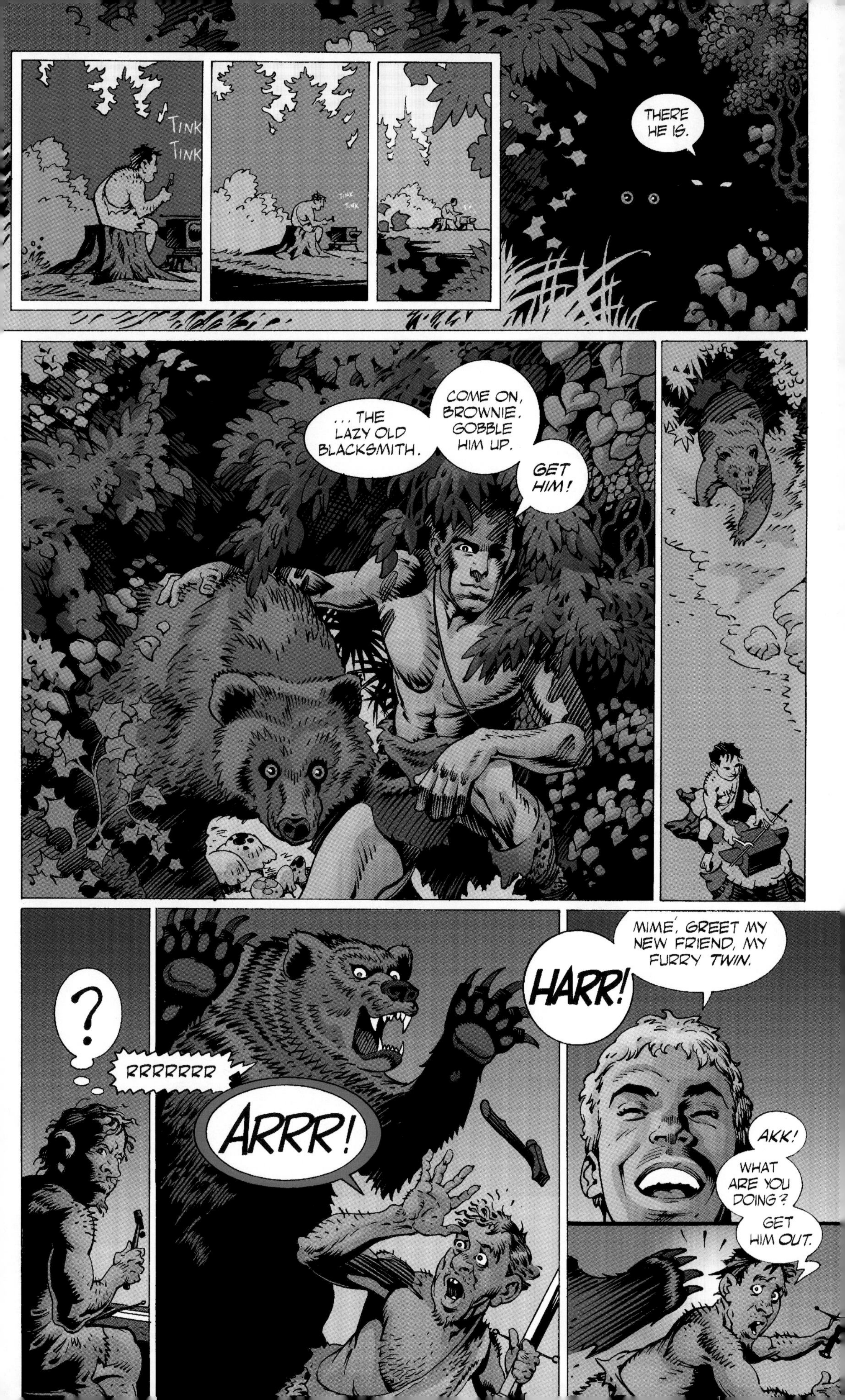
TINK
TINK
TINK
TINK
THERE HE IS.
...THE LAZY OLD BLACKSMITH.
COME ON, BROWNIE. GOBBLE HIM UP.
GET HIM!
?
RRRRRRR
ARRR!
HARR!
MIME, GREET MY NEW FRIEND, MY FURRY TWIN.
AKK!
WHAT ARE YOU DOING?
GET HIM OUT.

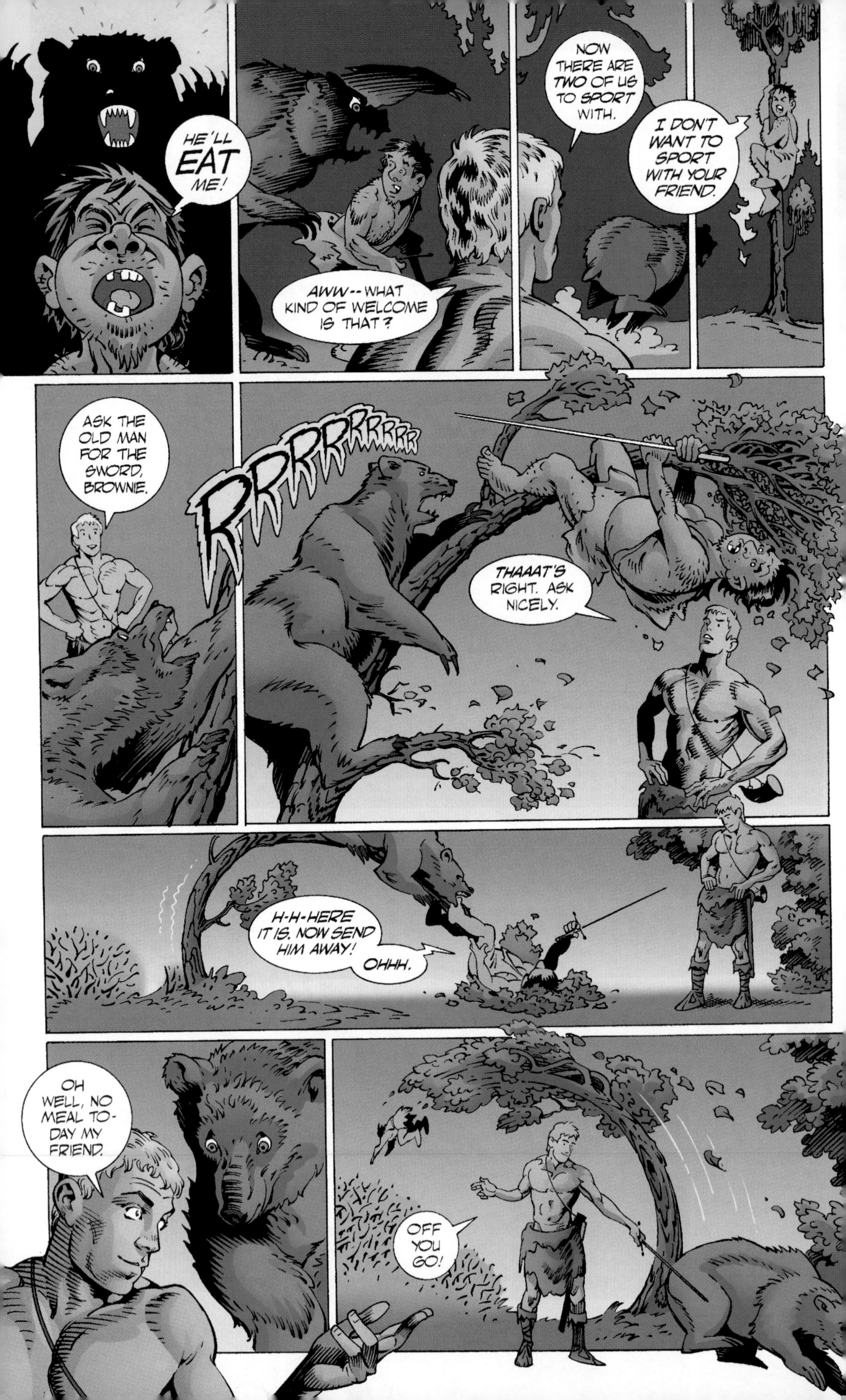
HE'LL EAT ME!
AWW--WHAT KIND OF WELCOME IS THAT?
NOW THERE ARE TWO OF US TO SPORT WITH.
I DON'T WANT TO SPORT WITH YOUR FRIEND.
ASK THE OLD MAN FOR THE SWORD, BROWNIE.
RRRRRRRRRRR
THAAAT'S RIGHT. ASK NICELY.
H-H-HERE IT IS. NOW SEND HIM AWAY!
OHHH.
OH WELL, NO MEAL TO-DAY MY FRIEND.
OFF YOU GO!

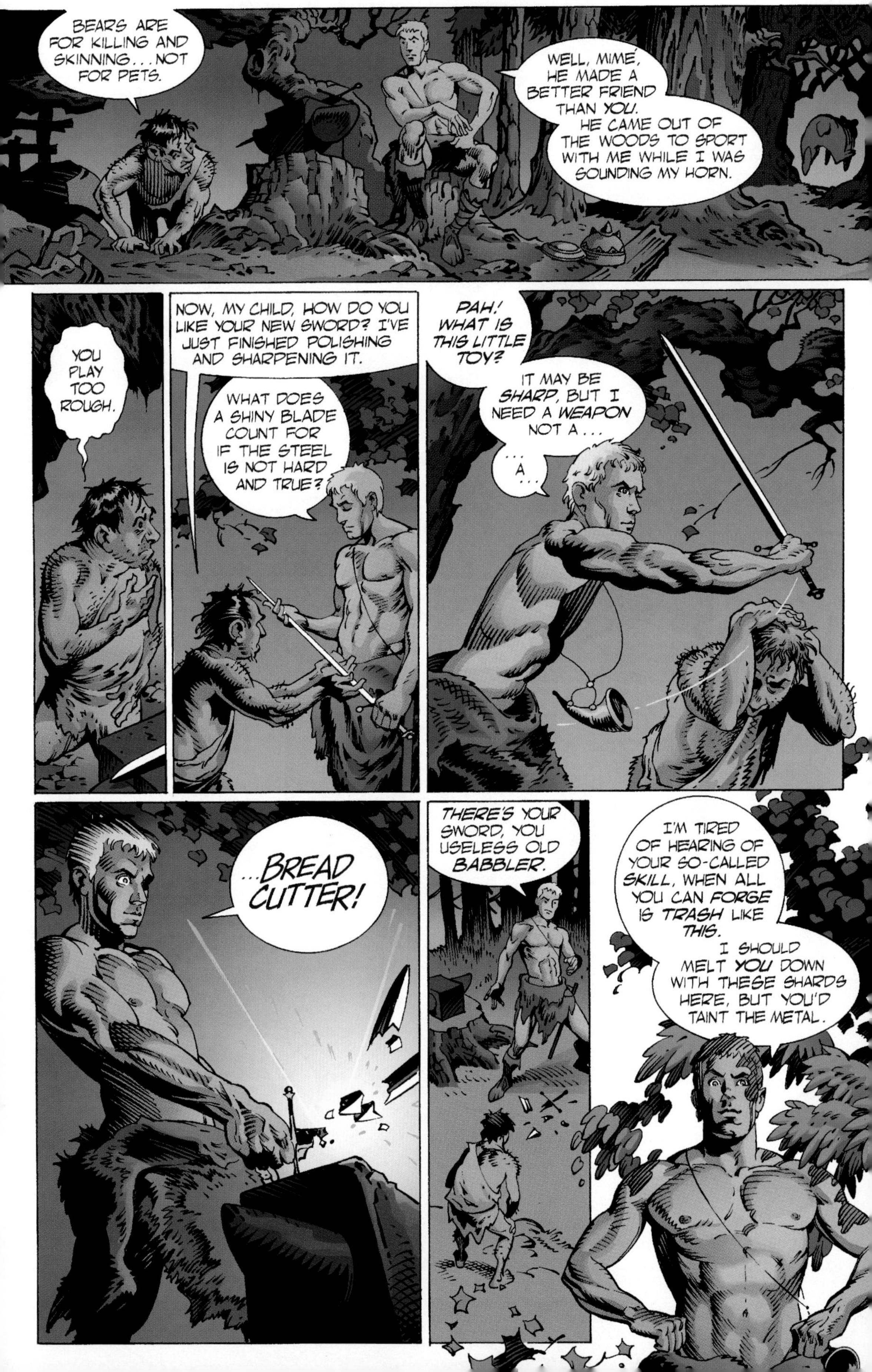
BEARS ARE FOR KILLING AND SKINNING... NOT FOR PETS.
WELL, MIMÉ, HE MADE A BETTER FRIEND THAN YOU.
HE CAME OUT OF THE WOODS TO SPORT WITH ME WHILE I WAS SOUNDING MY HORN.
YOU PLAY TOO ROUGH.
NOW, MY CHILD, HOW DO YOU LIKE YOUR NEW SWORD? I'VE JUST FINISHED POLISHING AND SHARPENING IT.
WHAT DOES A SHINY BLADE COUNT FOR IF THE STEEL IS NOT HARD AND TRUE?
PAH! WHAT IS THIS LITTLE TOY?
IT MAY BE SHARP, BUT I NEED A WEAPON NOT A...
... A ...
...BREAD CUTTER!
THERE'S YOUR SWORD, YOU USELESS OLD BABBLER.
I'M TIRED OF HEARING OF YOUR SO-CALLED SKILL, WHEN ALL YOU CAN FORGE IS TRASH LIKE THIS.
I SHOULD MELT YOU DOWN WITH THESE SHARDS HERE, BUT YOU'D TAINT THE METAL.

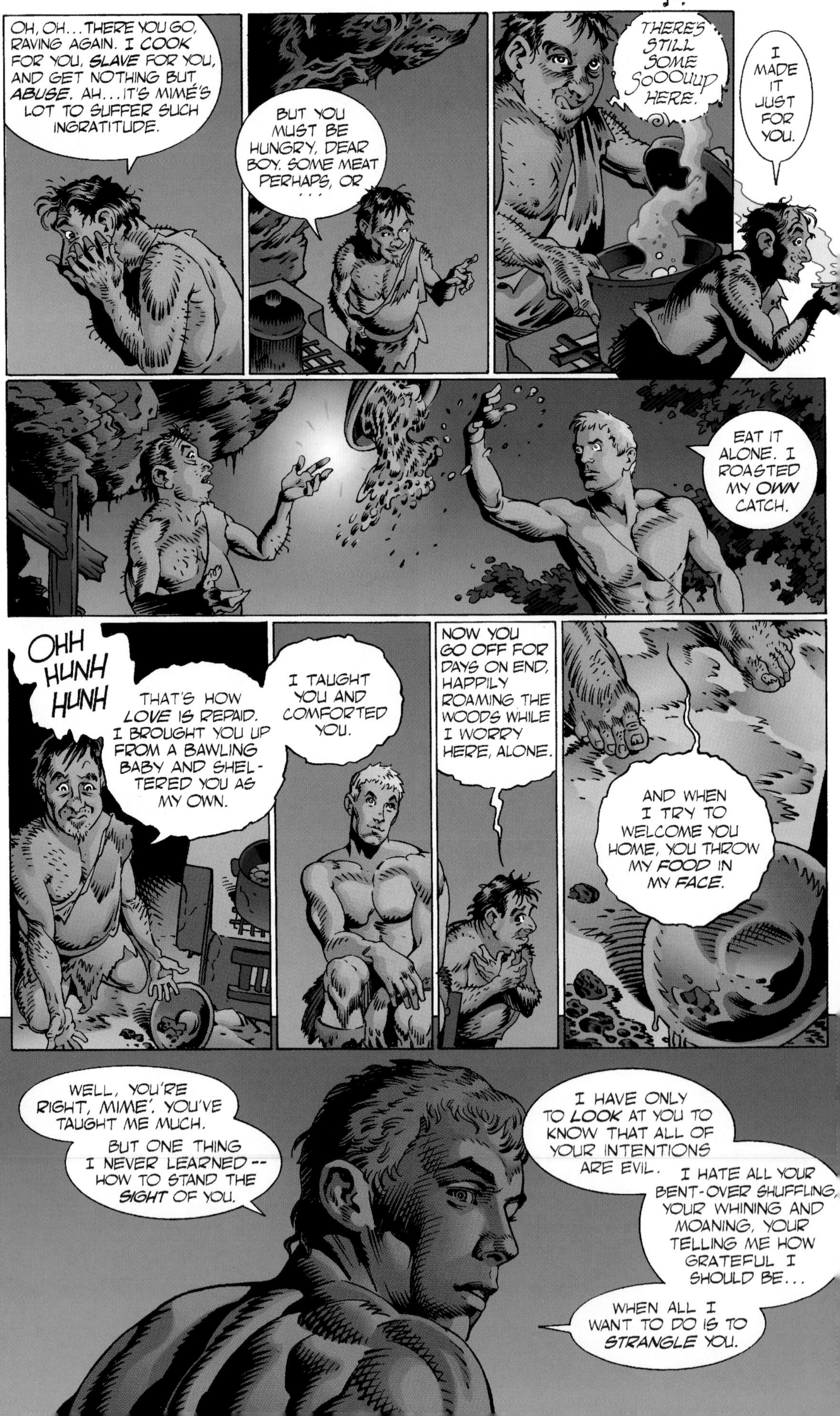
OH, OH...THERE YOU GO, RAVING AGAIN. I COOK FOR YOU, SLAVE FOR YOU, AND GET NOTHING BUT ABUSE. AH...IT'S MIMÉ'S LOT TO SUFFER SUCH INGRATITUDE.
BUT YOU MUST BE HUNGRY, DEAR BOY. SOME MEAT PERHAPS, OR ...
THERE'S STILL SOME SoOOuup HERE.
I MADE IT JUST FOR YOU.
EAT IT ALONE. I ROASTED MY OWN CATCH.
OHH HUNH HUNH
THAT'S HOW LOVE IS REPAID. I BROUGHT YOU UP FROM A BAWLING BABY AND SHEL-TERED YOU AS MY OWN.
I TAUGHT YOU AND COMFORTED YOU.
NOW YOU GO OFF FOR DAYS ON END, HAPPILY ROAMING THE WOODS WHILE I WORRY HERE, ALONE.
AND WHEN I TRY TO WELCOME YOU HOME, YOU THROW MY FOOD IN MY FACE.
WELL, YOU'RE RIGHT, MIME'. YOU'VE TAUGHT ME MUCH.
BUT ONE THING I NEVER LEARNED -- HOW TO STAND THE SIGHT OF YOU.
I HAVE ONLY TO LOOK AT YOU TO KNOW THAT ALL OF YOUR INTENTIONS ARE EVIL.
I HATE ALL YOUR BENT-OVER SHUFFLING, YOUR WHINING AND MOANING, YOUR TELLING ME HOW GRATEFUL I SHOULD BE...
WHEN ALL I WANT TO DO IS TO STRANGLE YOU.

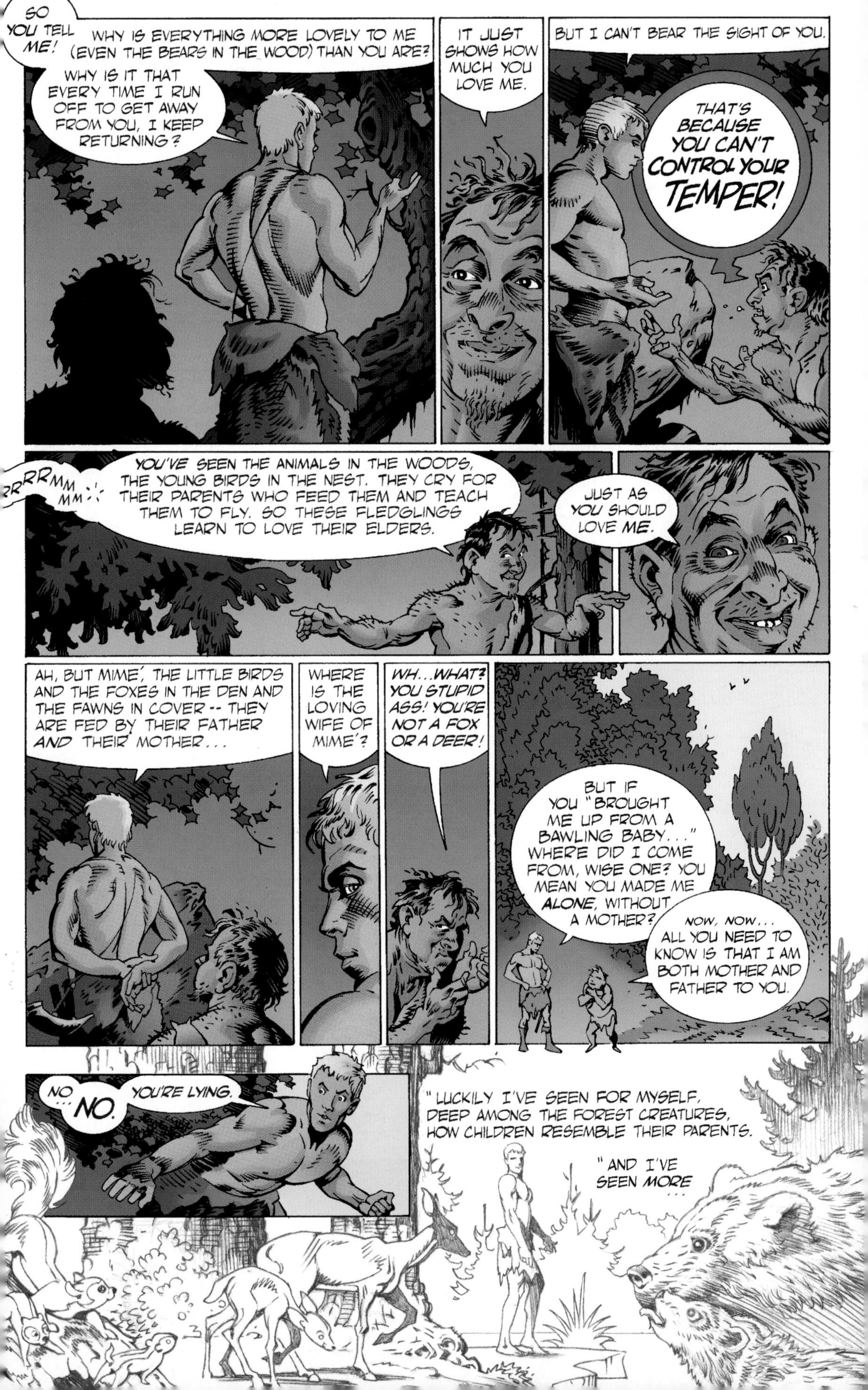

SO YOU TELL ME!
WHY IS EVERYTHING MORE LOVELY TO ME (EVEN THE BEARS IN THE WOOD) THAN YOU ARE?
WHY IS IT THAT EVERY TIME I RUN OFF TO GET AWAY FROM YOU, I KEEP RETURNING?
IT JUST SHOWS HOW MUCH YOU LOVE ME.
BUT I CAN'T BEAR THE SIGHT OF YOU.
THAT'S BECAUSE YOU CAN'T CONTROL YOUR TEMPER!
RRRRMM MM
YOU'VE SEEN THE ANIMALS IN THE WOODS, THE YOUNG BIRDS IN THE NEST. THEY CRY FOR THEIR PARENTS WHO FEED THEM AND TEACH THEM TO FLY. SO THESE FLEDGLINGS LEARN TO LOVE THEIR ELDERS.
JUST AS YOU SHOULD LOVE ME.
AH, BUT MIME, THE LITTLE BIRDS AND THE FOXES IN THE DEN AND THE FAWNS IN COVER -- THEY ARE FED BY THEIR FATHER AND THEIR MOTHER...
WHERE IS THE LOVING WIFE OF MIME?
WH...WHAT? YOU STUPID ASS! YOU'RE NOT A FOX OR A DEER!
BUT IF YOU "BROUGHT ME UP FROM A BAWLING BABY..." WHERE DID I COME FROM, WISE ONE? YOU MEAN YOU MADE ME ALONE, WITHOUT A MOTHER?
NOW, NOW... ALL YOU NEED TO KNOW IS THAT I AM BOTH MOTHER AND FATHER TO YOU.
NO... NO. YOU'RE LYING.
"LUCKILY I'VE SEEN FOR MYSELF, DEEP AMONG THE FOREST CREATURES, HOW CHILDREN RESEMBLE THEIR PARENTS.
"AND I'VE SEEN MORE ...

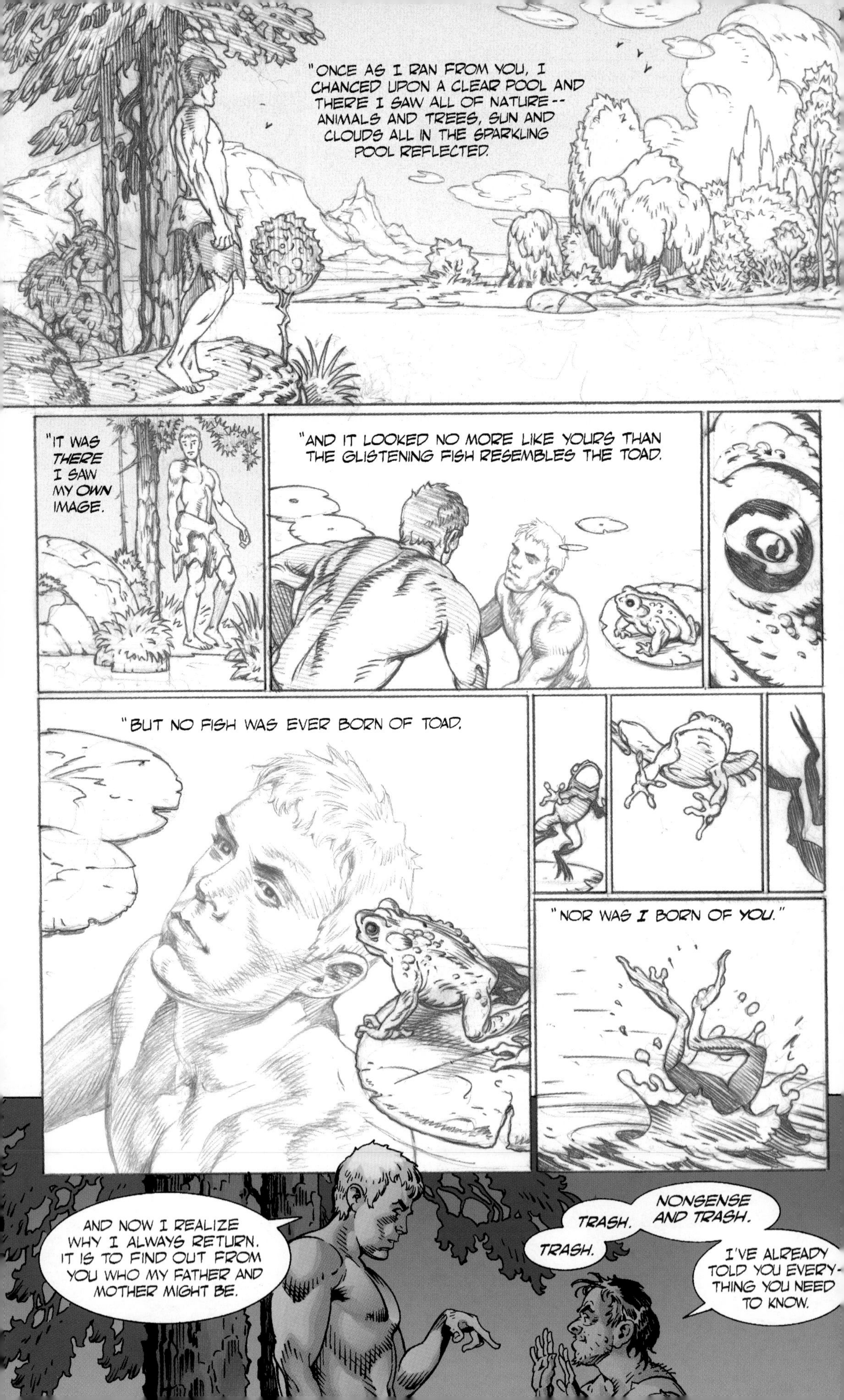
"ONCE AS I RAN FROM YOU, I CHANCED UPON A CLEAR POOL AND THERE I SAW ALL OF NATURE-- ANIMALS AND TREES, SUN AND CLOUDS ALL IN THE SPARKLING POOL REFLECTED.
"IT WAS THERE I SAW MY OWN IMAGE.
"AND IT LOOKED NO MORE LIKE YOURS THAN THE GLISTENING FISH RESEMBLES THE TOAD.
"BUT NO FISH WAS EVER BORN OF TOAD.
"NOR WAS I BORN OF YOU."
AND NOW I REALIZE WHY I ALWAYS RETURN. IT IS TO FIND OUT FROM YOU WHO MY FATHER AND MOTHER MIGHT BE.
NONSENSE AND TRASH.
TRASH.
TRASH.
I'VE ALREADY TOLD YOU EVERY-THING YOU NEED TO KNOW.

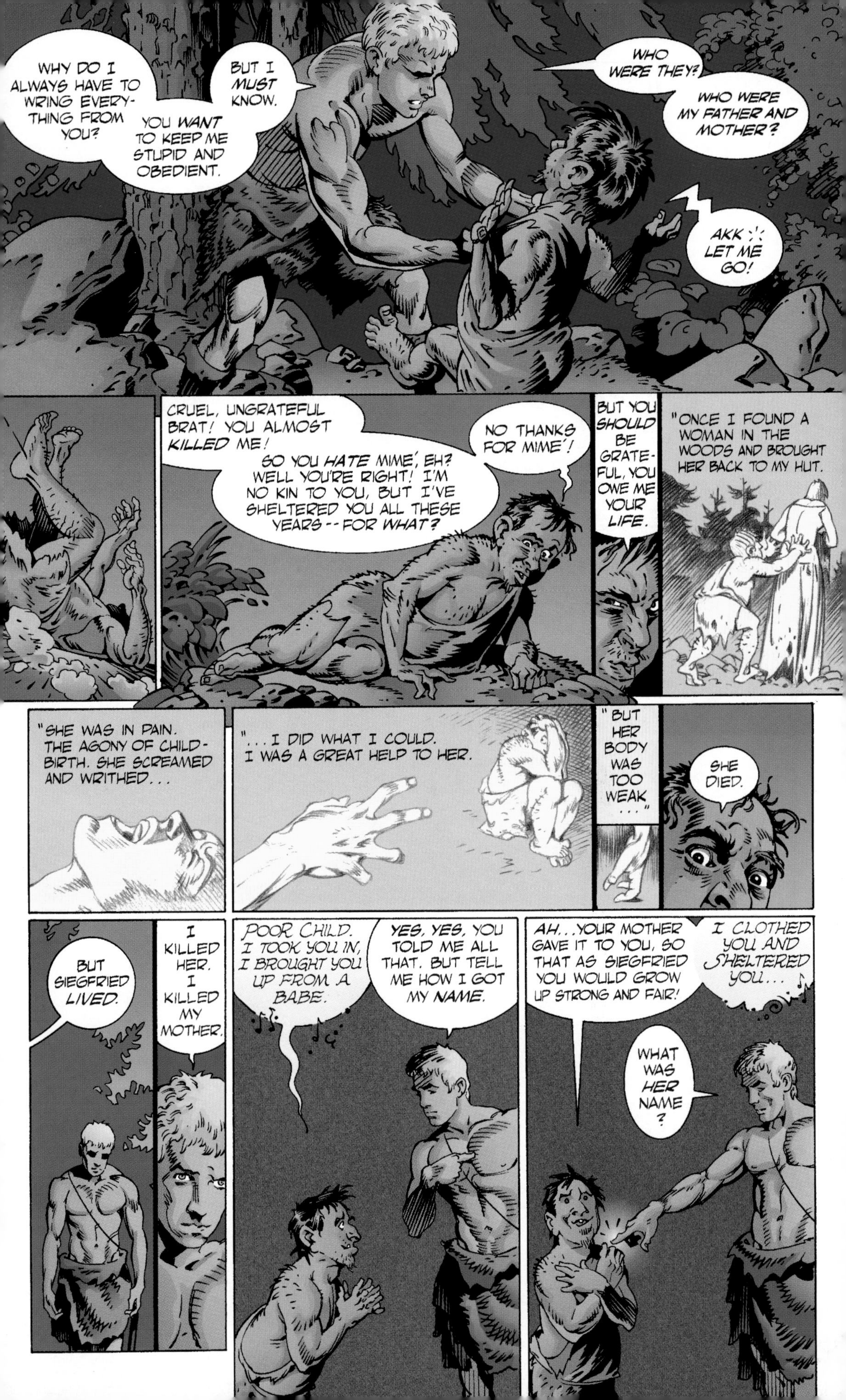

WHY DO I ALWAYS HAVE TO WRING EVERY-THING FROM YOU?
YOU WANT TO KEEP ME STUPID AND OBEDIENT.
BUT I MUST KNOW.
WHO WERE THEY?
WHO WERE MY FATHER AND MOTHER?
AKK! LET ME GO!
CRUEL, UNGRATEFUL BRAT! YOU ALMOST KILLED ME!
SO YOU HATE MIME, EH? WELL YOU'RE RIGHT! I'M NO KIN TO YOU, BUT I'VE SHELTERED YOU ALL THESE YEARS -- FOR WHAT?
NO THANKS FOR MIME!
BUT YOU SHOULD BE GRATE-FUL, YOU OWE ME YOUR LIFE.
"ONCE I FOUND A WOMAN IN THE WOODS AND BROUGHT HER BACK TO MY HUT.
"SHE WAS IN PAIN. THE AGONY OF CHILD-BIRTH. SHE SCREAMED AND WRITHED...
"...I DID WHAT I COULD. I WAS A GREAT HELP TO HER.
"BUT HER BODY WAS TOO WEAK..."
SHE DIED.
BUT SIEGFRIED LIVED.
I KILLED HER. I KILLED MY MOTHER.
POOR CHILD. I TOOK YOU IN, I BROUGHT YOU UP FROM A BABE.
YES, YES, YOU TOLD ME ALL THAT. BUT TELL ME HOW I GOT MY NAME.
AH...YOUR MOTHER GAVE IT TO YOU, SO THAT AS SIEGFRIED YOU WOULD GROW UP STRONG AND FAIR!
I CLOTHED YOU AND SHELTERED YOU...
WHAT WAS HER NAME?

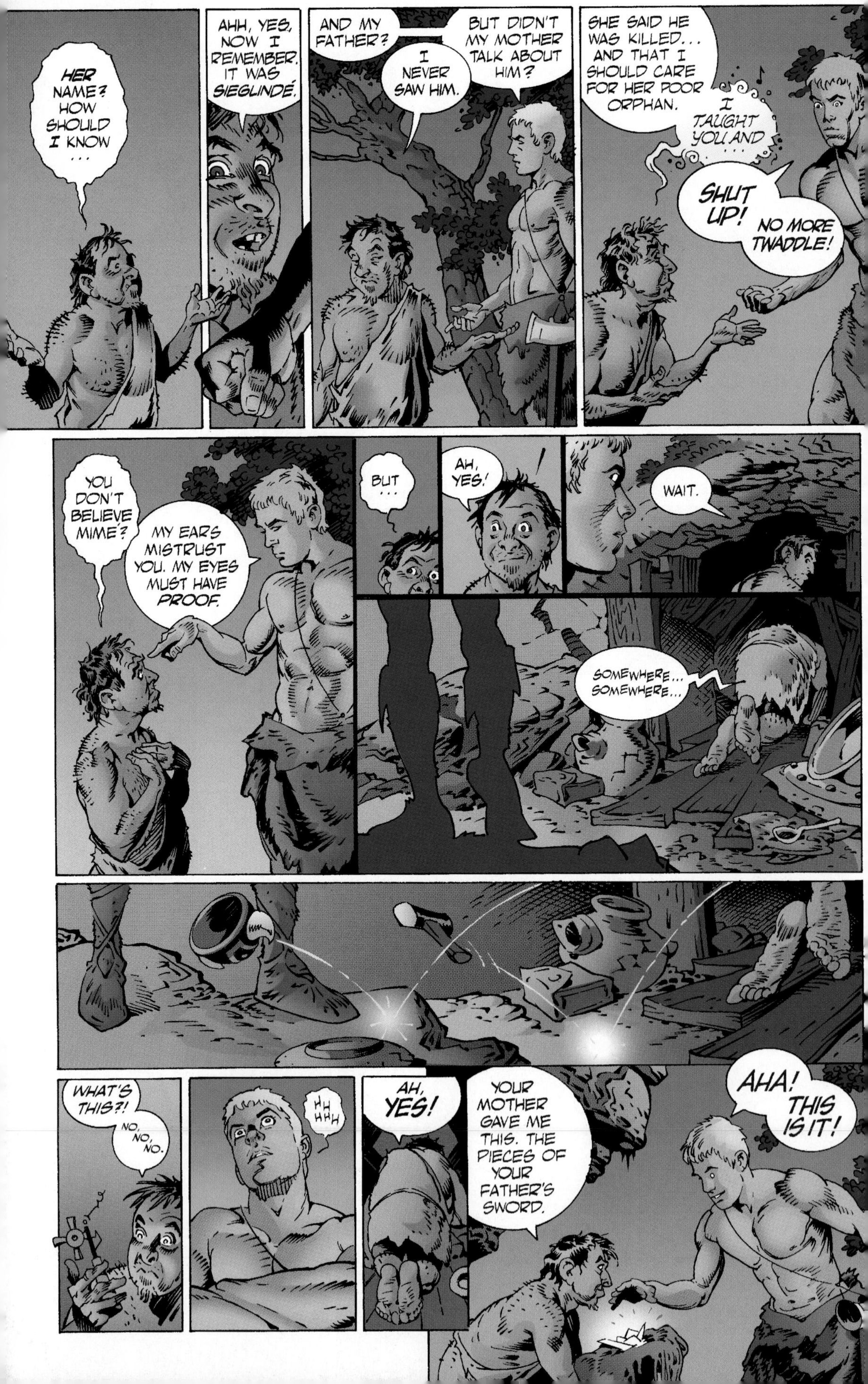
HER NAME? HOW SHOULD I KNOW . . .
AHH, YES, NOW I REMEMBER. IT WAS SIEGLINDÉ.
AND MY FATHER?
I NEVER SAW HIM.
BUT DIDN'T MY MOTHER TALK ABOUT HIM?
SHE SAID HE WAS KILLED... AND THAT I SHOULD CARE FOR HER POOR ORPHAN.
I TAUGHT YOU AND . . .
SHUT UP!
NO MORE TWADDLE!
YOU DON'T BELIEVE MIME?
MY EARS MISTRUST YOU. MY EYES MUST HAVE PROOF.
BUT . . .
AH, YES!
WAIT.
SOMEWHERE... SOMEWHERE...
WHAT'S THIS?!
NO, NO, NO.
HH HHH
AH, YES!
YOUR MOTHER GAVE ME THIS. THE PIECES OF YOUR FATHER'S SWORD.
AHA! THIS IS IT!

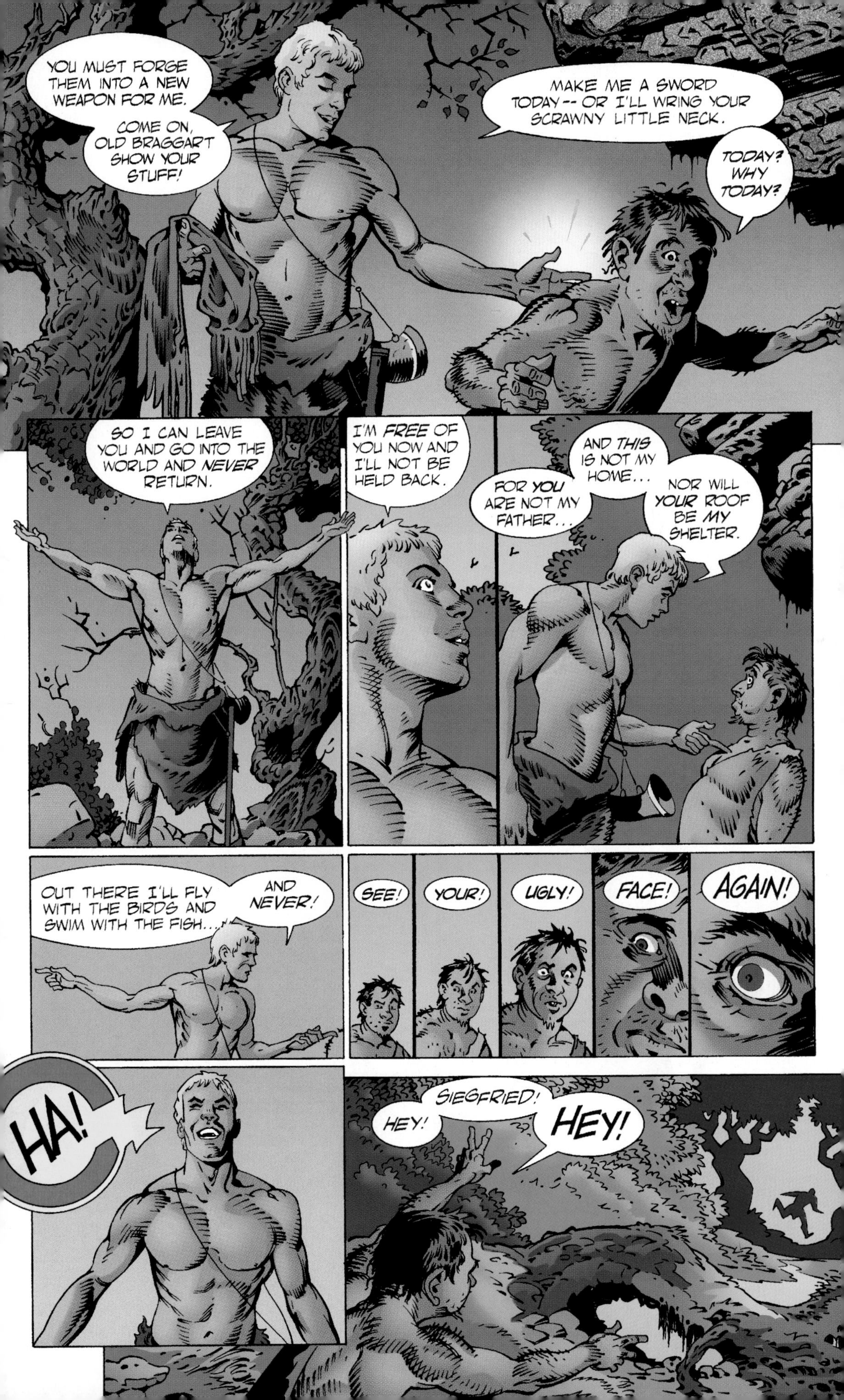
YOU MUST FORGE THEM INTO A NEW WEAPON FOR ME.
COME ON, OLD BRAGGART SHOW YOUR STUFF!
MAKE ME A SWORD TODAY-- OR I'LL WRING YOUR SCRAWNY LITTLE NECK.
TODAY? WHY TODAY?
SO I CAN LEAVE YOU AND GO INTO THE WORLD AND NEVER RETURN.
I'M FREE OF YOU NOW AND I'LL NOT BE HELD BACK.
FOR YOU ARE NOT MY FATHER...
AND THIS IS NOT MY HOME...
NOR WILL YOUR ROOF BE MY SHELTER.
OUT THERE I'LL FLY WITH THE BIRDS AND SWIM WITH THE FISH...
AND NEVER!
SEE!
YOUR!
UGLY!
FACE!
AGAIN!
HA!
HEY!
SIEGFRIED!
HEY!

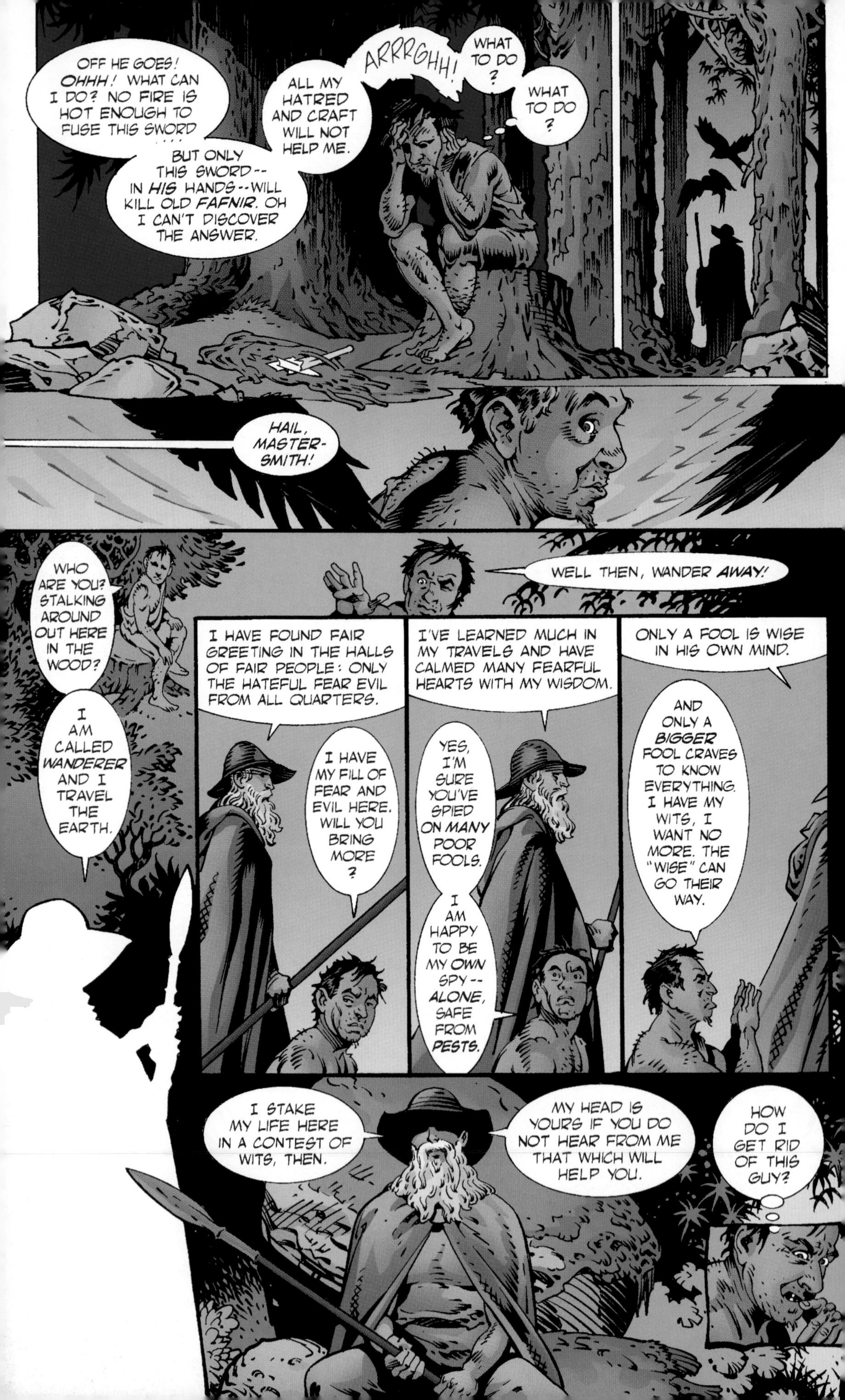
OFF HE GOES! OHHH! WHAT CAN I DO? NO FIRE IS HOT ENOUGH TO FUSE THIS SWORD . . . .
BUT ONLY THIS SWORD-- IN HIS HANDS--WILL KILL OLD FAFNIR. OH I CAN'T DISCOVER THE ANSWER.
ALL MY HATRED AND CRAFT WILL NOT HELP ME.
ARRRGHH!
WHAT TO DO ?
WHAT TO DO ?
HAIL, MASTER-SMITH!
WHO ARE YOU? STALKING AROUND OUT HERE IN THE WOOD?
I AM CALLED WANDERER AND I TRAVEL THE EARTH.
WELL THEN, WANDER AWAY!
I HAVE FOUND FAIR GREETING IN THE HALLS OF FAIR PEOPLE: ONLY THE HATEFUL FEAR EVIL FROM ALL QUARTERS.
I HAVE MY FILL OF FEAR AND EVIL HERE. WILL YOU BRING MORE ?
I'VE LEARNED MUCH IN MY TRAVELS AND HAVE CALMED MANY FEARFUL HEARTS WITH MY WISDOM.
YES, I'M SURE YOU'VE SPIED ON MANY POOR FOOLS.
I AM HAPPY TO BE MY OWN SPY-- ALONE, SAFE FROM PESTS.
ONLY A FOOL IS WISE IN HIS OWN MIND.
AND ONLY A BIGGER FOOL CRAVES TO KNOW EVERYTHING. I HAVE MY WITS, I WANT NO MORE. THE "WISE" CAN GO THEIR WAY.
I STAKE MY LIFE HERE IN A CONTEST OF WITS, THEN.
MY HEAD IS YOURS IF YOU DO NOT HEAR FROM ME THAT WHICH WILL HELP YOU.
HOW DO I GET RID OF THIS GUY?

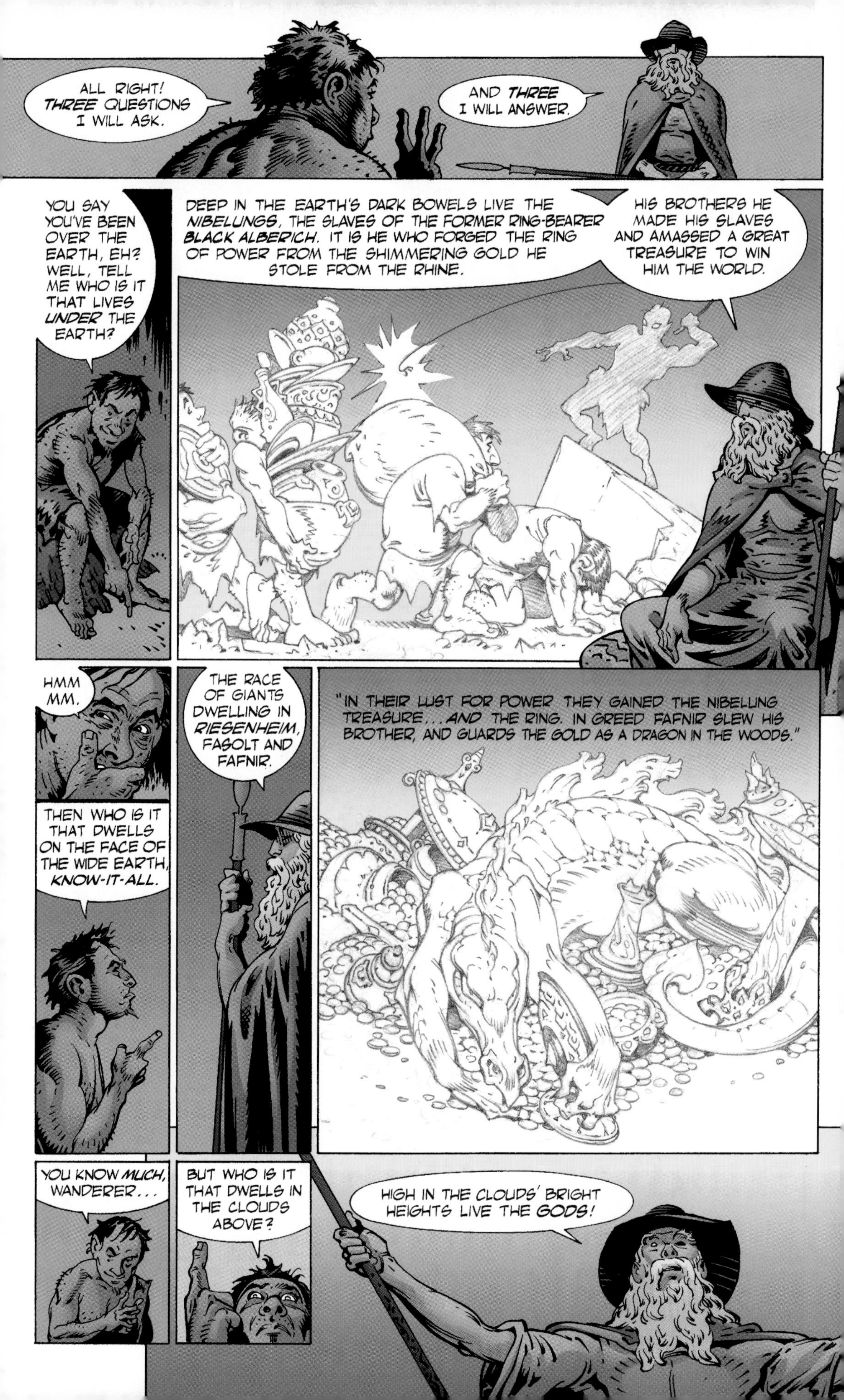
ALL RIGHT! THREE QUESTIONS I WILL ASK.
AND THREE I WILL ANSWER.
YOU SAY YOU'VE BEEN OVER THE EARTH, EH? WELL, TELL ME WHO IS IT THAT LIVES UNDER THE EARTH?
DEEP IN THE EARTH'S DARK BOWELS LIVE THE NIBELUNGS, THE SLAVES OF THE FORMER RING-BEARER BLACK ALBERICH. IT IS HE WHO FORGED THE RING OF POWER FROM THE SHIMMERING GOLD HE STOLE FROM THE RHINE.
HIS BROTHERS HE MADE HIS SLAVES AND AMASSED A GREAT TREASURE TO WIN HIM THE WORLD.
HMM MM.
THE RACE OF GIANTS DWELLING IN RIESENHEIM, FASOLT AND FAFNIR.
"IN THEIR LUST FOR POWER THEY GAINED THE NIBELUNG TREASURE... AND THE RING. IN GREED FAFNIR SLEW HIS BROTHER, AND GUARDS THE GOLD AS A DRAGON IN THE WOODS."
THEN WHO IS IT THAT DWELLS ON THE FACE OF THE WIDE EARTH, KNOW-IT-ALL.
YOU KNOW MUCH, WANDERER...
BUT WHO IS IT THAT DWELLS IN THE CLOUDS ABOVE?
HIGH IN THE CLOUDS' BRIGHT HEIGHTS LIVE THE GODS!

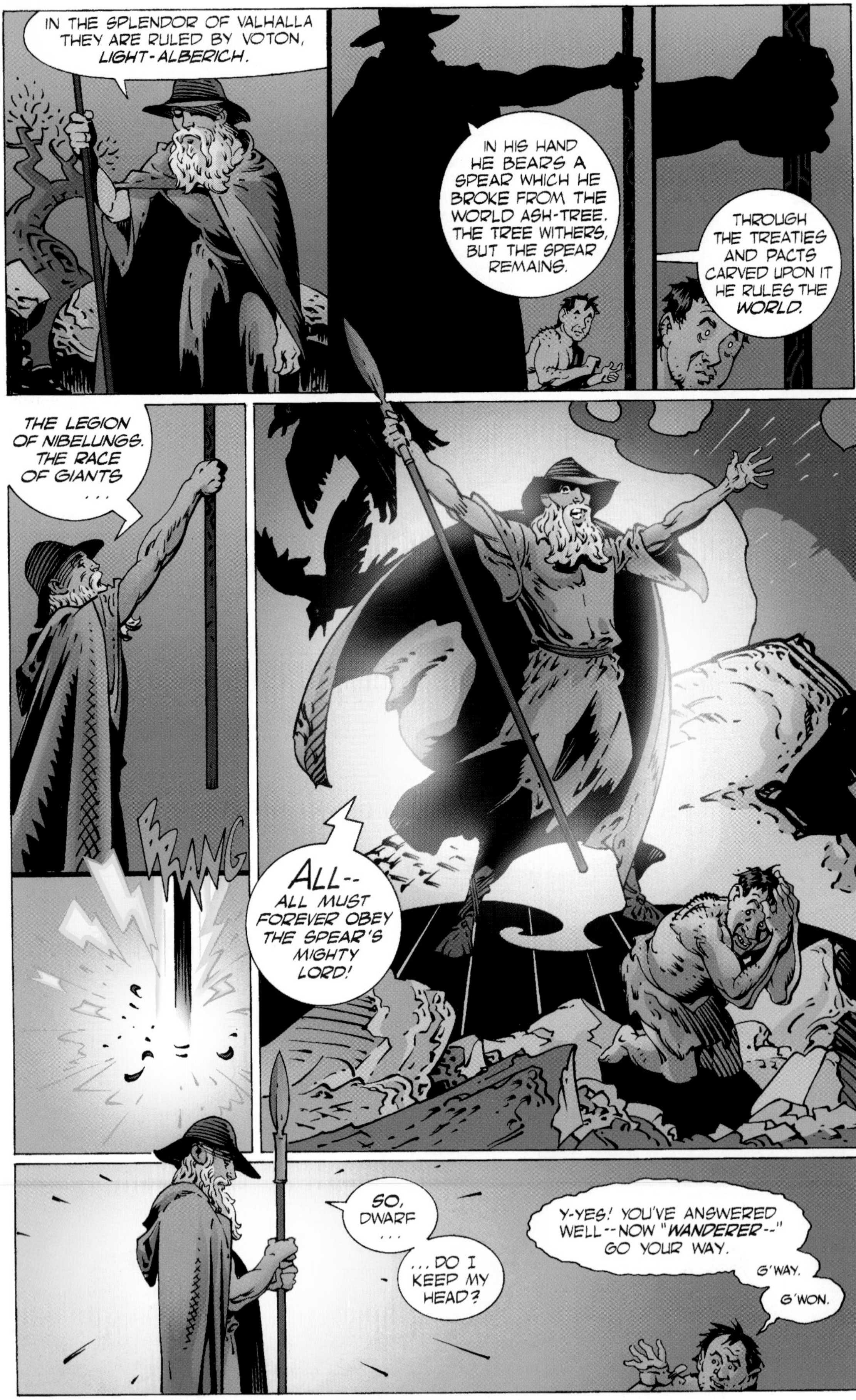

IN THE SPLENDOR OF VALHALLA THEY ARE RULED BY VOTON, *LIGHT-ALBERICH*.
IN HIS HAND HE BEARS A SPEAR WHICH HE BROKE FROM THE WORLD ASH-TREE. THE TREE WITHERS, BUT THE SPEAR REMAINS.
THROUGH THE TREATIES AND PACTS CARVED UPON IT HE RULES THE *WORLD*.
THE LEGION OF NIBELUNGS. THE RACE OF GIANTS . . .
BRANG
ALL--
ALL MUST FOREVER OBEY THE SPEAR'S MIGHTY LORD!
SO, DWARF . . .
. . . DO I KEEP MY HEAD?
Y-YES! YOU'VE ANSWERED WELL--NOW "*WANDERER*--" GO YOUR WAY.
G'WAY.
G'WON.

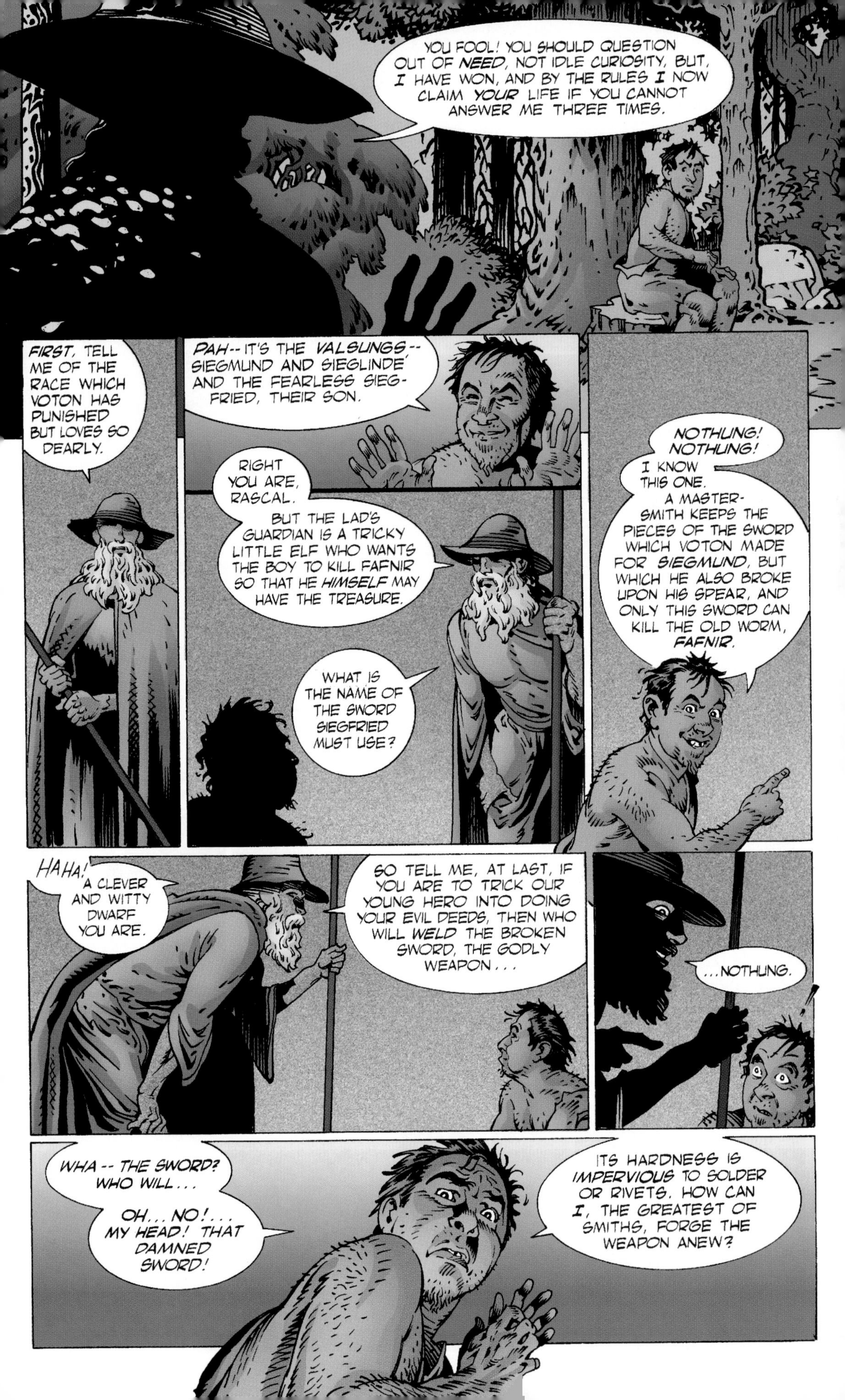
YOU FOOL! YOU SHOULD QUESTION OUT OF NEED, NOT IDLE CURIOSITY, BUT, I HAVE WON, AND BY THE RULES I NOW CLAIM YOUR LIFE IF YOU CANNOT ANSWER ME THREE TIMES.
FIRST, TELL ME OF THE RACE WHICH VOTON HAS PUNISHED BUT LOVES SO DEARLY.
PAH-- IT'S THE VALSUNGS-- SIEGMUND AND SIEGLINDE, AND THE FEARLESS SIEGFRIED, THEIR SON.
RIGHT YOU ARE, RASCAL.
BUT THE LAD'S GUARDIAN IS A TRICKY LITTLE ELF WHO WANTS THE BOY TO KILL FAFNIR SO THAT HE HIMSELF MAY HAVE THE TREASURE.
WHAT IS THE NAME OF THE SWORD SIEGFRIED MUST USE?
NOTHUNG! NOTHUNG!
I KNOW THIS ONE.
A MASTER-SMITH KEEPS THE PIECES OF THE SWORD WHICH VOTON MADE FOR SIEGMUND, BUT WHICH HE ALSO BROKE UPON HIS SPEAR, AND ONLY THIS SWORD CAN KILL THE OLD WORM, FAFNIR.
HAHA! A CLEVER AND WITTY DWARF YOU ARE.
SO TELL ME, AT LAST, IF YOU ARE TO TRICK OUR YOUNG HERO INTO DOING YOUR EVIL DEEDS, THEN WHO WILL WELD THE BROKEN SWORD, THE GODLY WEAPON . . .
. . . NOTHUNG.
WHA -- THE SWORD? WHO WILL . . .
OH . . . NO! . . . MY HEAD! THAT DAMNED SWORD!
ITS HARDNESS IS IMPERVIOUS TO SOLDER OR RIVETS. HOW CAN I, THE GREATEST OF SMITHS, FORGE THE WEAPON ANEW?

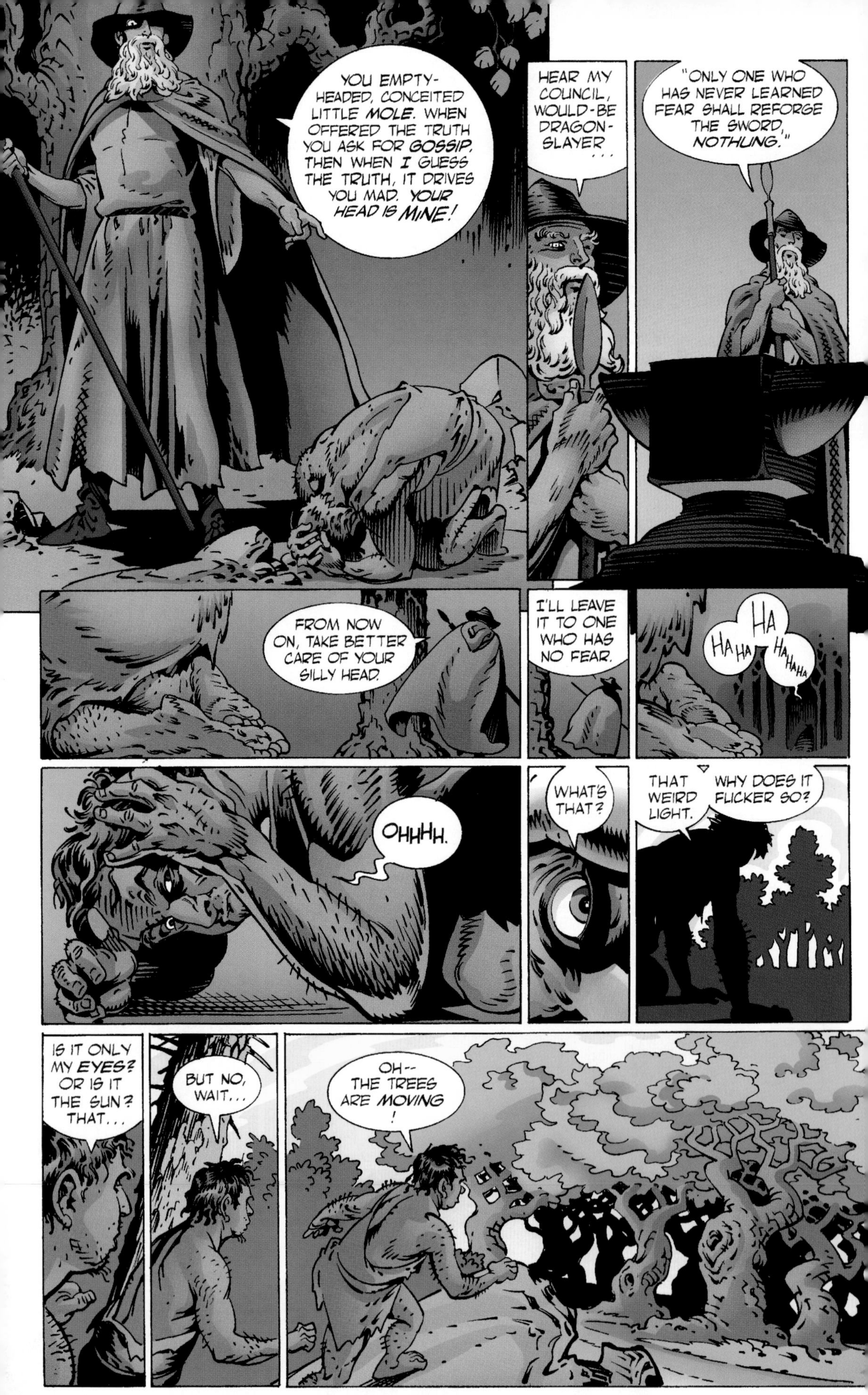
YOU EMPTY-HEADED, CONCEITED LITTLE MOLE. WHEN OFFERED THE TRUTH YOU ASK FOR GOSSIP, THEN WHEN I GUESS THE TRUTH, IT DRIVES YOU MAD. YOUR HEAD IS MINE!
HEAR MY COUNCIL, WOULD-BE DRAGON-SLAYER . . .
"ONLY ONE WHO HAS NEVER LEARNED FEAR SHALL REFORGE THE SWORD, NOTHUNG."
FROM NOW ON, TAKE BETTER CARE OF YOUR SILLY HEAD.
I'LL LEAVE IT TO ONE WHO HAS NO FEAR.
HA HA HA HA HA HA HA
OHHHH.
WHAT'S THAT?
THAT WEIRD LIGHT.
WHY DOES IT FLICKER SO?
IS IT ONLY MY EYES? OR IS IT THE SUN? THAT...
BUT NO, WAIT...
OH -- THE TREES ARE MOVING !

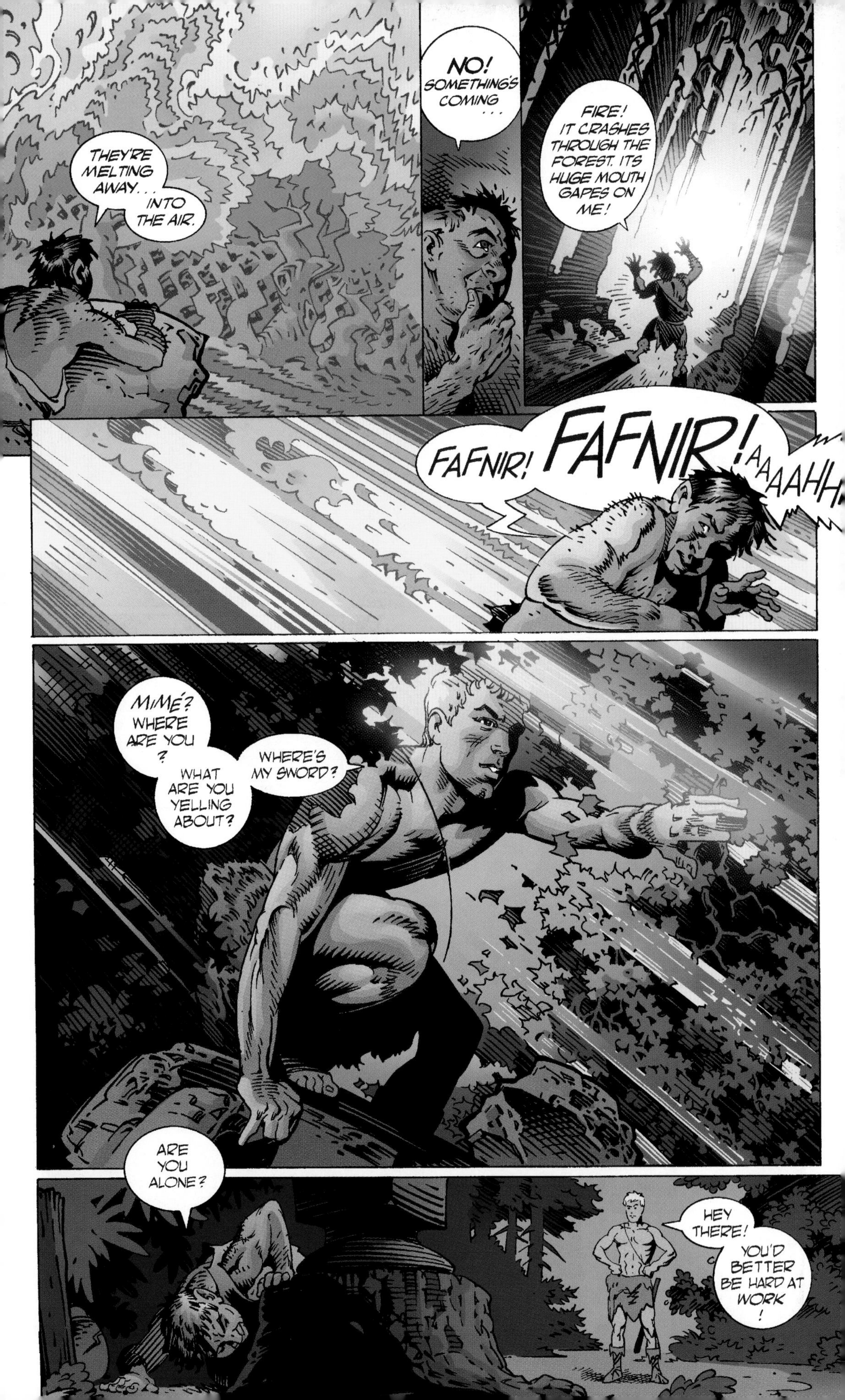
THEY'RE MELTING AWAY... INTO THE AIR.
NO! SOMETHING'S COMING...
FIRE! IT CRASHES THROUGH THE FOREST. ITS HUGE MOUTH GAPES ON ME!
FAFNIR! FAFNIR! AAAAHH
MIME? WHERE ARE YOU?
WHAT ARE YOU YELLING ABOUT?
WHERE'S MY SWORD?
ARE YOU ALONE?
HEY THERE!
YOU'D BETTER BE HARD AT WORK!

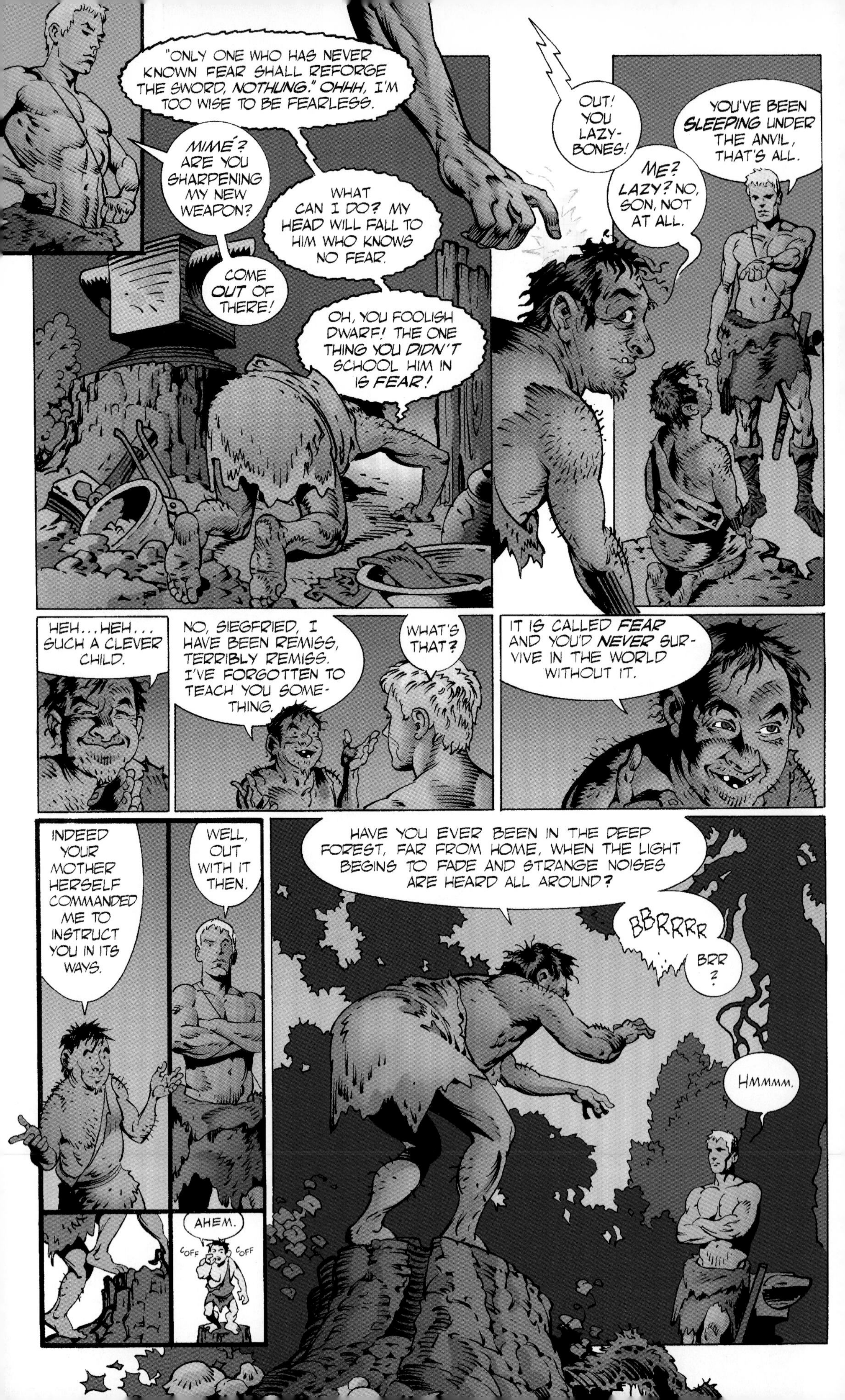
"ONLY ONE WHO HAS NEVER KNOWN FEAR SHALL REFORGE THE SWORD, NOTHUNG." OHHH, I'M TOO WISE TO BE FEARLESS.
MIMÉ? ARE YOU SHARPENING MY NEW WEAPON?
WHAT CAN I DO? MY HEAD WILL FALL TO HIM WHO KNOWS NO FEAR.
COME OUT OF THERE!
OH, YOU FOOLISH DWARF! THE ONE THING YOU DIDN'T SCHOOL HIM IN IS FEAR!
OUT! YOU LAZY-BONES!
YOU'VE BEEN SLEEPING UNDER THE ANVIL, THAT'S ALL.
ME? LAZY? NO, SON, NOT AT ALL.
HEH... HEH... SUCH A CLEVER CHILD.
NO, SIEGFRIED, I HAVE BEEN REMISS, TERRIBLY REMISS. I'VE FORGOTTEN TO TEACH YOU SOME-THING.
WHAT'S THAT?
IT IS CALLED FEAR AND YOU'D NEVER SUR-VIVE IN THE WORLD WITHOUT IT.
INDEED YOUR MOTHER HERSELF COMMANDED ME TO INSTRUCT YOU IN ITS WAYS.
WELL, OUT WITH IT THEN.
AHEM.
COFF COFF
HAVE YOU EVER BEEN IN THE DEEP FOREST, FAR FROM HOME, WHEN THE LIGHT BEGINS TO FADE AND STRANGE NOISES ARE HEARD ALL AROUND?
BBRRRRR
BRR?
HMMMM.

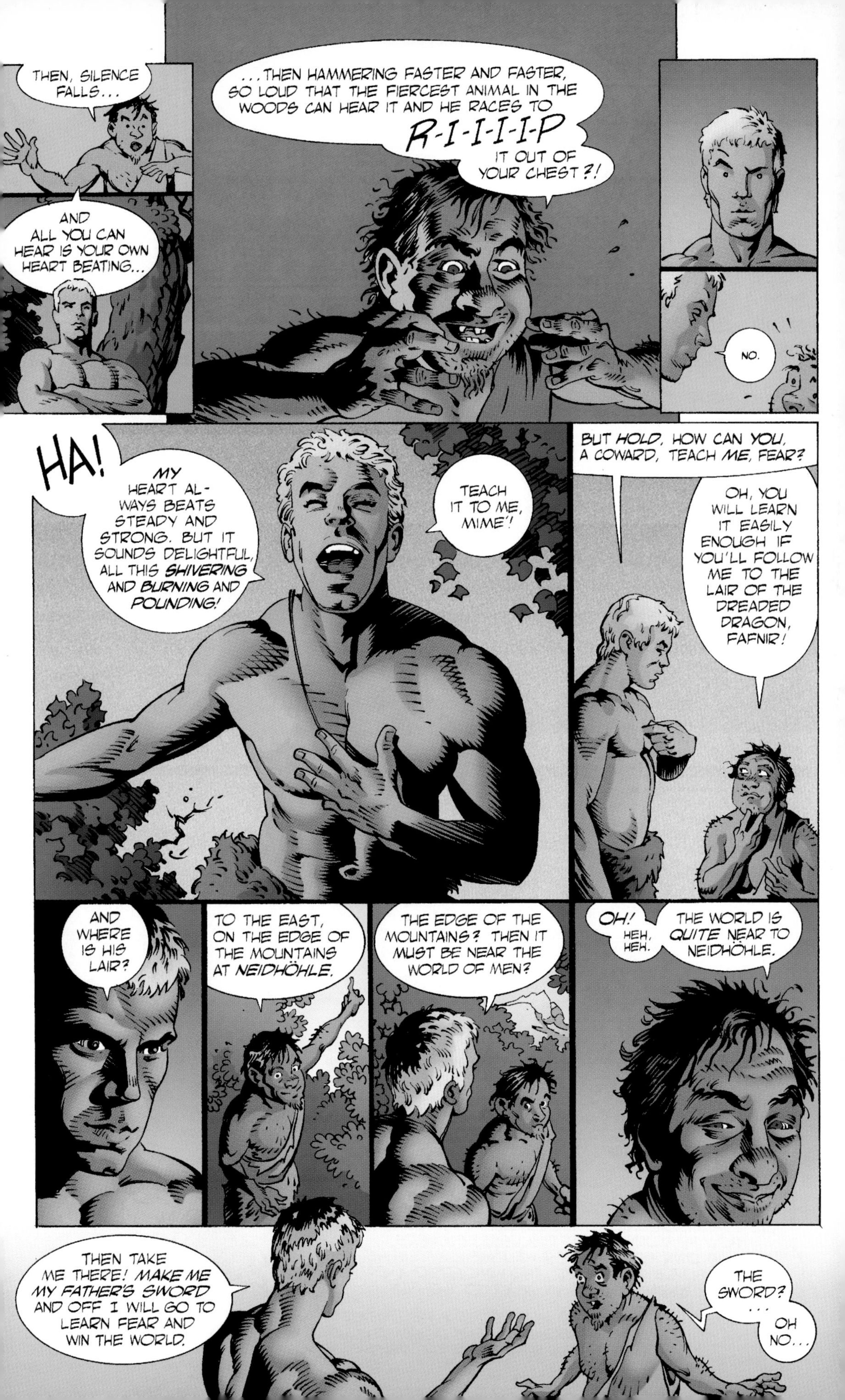
THEN, SILENCE FALLS...
...THEN HAMMERING FASTER AND FASTER, SO LOUD THAT THE FIERCEST ANIMAL IN THE WOODS CAN HEAR IT AND HE RACES TO
R-I-I-I-P
IT OUT OF YOUR CHEST?!
AND ALL YOU CAN HEAR IS YOUR OWN HEART BEATING...
NO.
HA!
MY HEART AL-WAYS BEATS STEADY AND STRONG. BUT IT SOUNDS DELIGHTFUL, ALL THIS SHIVERING AND BURNING AND POUNDING!
TEACH IT TO ME, MIME'!
BUT HOLD, HOW CAN YOU, A COWARD, TEACH ME, FEAR?
OH, YOU WILL LEARN IT EASILY ENOUGH IF YOU'LL FOLLOW ME TO THE LAIR OF THE DREADED DRAGON, FAFNIR!
AND WHERE IS HIS LAIR?
TO THE EAST, ON THE EDGE OF THE MOUNTAINS AT NEIDHÖHLE.
THE EDGE OF THE MOUNTAINS? THEN IT MUST BE NEAR THE WORLD OF MEN?
OH!
HEH, HEH.
THE WORLD IS QUITE NEAR TO NEIDHÖHLE.
THEN TAKE ME THERE! MAKE ME MY FATHER'S SWORD AND OFF I WILL GO TO LEARN FEAR AND WIN THE WORLD.
THE SWORD? ... OH NO...

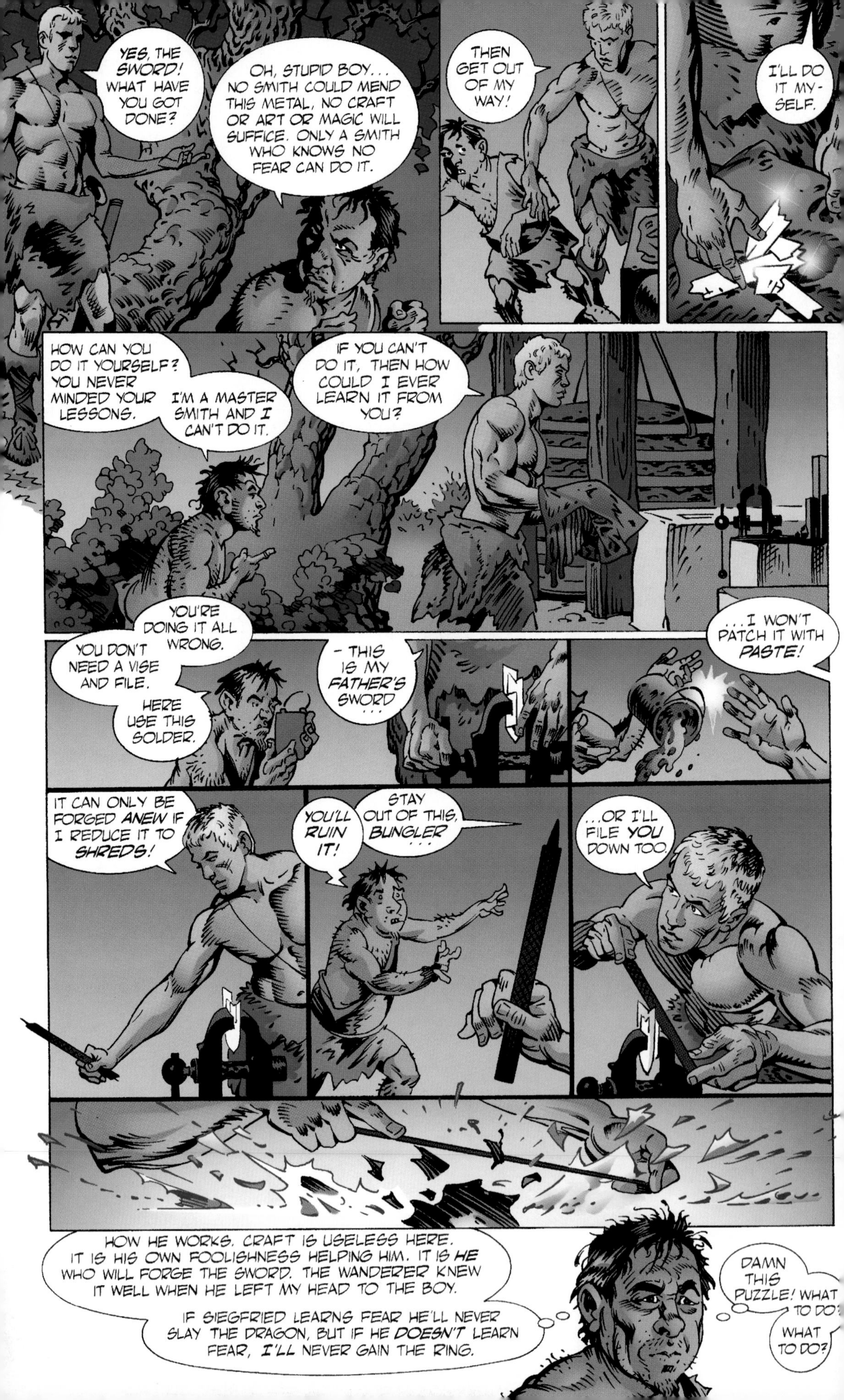
YES, THE SWORD! WHAT HAVE YOU GOT DONE?
OH, STUPID BOY... NO SMITH COULD MEND THIS METAL, NO CRAFT OR ART OR MAGIC WILL SUFFICE. ONLY A SMITH WHO KNOWS NO FEAR CAN DO IT.
THEN GET OUT OF MY WAY!
I'LL DO IT MY-SELF.
HOW CAN YOU DO IT YOURSELF? YOU NEVER MINDED YOUR LESSONS.
I'M A MASTER SMITH AND I CAN'T DO IT.
IF YOU CAN'T DO IT, THEN HOW COULD I EVER LEARN IT FROM YOU?
YOU'RE DOING IT ALL WRONG.
YOU DON'T NEED A VISE AND FILE.
HERE USE THIS SOLDER.
- THIS IS MY FATHER'S SWORD...
...I WON'T PATCH IT WITH PASTE!
IT CAN ONLY BE FORGED ANEW IF I REDUCE IT TO SHREDS!
YOU'LL RUIN IT!
STAY OUT OF THIS, BUNGLER...
...OR I'LL FILE YOU DOWN TOO.
HOW HE WORKS. CRAFT IS USELESS HERE. IT IS HIS OWN FOOLISHNESS HELPING HIM. IT IS HE WHO WILL FORGE THE SWORD. THE WANDERER KNEW IT WELL WHEN HE LEFT MY HEAD TO THE BOY.
IF SIEGFRIED LEARNS FEAR HE'LL NEVER SLAY THE DRAGON, BUT IF HE DOESN'T LEARN FEAR, I'LL NEVER GAIN THE RING.
DAMN THIS PUZZLE! WHAT TO DO?
WHAT TO DO?

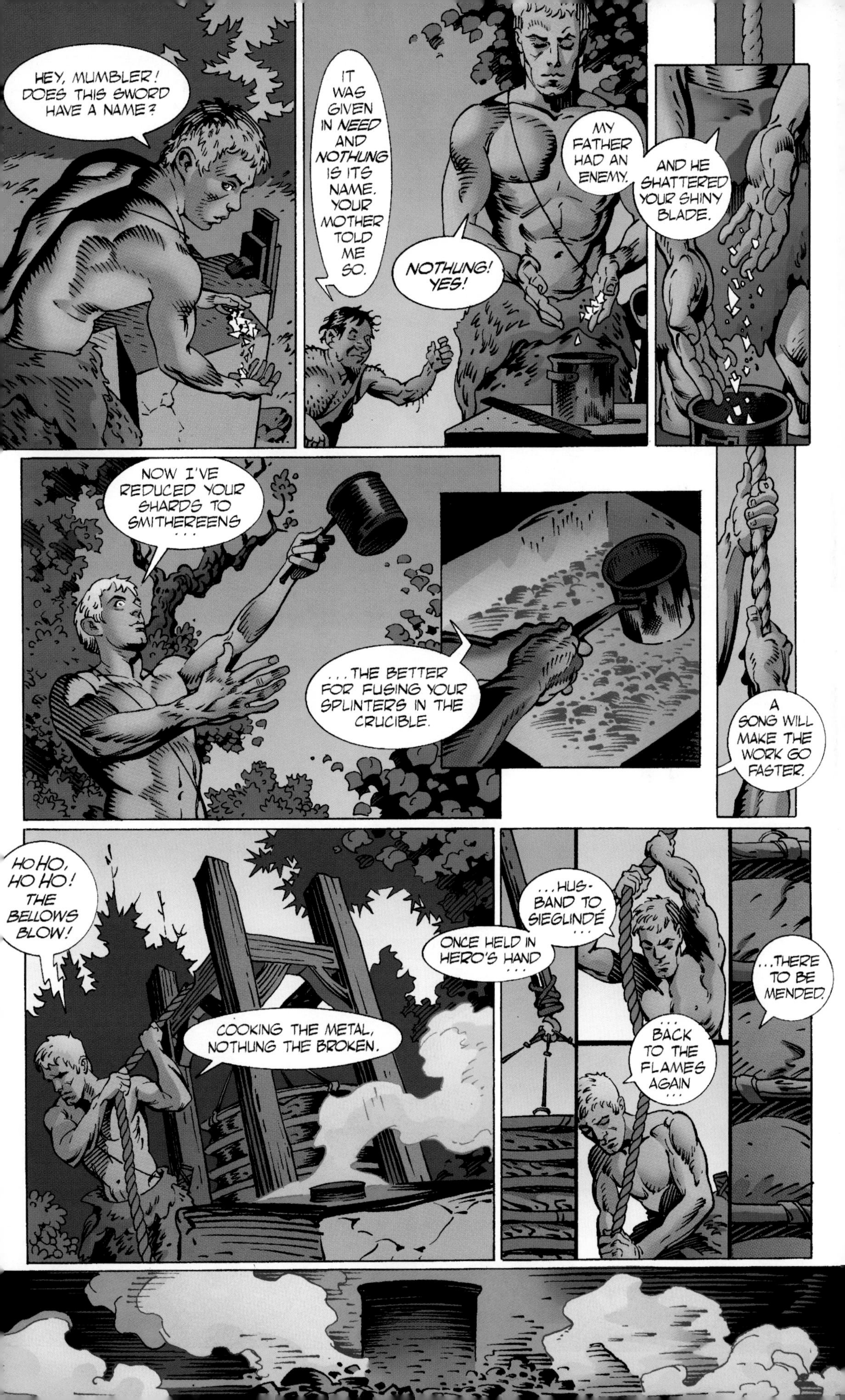
HEY, MUMBLER! DOES THIS SWORD HAVE A NAME?
IT WAS GIVEN IN NEED AND NOTHUNG IS ITS NAME. YOUR MOTHER TOLD ME SO.
NOTHUNG! YES!
MY FATHER HAD AN ENEMY.
AND HE SHATTERED YOUR SHINY BLADE.
NOW I'VE REDUCED YOUR SHARDS TO SMITHEREENS . . .
. . .THE BETTER FOR FUSING YOUR SPLINTERS IN THE CRUCIBLE.
A SONG WILL MAKE THE WORK GO FASTER.
HO HO, HO HO! THE BELLOWS BLOW!
COOKING THE METAL, NOTHUNG THE BROKEN.
. . .HUS-BAND TO SIEGLINDÉ . . .
ONCE HELD IN HERO'S HAND . . .
. . . BACK TO THE FLAMES AGAIN . . .
. . .THERE TO BE MENDED.

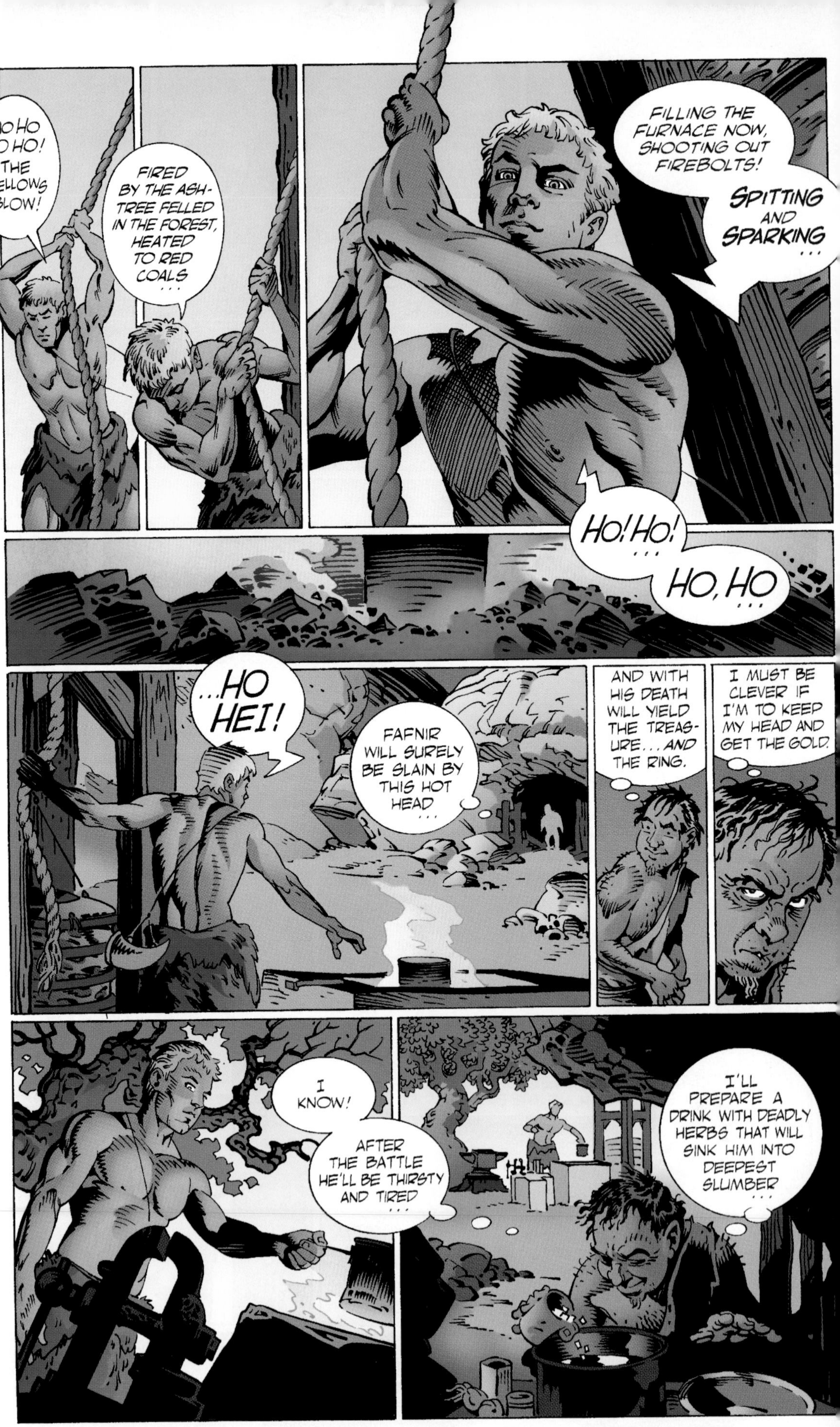
HO HO HO HO! THE BELLOWS BLOW!
FIRED BY THE ASH-TREE FELLED IN THE FOREST, HEATED TO RED COALS . . .
FILLING THE FURNACE NOW, SHOOTING OUT FIREBOLTS!
SPITTING AND SPARKING . . .
HO! HO! . . .
HO, HO . . .
...HO HEI!
FAFNIR WILL SURELY BE SLAIN BY THIS HOT HEAD . . .
AND WITH HIS DEATH WILL YIELD THE TREASURE... AND THE RING.
I MUST BE CLEVER IF I'M TO KEEP MY HEAD AND GET THE GOLD.
I KNOW!
AFTER THE BATTLE HE'LL BE THIRSTY AND TIRED . . .
I'LL PREPARE A DRINK WITH DEADLY HERBS THAT WILL SINK HIM INTO DEEPEST SLUMBER . . .

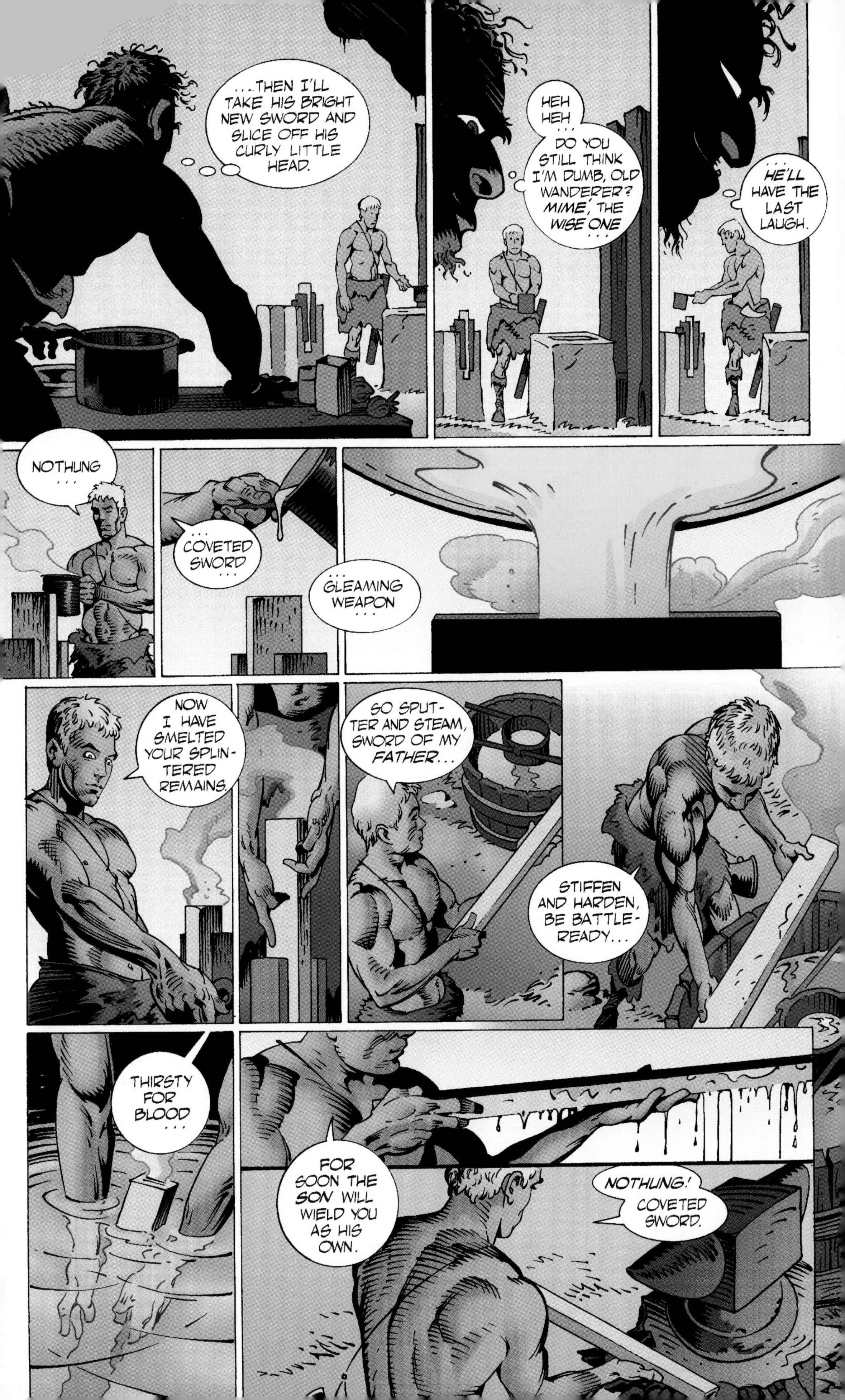

...THEN I'LL TAKE HIS BRIGHT NEW SWORD AND SLICE OFF HIS CURLY LITTLE HEAD.
HEH HEH ... DO YOU STILL THINK I'M DUMB, OLD WANDERER? MIME, THE WISE ONE ...
... HE'LL HAVE THE LAST LAUGH.
NOTHUNG ...
... COVETED SWORD ...
... GLEAMING WEAPON ...
NOW I HAVE SMELTED YOUR SPLINTERED REMAINS.
SO SPUTTER AND STEAM, SWORD OF MY FATHER...
STIFFEN AND HARDEN, BE BATTLE-READY...
THIRSTY FOR BLOOD ...
FOR SOON THE SON WILL WIELD YOU AS HIS OWN.
NOTHUNG! COVETED SWORD.

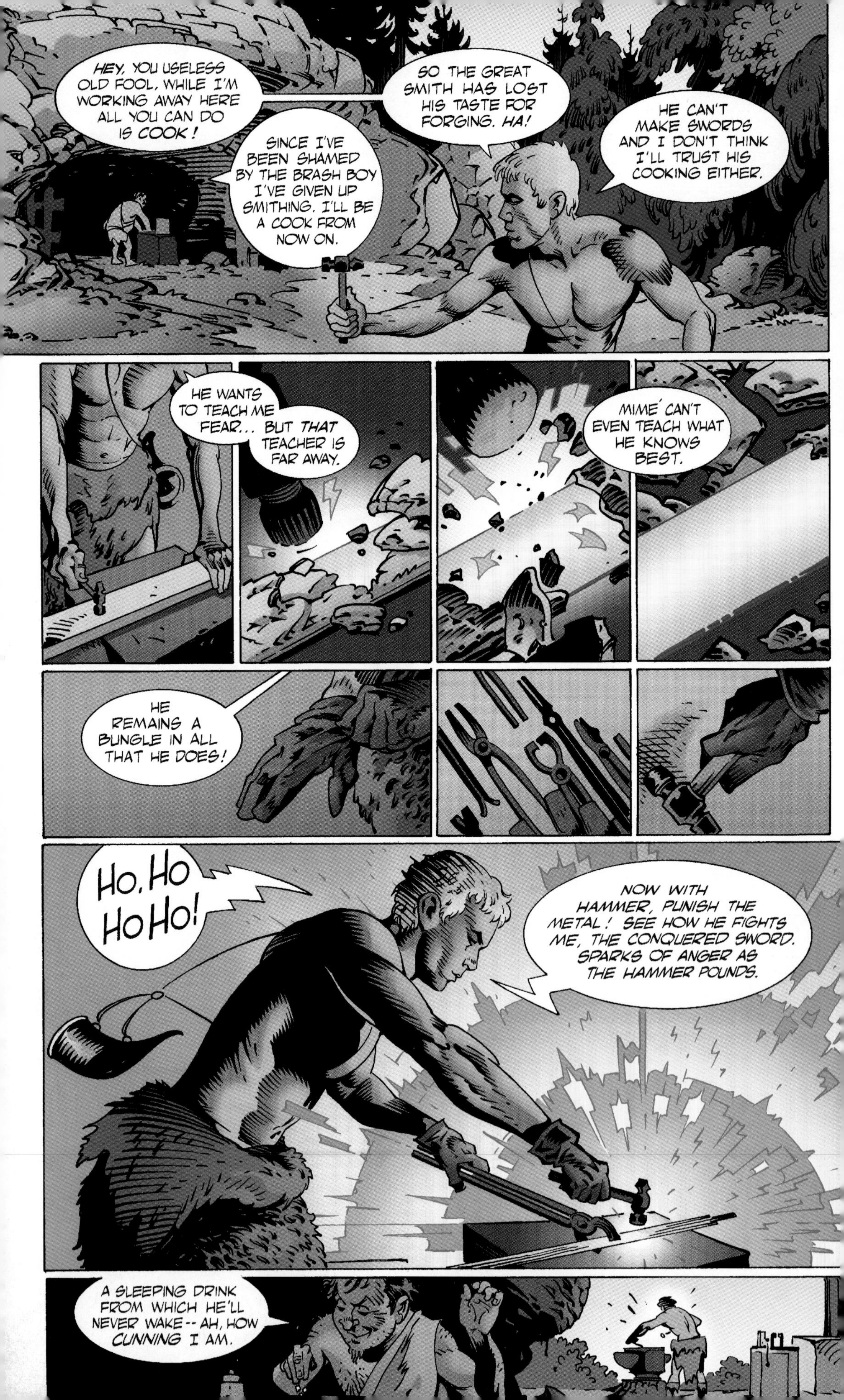
HEY, YOU USELESS OLD FOOL, WHILE I'M WORKING AWAY HERE ALL YOU CAN DO IS COOK!
SINCE I'VE BEEN SHAMED BY THE BRASH BOY I'VE GIVEN UP SMITHING. I'LL BE A COOK FROM NOW ON.
SO THE GREAT SMITH HAS LOST HIS TASTE FOR FORGING. HA!
HE CAN'T MAKE SWORDS AND I DON'T THINK I'LL TRUST HIS COOKING EITHER.
HE WANTS TO TEACH ME FEAR... BUT THAT TEACHER IS FAR AWAY.
MIMÉ CAN'T EVEN TEACH WHAT HE KNOWS BEST.
HE REMAINS A BUNGLE IN ALL THAT HE DOES!
Ho, Ho Ho Ho!
NOW WITH HAMMER, PUNISH THE METAL! SEE HOW HE FIGHTS ME, THE CONQUERED SWORD. SPARKS OF ANGER AS THE HAMMER POUNDS.
A SLEEPING DRINK FROM WHICH HE'LL NEVER WAKE -- AH, HOW CUNNING I AM.

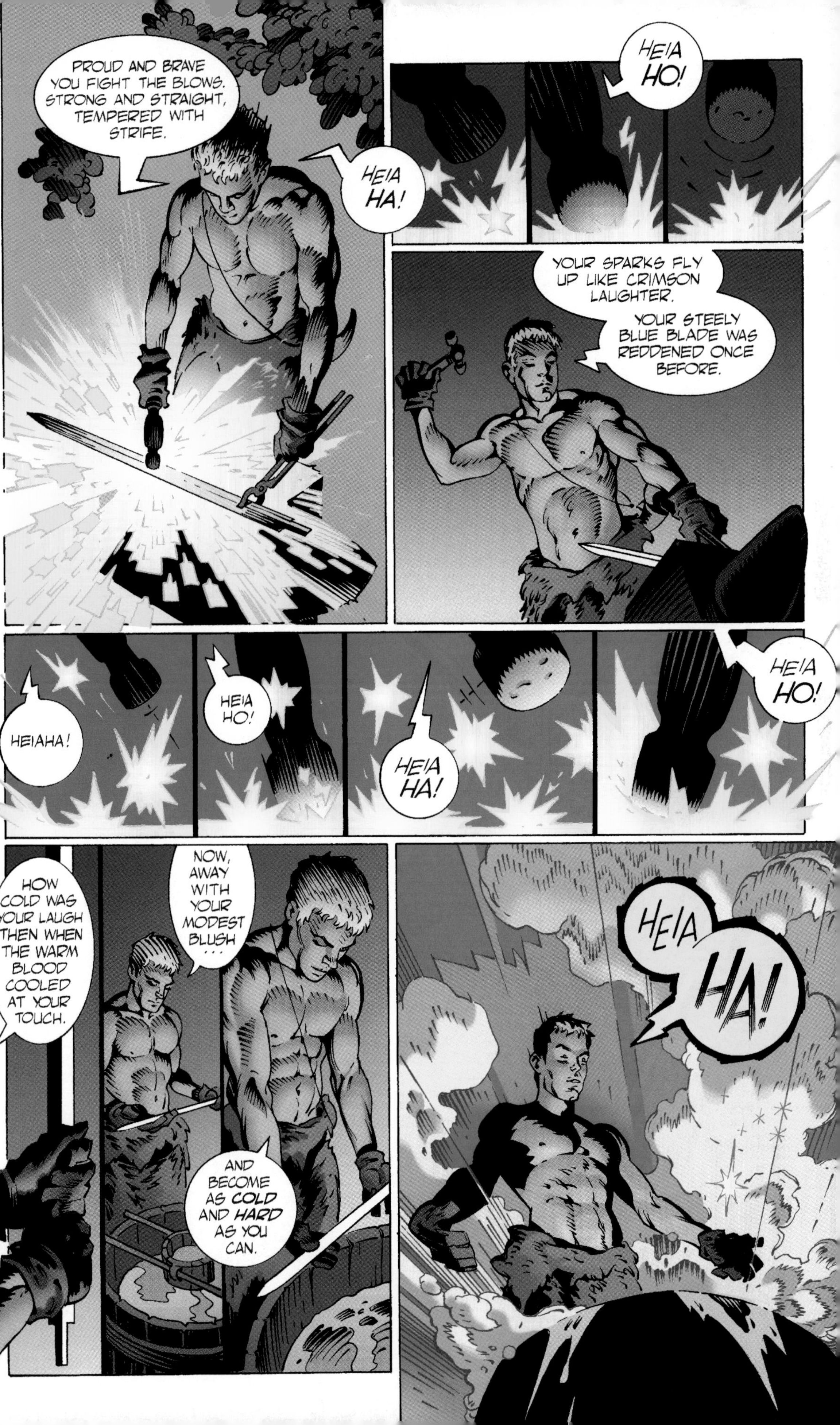
PROUD AND BRAVE YOU FIGHT THE BLOWS. STRONG AND STRAIGHT, TEMPERED WITH STRIFE.
HEIA HA!
HEIA HO!
YOUR SPARKS FLY UP LIKE CRIMSON LAUGHTER.
YOUR STEELY BLUE BLADE WAS REDDENED ONCE BEFORE.
HEIAHA!
HEIA HO!
HEIA HA!
HEIA HO!
HOW COLD WAS YOUR LAUGH THEN WHEN THE WARM BLOOD COOLED AT YOUR TOUCH.
NOW, AWAY WITH YOUR MODEST BLUSH . . .
AND BECOME AS **COLD** AND **HARD** AS YOU CAN.
HEIA HA!

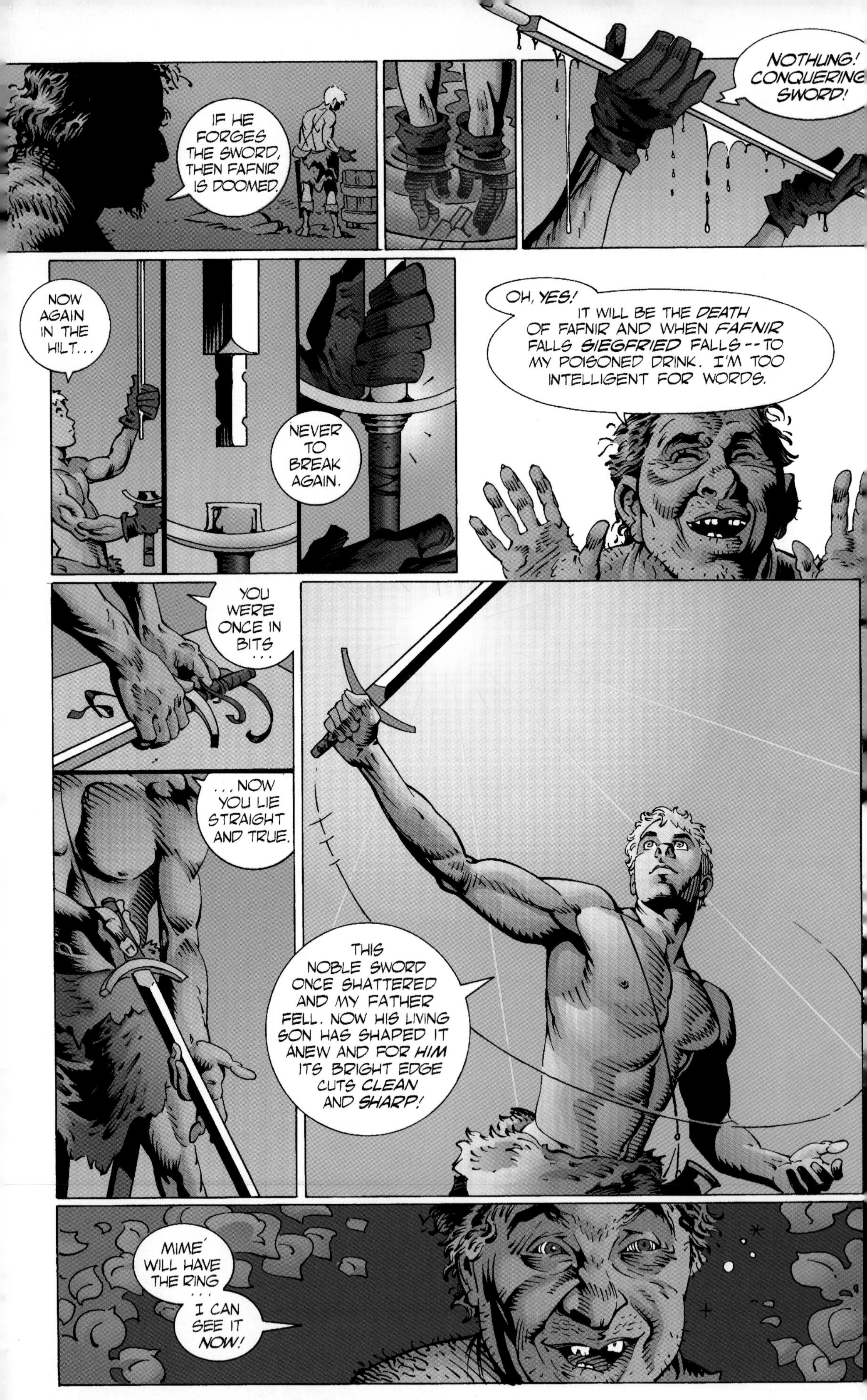
IF HE FORGES THE SWORD, THEN FAFNIR IS DOOMED.
NOTHUNG! CONQUERING SWORD!
NOW AGAIN IN THE HILT...
NEVER TO BREAK AGAIN.
OH, YES! IT WILL BE THE DEATH OF FAFNIR AND WHEN FAFNIR FALLS SIEGFRIED FALLS -- TO MY POISONED DRINK. I'M TOO INTELLIGENT FOR WORDS.
YOU WERE ONCE IN BITS ...
...NOW YOU LIE STRAIGHT AND TRUE.
THIS NOBLE SWORD ONCE SHATTERED AND MY FATHER FELL. NOW HIS LIVING SON HAS SHAPED IT ANEW AND FOR HIM ITS BRIGHT EDGE CUTS CLEAN AND SHARP!
MIMÉ WILL HAVE THE RING ...
I CAN SEE IT NOW!

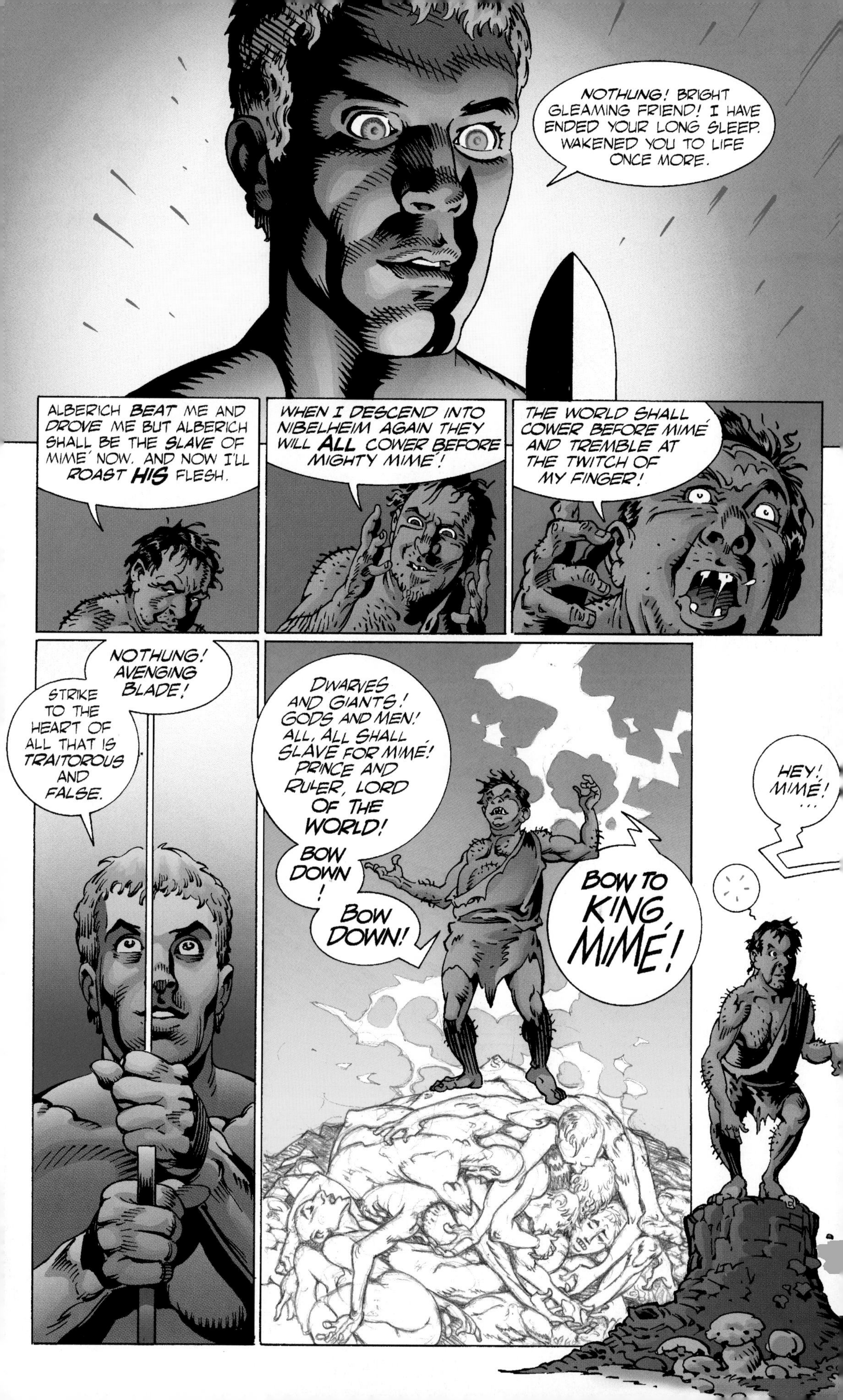

NOTHUNG! BRIGHT GLEAMING FRIEND! I HAVE ENDED YOUR LONG SLEEP. WAKENED YOU TO LIFE ONCE MORE.
ALBERICH BEAT ME AND DROVE ME BUT ALBERICH SHALL BE THE SLAVE OF MIMÉ NOW. AND NOW I'LL ROAST HIS FLESH.
WHEN I DESCEND INTO NIBELHEIM AGAIN THEY WILL ALL COWER BEFORE MIGHTY MIMÉ!
THE WORLD SHALL COWER BEFORE MIMÉ AND TREMBLE AT THE TWITCH OF MY FINGER!
NOTHUNG! AVENGING BLADE!
STRIKE TO THE HEART OF ALL THAT IS TRAITOROUS AND FALSE.
DWARVES AND GIANTS! GODS AND MEN! ALL, ALL SHALL SLAVE FOR MIMÉ! PRINCE AND RULER, LORD OF THE WORLD!
BOW DOWN!
BOW DOWN!
BOW TO KING MIMÉ!
HEY! MIMÉ! ...

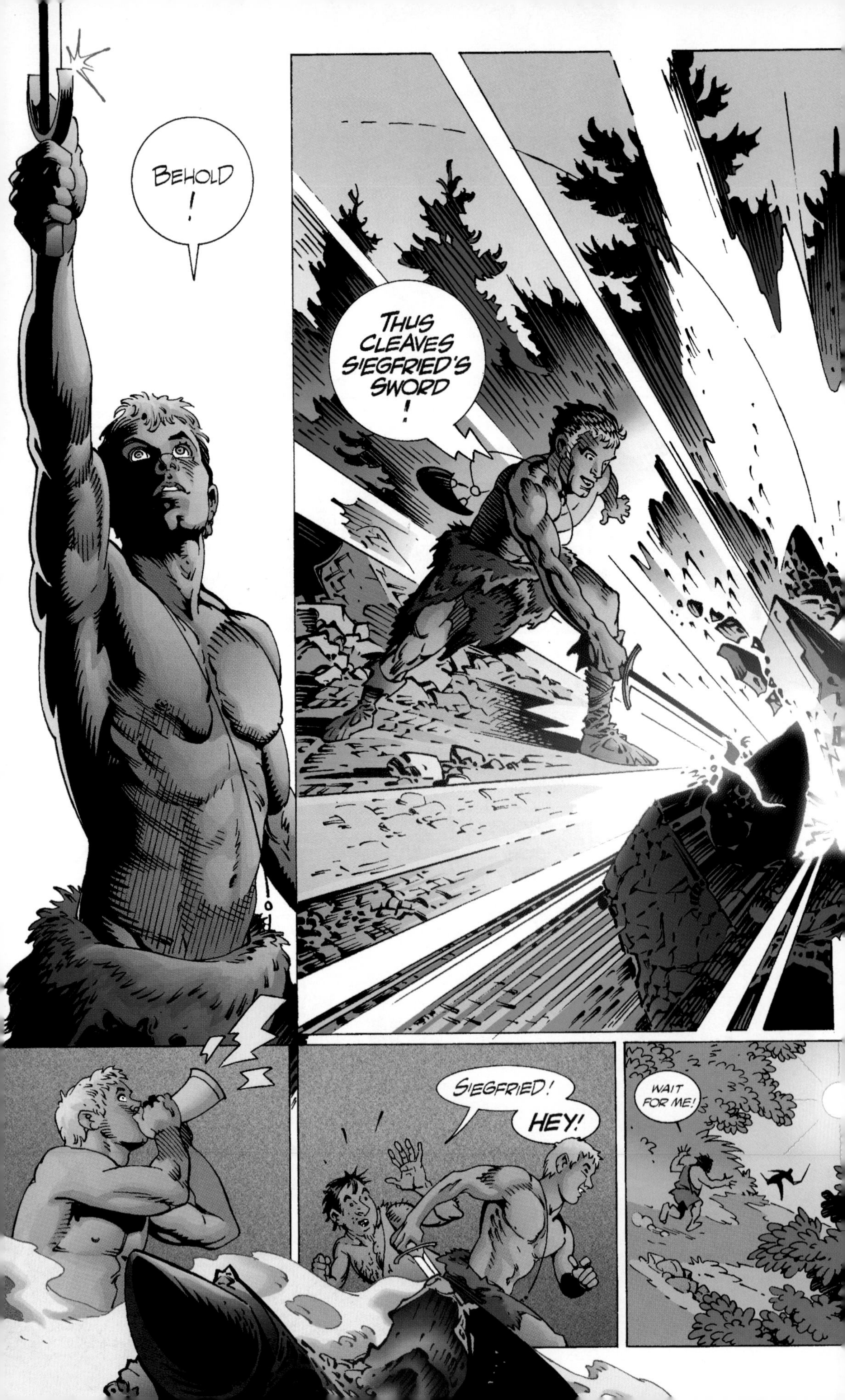
BEHOLD
!
THUS CLEAVES SIEGFRIED'S SWORD
!
SIEGFRIED!
HEY!
WAIT FOR ME!

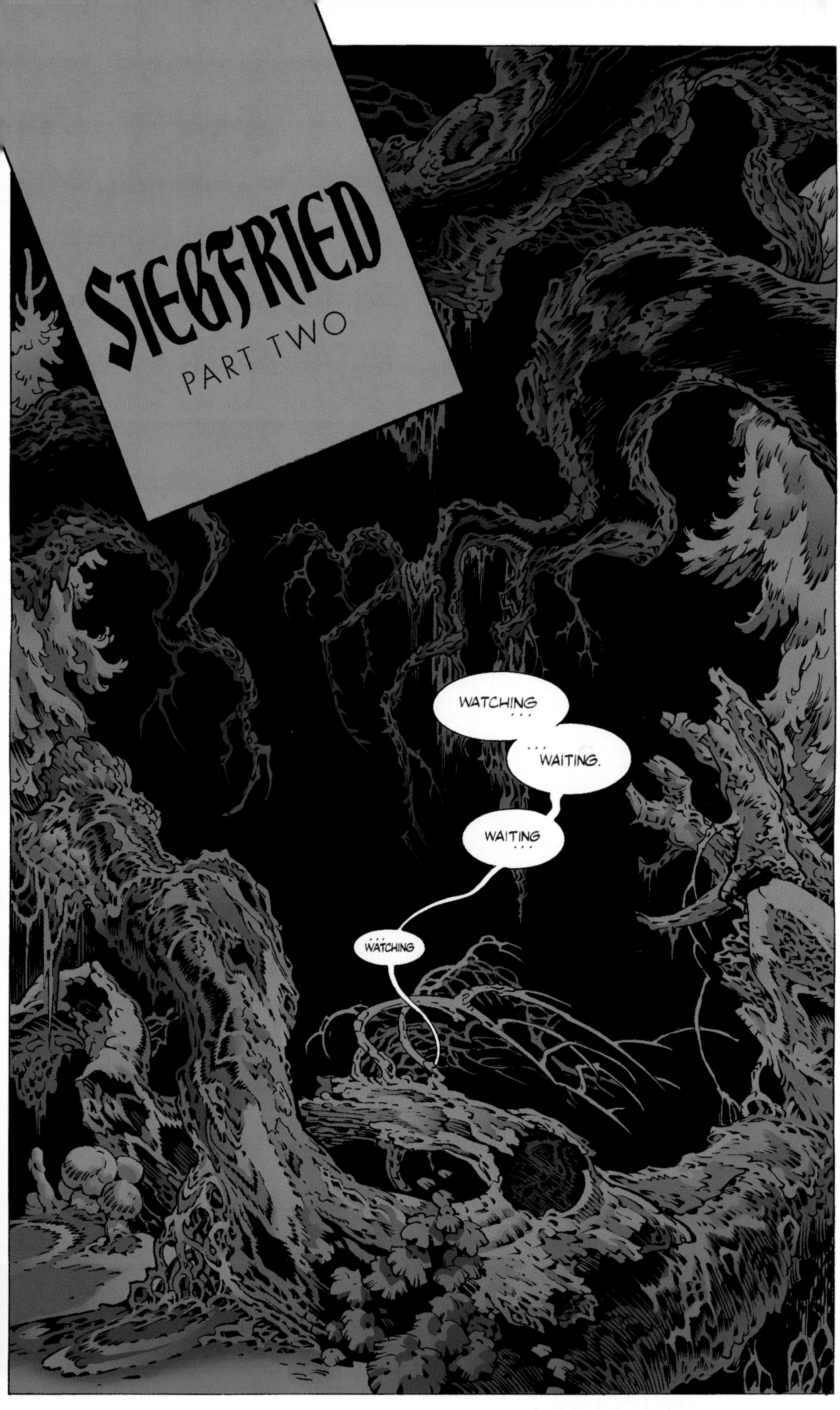
SIEGFRIED
PART TWO
WATCHING . . .
. . . WAITING.
WAITING . . .
. . . WATCHING

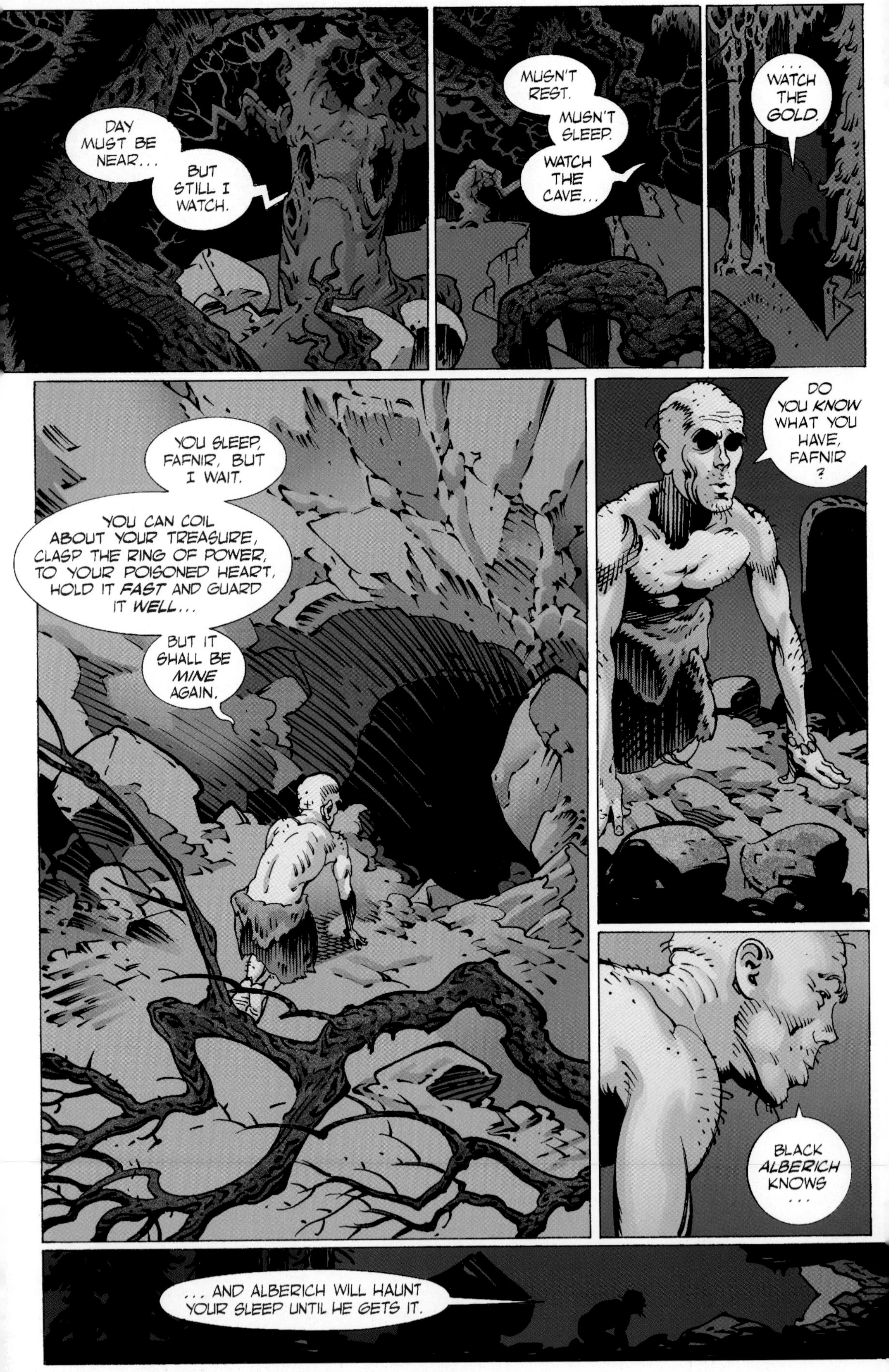
DAY MUST BE NEAR...
BUT STILL I WATCH.
MUSN'T REST.
MUSN'T SLEEP.
WATCH THE CAVE...
...WATCH THE GOLD.
YOU SLEEP, FAFNIR, BUT I WAIT.
YOU CAN COIL ABOUT YOUR TREASURE, CLASP THE RING OF POWER, TO YOUR POISONED HEART, HOLD IT *FAST* AND GUARD IT *WELL*...
BUT IT SHALL BE *MINE* AGAIN.
DO YOU *KNOW* WHAT YOU HAVE, FAFNIR?
BLACK *ALBERICH* KNOWS...
...AND ALBERICH WILL HAUNT YOUR SLEEP UNTIL HE GETS IT.

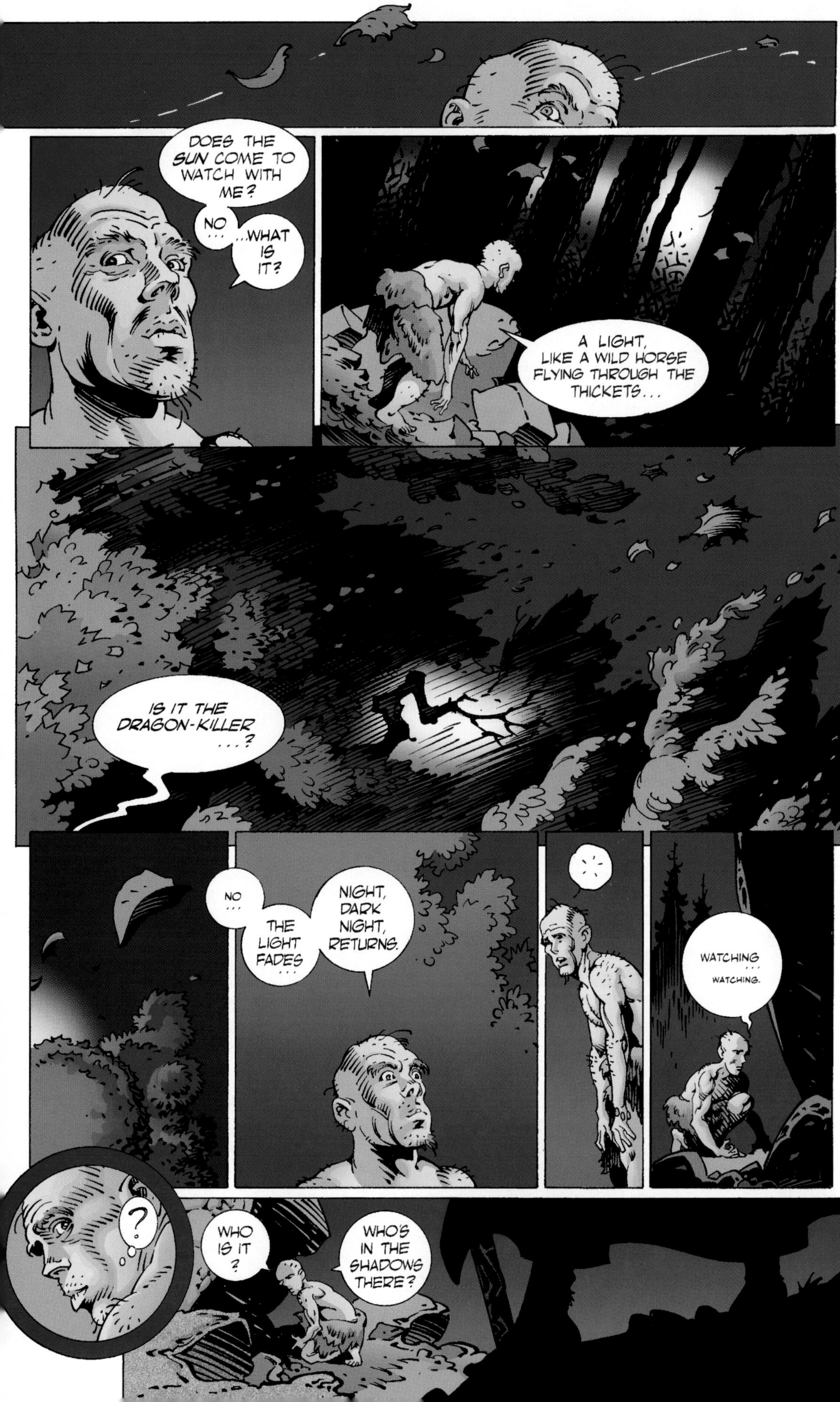
DOES THE SUN COME TO WATCH WITH ME?
NO . . .
...WHAT IS IT?
A LIGHT, LIKE A WILD HORSE FLYING THROUGH THE THICKETS...
IS IT THE DRAGON-KILLER . . . ?
NO . . .
THE LIGHT FADES . . .
NIGHT, DARK NIGHT, RETURNS.
WATCHING . . .
WATCHING.
?
WHO IS IT ?
WHO'S IN THE SHADOWS THERE?

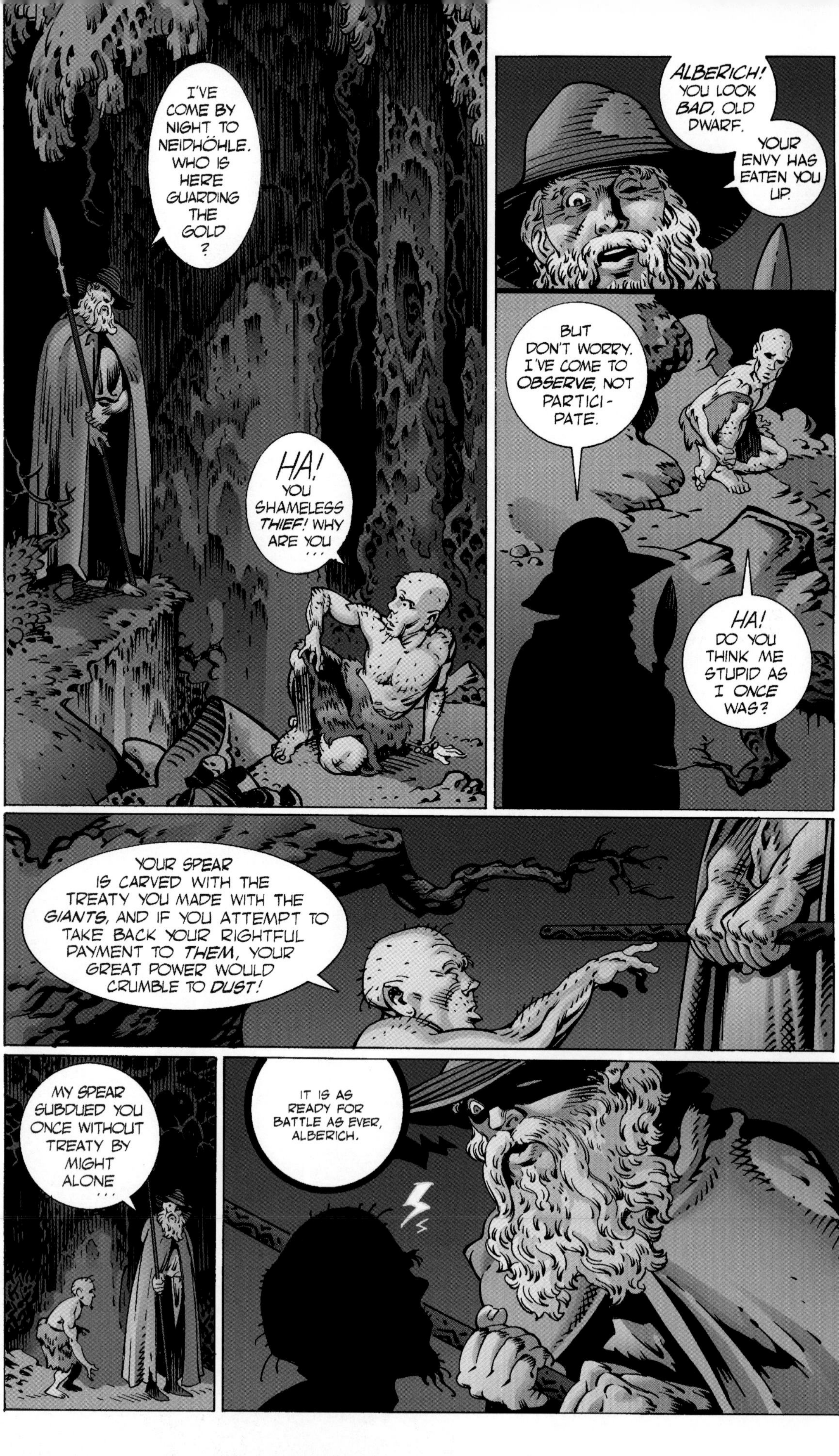
I'VE COME BY NIGHT TO NEIDHÖHLE. WHO IS HERE GUARDING THE GOLD ?
HA! YOU SHAMELESS THIEF! WHY ARE YOU . . .
ALBERICH! YOU LOOK BAD, OLD DWARF.
YOUR ENVY HAS EATEN YOU UP.
BUT DON'T WORRY. I'VE COME TO OBSERVE, NOT PARTICI-PATE.
HA! DO YOU THINK ME STUPID AS I ONCE WAS?
YOUR SPEAR IS CARVED WITH THE TREATY YOU MADE WITH THE GIANTS, AND IF YOU ATTEMPT TO TAKE BACK YOUR RIGHTFUL PAYMENT TO THEM, YOUR GREAT POWER WOULD CRUMBLE TO DUST!
MY SPEAR SUBDUED YOU ONCE WITHOUT TREATY BY MIGHT ALONE . . .
IT IS AS READY FOR BATTLE AS EVER, ALBERICH.

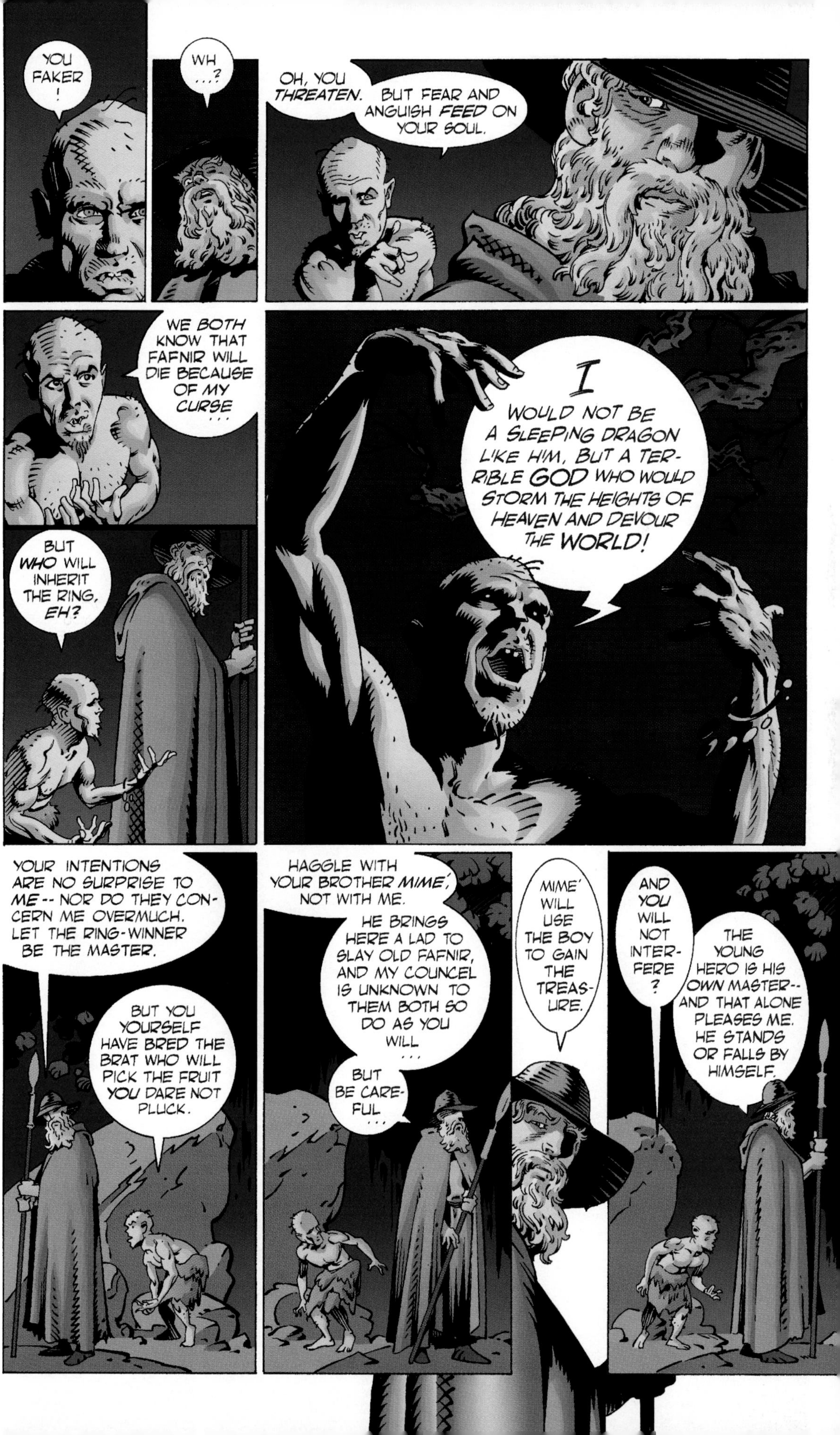
YOU FAKER!
WH...?
OH, YOU THREATEN.
BUT FEAR AND ANGUISH FEED ON YOUR SOUL.
WE BOTH KNOW THAT FAFNIR WILL DIE BECAUSE OF MY CURSE...
BUT WHO WILL INHERIT THE RING, EH?
I WOULD NOT BE A SLEEPING DRAGON LIKE HIM, BUT A TERRIBLE GOD WHO WOULD STORM THE HEIGHTS OF HEAVEN AND DEVOUR THE WORLD!
YOUR INTENTIONS ARE NO SURPRISE TO ME -- NOR DO THEY CONCERN ME OVERMUCH. LET THE RING-WINNER BE THE MASTER.
BUT YOU YOURSELF HAVE BRED THE BRAT WHO WILL PICK THE FRUIT YOU DARE NOT PLUCK.
HAGGLE WITH YOUR BROTHER MIME', NOT WITH ME.
HE BRINGS HERE A LAD TO SLAY OLD FAFNIR, AND MY COUNCEL IS UNKNOWN TO THEM BOTH SO DO AS YOU WILL...
BUT BE CAREFUL...
MIME' WILL USE THE BOY TO GAIN THE TREASURE.
AND YOU WILL NOT INTERFERE?
THE YOUNG HERO IS HIS OWN MASTER-- AND THAT ALONE PLEASES ME. HE STANDS OR FALLS BY HIMSELF.

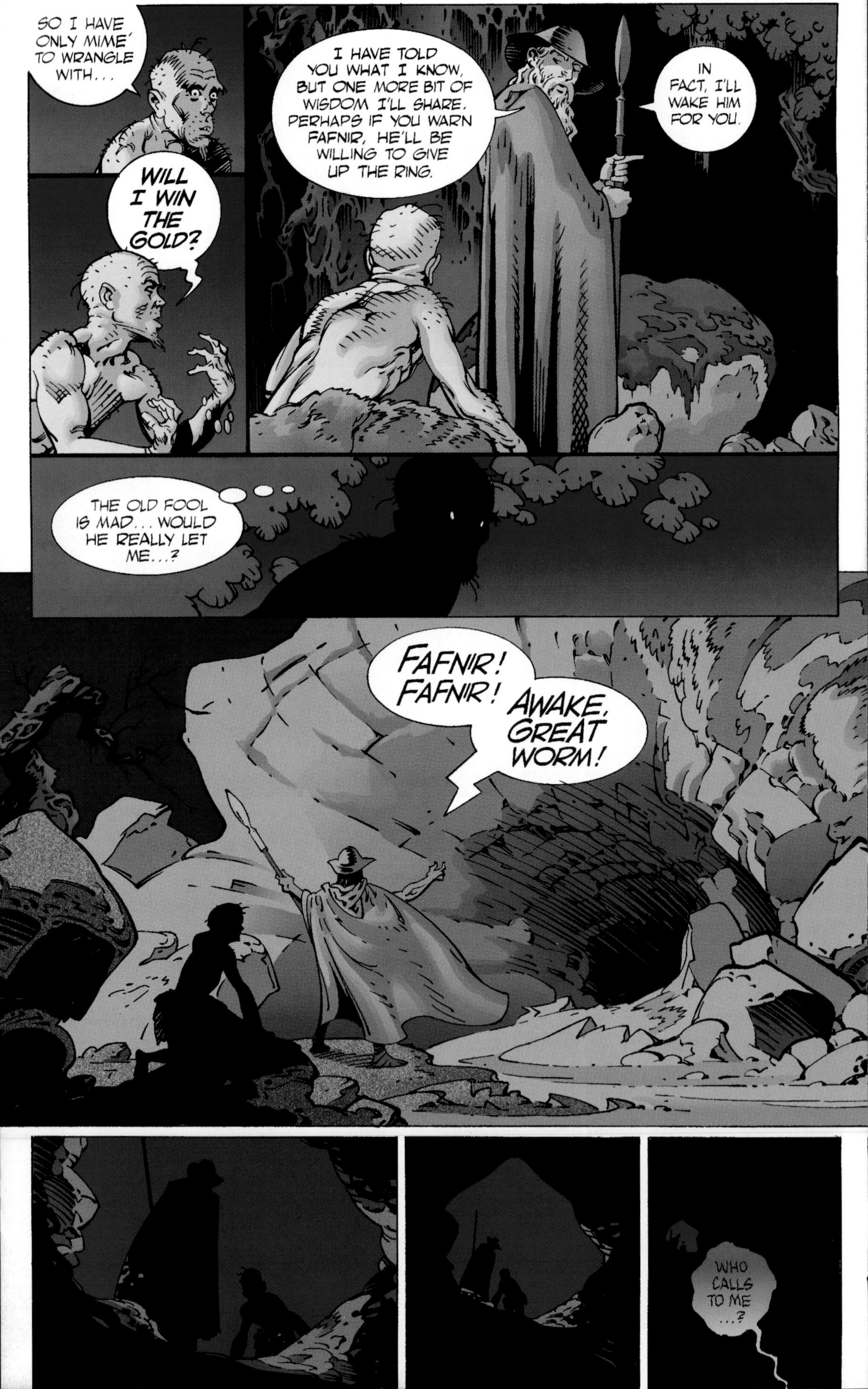
SO I HAVE ONLY MIME' TO WRANGLE WITH...
WILL I WIN THE GOLD?
I HAVE TOLD YOU WHAT I KNOW, BUT ONE MORE BIT OF WISDOM I'LL SHARE. PERHAPS IF YOU WARN FAFNIR, HE'LL BE WILLING TO GIVE UP THE RING.
IN FACT, I'LL WAKE HIM FOR YOU.
THE OLD FOOL IS MAD... WOULD HE REALLY LET ME...?
FAFNIR! FAFNIR!
AWAKE, GREAT WORM!
WHO CALLS TO ME ...?

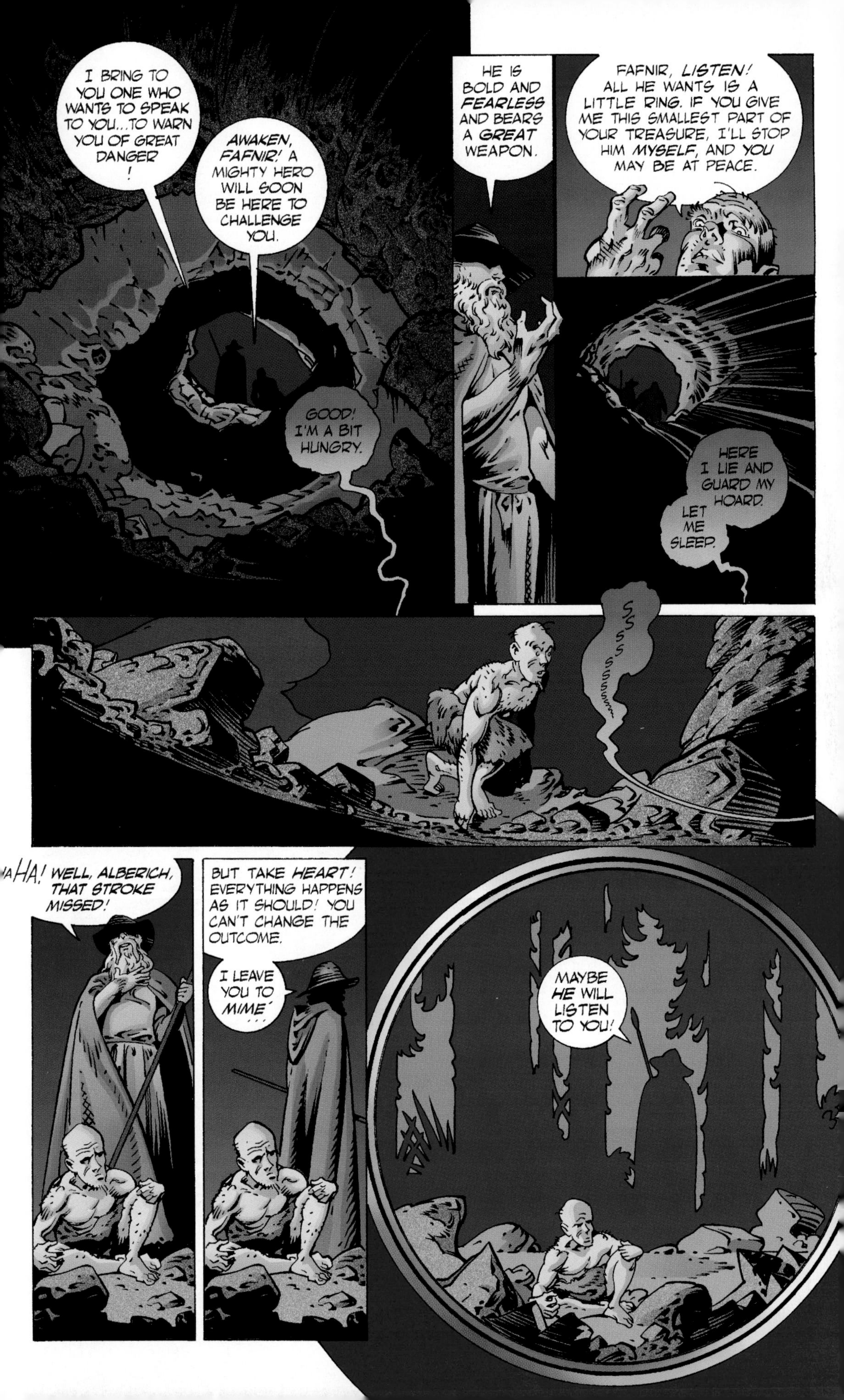
I BRING TO YOU ONE WHO WANTS TO SPEAK TO YOU...TO WARN YOU OF GREAT DANGER!
AWAKEN, FAFNIR! A MIGHTY HERO WILL SOON BE HERE TO CHALLENGE YOU.
GOOD! I'M A BIT HUNGRY.
HE IS BOLD AND FEARLESS AND BEARS A GREAT WEAPON.
FAFNIR, LISTEN! ALL HE WANTS IS A LITTLE RING. IF YOU GIVE ME THIS SMALLEST PART OF YOUR TREASURE, I'LL STOP HIM MYSELF, AND YOU MAY BE AT PEACE.
HERE I LIE AND GUARD MY HOARD.
LET ME SLEEP.
SSSSSSSSSS
HA HA! WELL, ALBERICH, THAT STROKE MISSED!
BUT TAKE HEART! EVERYTHING HAPPENS AS IT SHOULD! YOU CAN'T CHANGE THE OUTCOME.
I LEAVE YOU TO MIME...
MAYBE HE WILL LISTEN TO YOU!

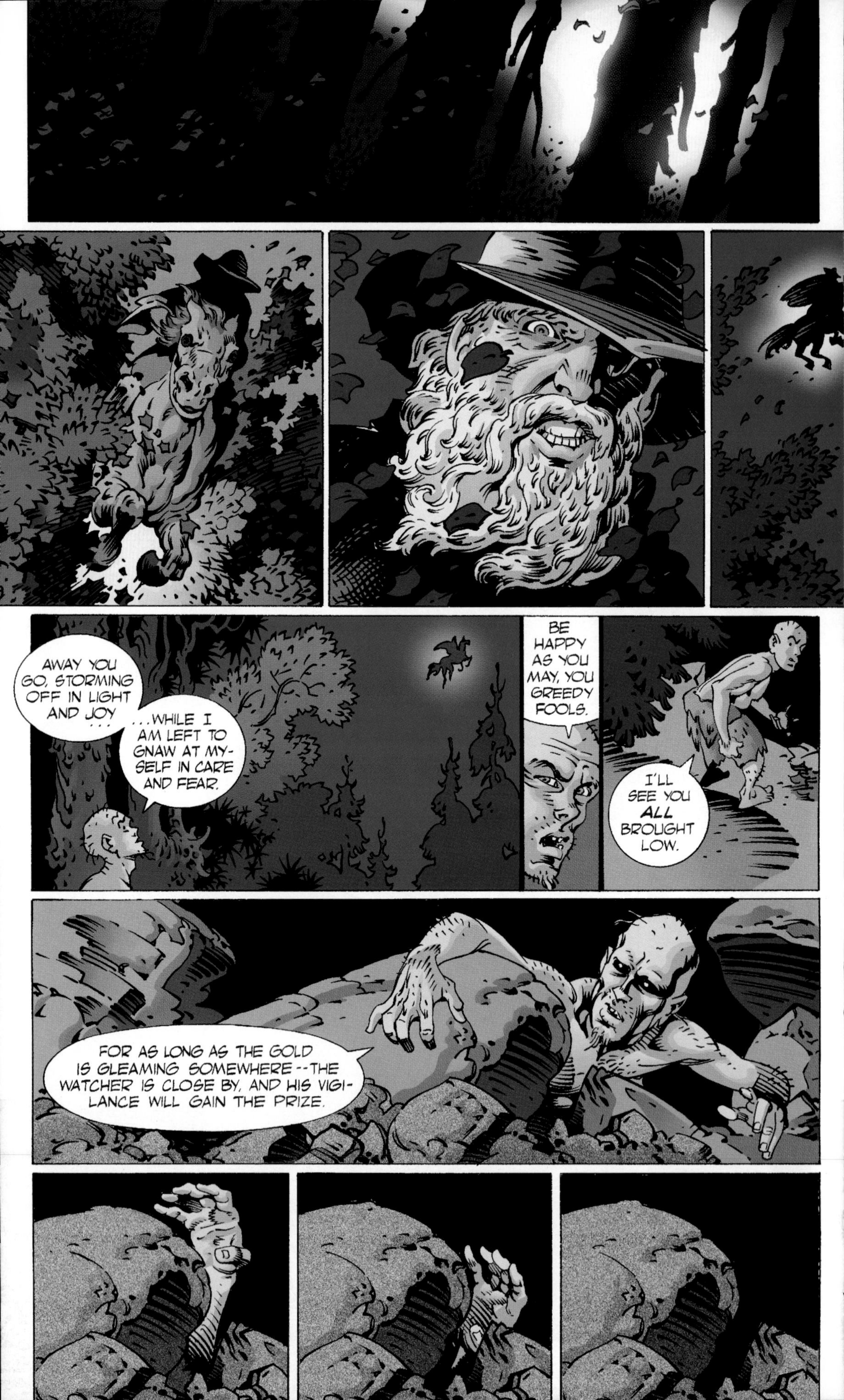
AWAY YOU GO, STORMING OFF IN LIGHT AND JOY . . .
. . .WHILE I AM LEFT TO GNAW AT MY-SELF IN CARE AND FEAR.
BE HAPPY AS YOU MAY, YOU GREEDY FOOLS.
I'LL SEE YOU **ALL** BROUGHT LOW.
FOR AS LONG AS THE GOLD IS GLEAMING SOMEWHERE--THE WATCHER IS CLOSE BY, AND HIS VIGI-LANCE WILL GAIN THE PRIZE.

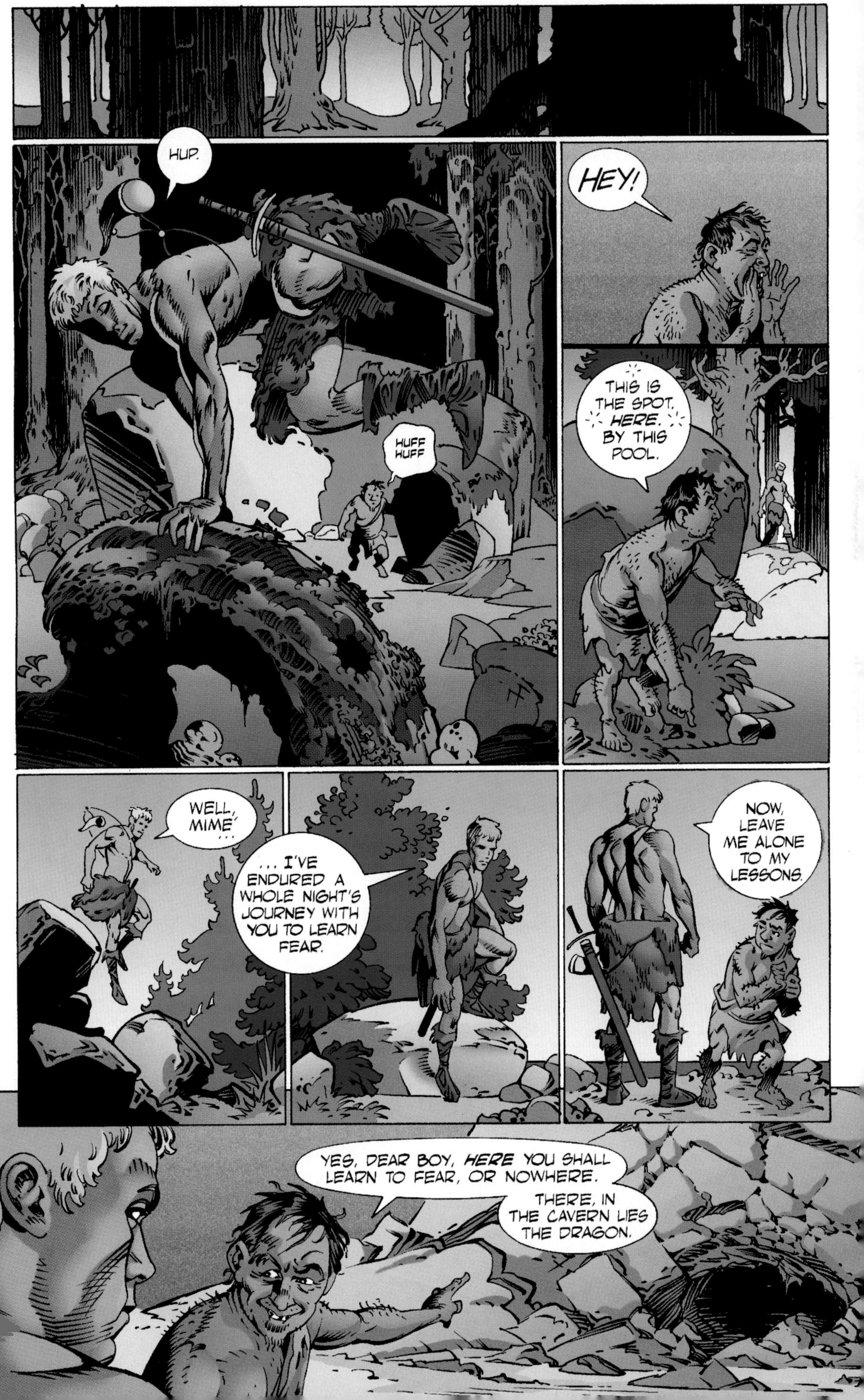
HUP.
HUFF HUFF
HEY!
THIS IS THE SPOT. HERE. BY THIS POOL.
WELL, MIME...
...I'VE ENDURED A WHOLE NIGHT'S JOURNEY WITH YOU TO LEARN FEAR.
NOW, LEAVE ME ALONE TO MY LESSONS.
YES, DEAR BOY, HERE YOU SHALL LEARN TO FEAR, OR NOWHERE.
THERE, IN THE CAVERN LIES THE DRAGON.

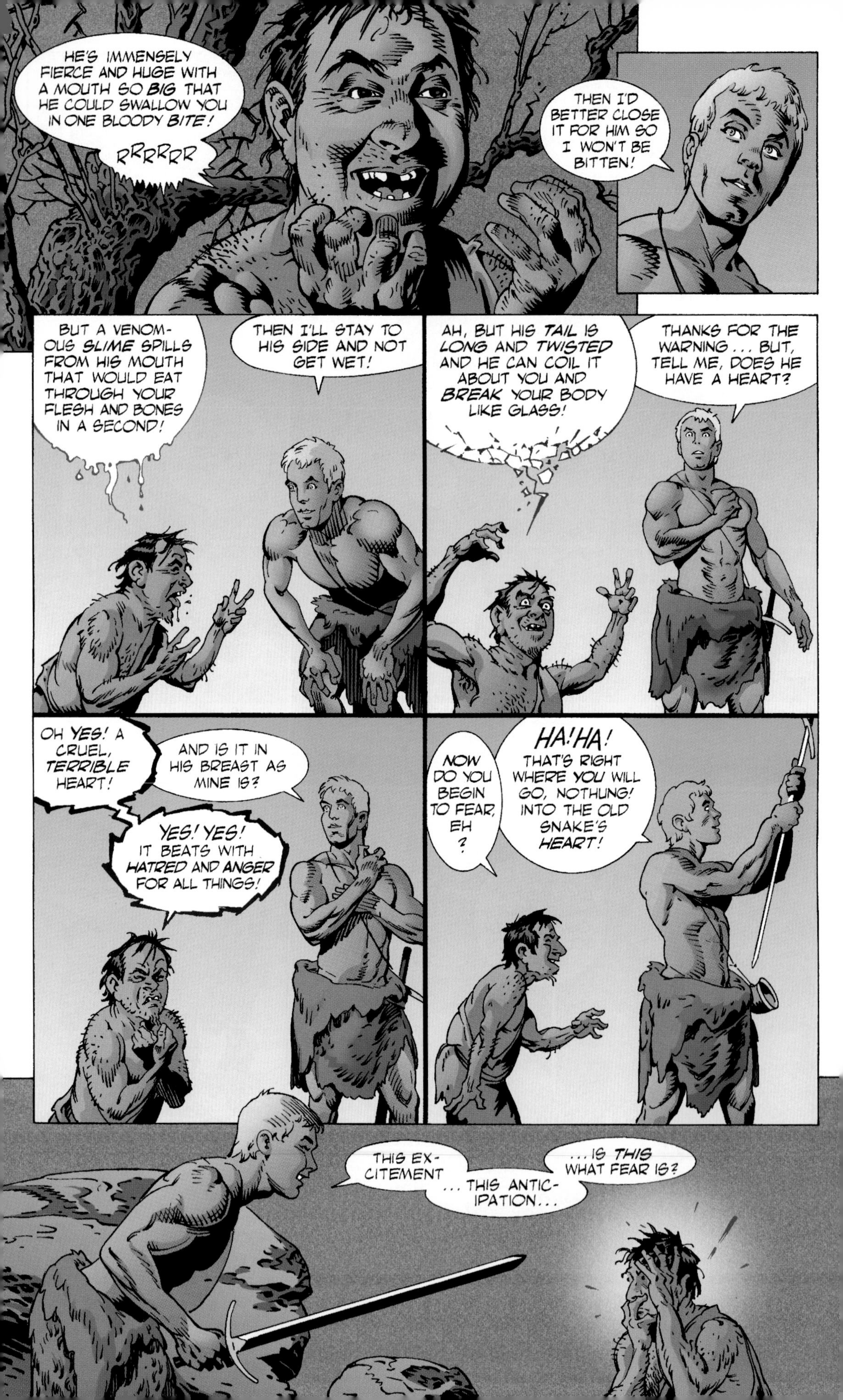
HE'S IMMENSELY FIERCE AND HUGE WITH A MOUTH SO BIG THAT HE COULD SWALLOW YOU IN ONE BLOODY BITE!
RRRRRR
THEN I'D BETTER CLOSE IT FOR HIM SO I WON'T BE BITTEN!
BUT A VENOMOUS SLIME SPILLS FROM HIS MOUTH THAT WOULD EAT THROUGH YOUR FLESH AND BONES IN A SECOND!
THEN I'LL STAY TO HIS SIDE AND NOT GET WET!
AH, BUT HIS TAIL IS LONG AND TWISTED AND HE CAN COIL IT ABOUT YOU AND BREAK YOUR BODY LIKE GLASS!
THANKS FOR THE WARNING ... BUT, TELL ME, DOES HE HAVE A HEART?
OH YES! A CRUEL, TERRIBLE HEART!
AND IS IT IN HIS BREAST AS MINE IS?
YES! YES! IT BEATS WITH HATRED AND ANGER FOR ALL THINGS!
NOW DO YOU BEGIN TO FEAR, EH?
HA! HA! THAT'S RIGHT WHERE YOU WILL GO, NOTHUNG! INTO THE OLD SNAKE'S HEART!
THIS EXCITEMENT
... THIS ANTICIPATION...
... IS THIS WHAT FEAR IS?

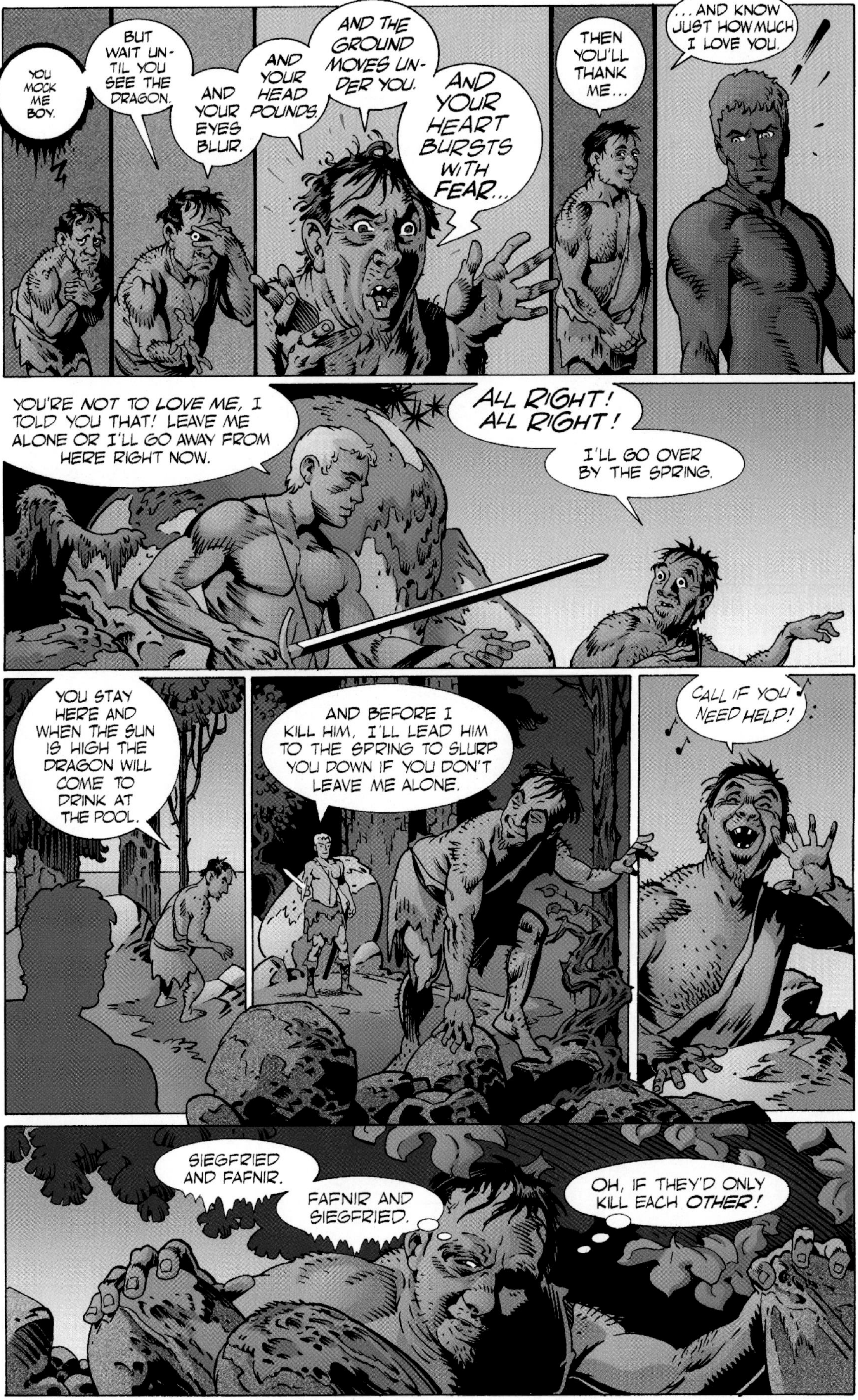
YOU MOCK ME BOY.
BUT WAIT UNTIL YOU SEE THE DRAGON.
AND YOUR EYES BLUR.
AND YOUR HEAD POUNDS.
AND THE GROUND MOVES UNDER YOU.
AND YOUR HEART BURSTS WITH FEAR...
THEN YOU'LL THANK ME...
...AND KNOW JUST HOW MUCH I LOVE YOU.
YOU'RE NOT TO LOVE ME, I TOLD YOU THAT! LEAVE ME ALONE OR I'LL GO AWAY FROM HERE RIGHT NOW.
ALL RIGHT! ALL RIGHT!
I'LL GO OVER BY THE SPRING.
YOU STAY HERE AND WHEN THE SUN IS HIGH THE DRAGON WILL COME TO DRINK AT THE POOL.
AND BEFORE I KILL HIM, I'LL LEAD HIM TO THE SPRING TO SLURP YOU DOWN IF YOU DON'T LEAVE ME ALONE.
CALL IF YOU NEED HELP!
SIEGFRIED AND FAFNIR.
FAFNIR AND SIEGFRIED.
OH, IF THEY'D ONLY KILL EACH OTHER!

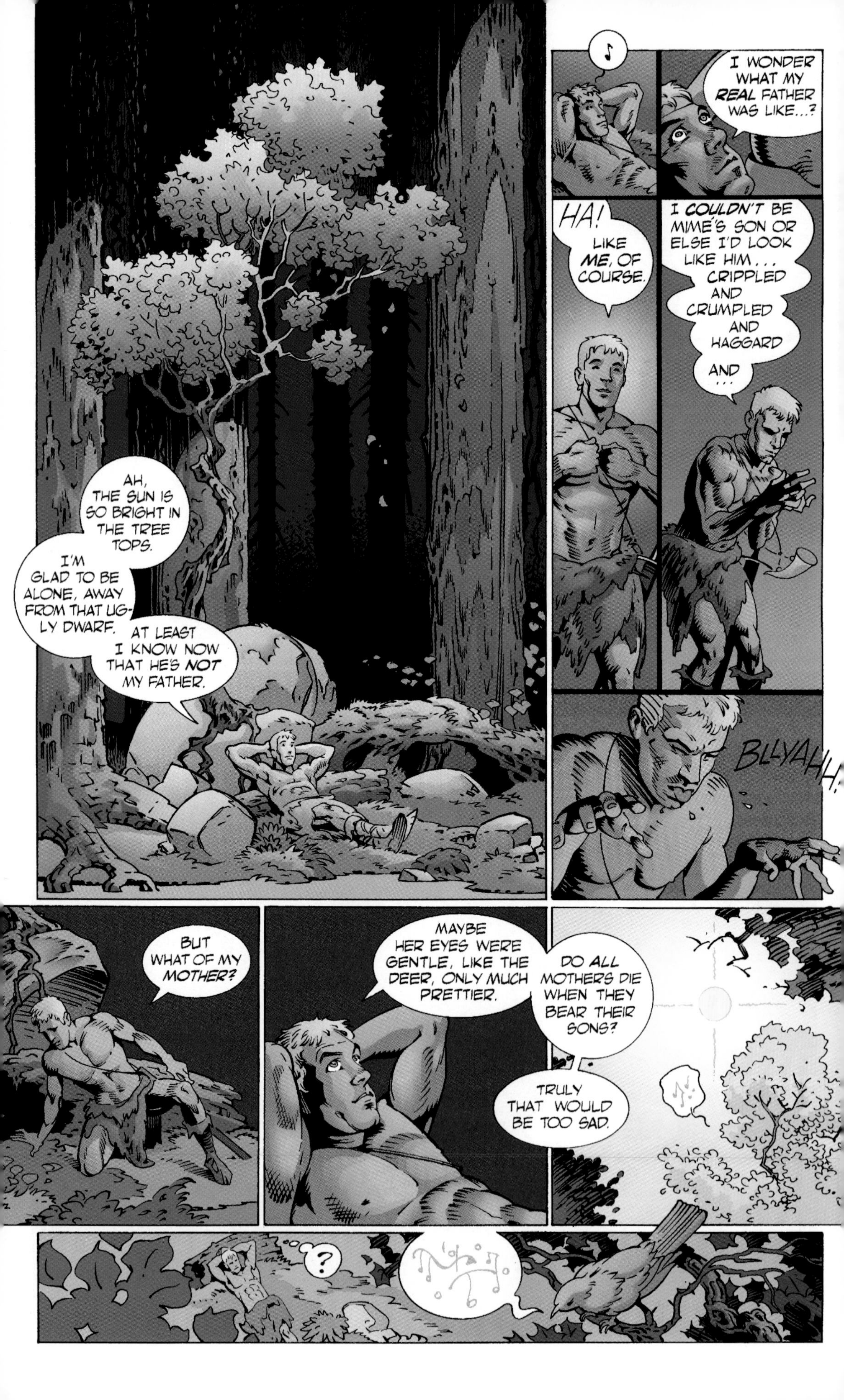
AH, THE SUN IS SO BRIGHT IN THE TREE TOPS.
I'M GLAD TO BE ALONE, AWAY FROM THAT UG-LY DWARF.
AT LEAST I KNOW NOW THAT HE'S NOT MY FATHER.
♪
I WONDER WHAT MY REAL FATHER WAS LIKE...?
HA!
LIKE ME, OF COURSE.
I COULDN'T BE MIME'S SON OR ELSE I'D LOOK LIKE HIM... CRIPPLED AND CRUMPLED AND HAGGARD
AND...
BLLYAHH!
BUT WHAT OF MY MOTHER?
MAYBE HER EYES WERE GENTLE, LIKE THE DEER, ONLY MUCH PRETTIER.
DO ALL MOTHERS DIE WHEN THEY BEAR THEIR SONS?
TRULY THAT WOULD BE TOO SAD.
?

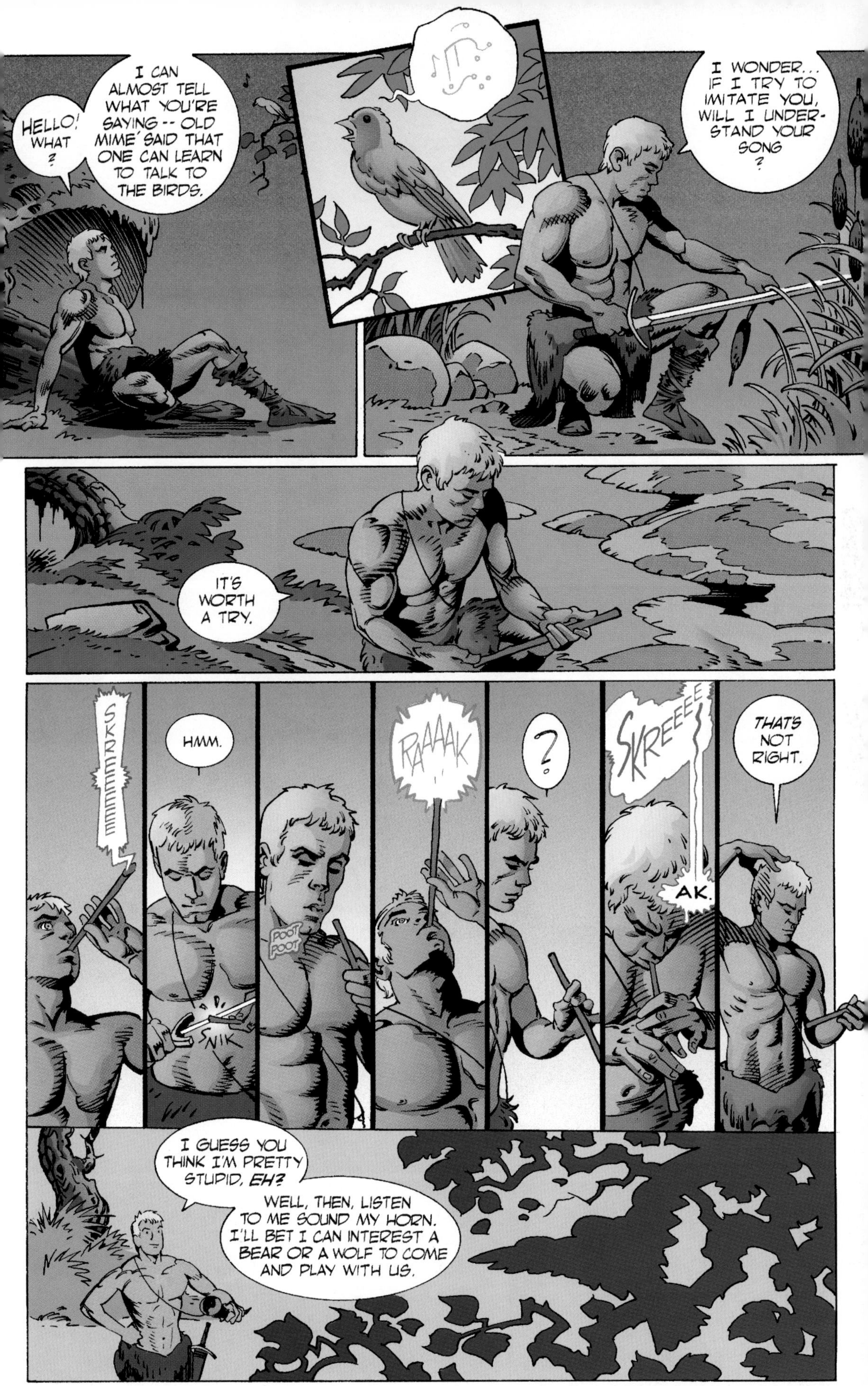
HELLO! WHAT ?
I CAN ALMOST TELL WHAT YOU'RE SAYING -- OLD MIME' SAID THAT ONE CAN LEARN TO TALK TO THE BIRDS.
I WONDER... IF I TRY TO IMITATE YOU, WILL I UNDERSTAND YOUR SONG ?
IT'S WORTH A TRY.
SKREEEEEE
HMM.
SNIK
POOT POOT
RAAAAK
?
SKREEEE
AK.
THAT'S NOT RIGHT.
I GUESS YOU THINK I'M PRETTY STUPID, EH?
WELL, THEN, LISTEN TO ME SOUND MY HORN. I'LL BET I CAN INTEREST A BEAR OR A WOLF TO COME AND PLAY WITH US.

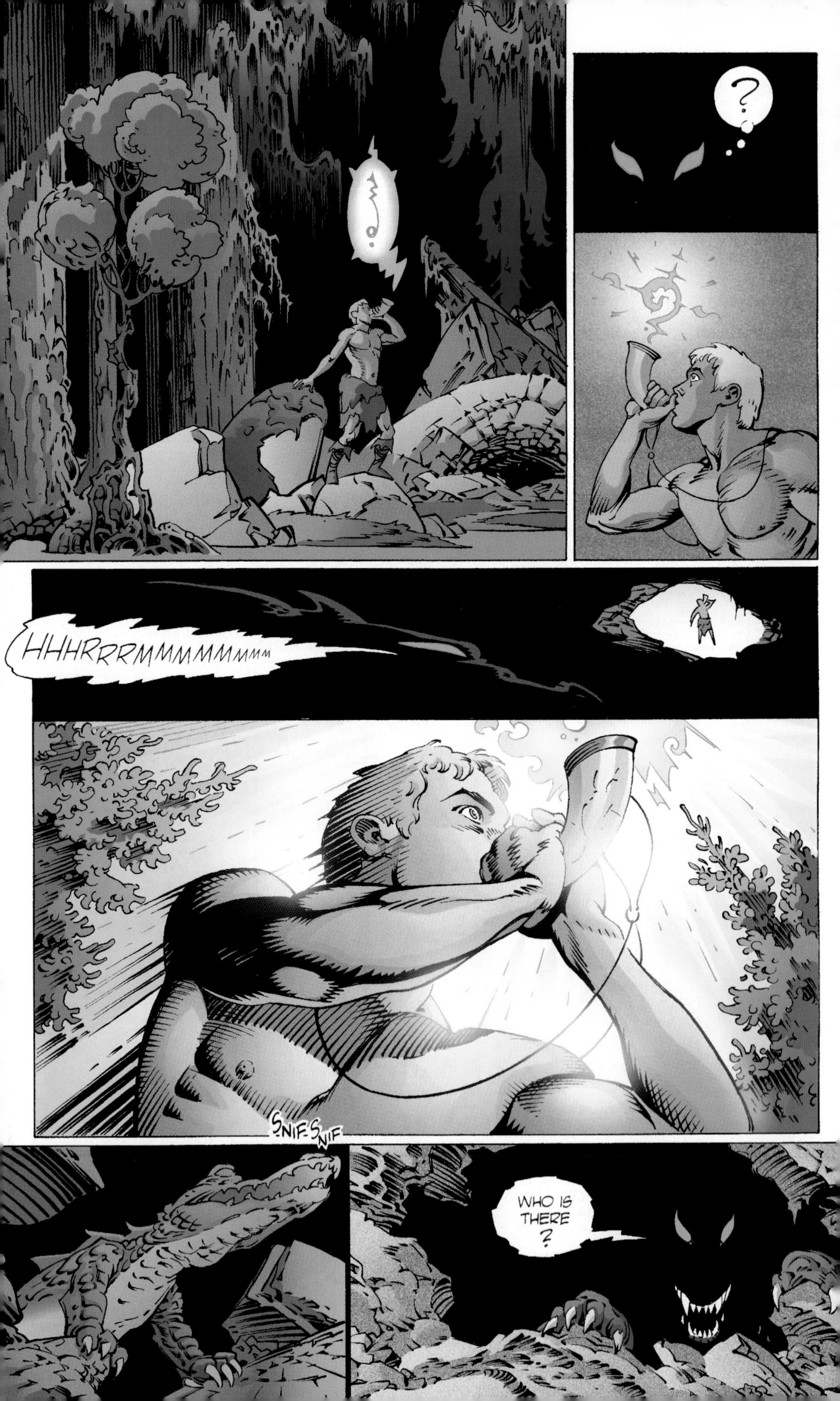
?
HHHRRRMMMMMMMmmm
SNIF SNIF
WHO IS THERE ?

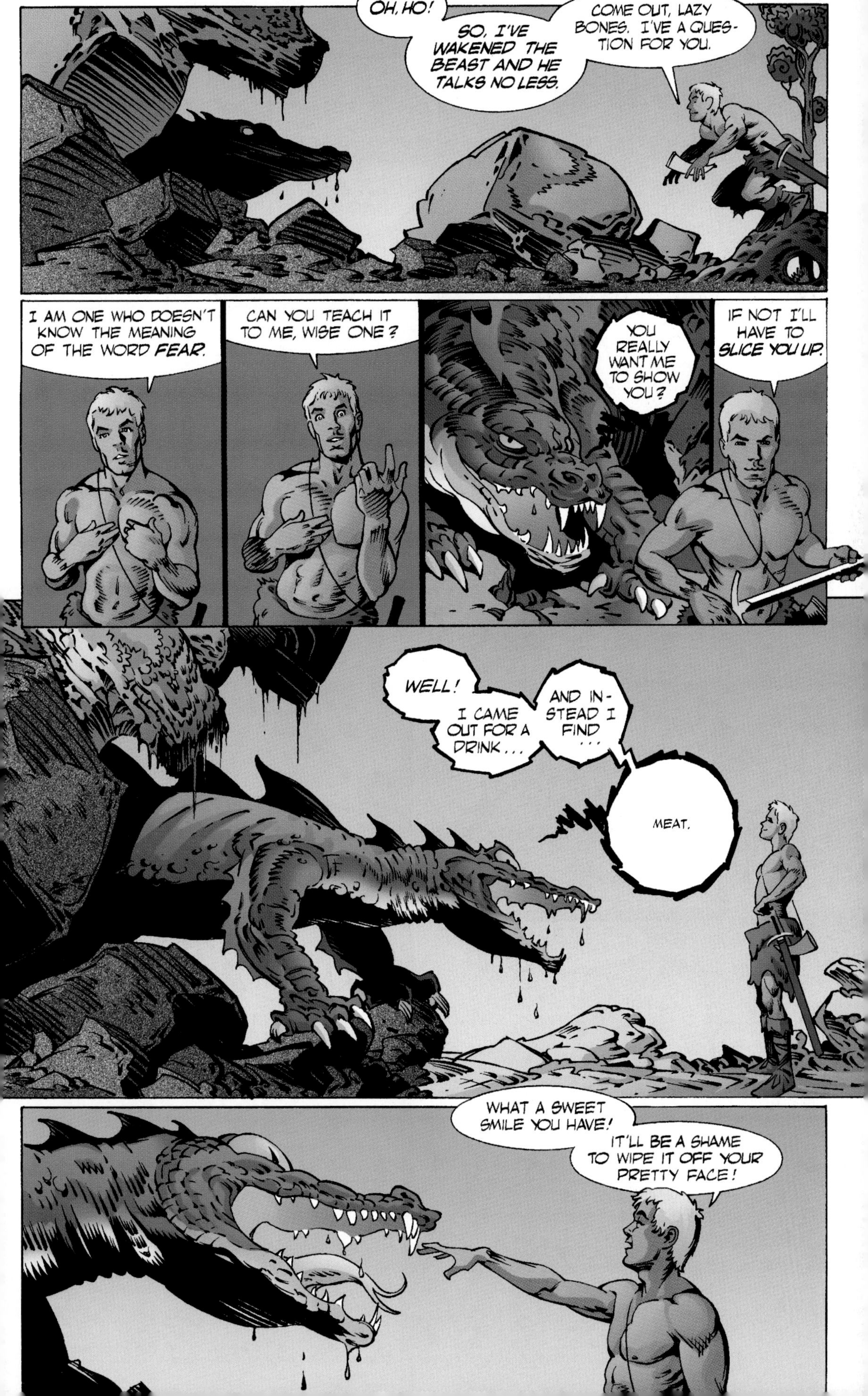
OH, HO!
SO, I'VE WAKENED THE BEAST AND HE TALKS NO LESS.
COME OUT, LAZY BONES. I'VE A QUES-TION FOR YOU.
I AM ONE WHO DOESN'T KNOW THE MEANING OF THE WORD FEAR.
CAN YOU TEACH IT TO ME, WISE ONE?
YOU REALLY WANT ME TO SHOW YOU?
IF NOT I'LL HAVE TO SLICE YOU UP.
WELL!
I CAME OUT FOR A DRINK . . .
AND IN-STEAD I FIND . . .
MEAT.
WHAT A SWEET SMILE YOU HAVE!
IT'LL BE A SHAME TO WIPE IT OFF YOUR PRETTY FACE!

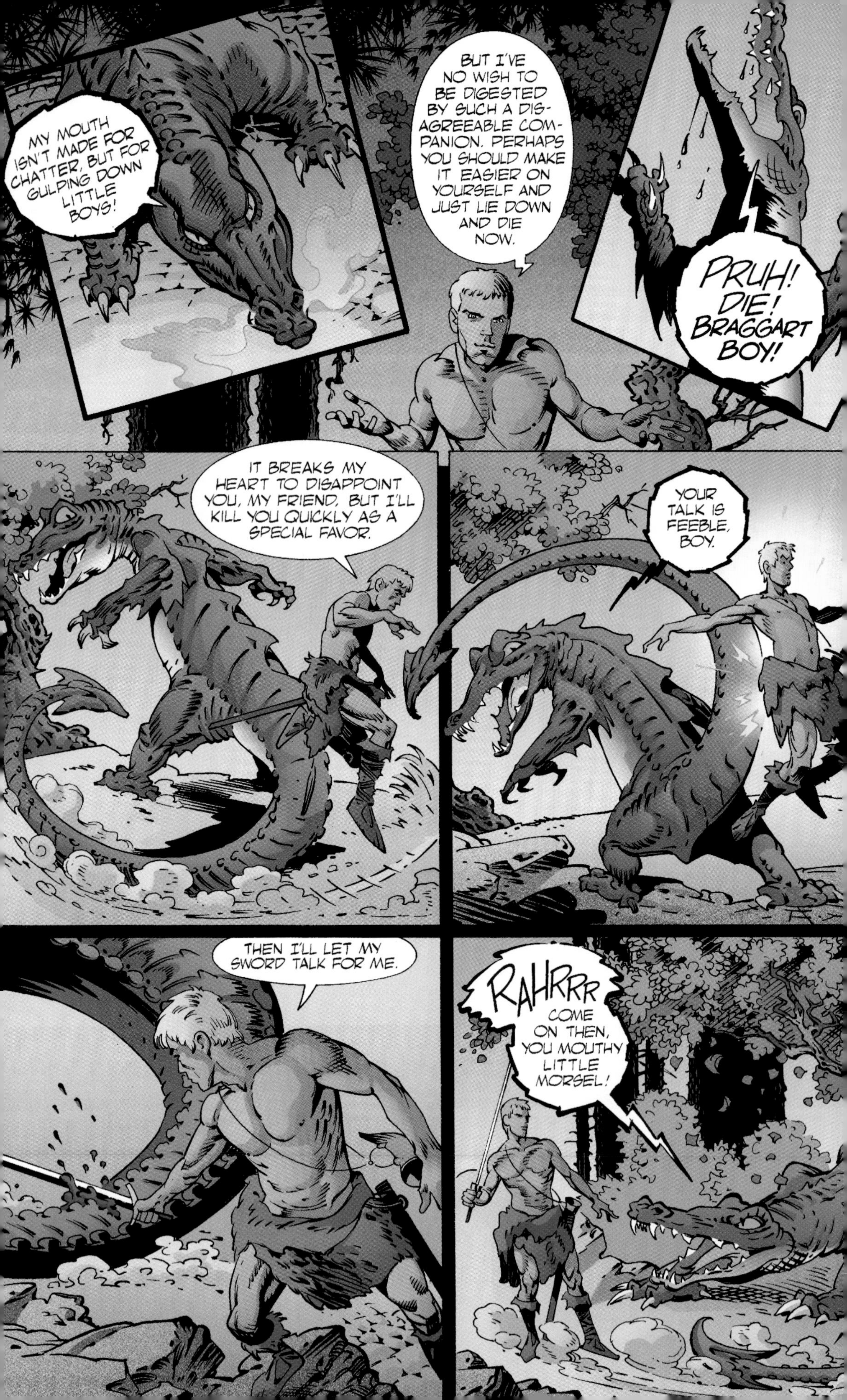
MY MOUTH ISN'T MADE FOR CHATTER, BUT FOR GULPING DOWN LITTLE BOYS!
BUT I'VE NO WISH TO BE DIGESTED BY SUCH A DIS-AGREEABLE COM-PANION. PERHAPS YOU SHOULD MAKE IT EASIER ON YOURSELF AND JUST LIE DOWN AND DIE NOW.
PRUH! DIE! BRAGGART BOY!
IT BREAKS MY HEART TO DISAPPOINT YOU, MY FRIEND, BUT I'LL KILL YOU QUICKLY AS A SPECIAL FAVOR.
YOUR TALK IS FEEBLE, BOY.
THEN I'LL LET MY SWORD TALK FOR ME.
RAHRRR
COME ON THEN, YOU MOUTHY LITTLE MORSEL!

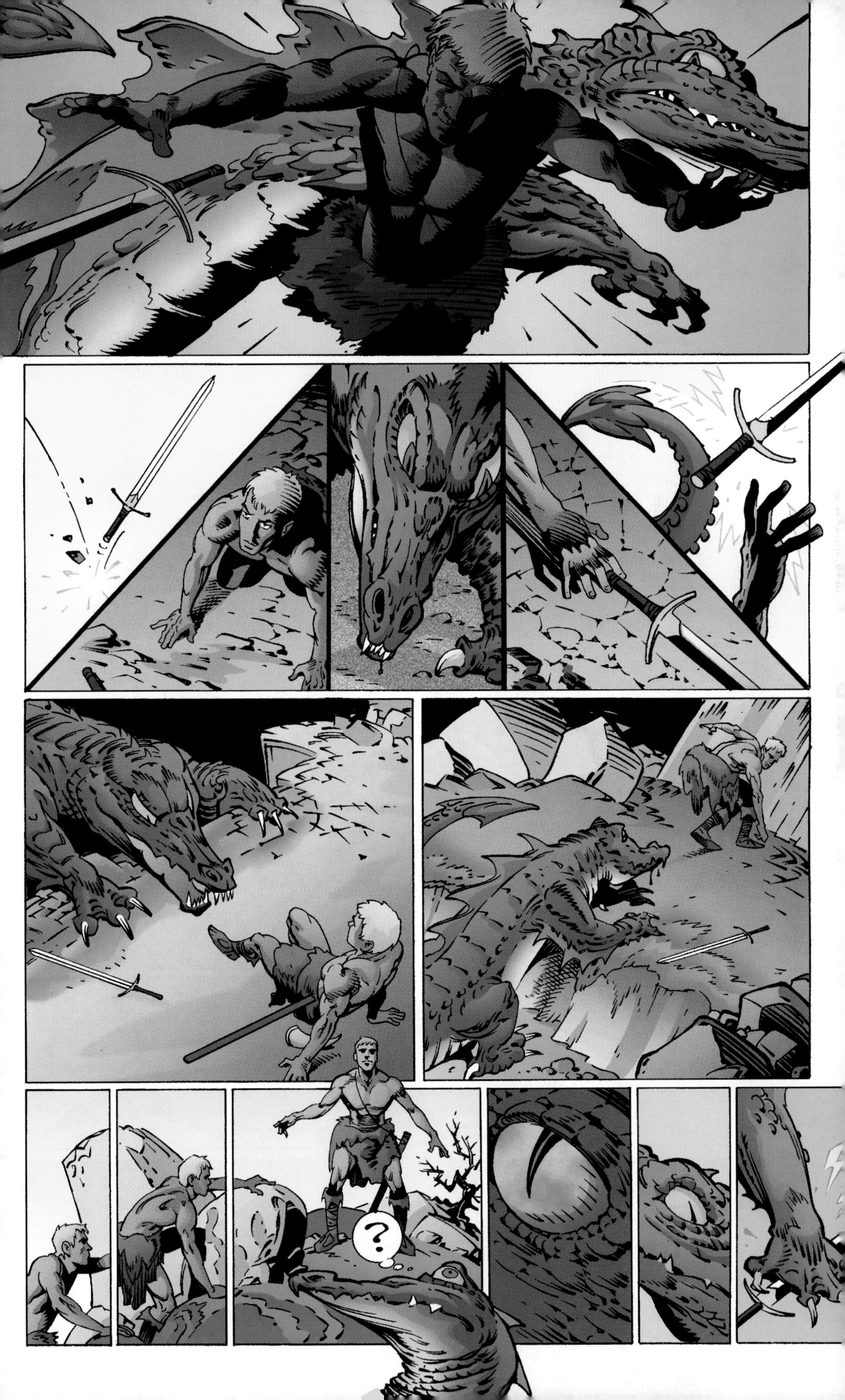
?

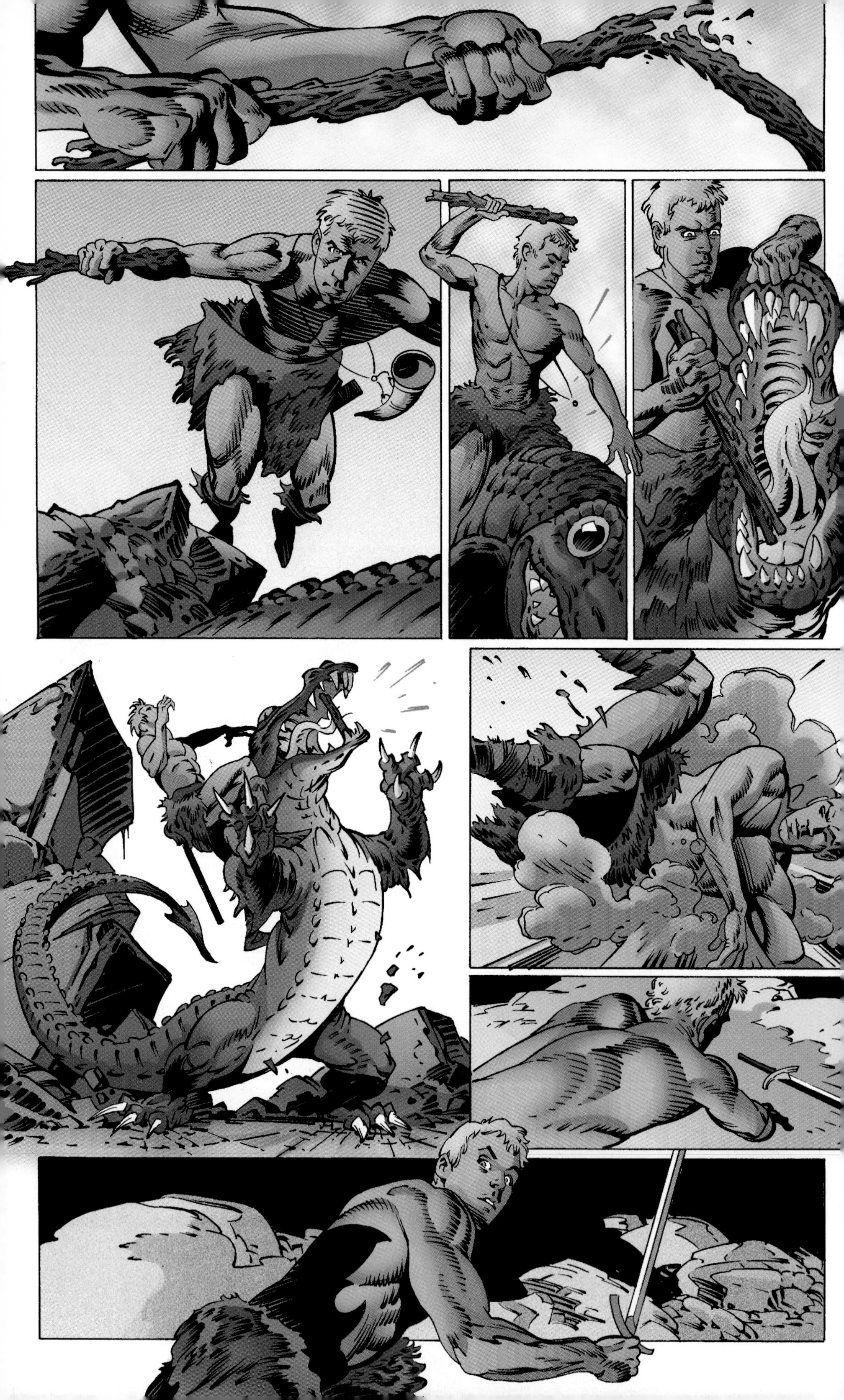

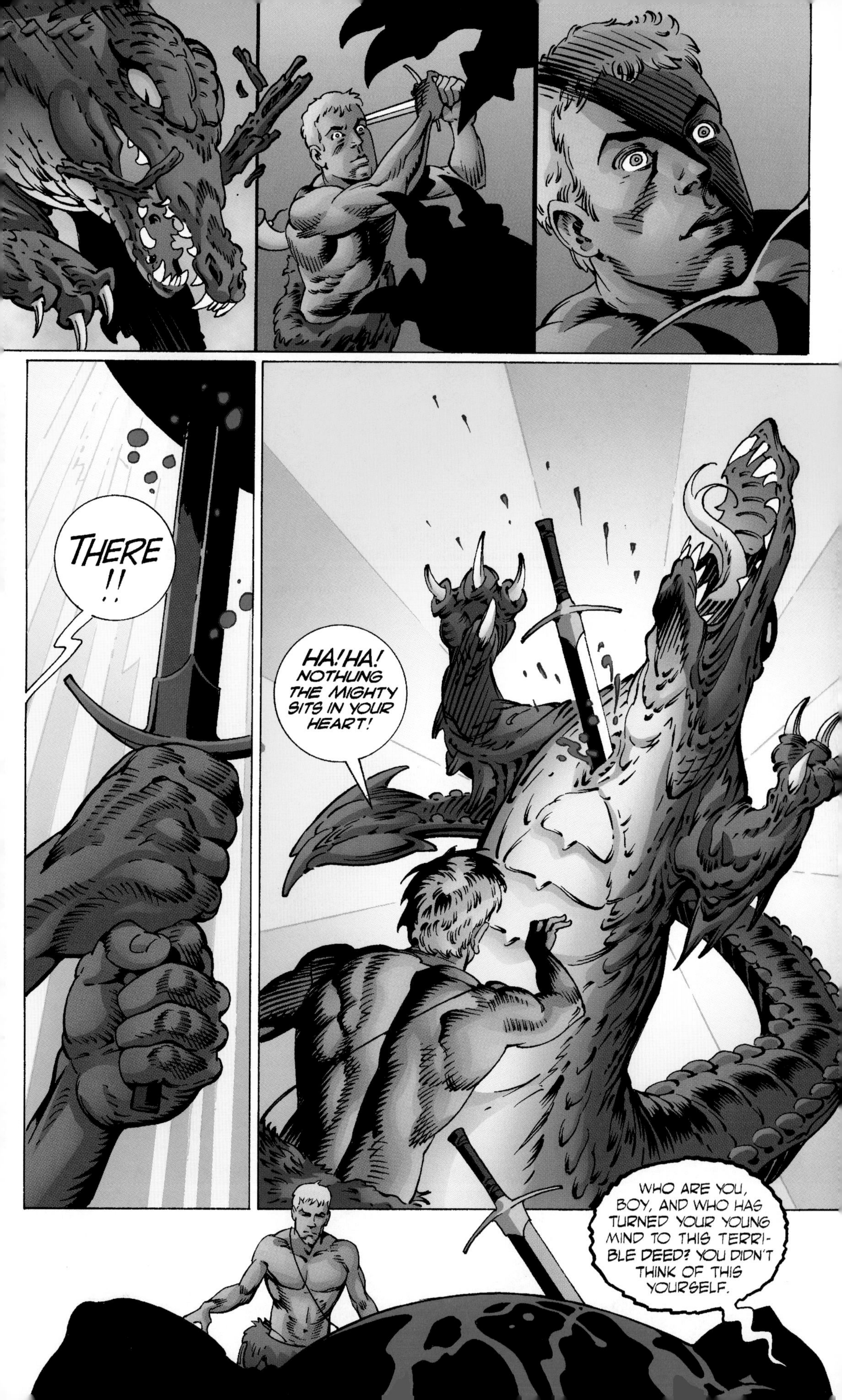
THERE !!
HA!HA! NOTHUNG THE MIGHTY SITS IN YOUR HEART!
WHO ARE YOU, BOY, AND WHO HAS TURNED YOUR YOUNG MIND TO THIS TERRI-BLE DEED? YOU DIDN'T THINK OF THIS YOURSELF.

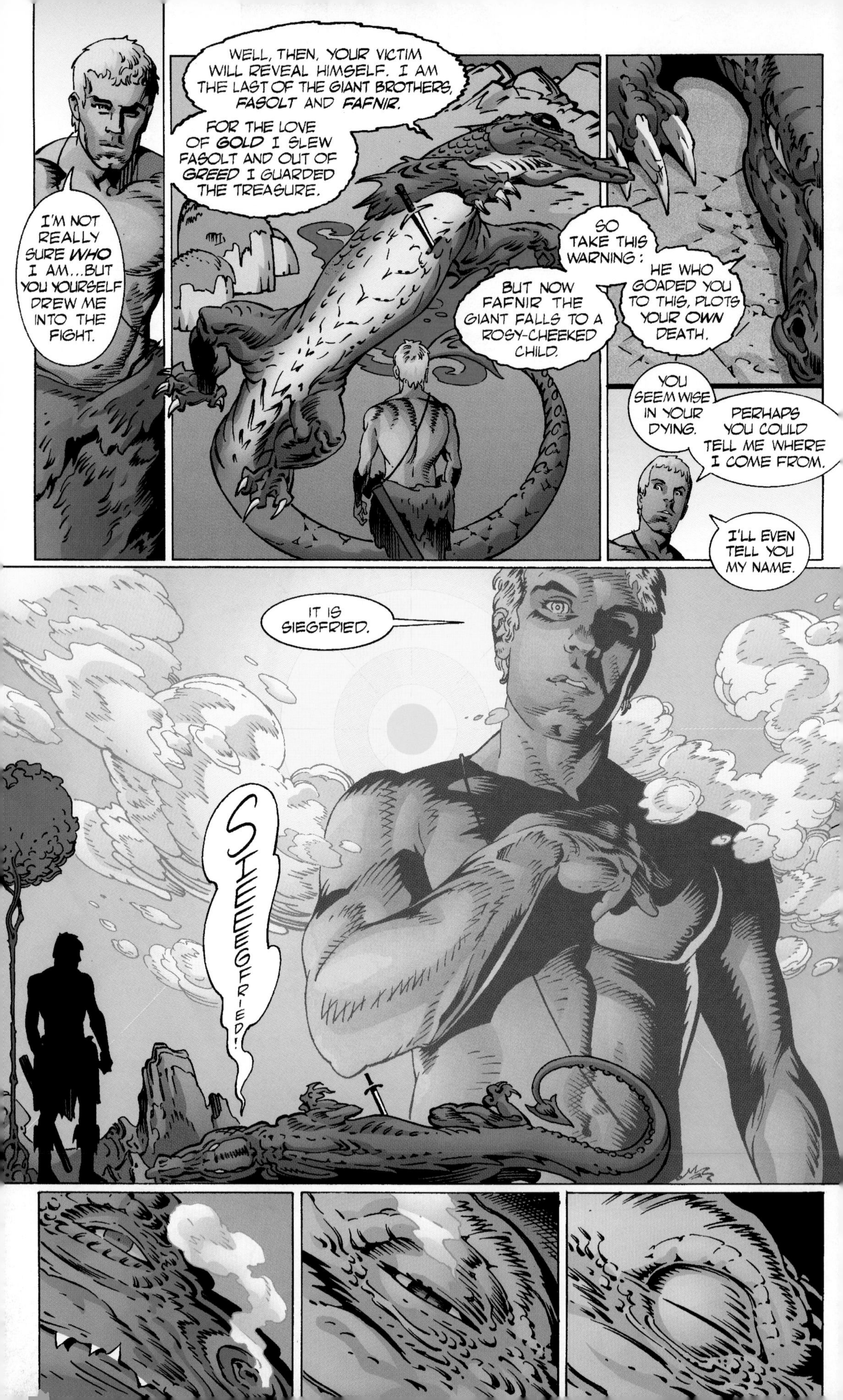
I'M NOT REALLY SURE WHO I AM...BUT YOU YOURSELF DREW ME INTO THE FIGHT.
WELL, THEN, YOUR VICTIM WILL REVEAL HIMSELF. I AM THE LAST OF THE GIANT BROTHERS, FASOLT AND FAFNIR.
FOR THE LOVE OF GOLD I SLEW FASOLT AND OUT OF GREED I GUARDED THE TREASURE.
BUT NOW FAFNIR THE GIANT FALLS TO A ROSY-CHEEKED CHILD.
SO TAKE THIS WARNING:
HE WHO GOADED YOU TO THIS, PLOTS YOUR OWN DEATH.
YOU SEEM WISE IN YOUR DYING.
PERHAPS YOU COULD TELL ME WHERE I COME FROM.
I'LL EVEN TELL YOU MY NAME.
IT IS SIEGFRIED.
SIEEEGFRIED!

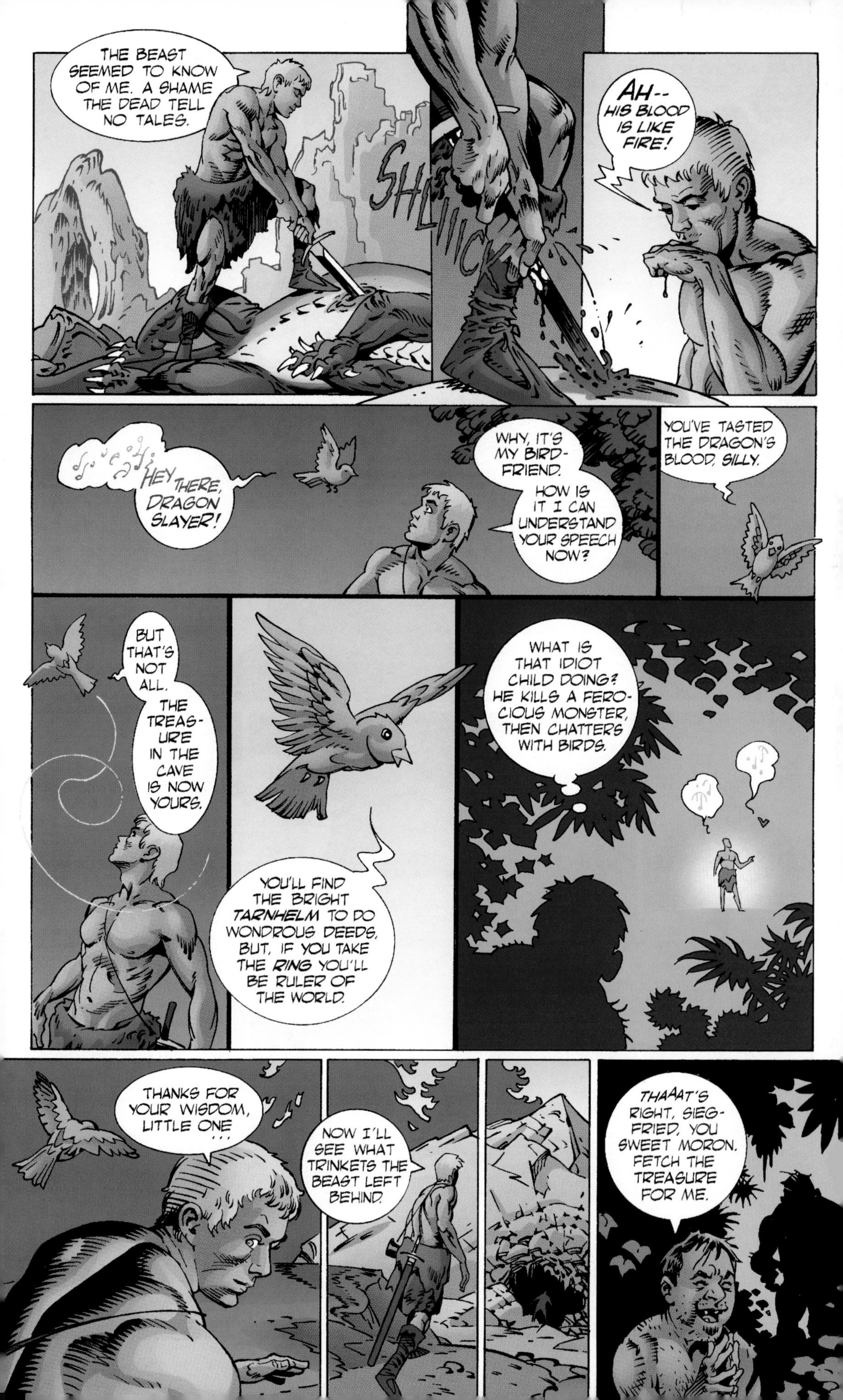
THE BEAST SEEMED TO KNOW OF ME. A SHAME THE DEAD TELL NO TALES.
SHLIICK
AH-- HIS BLOOD IS LIKE FIRE!
HEY THERE, DRAGON SLAYER!
WHY, IT'S MY BIRD-FRIEND.
HOW IS IT I CAN UNDERSTAND YOUR SPEECH NOW?
YOU'VE TASTED THE DRAGON'S BLOOD, SILLY.
BUT THAT'S NOT ALL.
THE TREAS-URE IN THE CAVE IS NOW YOURS.
YOU'LL FIND THE BRIGHT TARNHELM TO DO WONDROUS DEEDS, BUT, IF YOU TAKE THE RING YOU'LL BE RULER OF THE WORLD.
WHAT IS THAT IDIOT CHILD DOING? HE KILLS A FERO-CIOUS MONSTER, THEN CHATTERS WITH BIRDS.
THANKS FOR YOUR WISDOM, LITTLE ONE . . .
NOW I'LL SEE WHAT TRINKETS THE BEAST LEFT BEHIND.
THAAAT'S RIGHT, SIEG-FRIED, YOU SWEET MORON. FETCH THE TREASURE FOR ME.

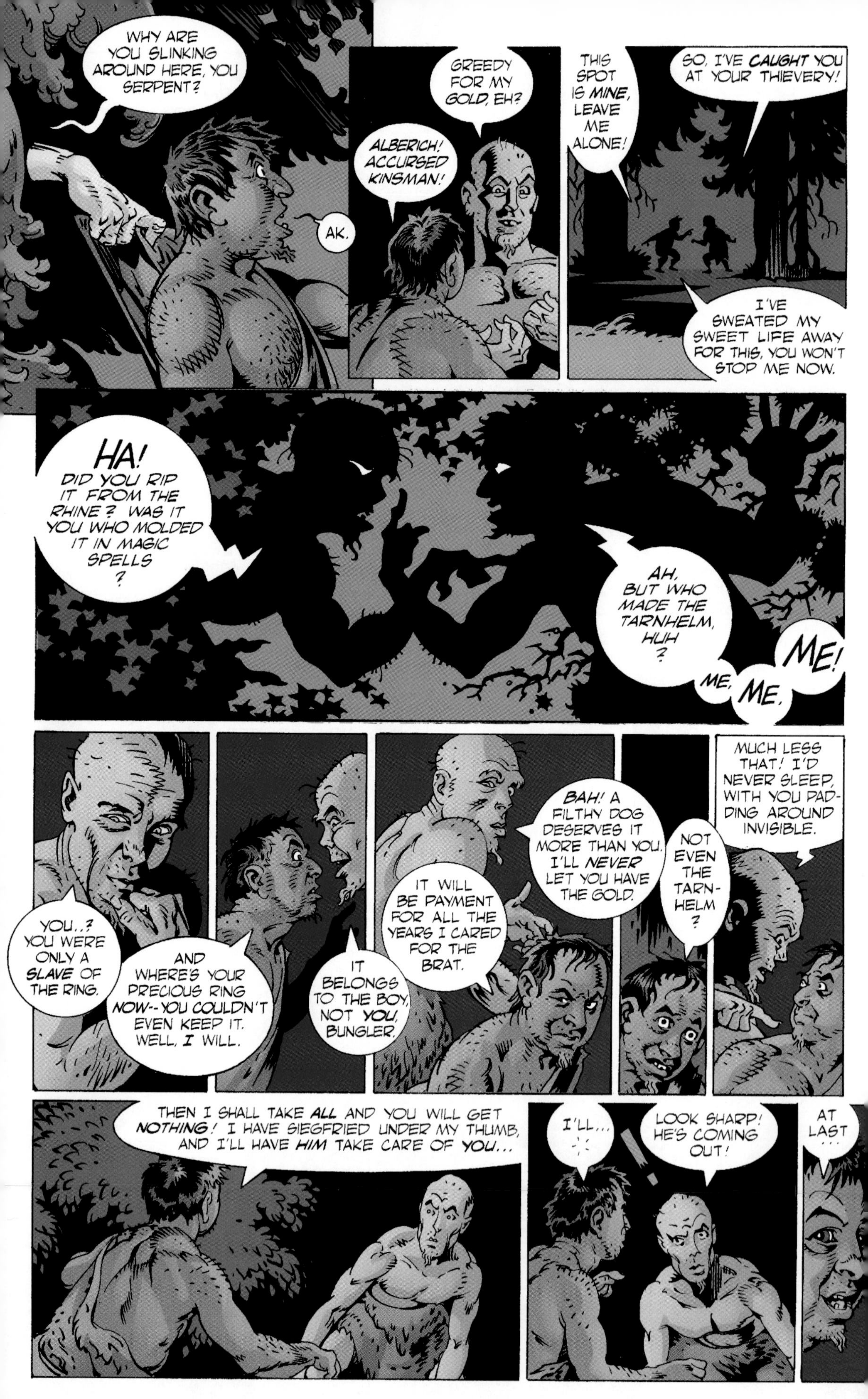
WHY ARE YOU SLINKING AROUND HERE, YOU SERPENT?
AK.
GREEDY FOR MY GOLD, EH?
ALBERICH! ACCURSED KINSMAN!
THIS SPOT IS MINE, LEAVE ME ALONE!
SO, I'VE CAUGHT YOU AT YOUR THIEVERY!
I'VE SWEATED MY SWEET LIFE AWAY FOR THIS, YOU WON'T STOP ME NOW.
HA! DID YOU RIP IT FROM THE RHINE? WAS IT YOU WHO MOLDED IT IN MAGIC SPELLS?
AH, BUT WHO MADE THE TARNHELM, HUH?
ME, ME, ME!
YOU..? YOU WERE ONLY A SLAVE OF THE RING.
AND WHERE'S YOUR PRECIOUS RING NOW--YOU COULDN'T EVEN KEEP IT. WELL, I WILL.
IT BELONGS TO THE BOY, NOT YOU, BUNGLER.
IT WILL BE PAYMENT FOR ALL THE YEARS I CARED FOR THE BRAT.
BAH! A FILTHY DOG DESERVES IT MORE THAN YOU. I'LL NEVER LET YOU HAVE THE GOLD.
NOT EVEN THE TARNHELM?
MUCH LESS THAT! I'D NEVER SLEEP, WITH YOU PADDING AROUND INVISIBLE.
THEN I SHALL TAKE ALL AND YOU WILL GET NOTHING! I HAVE SIEGFRIED UNDER MY THUMB, AND I'LL HAVE HIM TAKE CARE OF YOU...
I'LL...
LOOK SHARP! HE'S COMING OUT!
AT LAST...

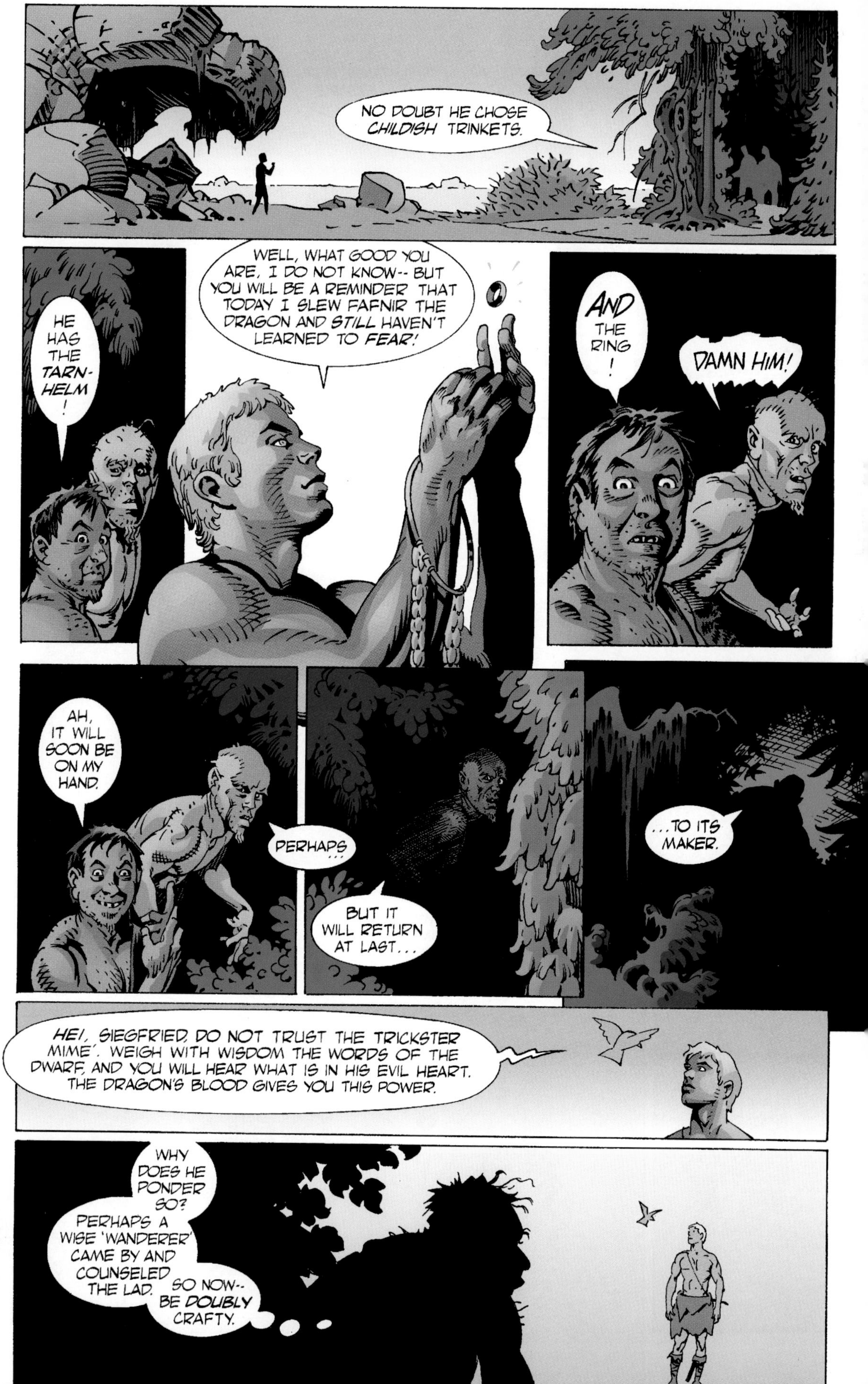
NO DOUBT HE CHOSE CHILDISH TRINKETS.
HE HAS THE TARN-HELM!
WELL, WHAT GOOD YOU ARE, I DO NOT KNOW-- BUT YOU WILL BE A REMINDER THAT TODAY I SLEW FAFNIR THE DRAGON AND STILL HAVEN'T LEARNED TO FEAR!
AND THE RING!
DAMN HIM!
AH, IT WILL SOON BE ON MY HAND.
PERHAPS...
BUT IT WILL RETURN AT LAST...
...TO ITS MAKER.
HEI, SIEGFRIED, DO NOT TRUST THE TRICKSTER MIME´. WEIGH WITH WISDOM THE WORDS OF THE DWARF, AND YOU WILL HEAR WHAT IS IN HIS EVIL HEART. THE DRAGON'S BLOOD GIVES YOU THIS POWER.
WHY DOES HE PONDER SO? PERHAPS A WISE 'WANDERER' CAME BY AND COUNSELED THE LAD.
SO NOW-- BE DOUBLY CRAFTY.

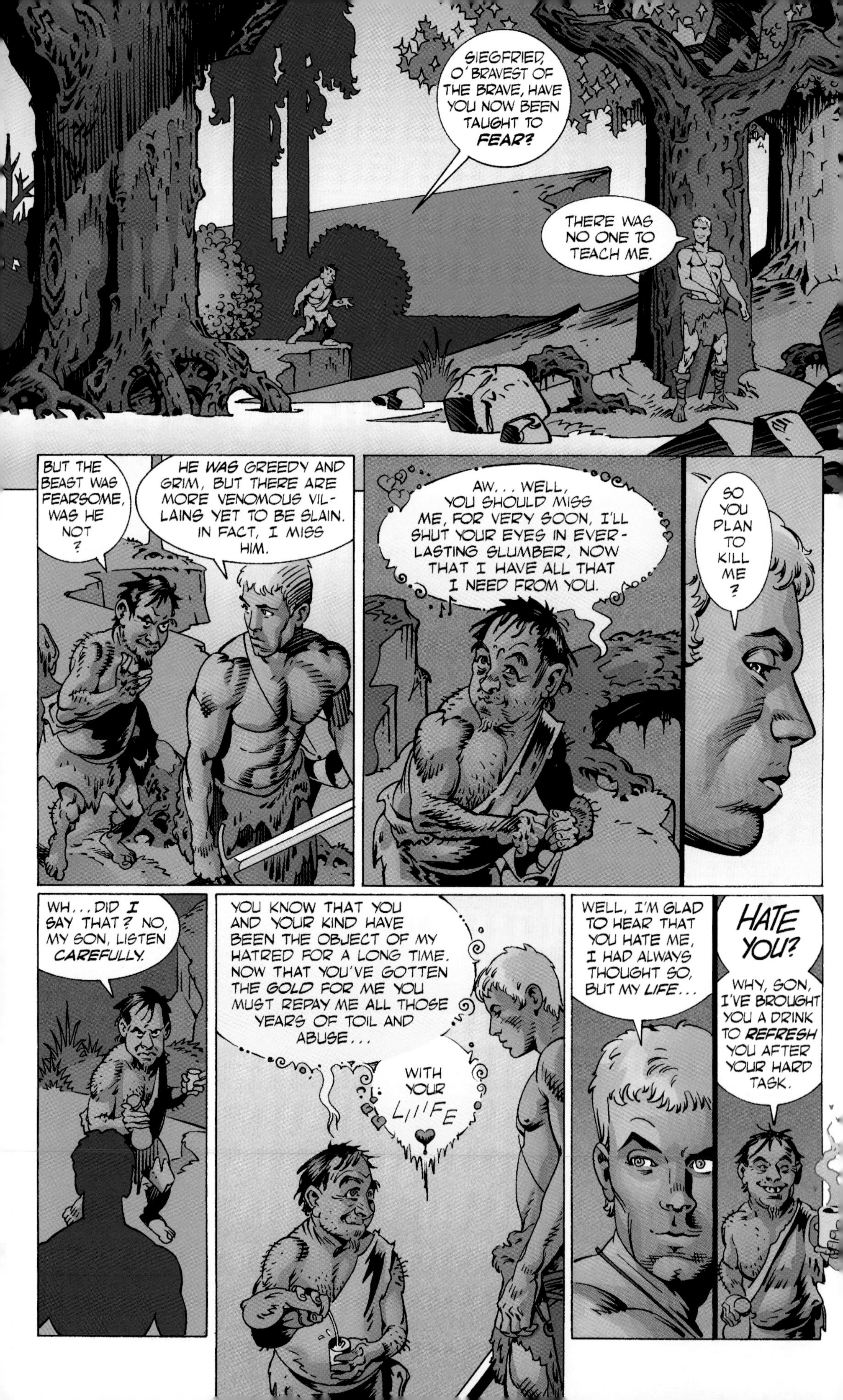
SIEGFRIED, O' BRAVEST OF THE BRAVE, HAVE YOU NOW BEEN TAUGHT TO FEAR?
THERE WAS NO ONE TO TEACH ME.
BUT THE BEAST WAS FEARSOME, WAS HE NOT?
HE WAS GREEDY AND GRIM, BUT THERE ARE MORE VENOMOUS VIL-LAINS YET TO BE SLAIN. IN FACT, I MISS HIM.
AW... WELL, YOU SHOULD MISS ME, FOR VERY SOON, I'LL SHUT YOUR EYES IN EVER-LASTING SLUMBER, NOW THAT I HAVE ALL THAT I NEED FROM YOU.
SO YOU PLAN TO KILL ME?
WH... DID I SAY THAT? NO, MY SON, LISTEN CAREFULLY.
YOU KNOW THAT YOU AND YOUR KIND HAVE BEEN THE OBJECT OF MY HATRED FOR A LONG TIME. NOW THAT YOU'VE GOTTEN THE GOLD FOR ME YOU MUST REPAY ME ALL THOSE YEARS OF TOIL AND ABUSE...
WITH YOUR LIIIFE
WELL, I'M GLAD TO HEAR THAT YOU HATE ME, I HAD ALWAYS THOUGHT SO, BUT MY LIFE...
HATE YOU?
WHY, SON, I'VE BROUGHT YOU A DRINK TO REFRESH YOU AFTER YOUR HARD TASK.

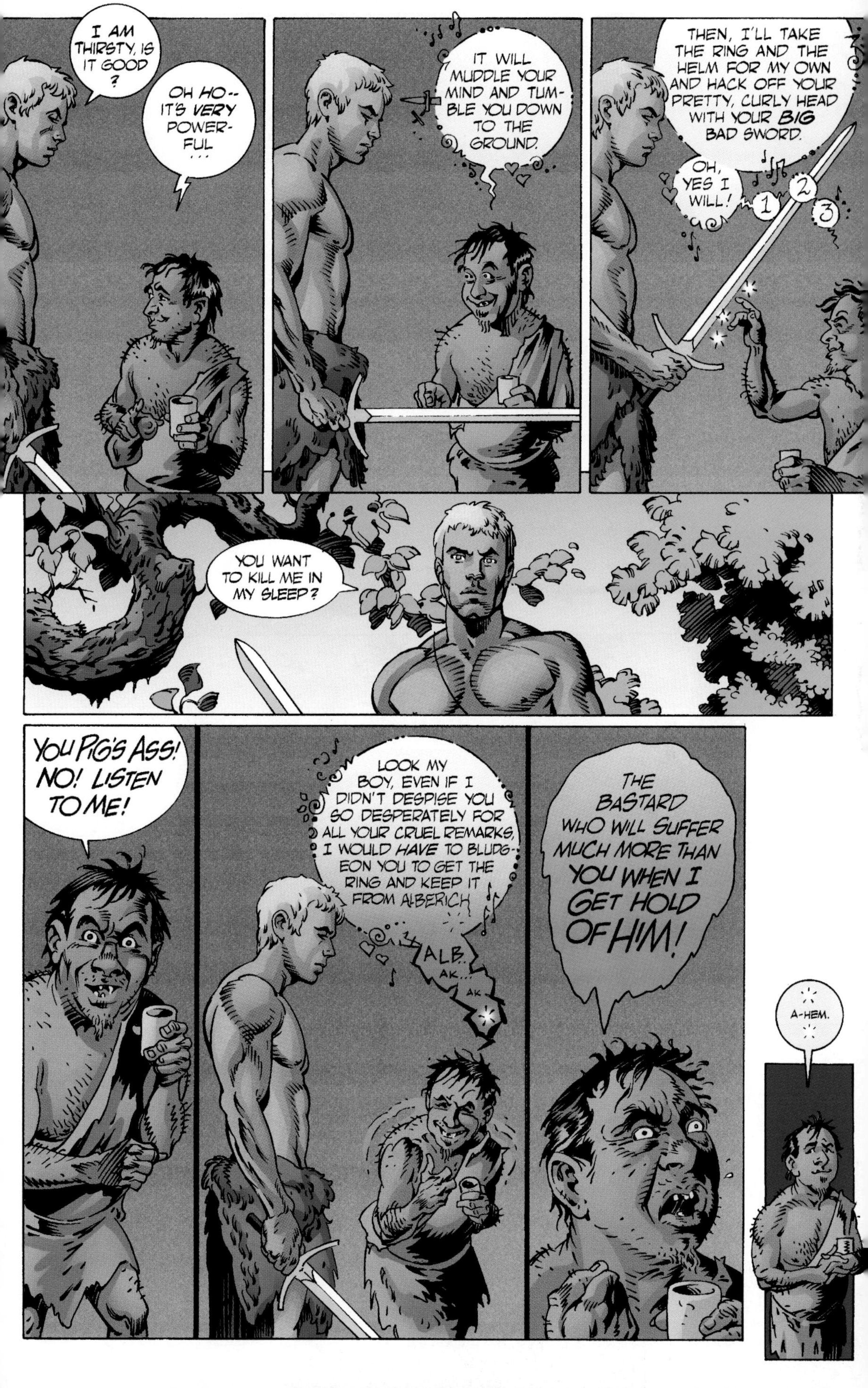
I AM THIRSTY, IS IT GOOD?
OH HO-- IT'S VERY POWERFUL...
IT WILL MUDDLE YOUR MIND AND TUMBLE YOU DOWN TO THE GROUND.
THEN, I'LL TAKE THE RING AND THE HELM FOR MY OWN AND HACK OFF YOUR PRETTY, CURLY HEAD WITH YOUR BIG BAD SWORD.
OH, YES I WILL!
1
2
3
YOU WANT TO KILL ME IN MY SLEEP?
YOU PIG'S ASS! NO! LISTEN TO ME!
LOOK MY BOY, EVEN IF I DIDN'T DESPISE YOU SO DESPERATELY FOR ALL YOUR CRUEL REMARKS, I WOULD HAVE TO BLUDGEON YOU TO GET THE RING AND KEEP IT FROM ALBERICH
ALB. AK... AK
THE BASTARD WHO WILL SUFFER MUCH MORE THAN YOU WHEN I GET HOLD OF HIM!
A-HEM.

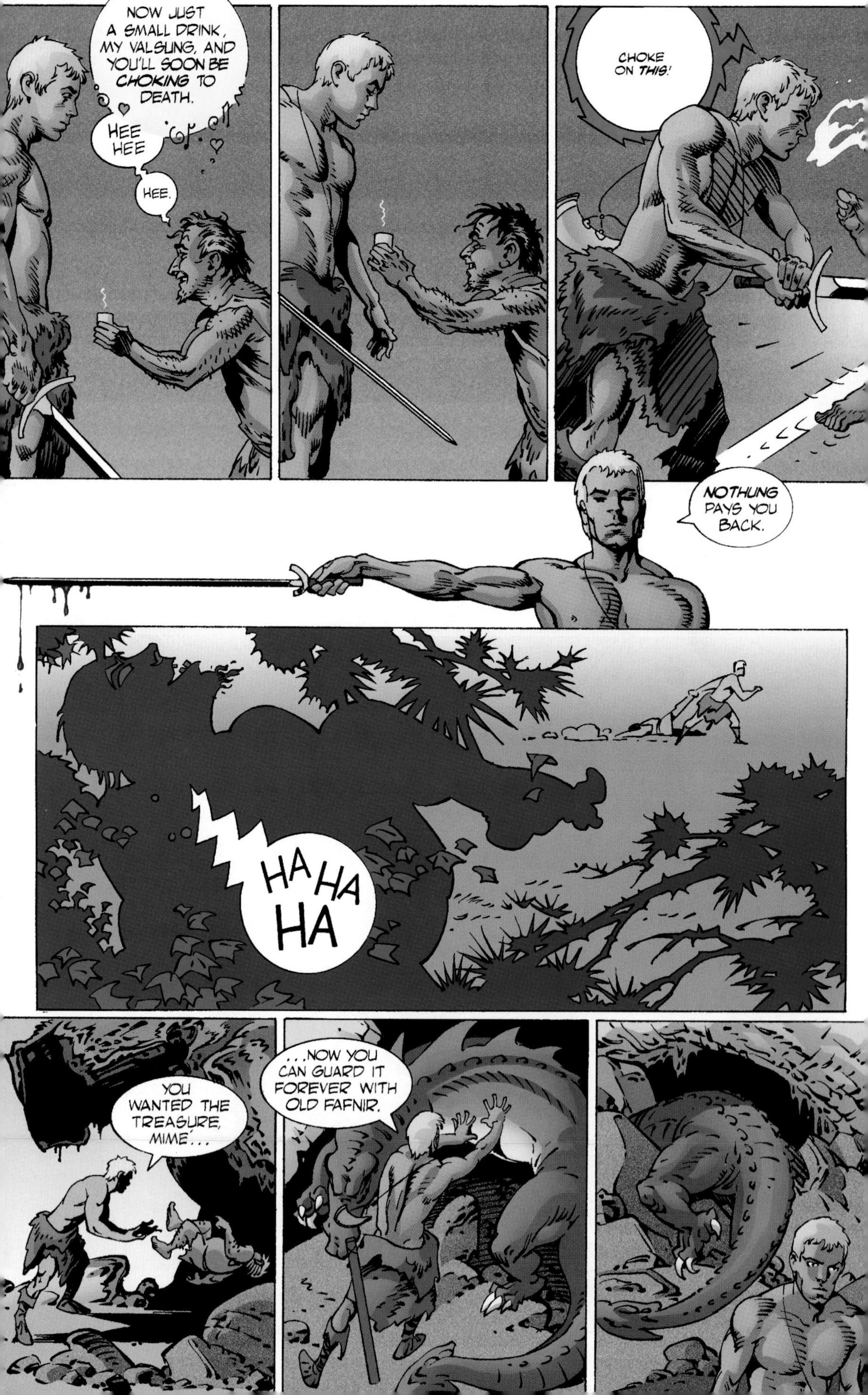
NOW JUST A SMALL DRINK, MY VALSUNG, AND YOU'LL SOON BE *CHOKING* TO DEATH.
HEE HEE
HEE.
CHOKE ON *THIS!*
NOTHUNG PAYS YOU BACK.
HA HA HA
YOU WANTED THE TREASURE, MIME...
...NOW YOU CAN GUARD IT FOREVER WITH OLD FAFNIR.

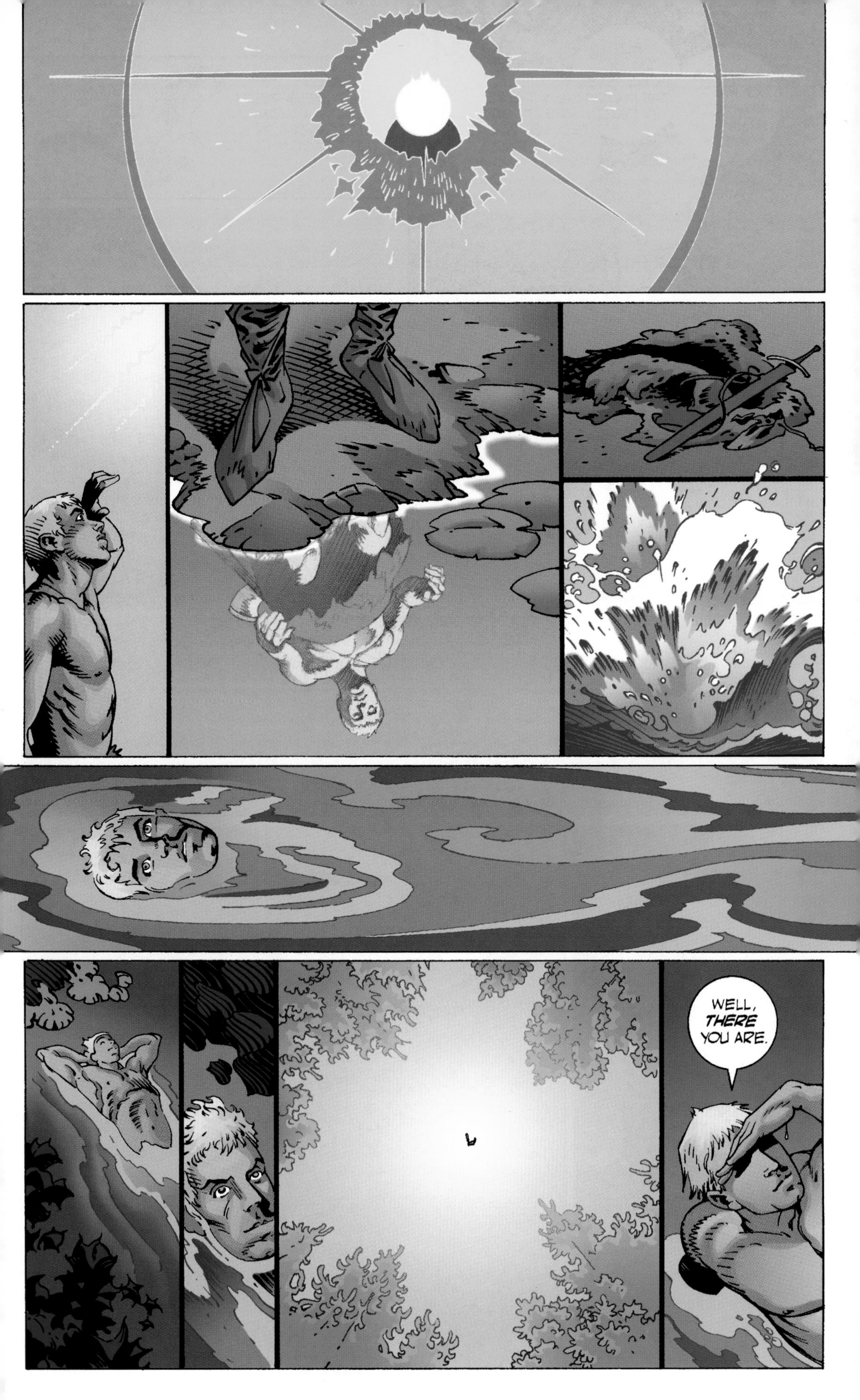
WELL, *THERE* YOU ARE.

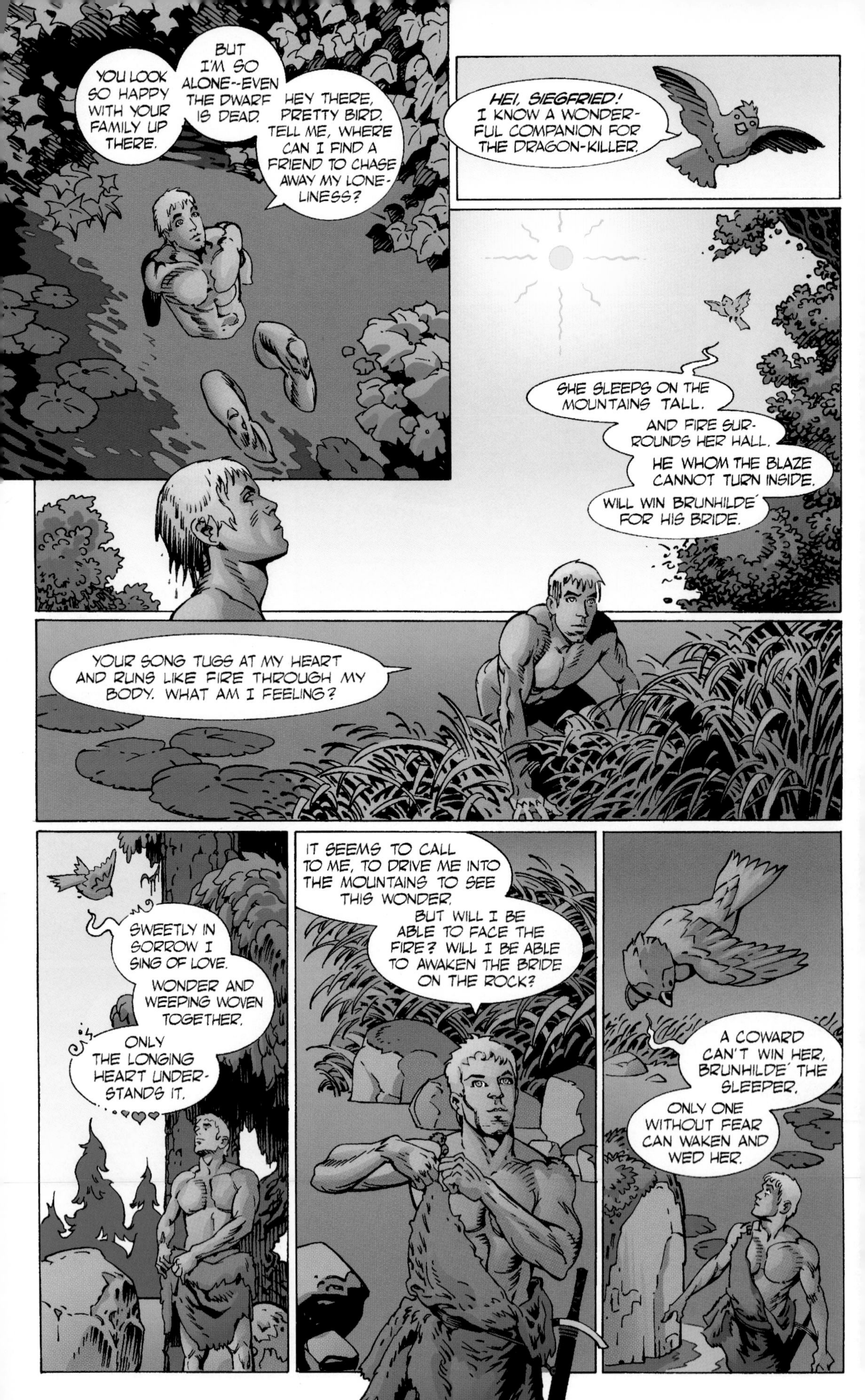
YOU LOOK SO HAPPY WITH YOUR FAMILY UP THERE.
BUT I'M SO ALONE--EVEN THE DWARF IS DEAD.
HEY THERE, PRETTY BIRD. TELL ME, WHERE CAN I FIND A FRIEND TO CHASE AWAY MY LONE-LINESS?
HEI, SIEGFRIED! I KNOW A WONDER-FUL COMPANION FOR THE DRAGON-KILLER.
SHE SLEEPS ON THE MOUNTAINS TALL.
AND FIRE SUR-ROUNDS HER HALL.
HE WHOM THE BLAZE CANNOT TURN INSIDE,
WILL WIN BRUNHILDÉ FOR HIS BRIDE.
YOUR SONG TUGS AT MY HEART AND RUNS LIKE FIRE THROUGH MY BODY. WHAT AM I FEELING?
SWEETLY IN SORROW I SING OF LOVE.
WONDER AND WEEPING WOVEN TOGETHER.
ONLY THE LONGING HEART UNDER-STANDS IT.
IT SEEMS TO CALL TO ME, TO DRIVE ME INTO THE MOUNTAINS TO SEE THIS WONDER.
BUT WILL I BE ABLE TO FACE THE FIRE? WILL I BE ABLE TO AWAKEN THE BRIDE ON THE ROCK?
A COWARD CAN'T WIN HER, BRUNHILDÉ THE SLEEPER.
ONLY ONE WITHOUT FEAR CAN WAKEN AND WED HER.

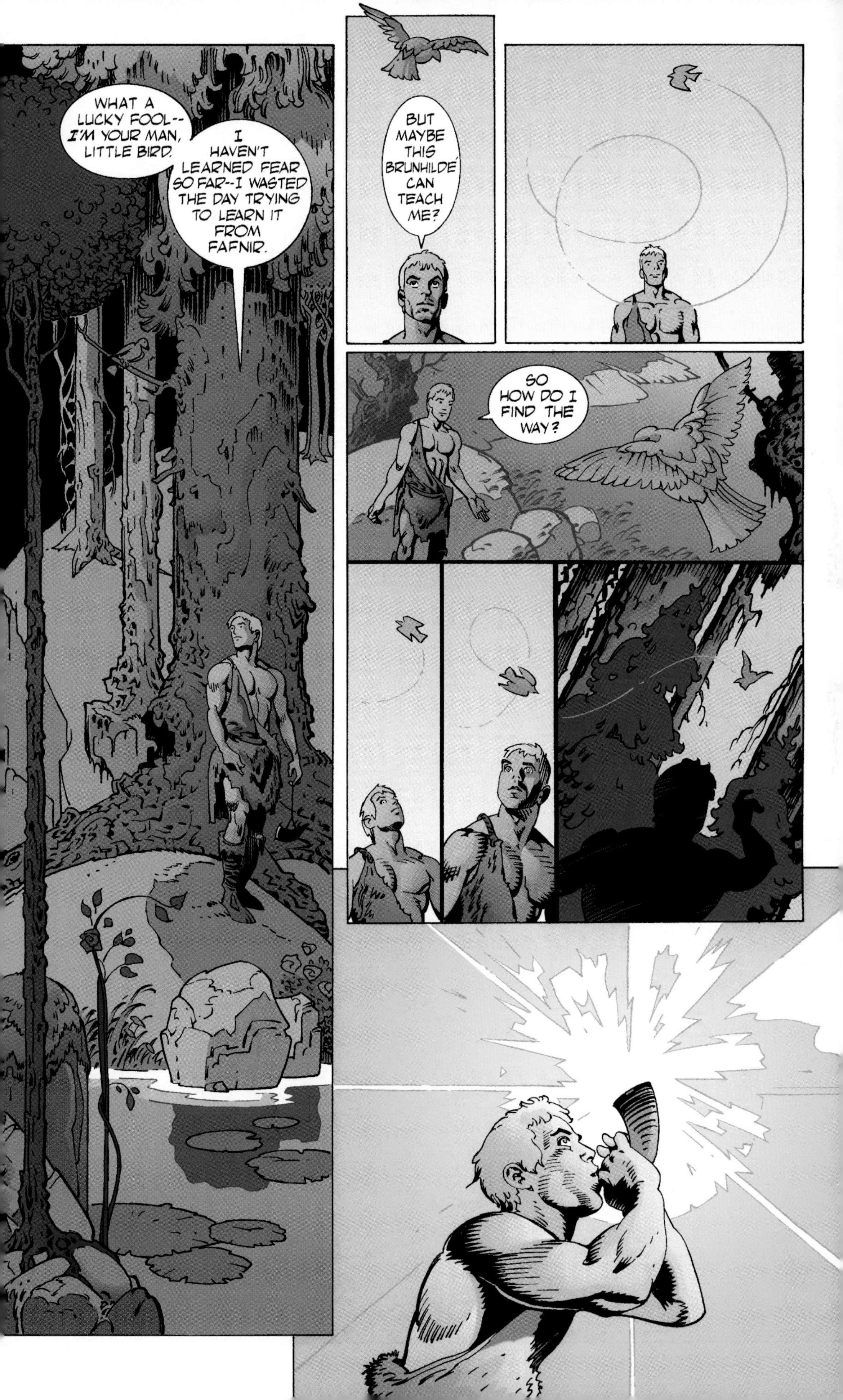
WHAT A LUCKY FOOL-- I'M YOUR MAN, LITTLE BIRD.
I HAVEN'T LEARNED FEAR SO FAR--I WASTED THE DAY TRYING TO LEARN IT FROM FAFNIR.
BUT MAYBE THIS BRUNHILDE CAN TEACH ME?
SO HOW DO I FIND THE WAY?

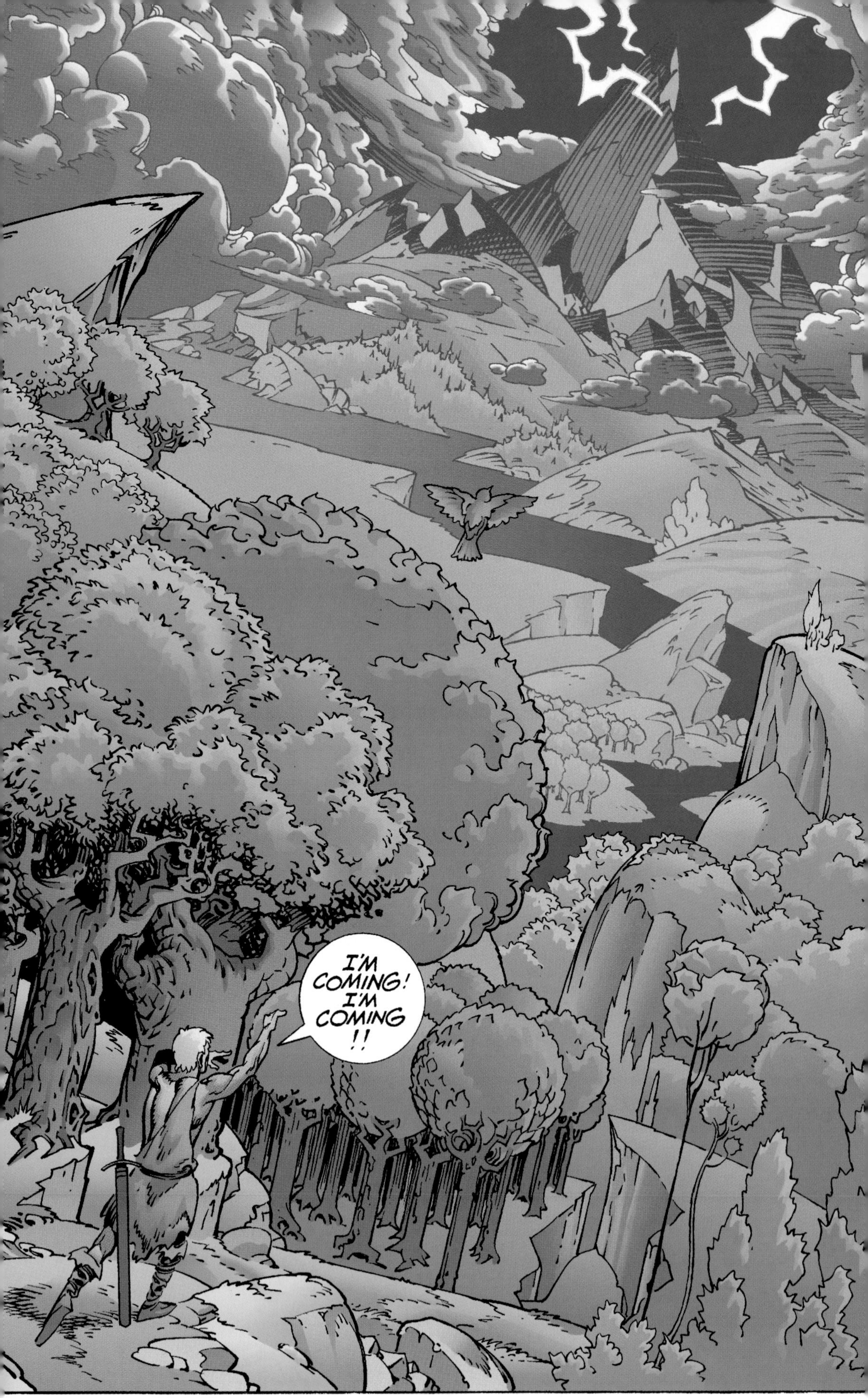
I'M COMING! I'M COMING !!

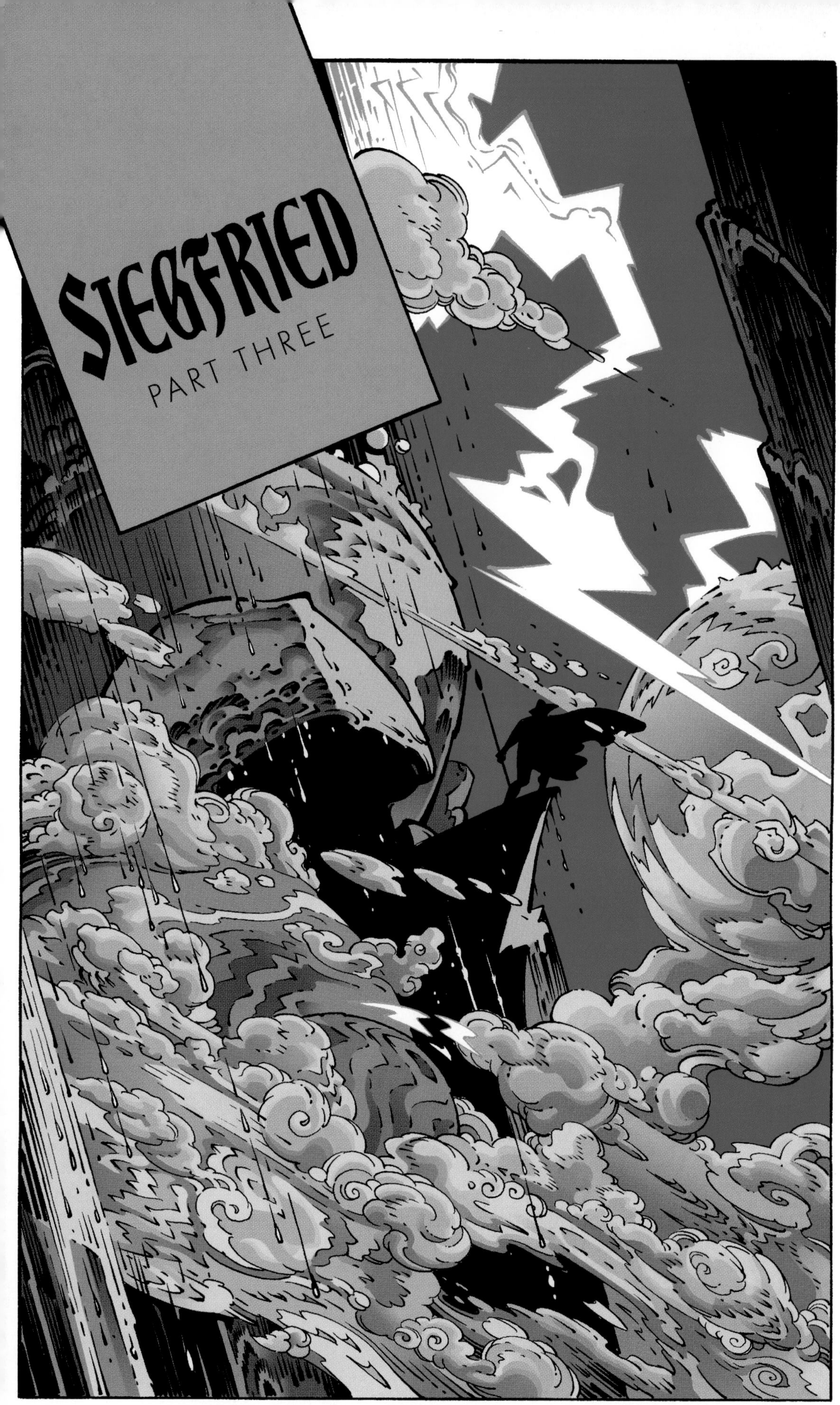
SIEGFRIED
PART THREE

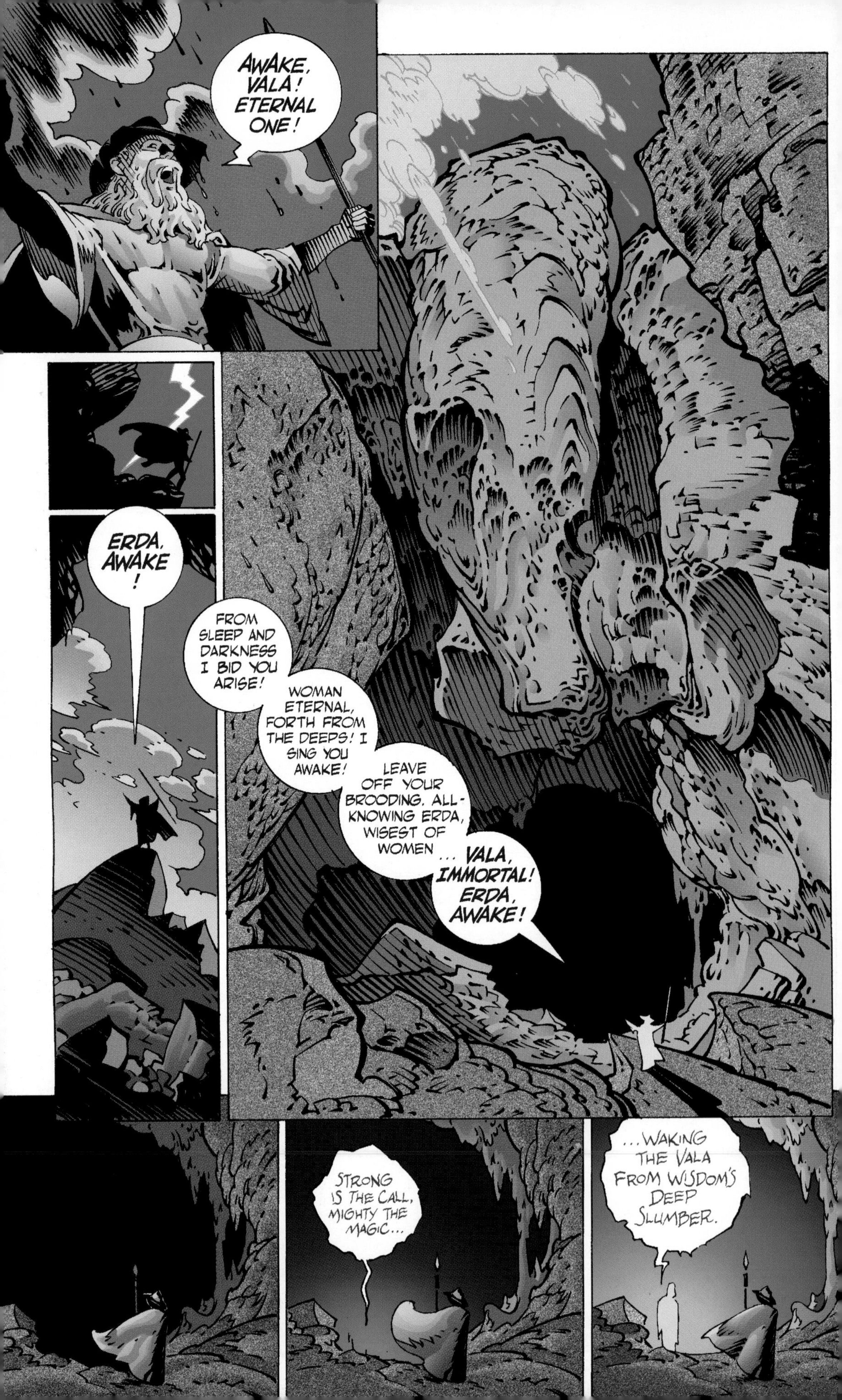
AWAKE, VALA! ETERNAL ONE!
ERDA, AWAKE!
FROM SLEEP AND DARKNESS I BID YOU ARISE!
WOMAN ETERNAL, FORTH FROM THE DEEPS! I SING YOU AWAKE!
LEAVE OFF YOUR BROODING, ALL-KNOWING ERDA, WISEST OF WOMEN ... VALA, IMMORTAL! ERDA, AWAKE!
STRONG IS THE CALL, MIGHTY THE MAGIC...
...WAKING THE VALA FROM WISDOM'S DEEP SLUMBER.

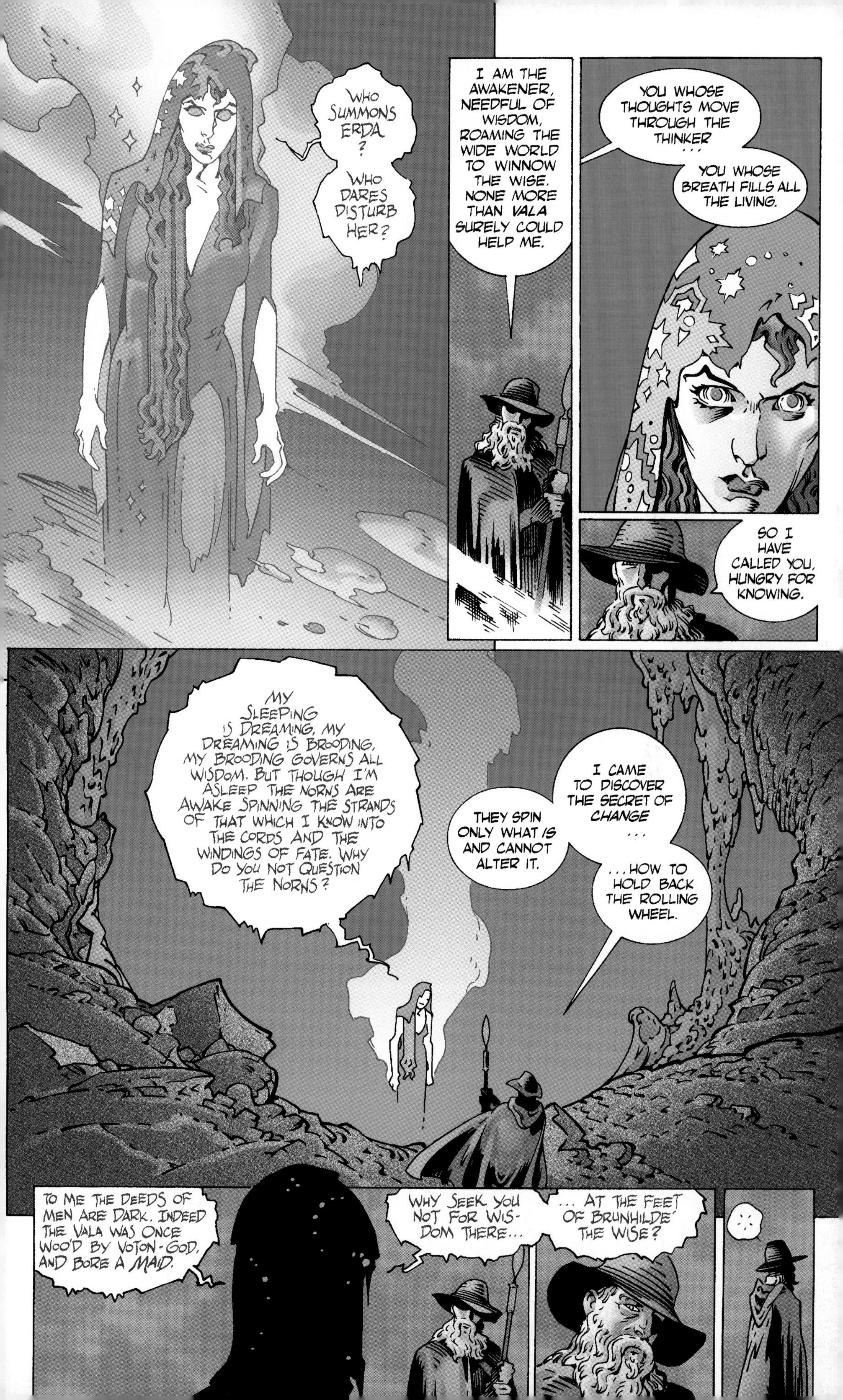
WHO SUMMONS ERDA?
WHO DARES DISTURB HER?
I AM THE AWAKENER, NEEDFUL OF WISDOM, ROAMING THE WIDE WORLD TO WINNOW THE WISE. NONE MORE THAN VALA SURELY COULD HELP ME.
YOU WHOSE THOUGHTS MOVE THROUGH THE THINKER . . .
YOU WHOSE BREATH FILLS ALL THE LIVING.
SO I HAVE CALLED YOU, HUNGRY FOR KNOWING.
MY SLEEPING IS DREAMING, MY DREAMING IS BROODING, MY BROODING GOVERNS ALL WISDOM. BUT THOUGH I'M ASLEEP THE NORNS ARE AWAKE SPINNING THE STRANDS OF THAT WHICH I KNOW INTO THE CORDS AND THE WINDINGS OF FATE. WHY DO YOU NOT QUESTION THE NORNS?
THEY SPIN ONLY WHAT IS AND CANNOT ALTER IT.
I CAME TO DISCOVER THE SECRET OF CHANGE . . .
. . . HOW TO HOLD BACK THE ROLLING WHEEL.
TO ME THE DEEDS OF MEN ARE DARK. INDEED THE VALA WAS ONCE WOO'D BY VOTON-GOD, AND BORE A MAID.
WHY SEEK YOU NOT FOR WISDOM THERE...
... AT THE FEET OF BRUNHILDE THE WISE?
. . .

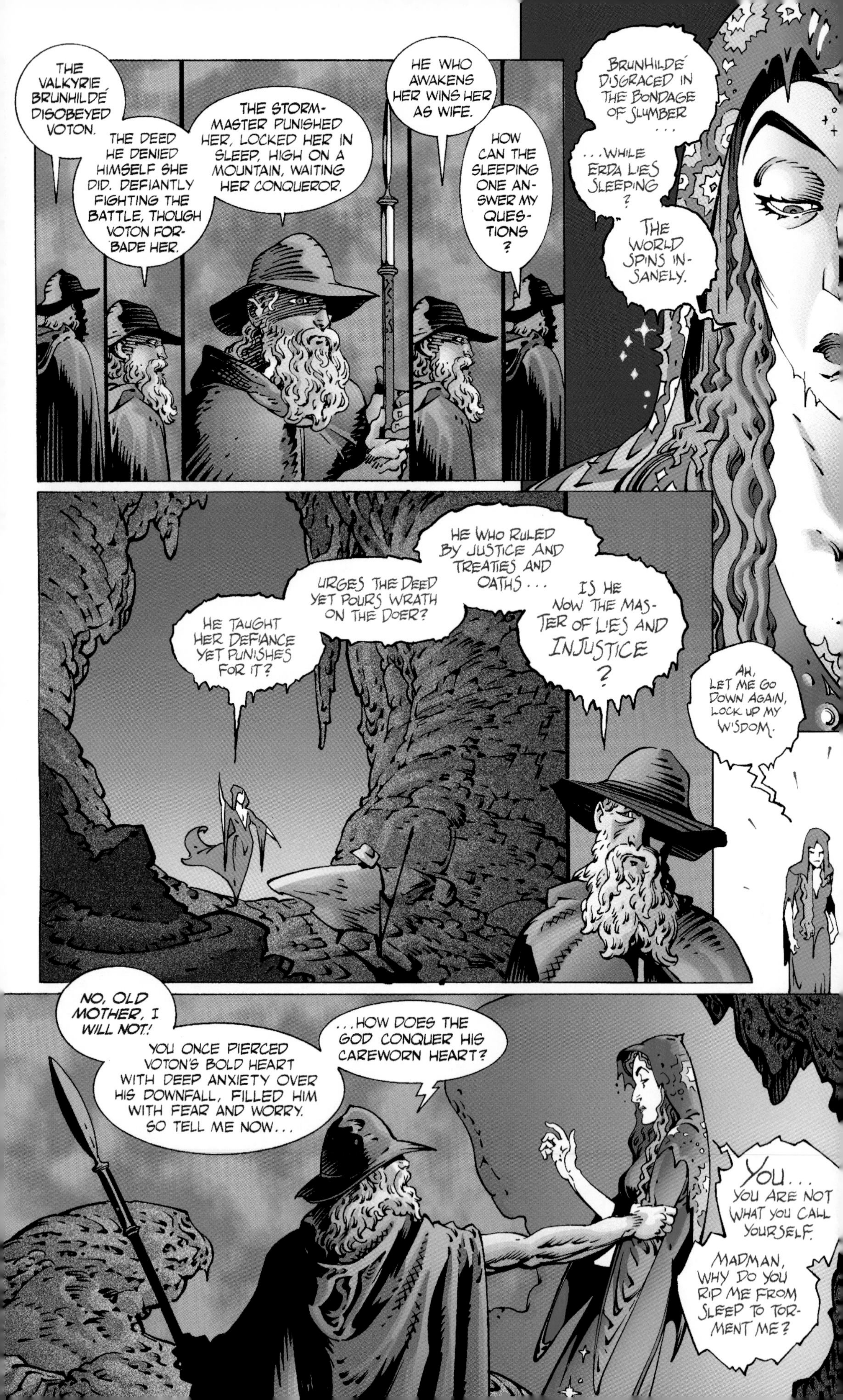
THE VALKYRIE BRUNHILDÉ DISOBEYED VOTON.
THE DEED HE DENIED HIMSELF SHE DID. DEFIANTLY FIGHTING THE BATTLE, THOUGH VOTON FOR-BADE HER.
THE STORM-MASTER PUNISHED HER, LOCKED HER IN SLEEP, HIGH ON A MOUNTAIN, WAITING HER CONQUEROR.
HE WHO AWAKENS HER WINS HER AS WIFE.
HOW CAN THE SLEEPING ONE AN-SWER MY QUES-TIONS?
BRUNHILDÉ DISGRACED IN THE BONDAGE OF SLUMBER . . .
. . . WHILE ERDA LIES SLEEPING?
THE WORLD SPINS IN-SANELY.
HE TAUGHT HER DEFIANCE YET PUNISHES FOR IT?
URGES THE DEED YET POURS WRATH ON THE DOER?
HE WHO RULED BY JUSTICE AND TREATIES AND OATHS . . .
IS HE NOW THE MAS-TER OF LIES AND INJUSTICE?
AH, LET ME GO DOWN AGAIN, LOCK UP MY WISDOM.
NO, OLD MOTHER, I WILL NOT!
YOU ONCE PIERCED VOTON'S BOLD HEART WITH DEEP ANXIETY OVER HIS DOWNFALL, FILLED HIM WITH FEAR AND WORRY. SO TELL ME NOW . . .
. . . HOW DOES THE GOD CONQUER HIS CAREWORN HEART?
YOU . . . YOU ARE NOT WHAT YOU CALL YOURSELF.
MADMAN, WHY DO YOU RIP ME FROM SLEEP TO TOR-MENT ME?

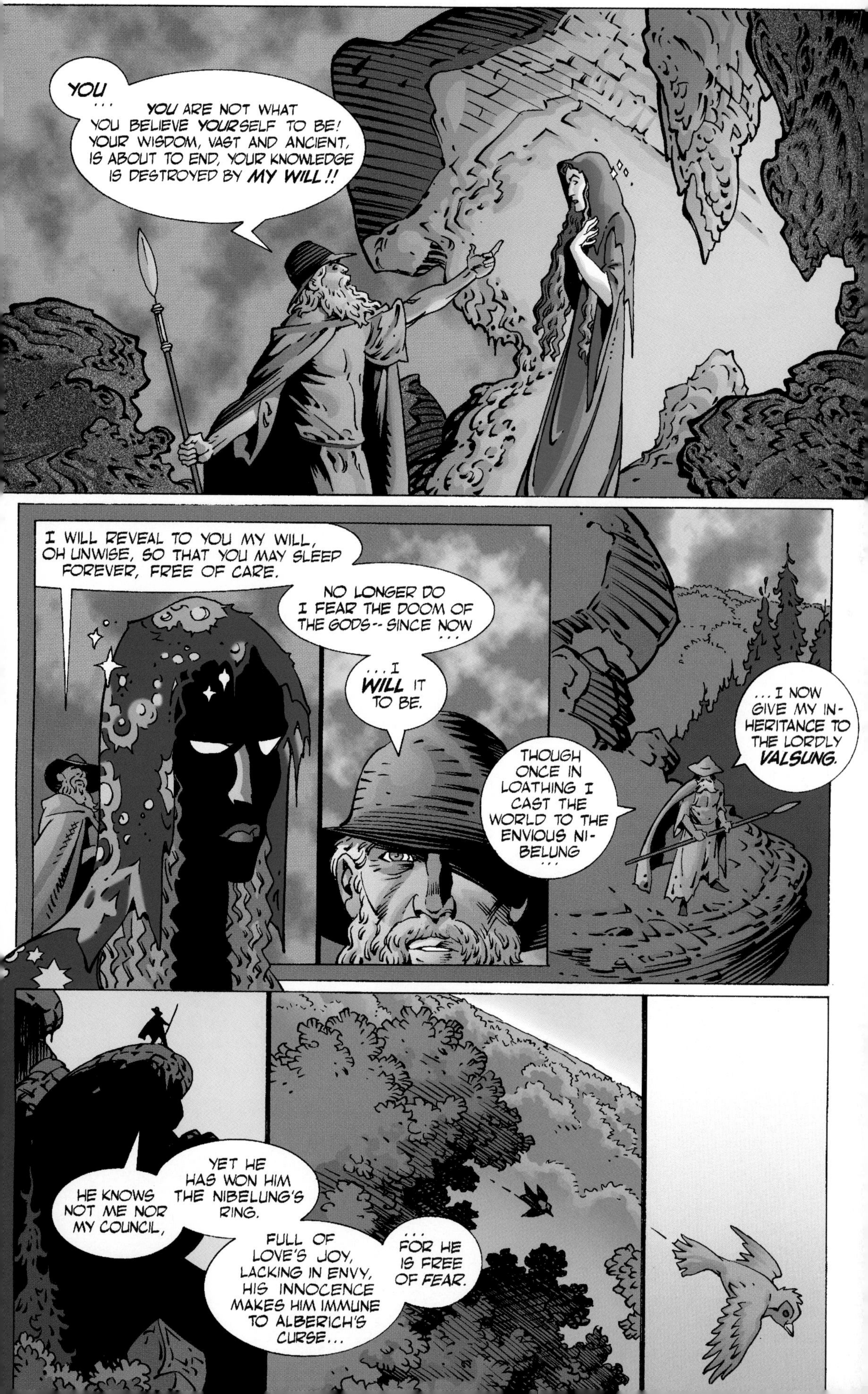
YOU . . . YOU ARE NOT WHAT YOU BELIEVE YOURSELF TO BE! YOUR WISDOM, VAST AND ANCIENT, IS ABOUT TO END, YOUR KNOWLEDGE IS DESTROYED BY MY WILL!!
I WILL REVEAL TO YOU MY WILL, OH UNWISE, SO THAT YOU MAY SLEEP FOREVER, FREE OF CARE.
NO LONGER DO I FEAR THE DOOM OF THE GODS-- SINCE NOW . . .
. . . I WILL IT TO BE.
THOUGH ONCE IN LOATHING I CAST THE WORLD TO THE ENVIOUS NI-BELUNG . . .
. . . I NOW GIVE MY IN-HERITANCE TO THE LORDLY VALSUNG.
HE KNOWS NOT ME NOR MY COUNCIL,
YET HE HAS WON HIM THE NIBELUNG'S RING.
FULL OF LOVE'S JOY, LACKING IN ENVY, HIS INNOCENCE MAKES HIM IMMUNE TO ALBERICH'S CURSE . . .
. . . FOR HE IS FREE OF FEAR.

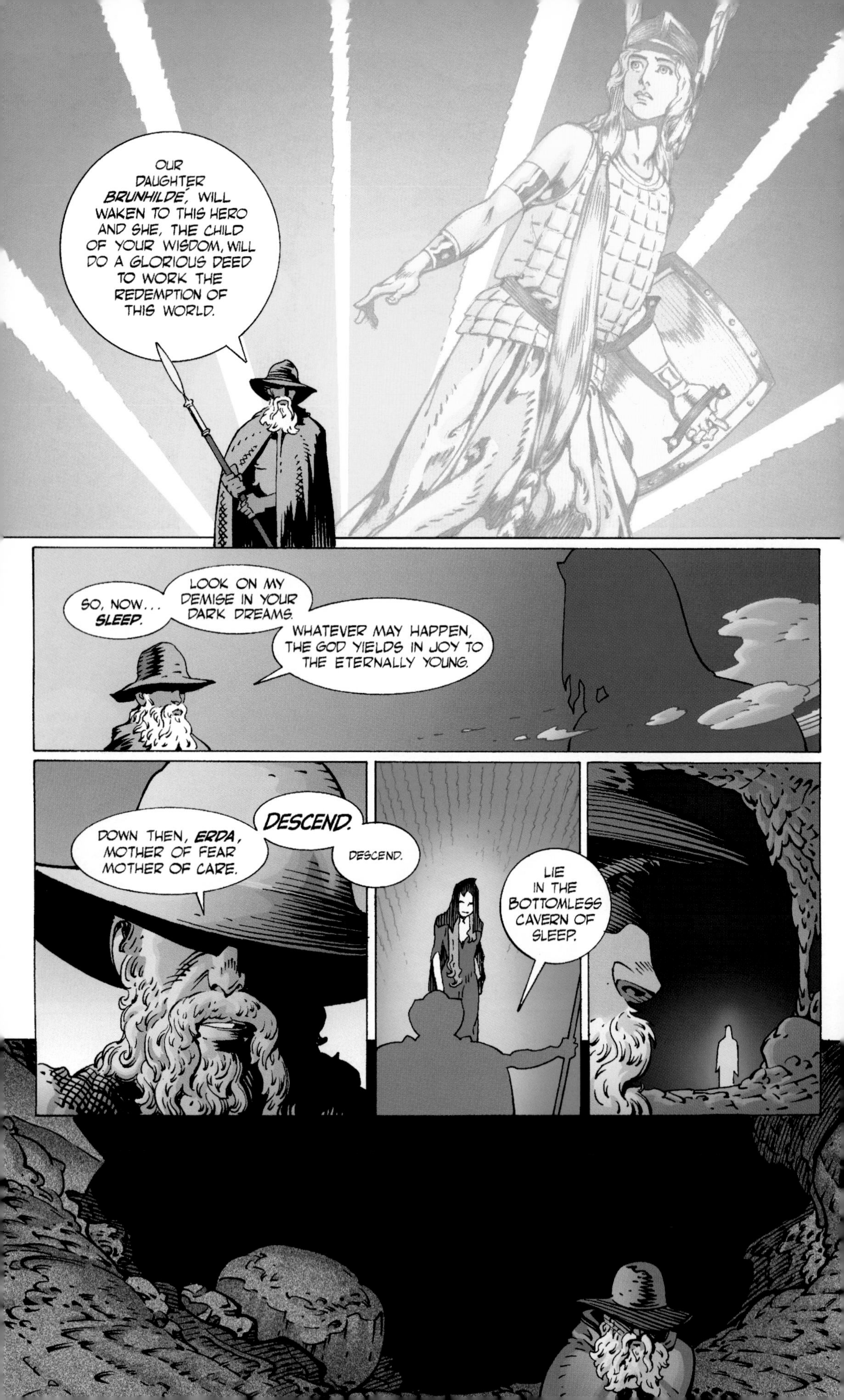
OUR DAUGHTER BRUNHILDE, WILL WAKEN TO THIS HERO AND SHE, THE CHILD OF YOUR WISDOM, WILL DO A GLORIOUS DEED TO WORK THE REDEMPTION OF THIS WORLD.
SO, NOW... SLEEP.
LOOK ON MY DEMISE IN YOUR DARK DREAMS.
WHATEVER MAY HAPPEN, THE GOD YIELDS IN JOY TO THE ETERNALLY YOUNG.
DOWN THEN, ERDA, MOTHER OF FEAR MOTHER OF CARE.
DESCEND.
DESCEND.
LIE IN THE BOTTOMLESS CAVERN OF SLEEP.

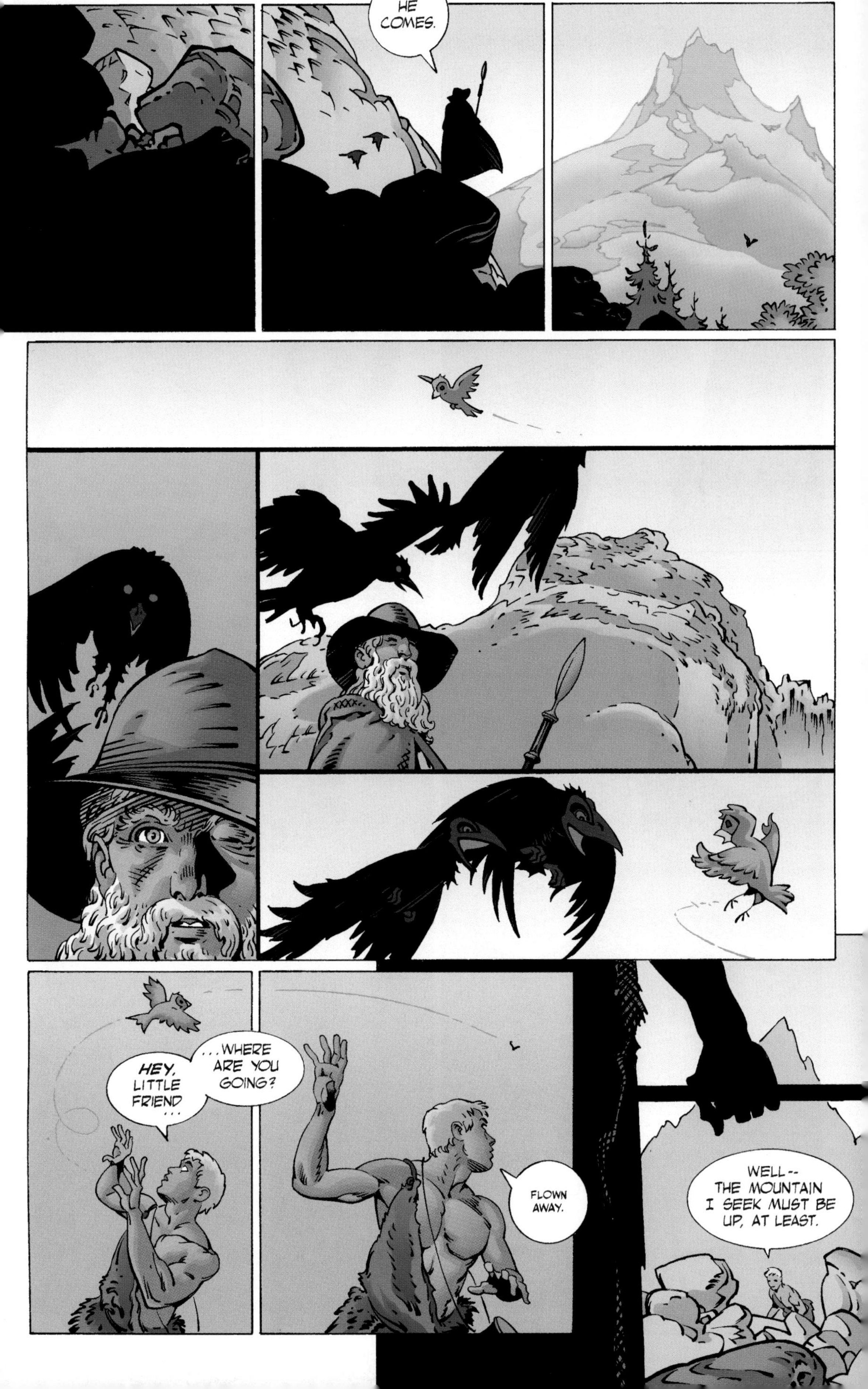
HE COMES.
HEY, LITTLE FRIEND...
...WHERE ARE YOU GOING?
FLOWN AWAY.
WELL-- THE MOUNTAIN I SEEK MUST BE UP, AT LEAST.

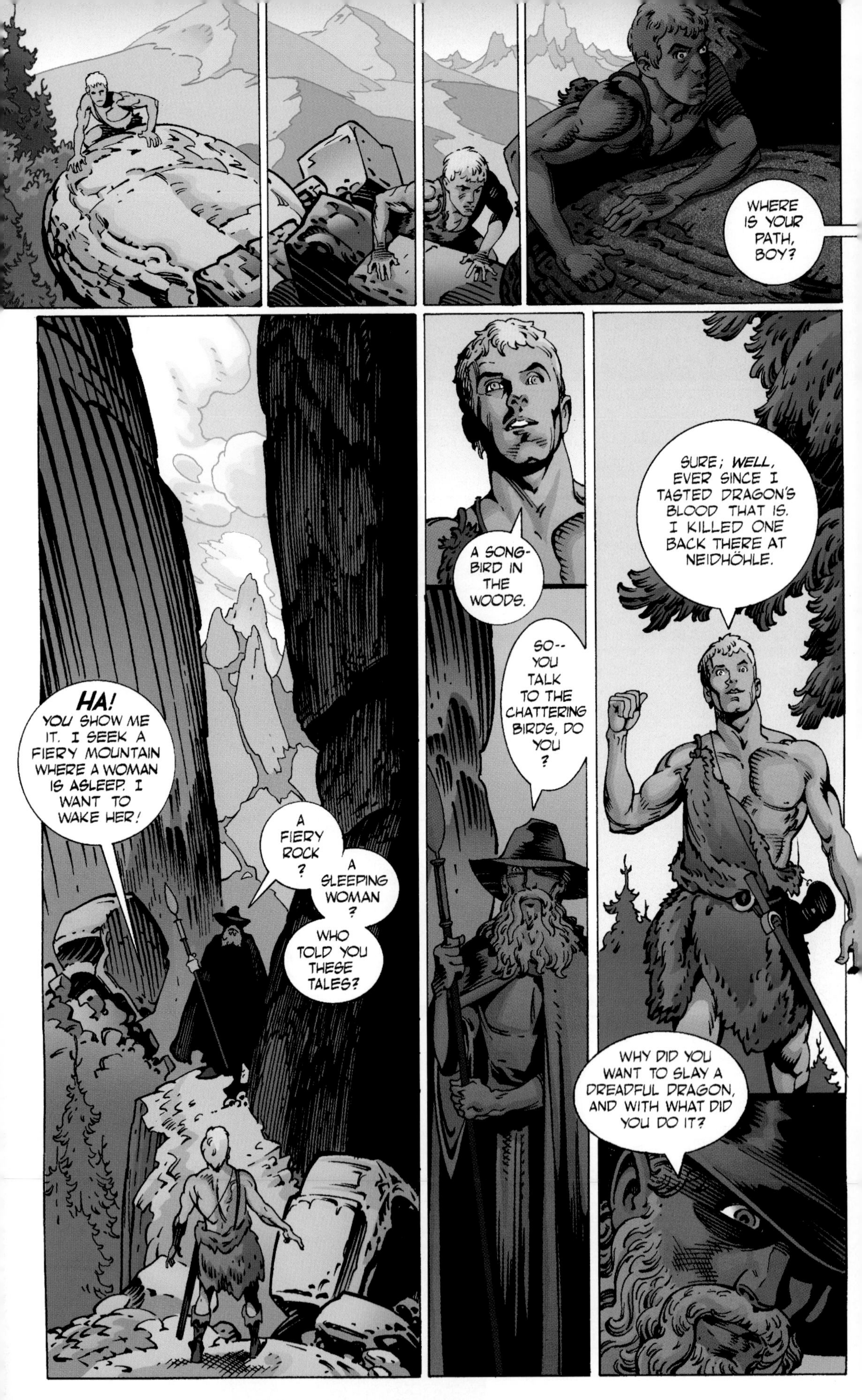
WHERE IS YOUR PATH, BOY?
HA! YOU SHOW ME IT. I SEEK A FIERY MOUNTAIN WHERE A WOMAN IS ASLEEP. I WANT TO WAKE HER!
A FIERY ROCK?
A SLEEPING WOMAN?
WHO TOLD YOU THESE TALES?
A SONG-BIRD IN THE WOODS.
SO-- YOU TALK TO THE CHATTERING BIRDS, DO YOU?
SURE; WELL, EVER SINCE I TASTED DRAGON'S BLOOD THAT IS. I KILLED ONE BACK THERE AT NEIDHÖHLE.
WHY DID YOU WANT TO SLAY A DREADFUL DRAGON, AND WITH WHAT DID YOU DO IT?

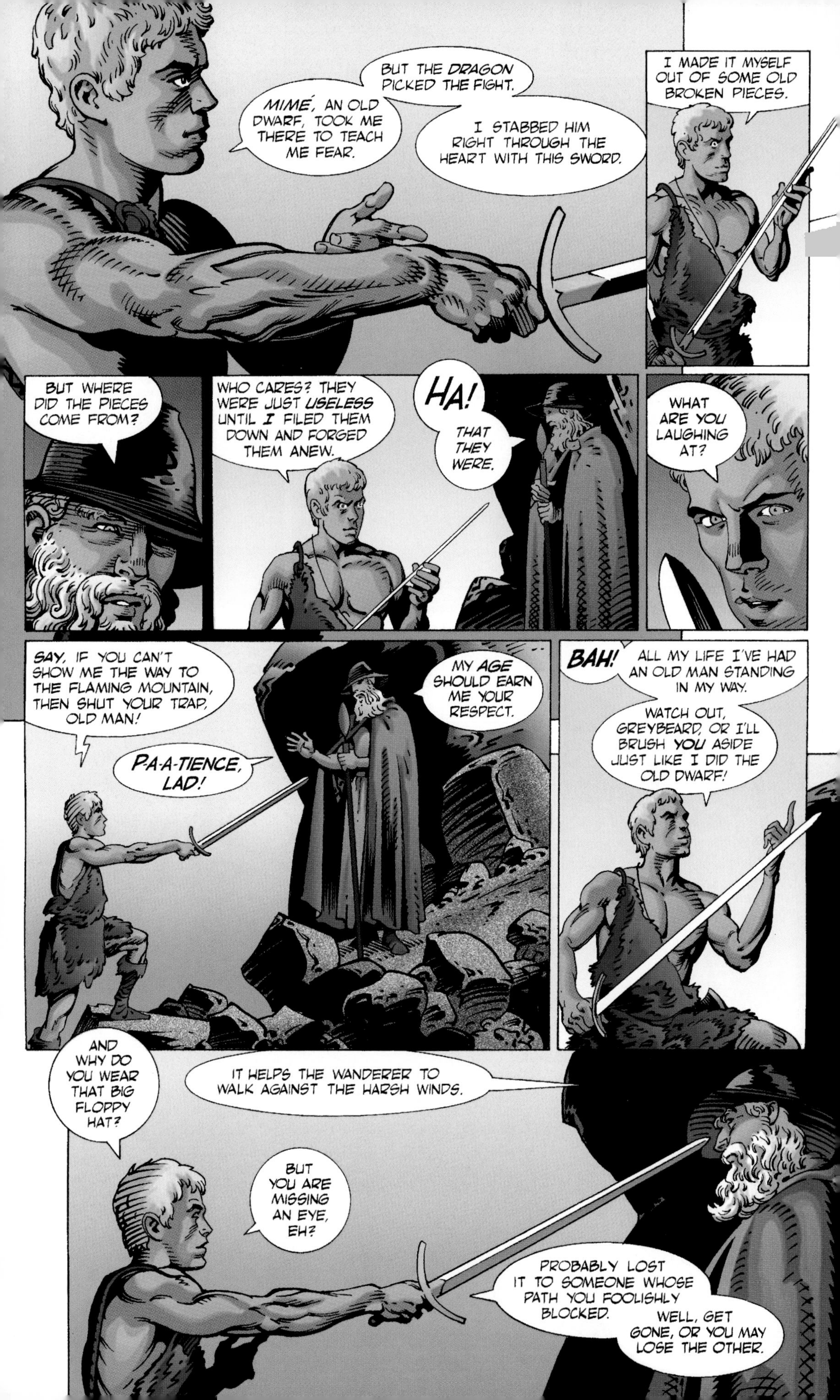
MIMÉ, AN OLD DWARF, TOOK ME THERE TO TEACH ME FEAR.
BUT THE DRAGON PICKED THE FIGHT.
I STABBED HIM RIGHT THROUGH THE HEART WITH THIS SWORD.
I MADE IT MYSELF OUT OF SOME OLD BROKEN PIECES.
BUT WHERE DID THE PIECES COME FROM?
WHO CARES? THEY WERE JUST USELESS UNTIL I FILED THEM DOWN AND FORGED THEM ANEW.
HA!
THAT THEY WERE.
WHAT ARE YOU LAUGHING AT?
SAY, IF YOU CAN'T SHOW ME THE WAY TO THE FLAMING MOUNTAIN, THEN SHUT YOUR TRAP, OLD MAN!
MY AGE SHOULD EARN ME YOUR RESPECT.
P-A-A-TIENCE, LAD!
BAH!
ALL MY LIFE I'VE HAD AN OLD MAN STANDING IN MY WAY.
WATCH OUT, GREYBEARD, OR I'LL BRUSH YOU ASIDE JUST LIKE I DID THE OLD DWARF!
AND WHY DO YOU WEAR THAT BIG FLOPPY HAT?
IT HELPS THE WANDERER TO WALK AGAINST THE HARSH WINDS.
BUT YOU ARE MISSING AN EYE, EH?
PROBABLY LOST IT TO SOMEONE WHOSE PATH YOU FOOLISHLY BLOCKED.
WELL, GET GONE, OR YOU MAY LOSE THE OTHER.

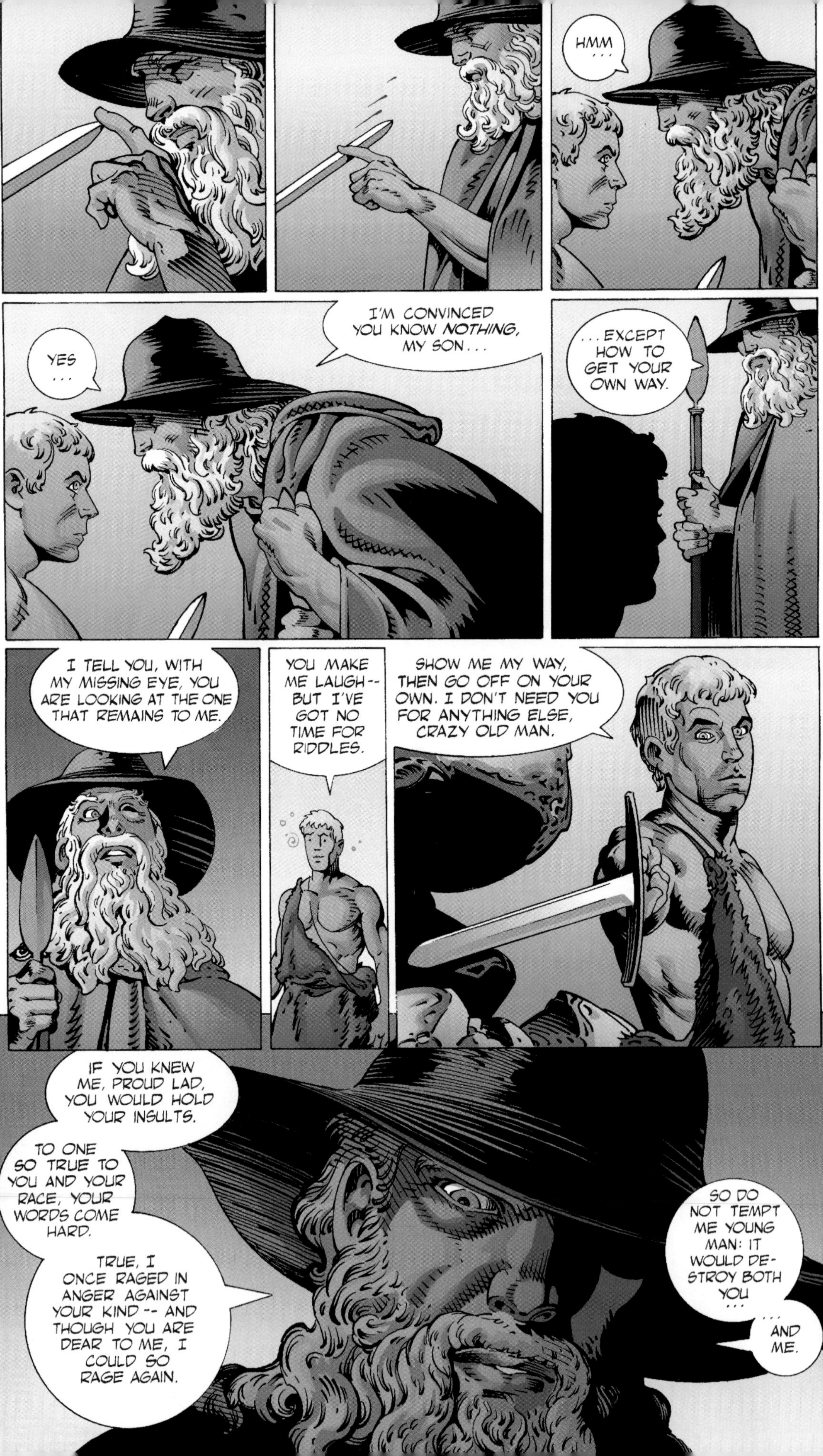
HMM ...
YES ...
I'M CONVINCED YOU KNOW NOTHING, MY SON...
...EXCEPT HOW TO GET YOUR OWN WAY.
I TELL YOU, WITH MY MISSING EYE, YOU ARE LOOKING AT THE ONE THAT REMAINS TO ME.
YOU MAKE ME LAUGH-- BUT I'VE GOT NO TIME FOR RIDDLES.
SHOW ME MY WAY, THEN GO OFF ON YOUR OWN. I DON'T NEED YOU FOR ANYTHING ELSE, CRAZY OLD MAN.
IF YOU KNEW ME, PROUD LAD, YOU WOULD HOLD YOUR INSULTS.
TO ONE SO TRUE TO YOU AND YOUR RACE, YOUR WORDS COME HARD.
TRUE, I ONCE RAGED IN ANGER AGAINST YOUR KIND -- AND THOUGH YOU ARE DEAR TO ME, I COULD SO RAGE AGAIN.
SO DO NOT TEMPT ME YOUNG MAN: IT WOULD DE-STROY BOTH YOU ...
... AND ME.

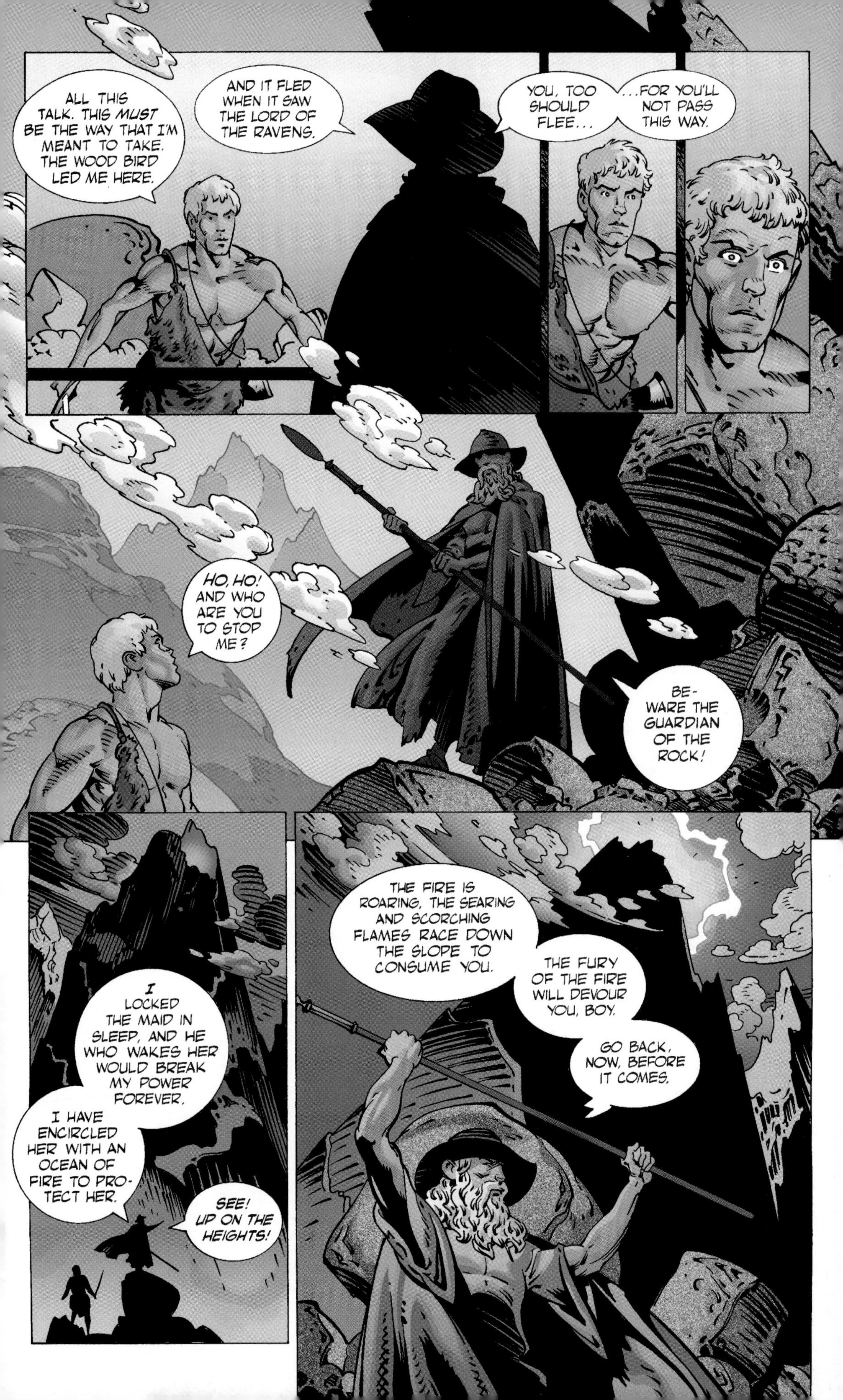
ALL THIS TALK. THIS MUST BE THE WAY THAT I'M MEANT TO TAKE. THE WOOD BIRD LED ME HERE.
AND IT FLED WHEN IT SAW THE LORD OF THE RAVENS.
YOU, TOO SHOULD FLEE...
...FOR YOU'LL NOT PASS THIS WAY.
HO, HO! AND WHO ARE YOU TO STOP ME?
BE-WARE THE GUARDIAN OF THE ROCK!
I LOCKED THE MAID IN SLEEP, AND HE WHO WAKES HER WOULD BREAK MY POWER FOREVER.
I HAVE ENCIRCLED HER WITH AN OCEAN OF FIRE TO PROTECT HER.
SEE! UP ON THE HEIGHTS!
THE FIRE IS ROARING, THE SEARING AND SCORCHING FLAMES RACE DOWN THE SLOPE TO CONSUME YOU.
THE FURY OF THE FIRE WILL DEVOUR YOU, BOY.
GO BACK, NOW, BEFORE IT COMES.

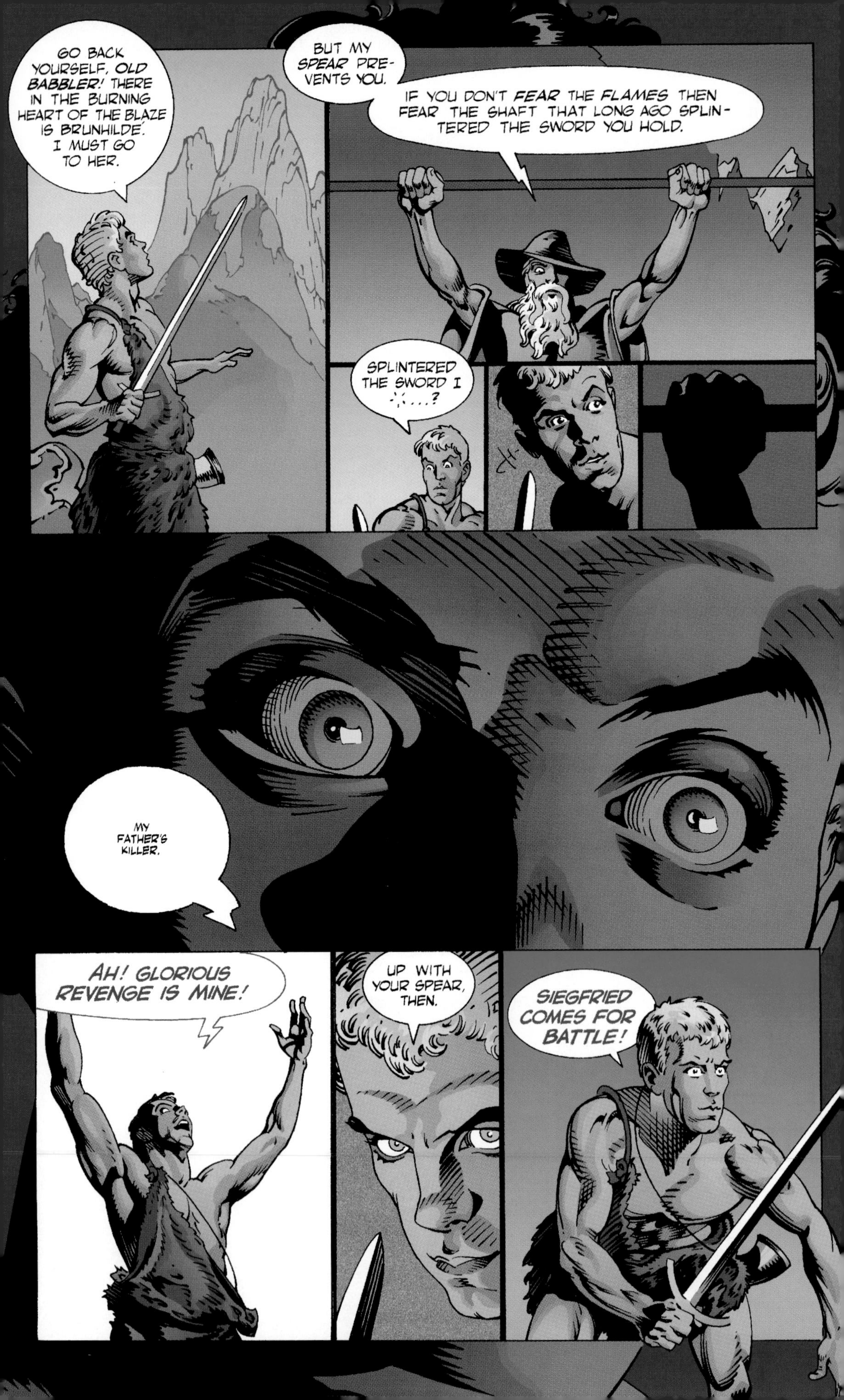

GO BACK YOURSELF, OLD BABBLER! THERE IN THE BURNING HEART OF THE BLAZE IS BRUNHILDE. I MUST GO TO HER.
BUT MY SPEAR PREVENTS YOU.
IF YOU DON'T FEAR THE FLAMES THEN FEAR THE SHAFT THAT LONG AGO SPLINTERED THE SWORD YOU HOLD.
SPLINTERED THE SWORD I ...?
MY FATHER'S KILLER.
AH! GLORIOUS REVENGE IS MINE!
UP WITH YOUR SPEAR, THEN.
SIEGFRIED COMES FOR BATTLE!

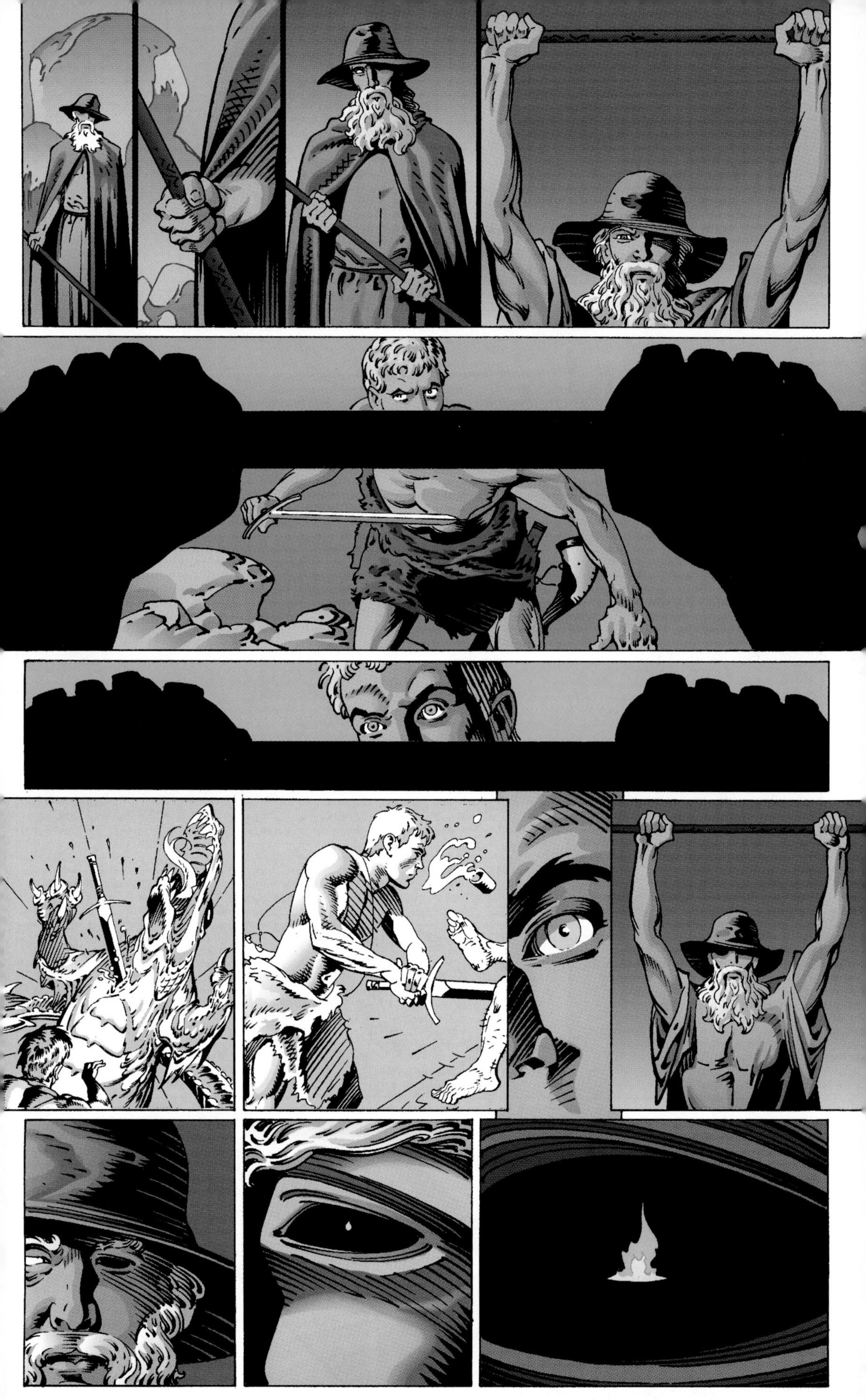

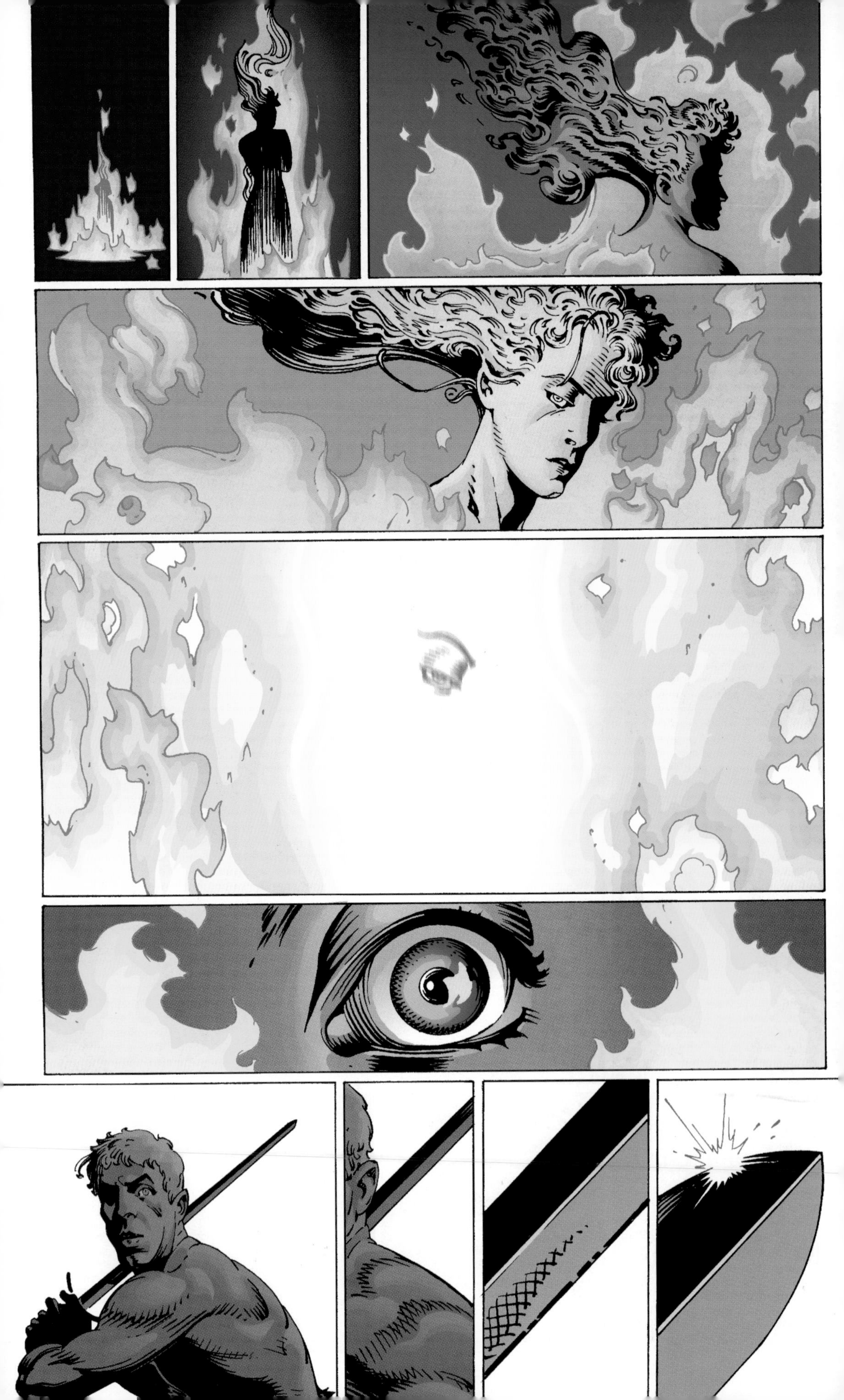

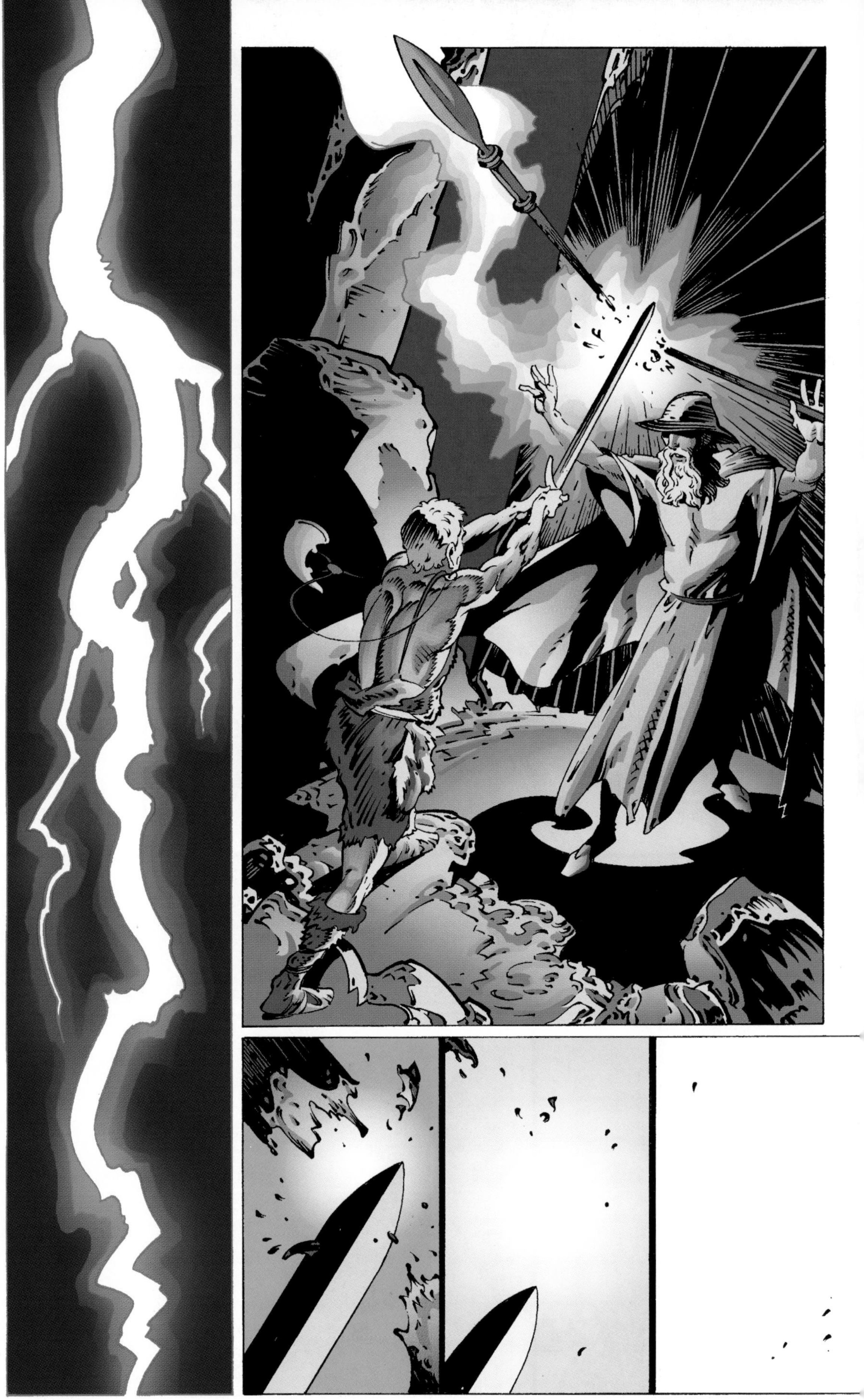

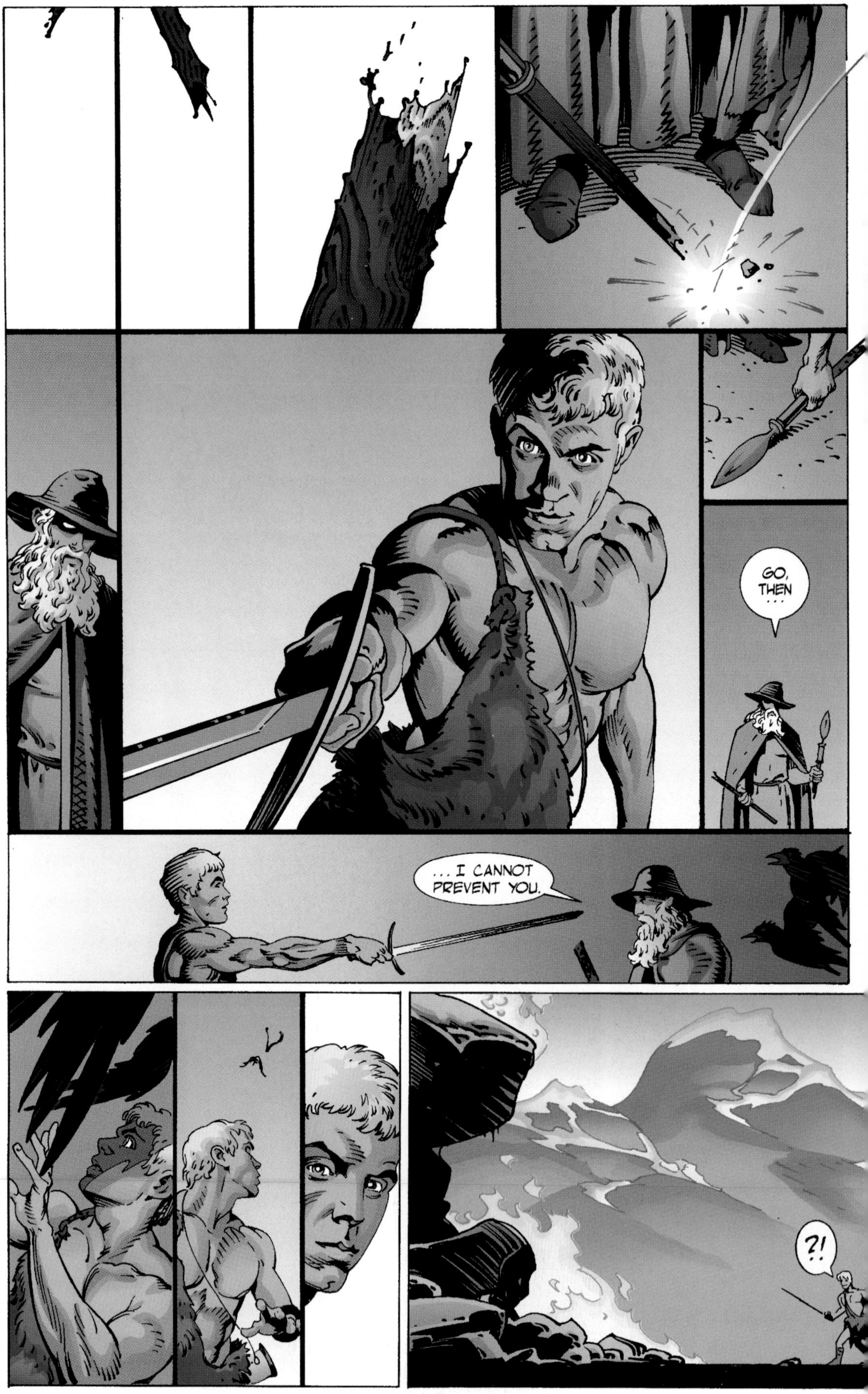
GO, THEN . . .
. . . I CANNOT PREVENT YOU.
?!

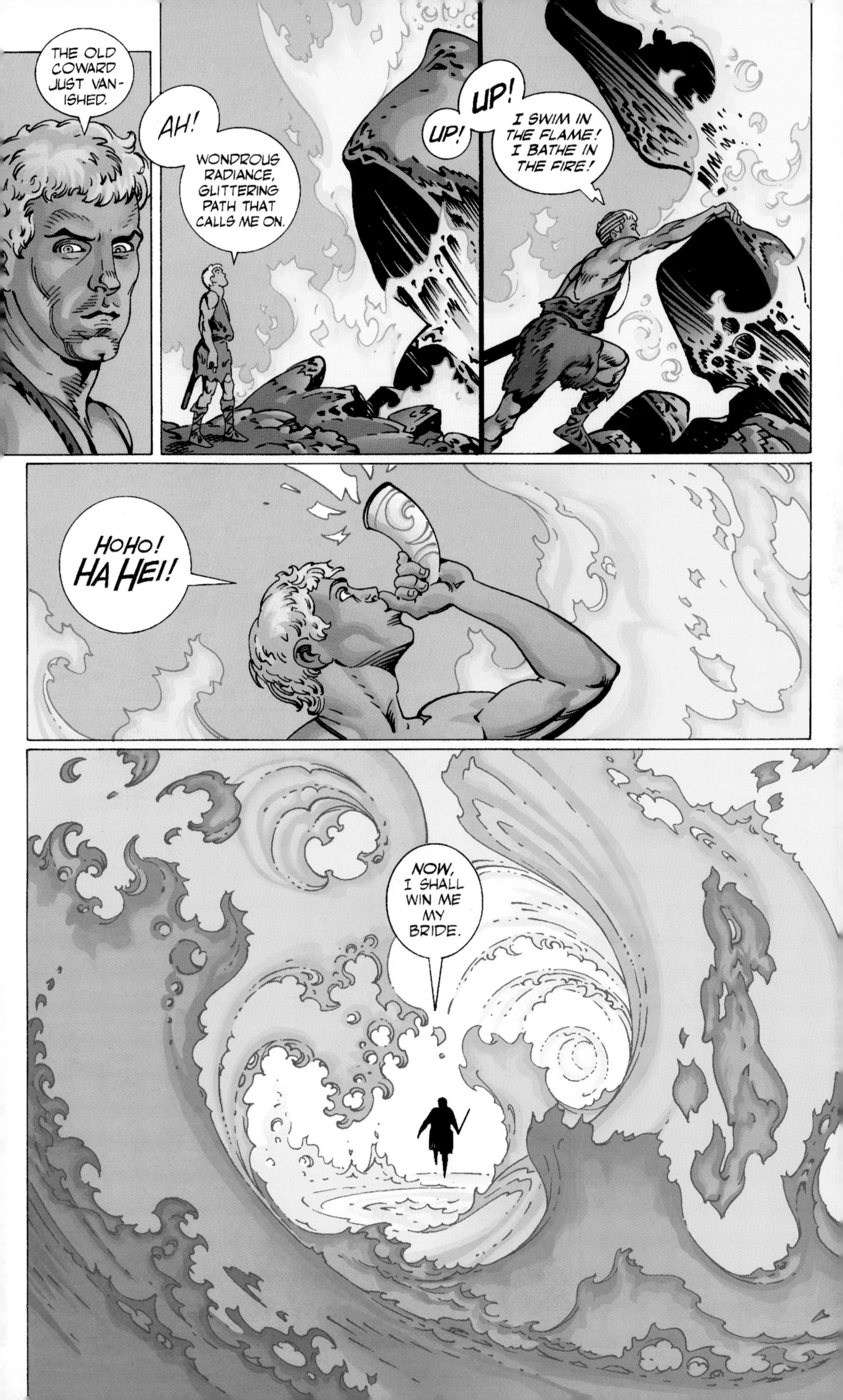
THE OLD COWARD JUST VAN-ISHED.
AH!
WONDROUS RADIANCE, GLITTERING PATH THAT CALLS ME ON.
UP!
UP!
I SWIM IN THE FLAME! I BATHE IN THE FIRE!
HOHO! HA HEI!
NOW, I SHALL WIN ME MY BRIDE.

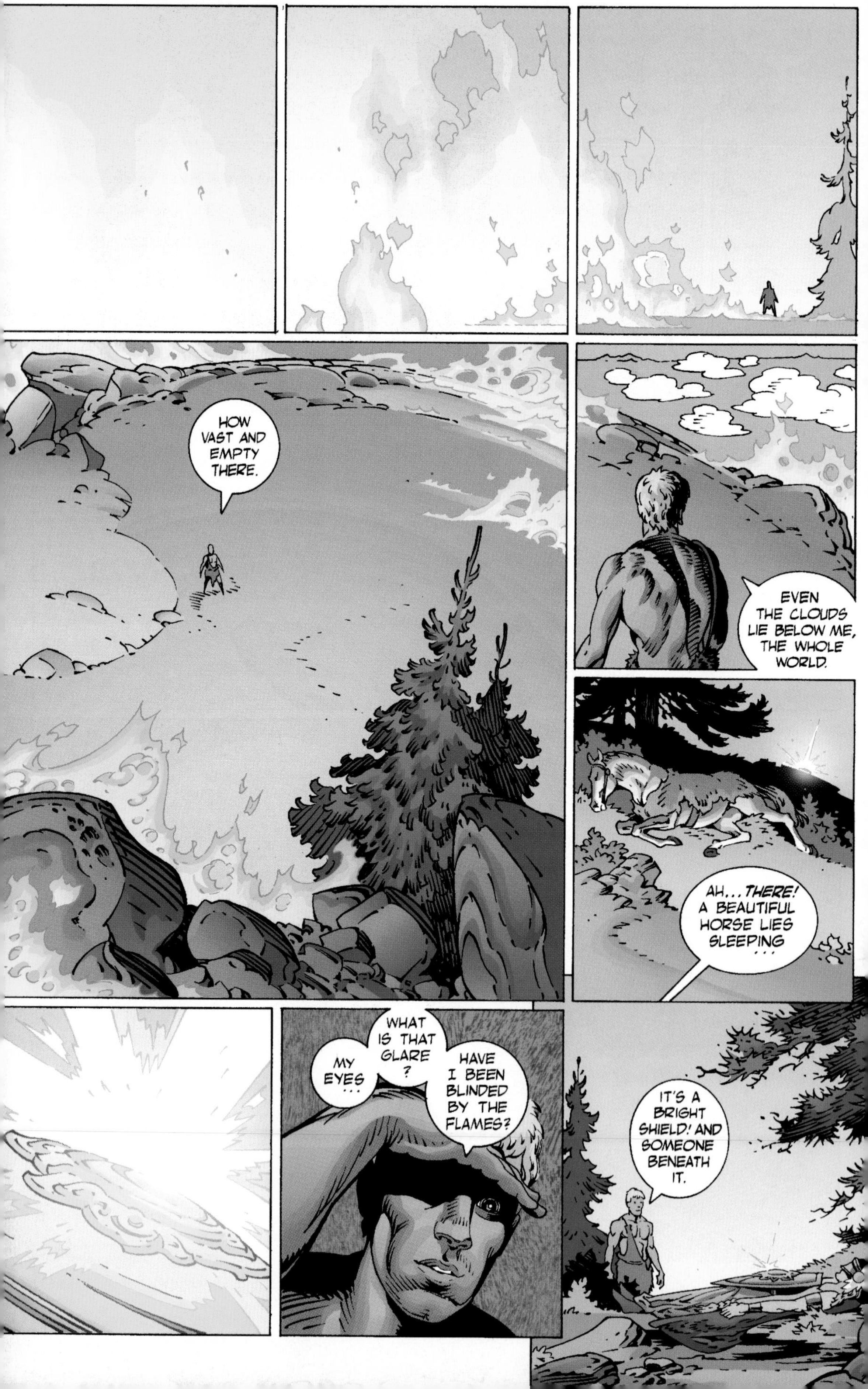
HOW VAST AND EMPTY THERE.
EVEN THE CLOUDS LIE BELOW ME, THE WHOLE WORLD.
AH... THERE! A BEAUTIFUL HORSE LIES SLEEPING ...
MY EYES ...
WHAT IS THAT GLARE ?
HAVE I BEEN BLINDED BY THE FLAMES?
IT'S A BRIGHT SHIELD! AND SOMEONE BENEATH IT.

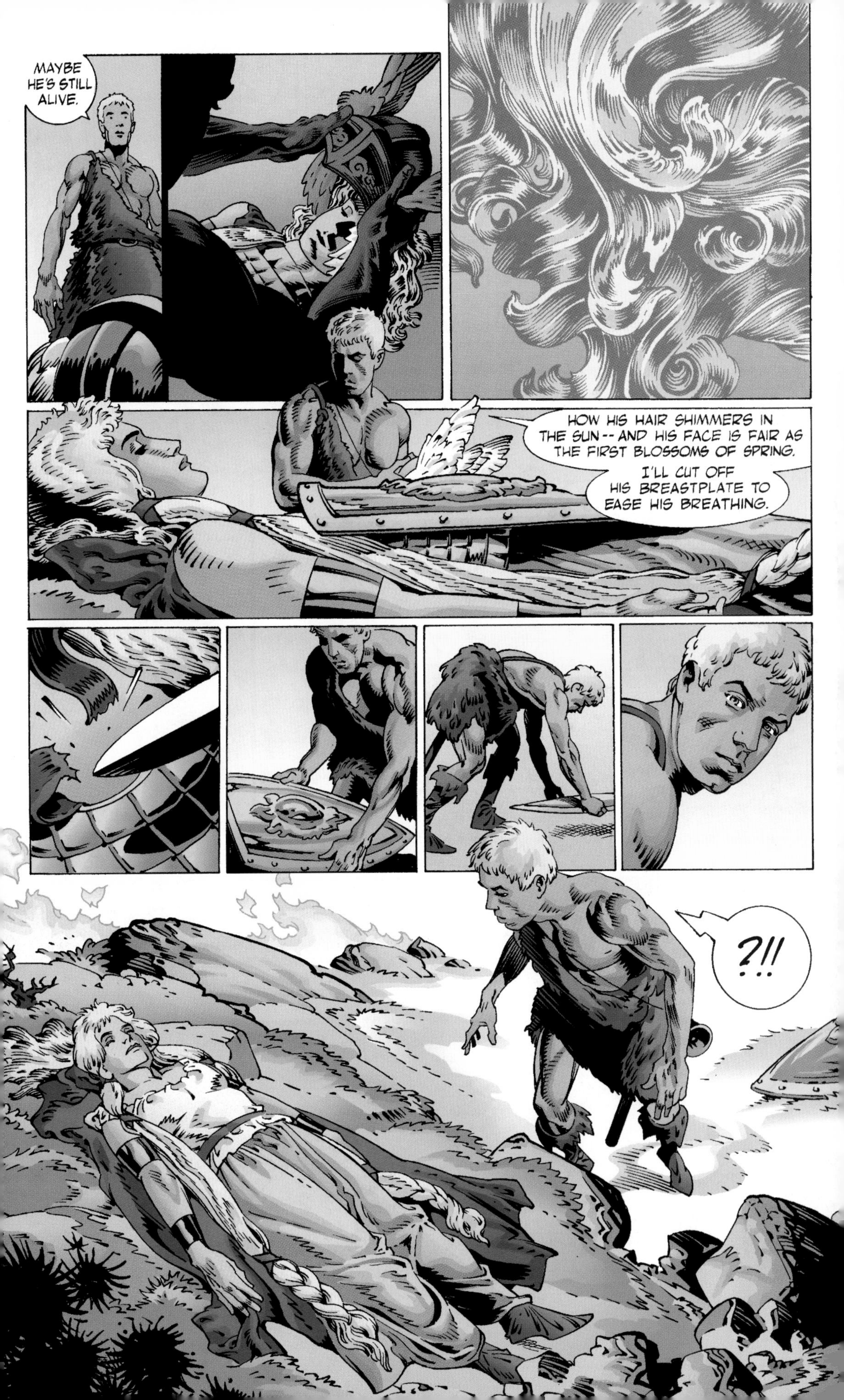
MAYBE HE'S STILL ALIVE.
HOW HIS HAIR SHIMMERS IN THE SUN -- AND HIS FACE IS FAIR AS THE FIRST BLOSSOMS OF SPRING.
I'LL CUT OFF HIS BREASTPLATE TO EASE HIS BREATHING.
?!!

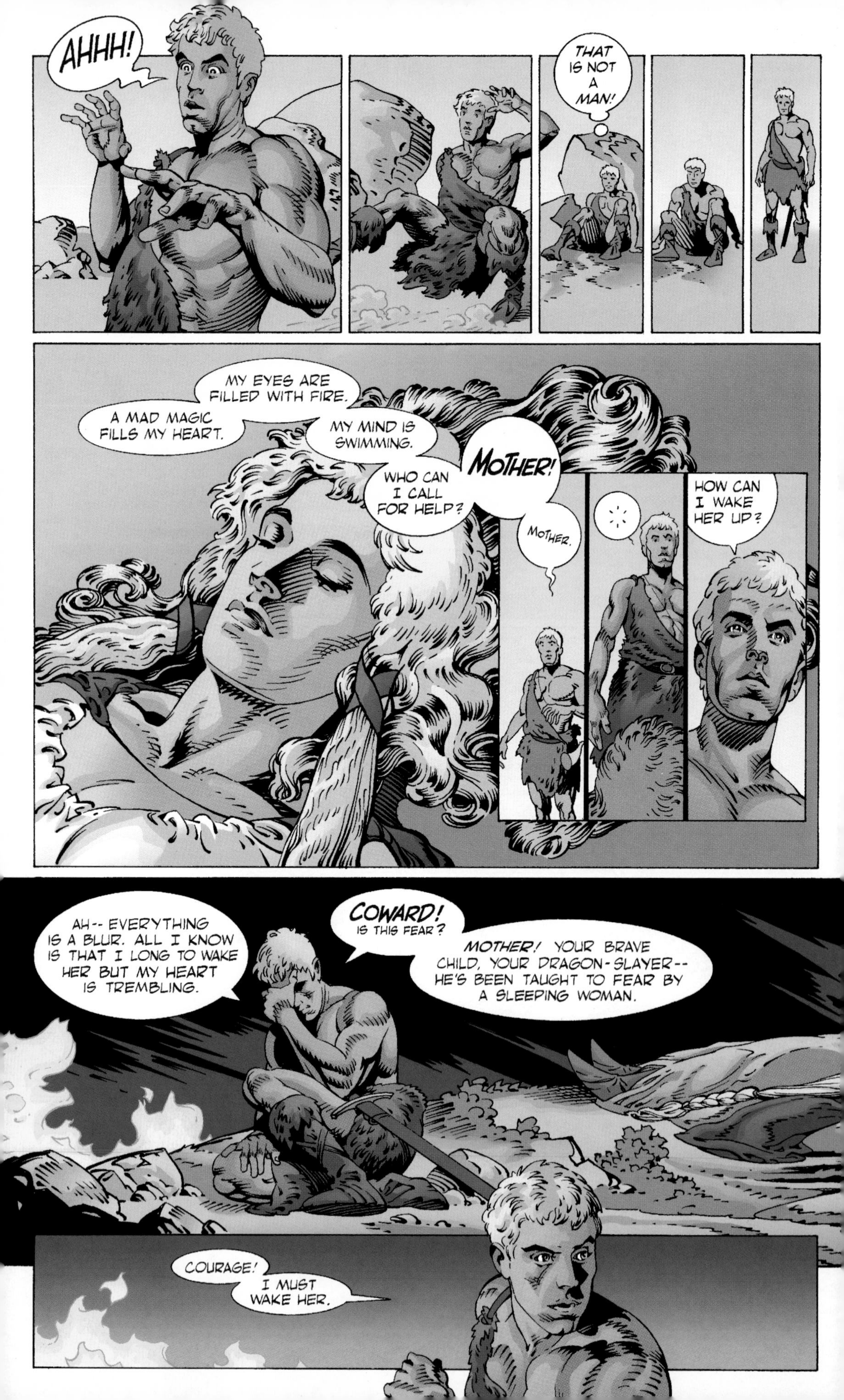
AHHH!
THAT IS NOT A MAN!
MY EYES ARE FILLED WITH FIRE.
A MAD MAGIC FILLS MY HEART.
MY MIND IS SWIMMING.
WHO CAN I CALL FOR HELP?
MOTHER!
MOTHER.
HOW CAN I WAKE HER UP?
AH-- EVERYTHING IS A BLUR. ALL I KNOW IS THAT I LONG TO WAKE HER BUT MY HEART IS TREMBLING.
COWARD! IS THIS FEAR?
MOTHER! YOUR BRAVE CHILD, YOUR DRAGON-SLAYER-- HE'S BEEN TAUGHT TO FEAR BY A SLEEPING WOMAN.
COURAGE!
I MUST WAKE HER.

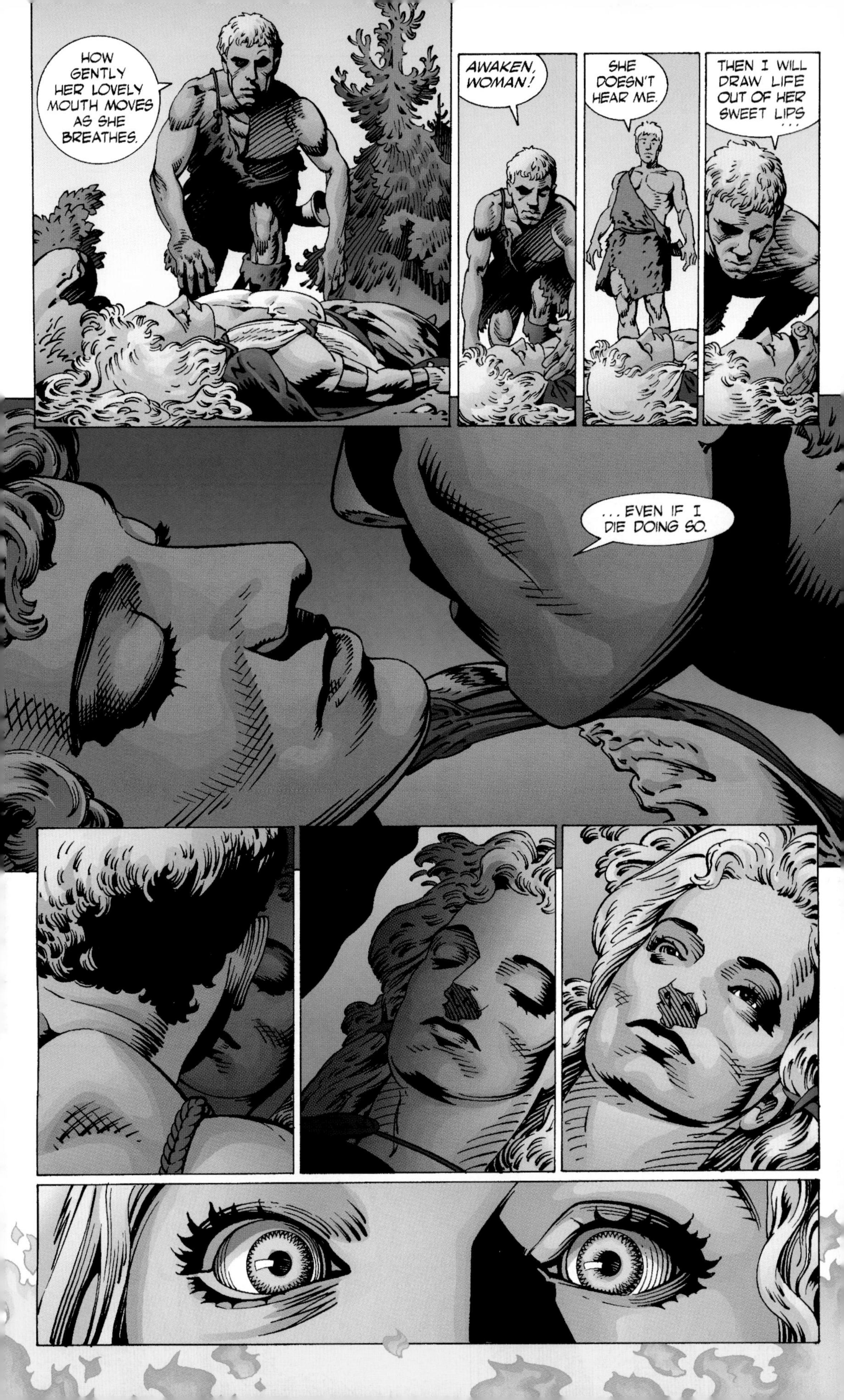
HOW GENTLY HER LOVELY MOUTH MOVES AS SHE BREATHES.
AWAKEN, WOMAN!
SHE DOESN'T HEAR ME.
THEN I WILL DRAW LIFE OUT OF HER SWEET LIPS . . .
. . . EVEN IF I DIE DOING SO.

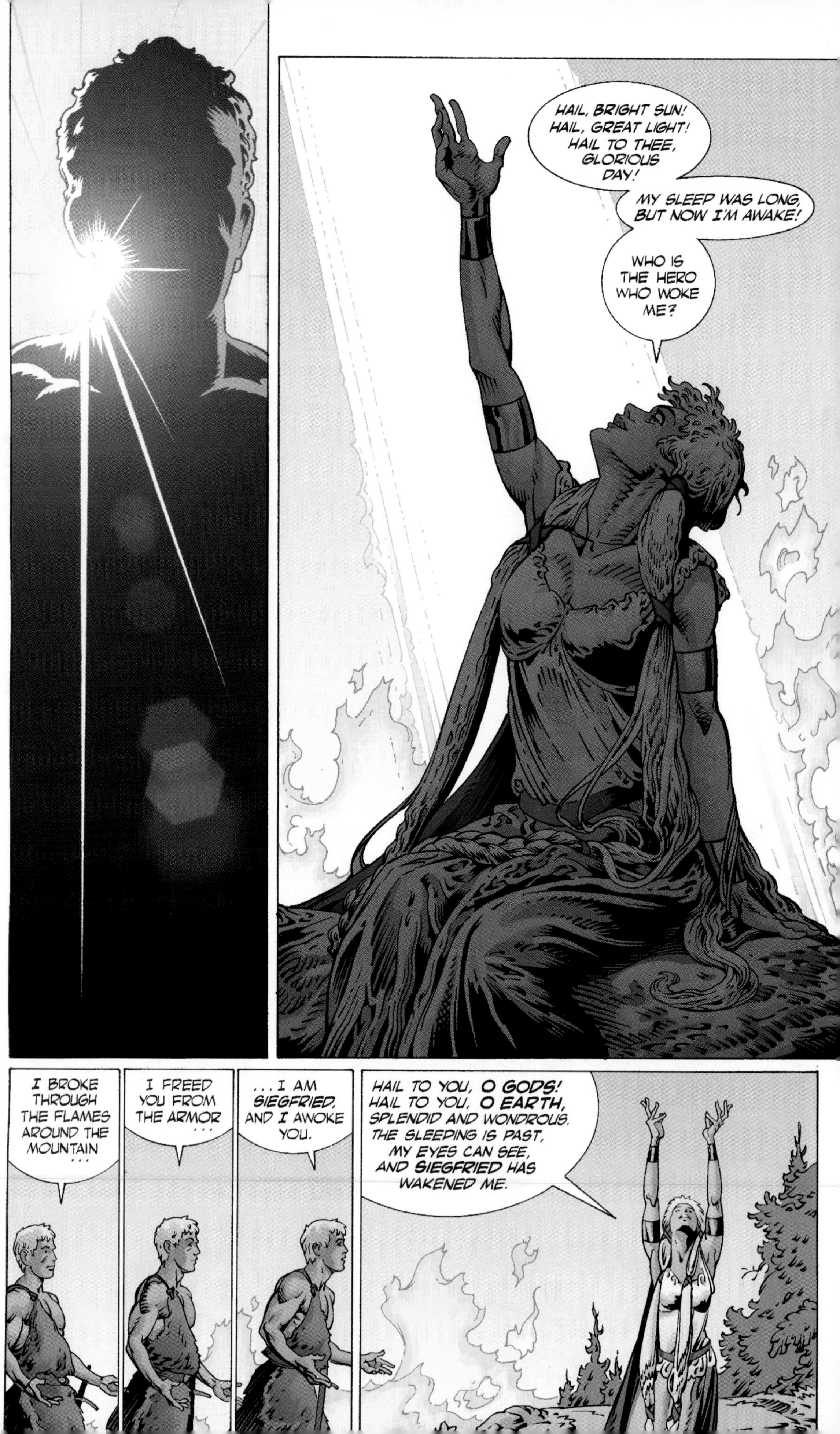
HAIL, BRIGHT SUN! HAIL, GREAT LIGHT! HAIL TO THEE, GLORIOUS DAY!
MY SLEEP WAS LONG, BUT NOW I'M AWAKE!
WHO IS THE HERO WHO WOKE ME?
I BROKE THROUGH THE FLAMES AROUND THE MOUNTAIN . . .
I FREED YOU FROM THE ARMOR . . .
. . . I AM SIEGFRIED, AND I AWOKE YOU.
HAIL TO YOU, O GODS! HAIL TO YOU, O EARTH, SPLENDID AND WONDROUS. THE SLEEPING IS PAST, MY EYES CAN SEE, AND SIEGFRIED HAS WAKENED ME.

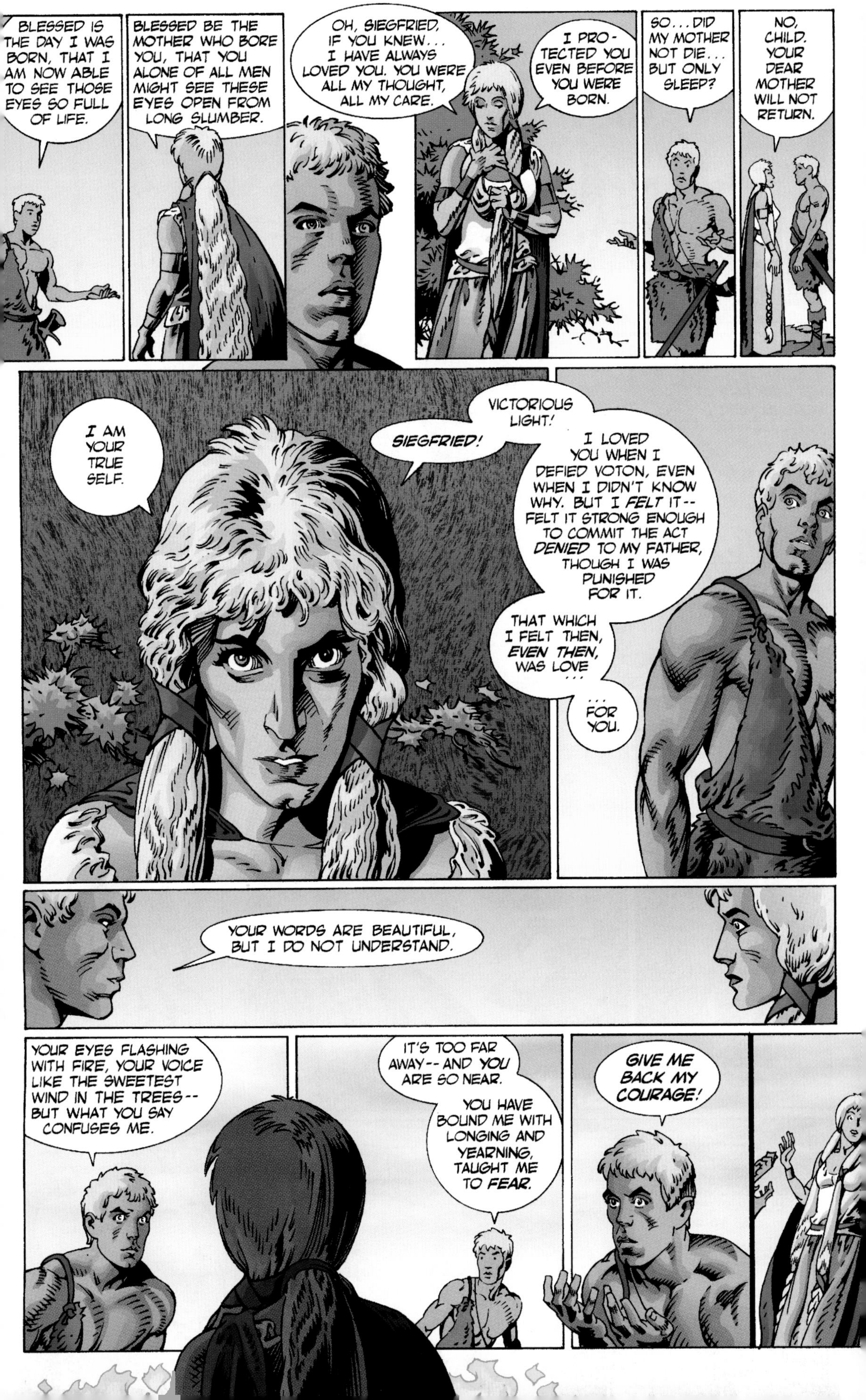
BLESSED IS THE DAY I WAS BORN, THAT I AM NOW ABLE TO SEE THOSE EYES SO FULL OF LIFE.
BLESSED BE THE MOTHER WHO BORE YOU, THAT YOU ALONE OF ALL MEN MIGHT SEE THESE EYES OPEN FROM LONG SLUMBER.
OH, SIEGFRIED, IF YOU KNEW... I HAVE ALWAYS LOVED YOU. YOU WERE ALL MY THOUGHT, ALL MY CARE.
I PROTECTED YOU EVEN BEFORE YOU WERE BORN.
SO...DID MY MOTHER NOT DIE... BUT ONLY SLEEP?
NO, CHILD. YOUR DEAR MOTHER WILL NOT RETURN.
I AM YOUR TRUE SELF.
SIEGFRIED!
VICTORIOUS LIGHT!
I LOVED YOU WHEN I DEFIED VOTON, EVEN WHEN I DIDN'T KNOW WHY. BUT I FELT IT-- FELT IT STRONG ENOUGH TO COMMIT THE ACT DENIED TO MY FATHER, THOUGH I WAS PUNISHED FOR IT.
THAT WHICH I FELT THEN, EVEN THEN, WAS LOVE...
...FOR YOU.
YOUR WORDS ARE BEAUTIFUL, BUT I DO NOT UNDERSTAND.
YOUR EYES FLASHING WITH FIRE, YOUR VOICE LIKE THE SWEETEST WIND IN THE TREES-- BUT WHAT YOU SAY CONFUSES ME.
IT'S TOO FAR AWAY-- AND YOU ARE SO NEAR.
YOU HAVE BOUND ME WITH LONGING AND YEARNING, TAUGHT ME TO FEAR.
GIVE ME BACK MY COURAGE!

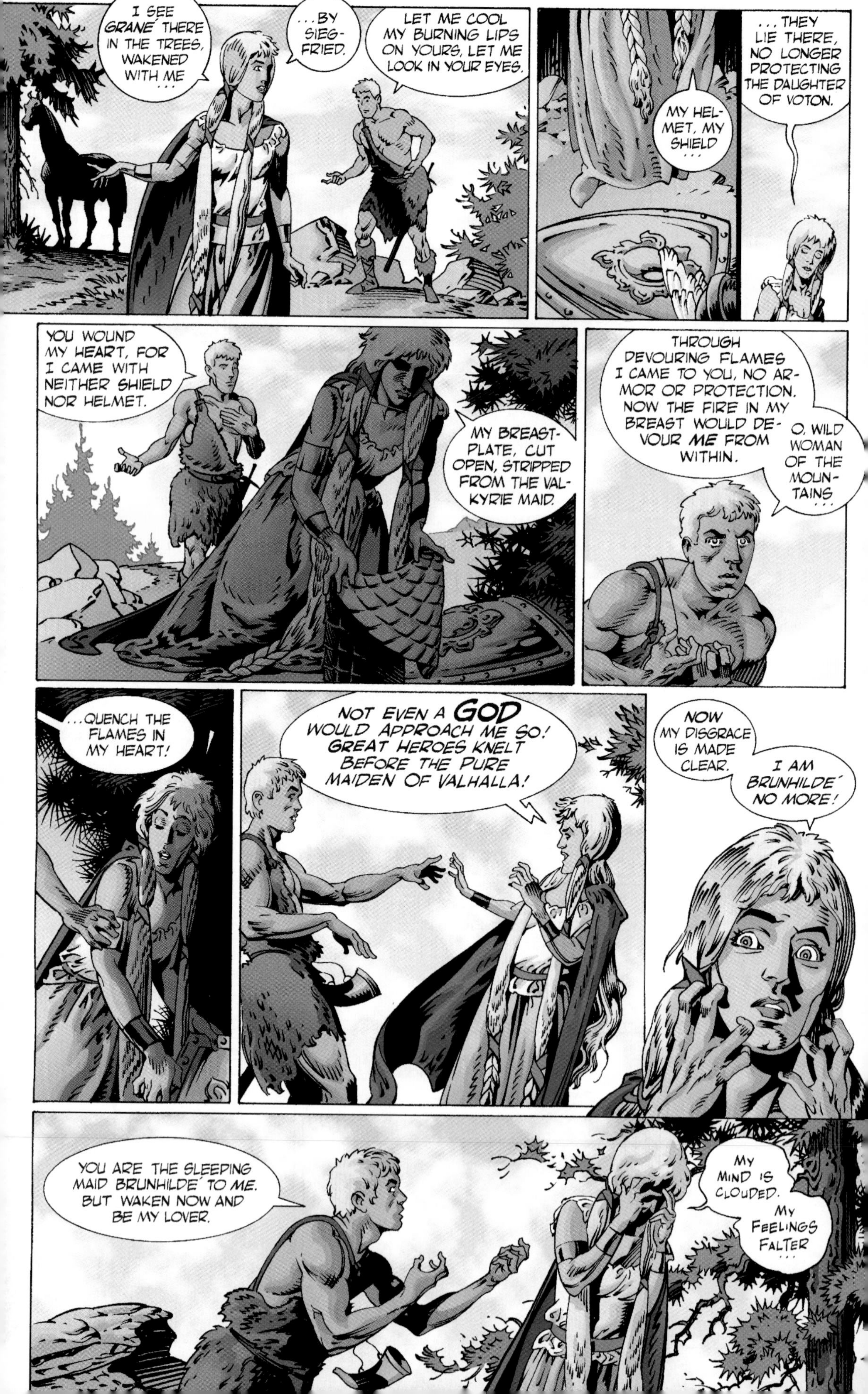
I SEE GRANE THERE IN THE TREES, WAKENED WITH ME . . .
. . . BY SIEG-FRIED.
LET ME COOL MY BURNING LIPS ON YOURS, LET ME LOOK IN YOUR EYES.
MY HEL-MET, MY SHIELD . . .
. . . THEY LIE THERE, NO LONGER PROTECTING THE DAUGHTER OF VOTON.
YOU WOUND MY HEART, FOR I CAME WITH NEITHER SHIELD NOR HELMET.
MY BREAST-PLATE, CUT OPEN, STRIPPED FROM THE VAL-KYRIE MAID.
THROUGH DEVOURING FLAMES I CAME TO YOU, NO AR-MOR OR PROTECTION. NOW THE FIRE IN MY BREAST WOULD DE-VOUR ME FROM WITHIN.
O, WILD WOMAN OF THE MOUN-TAINS . . .
. . . QUENCH THE FLAMES IN MY HEART!
NOT EVEN A GOD WOULD APPROACH ME SO! GREAT HEROES KNELT BEFORE THE PURE MAIDEN OF VALHALLA!
NOW MY DISGRACE IS MADE CLEAR.
I AM BRUNHILDE NO MORE!
YOU ARE THE SLEEPING MAID BRUNHILDE TO ME. BUT WAKEN NOW AND BE MY LOVER.
MY MIND IS CLOUDED.
MY FEELINGS FALTER . . .

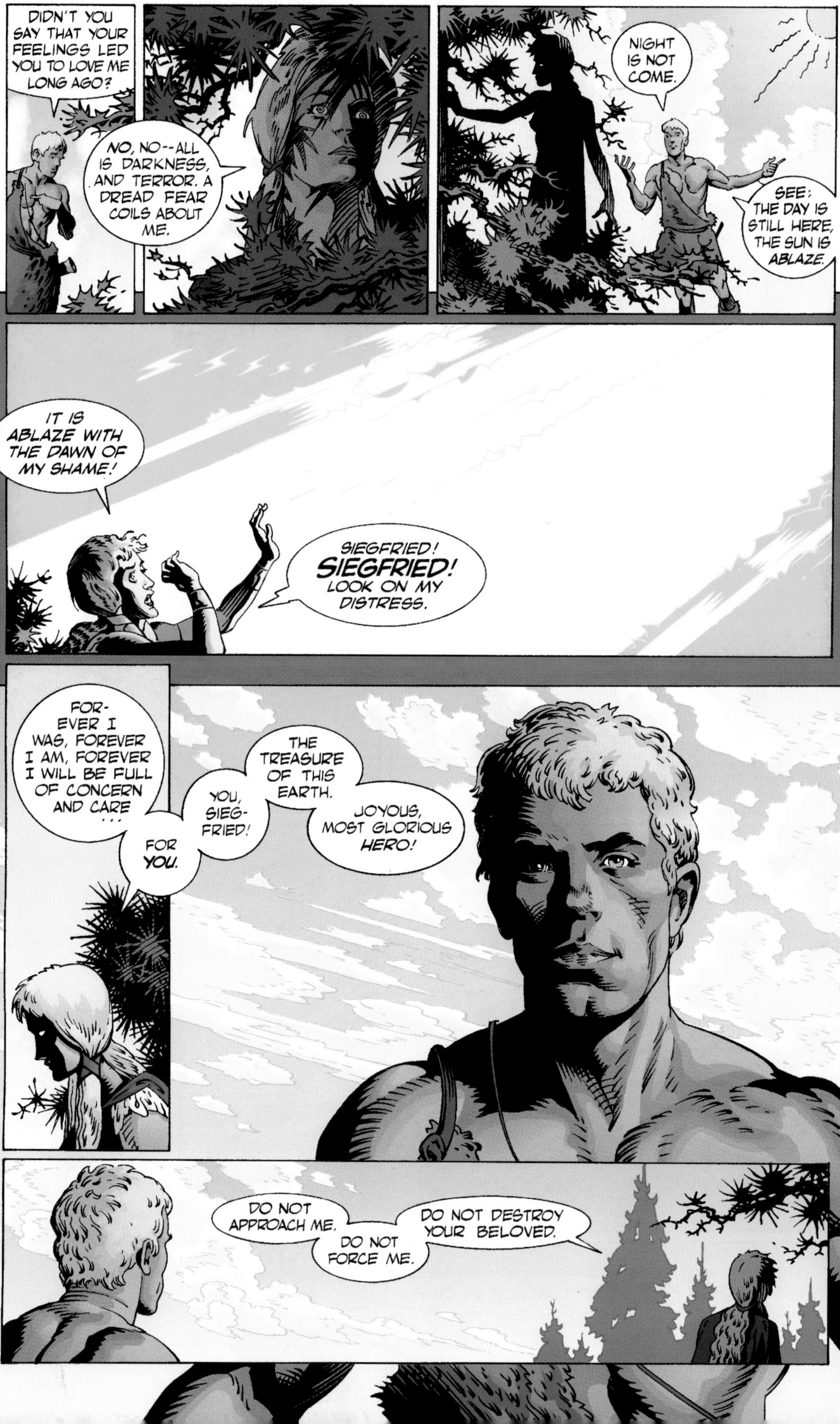
DIDN'T YOU SAY THAT YOUR FEELINGS LED YOU TO LOVE ME LONG AGO?
NO, NO--ALL IS DARKNESS, AND TERROR. A DREAD FEAR COILS ABOUT ME.
NIGHT IS NOT COME.
SEE: THE DAY IS STILL HERE, THE SUN IS ABLAZE.
IT IS ABLAZE WITH THE DAWN OF MY SHAME!
SIEGFRIED! SIEGFRIED! LOOK ON MY DISTRESS.
FOR-EVER I WAS, FOREVER I AM, FOREVER I WILL BE FULL OF CONCERN AND CARE . . .
FOR YOU.
YOU, SIEG-FRIED!
THE TREASURE OF THIS EARTH.
JOYOUS, MOST GLORIOUS HERO!
DO NOT APPROACH ME.
DO NOT FORCE ME.
DO NOT DESTROY YOUR BELOVED.

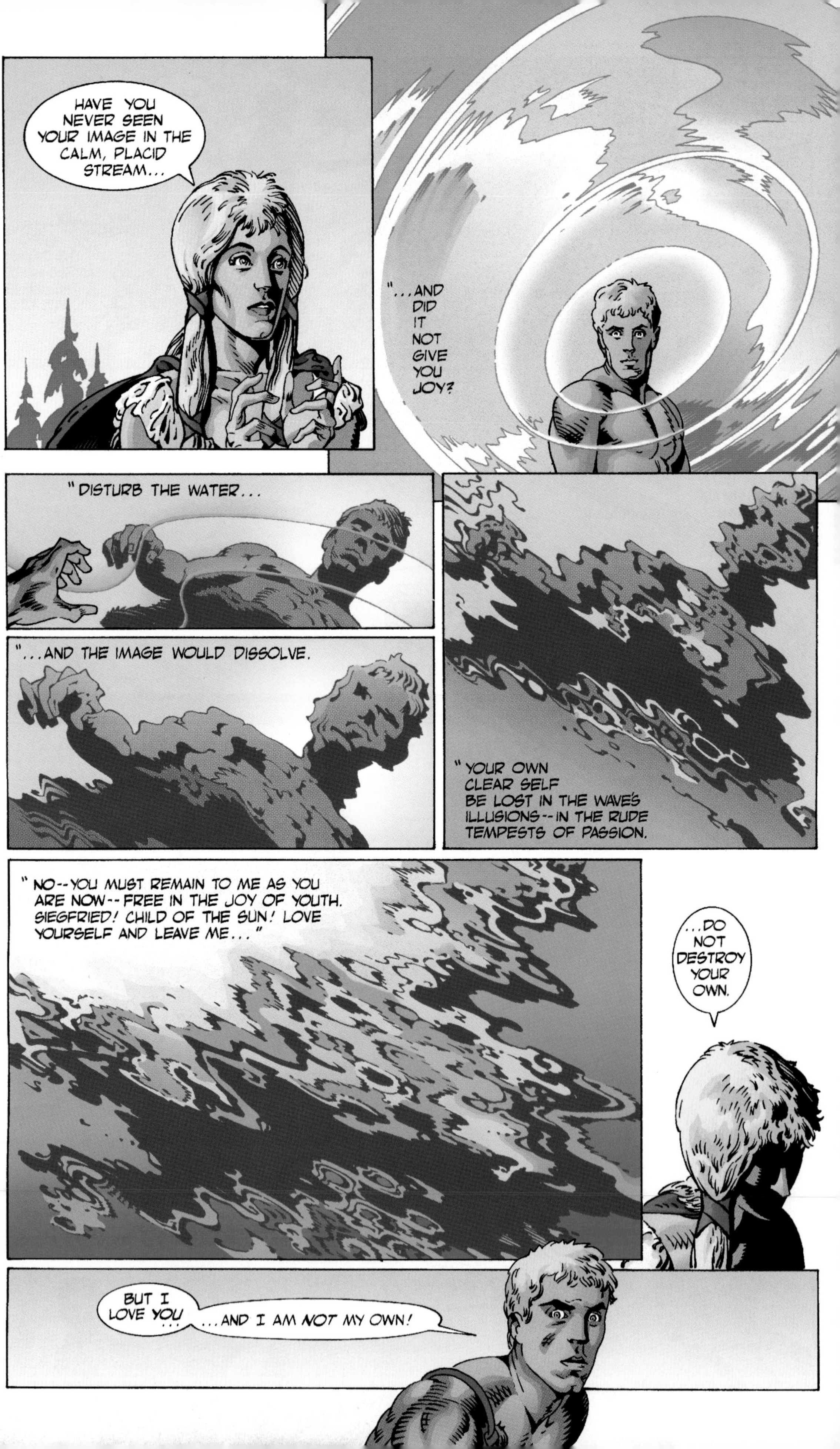
HAVE YOU NEVER SEEN YOUR IMAGE IN THE CALM, PLACID STREAM...
"...AND DID IT NOT GIVE YOU JOY?
"DISTURB THE WATER...
"...AND THE IMAGE WOULD DISSOLVE.
"YOUR OWN CLEAR SELF BE LOST IN THE WAVE'S ILLUSIONS--IN THE RUDE TEMPESTS OF PASSION.
" NO--YOU MUST REMAIN TO ME AS YOU ARE NOW--FREE IN THE JOY OF YOUTH. SIEGFRIED! CHILD OF THE SUN! LOVE YOURSELF AND LEAVE ME..."
...DO NOT DESTROY YOUR OWN.
BUT I LOVE *YOU*...
...AND I AM *NOT* MY OWN!

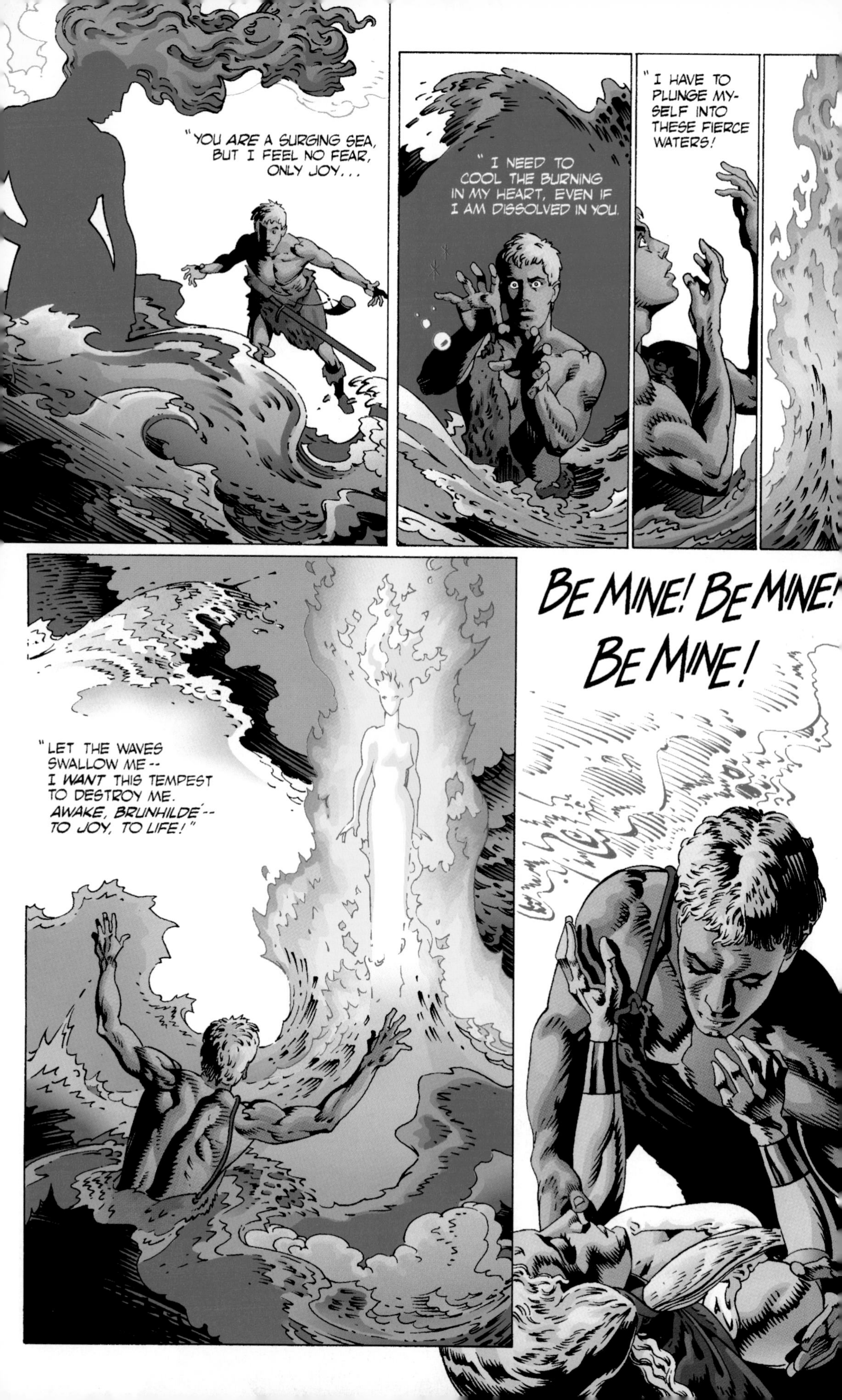
"YOU ARE A SURGING SEA, BUT I FEEL NO FEAR, ONLY JOY...
" I NEED TO COOL THE BURNING IN MY HEART, EVEN IF I AM DISSOLVED IN YOU.
" I HAVE TO PLUNGE MY-SELF INTO THESE FIERCE WATERS!
"LET THE WAVES SWALLOW ME -- I WANT THIS TEMPEST TO DESTROY ME. AWAKE, BRUNHILDE -- TO JOY, TO LIFE!"
BE MINE! BE MINE! BE MINE!

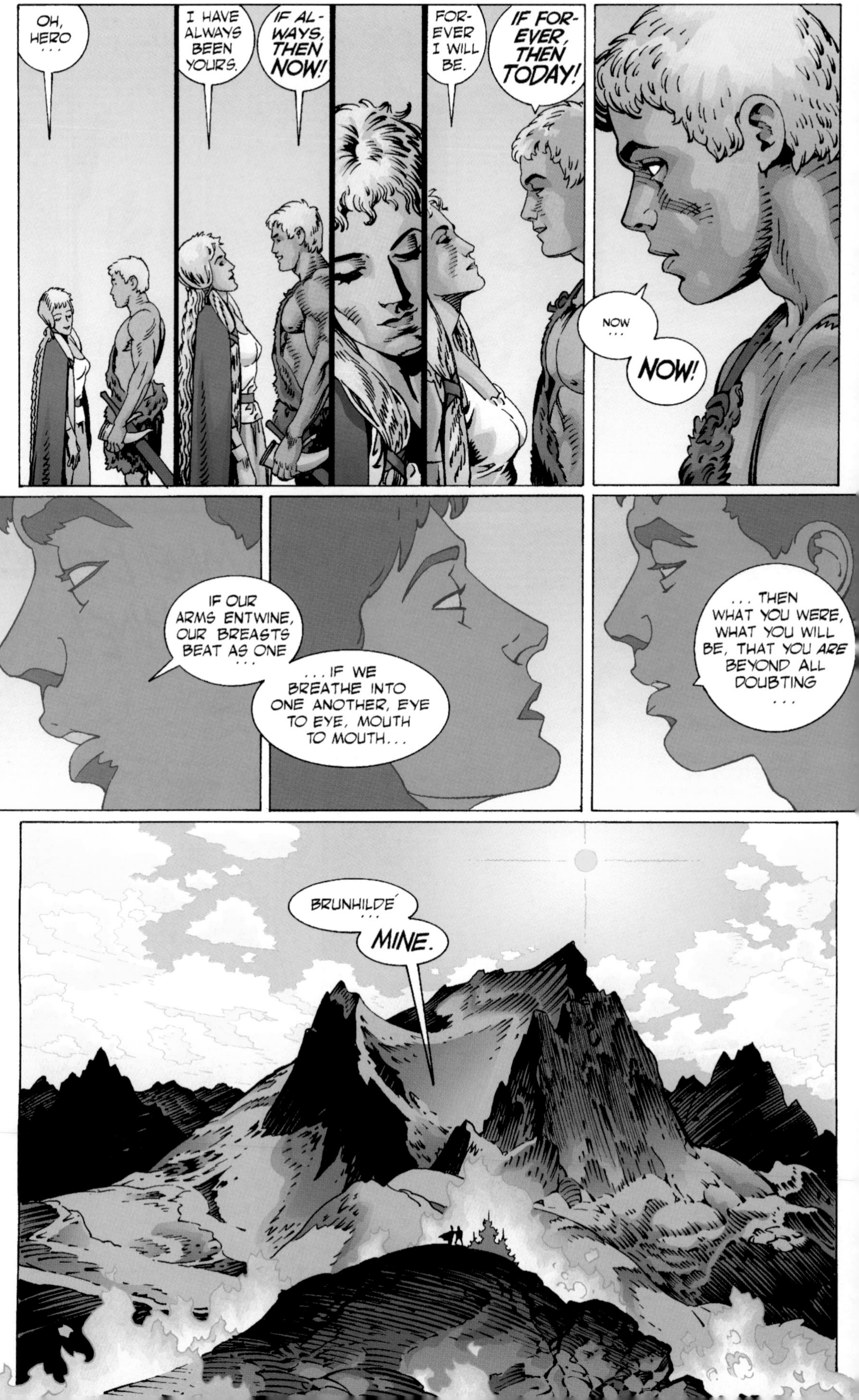
OH, HERO . . .
I HAVE ALWAYS BEEN YOURS.
IF ALWAYS, THEN NOW!
FOREVER I WILL BE.
IF FOREVER, THEN TODAY!
NOW . . .
NOW!
IF OUR ARMS ENTWINE, OUR BREASTS BEAT AS ONE . . .
. . . IF WE BREATHE INTO ONE ANOTHER, EYE TO EYE, MOUTH TO MOUTH . . .
. . . THEN WHAT YOU WERE, WHAT YOU WILL BE, THAT YOU *ARE* BEYOND ALL DOUBTING . . .
BRUNHILDÉ . . .
MINE.

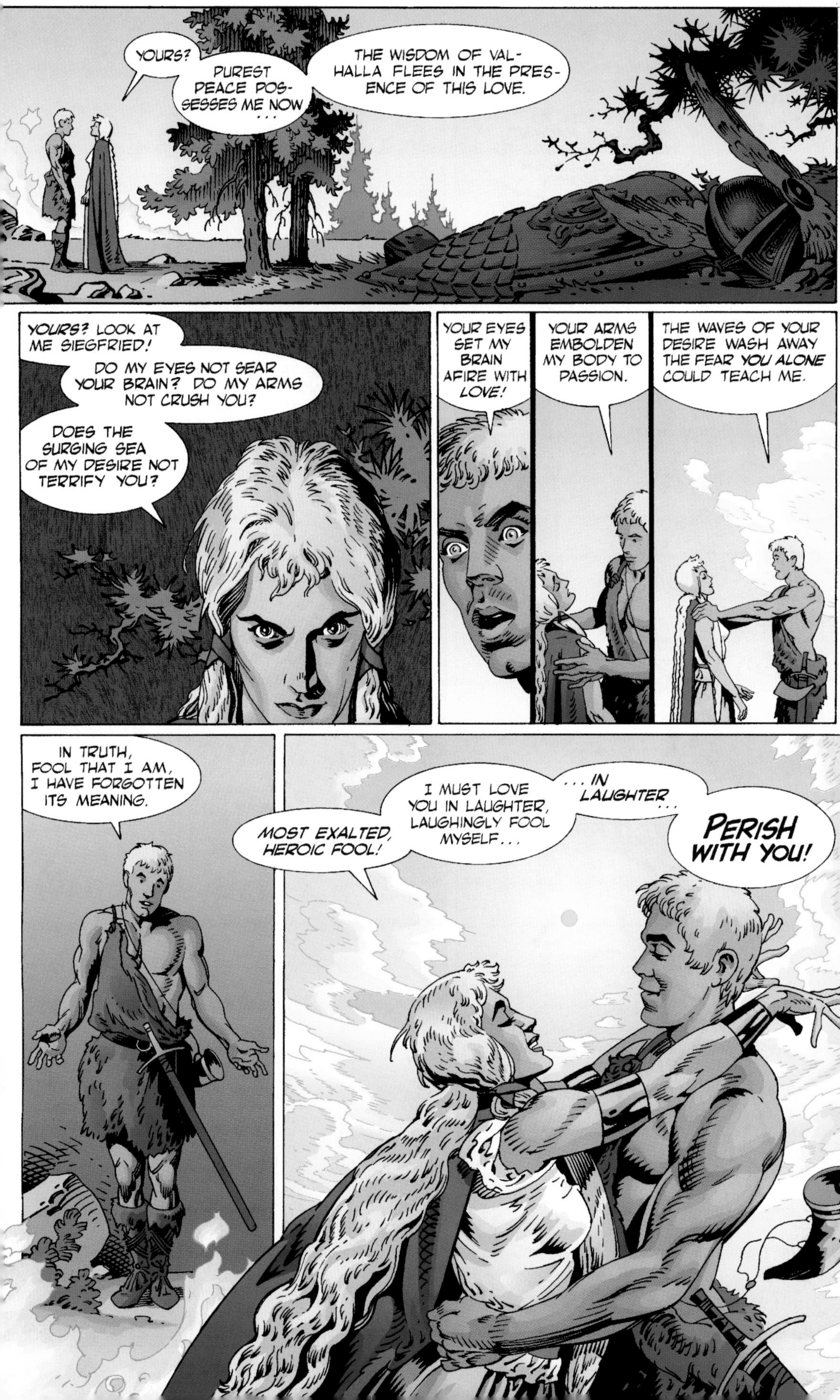
YOURS?
PUREST PEACE POSSESSES ME NOW . . .
THE WISDOM OF VALHALLA FLEES IN THE PRESENCE OF THIS LOVE.
YOURS? LOOK AT ME SIEGFRIED!
DO MY EYES NOT SEAR YOUR BRAIN? DO MY ARMS NOT CRUSH YOU?
DOES THE SURGING SEA OF MY DESIRE NOT TERRIFY YOU?
YOUR EYES SET MY BRAIN AFIRE WITH LOVE!
YOUR ARMS EMBOLDEN MY BODY TO PASSION.
THE WAVES OF YOUR DESIRE WASH AWAY THE FEAR YOU ALONE COULD TEACH ME.
IN TRUTH, FOOL THAT I AM, I HAVE FORGOTTEN ITS MEANING.
MOST EXALTED, HEROIC FOOL!
I MUST LOVE YOU IN LAUGHTER, LAUGHINGLY FOOL MYSELF . . .
. . . IN LAUGHTER . . .
PERISH WITH YOU!

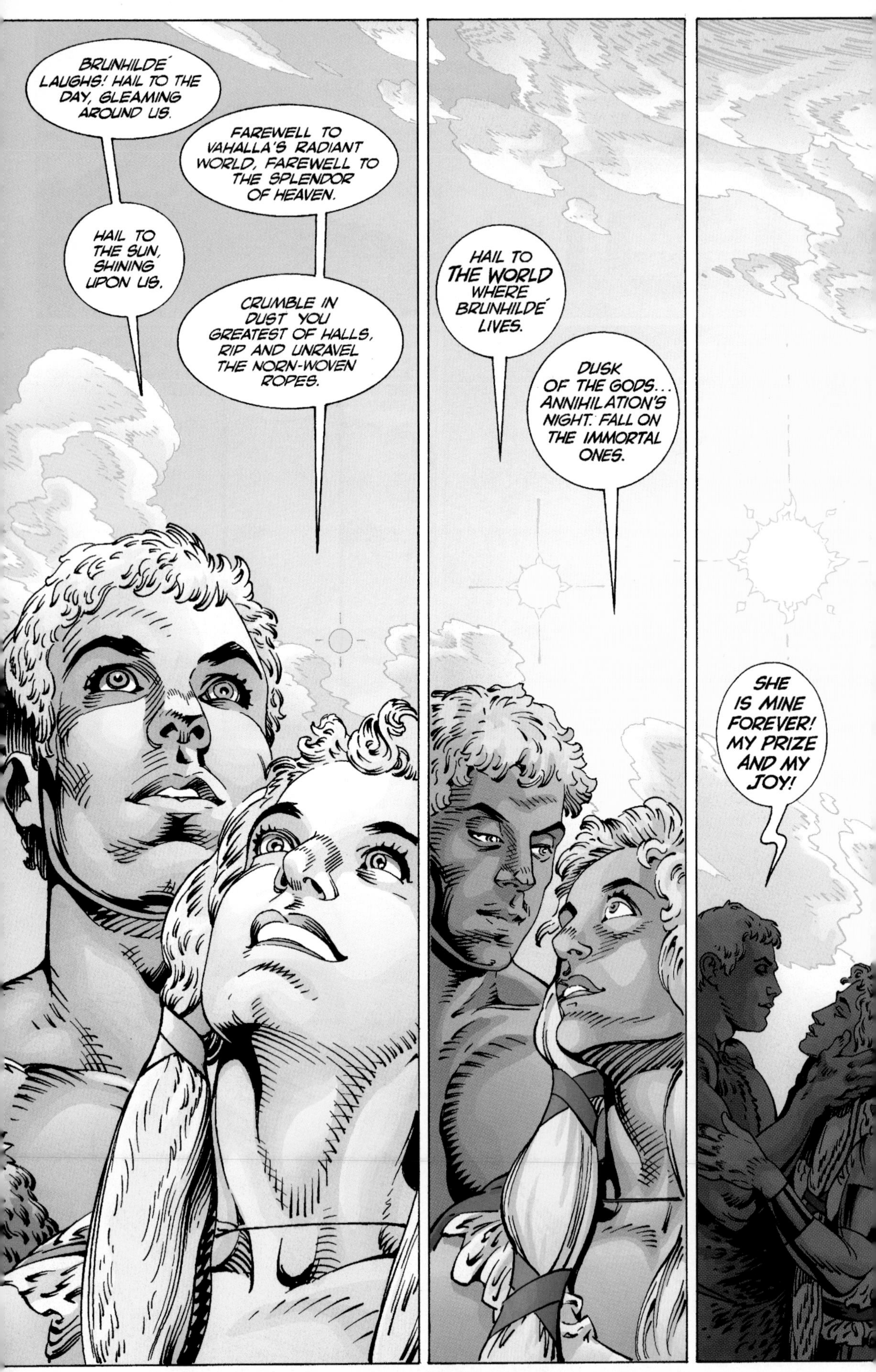
BRUNHILDE´ LAUGHS! HAIL TO THE DAY, GLEAMING AROUND US.
FAREWELL TO VAHALLA'S RADIANT WORLD, FAREWELL TO THE SPLENDOR OF HEAVEN.
HAIL TO THE SUN, SHINING UPON US.
CRUMBLE IN DUST YOU GREATEST OF HALLS, RIP AND UNRAVEL THE NORN-WOVEN ROPES.
HAIL TO THE WORLD WHERE BRUNHILDE´ LIVES.
DUSK OF THE GODS... ANNIHILATION'S NIGHT. FALL ON THE IMMORTAL ONES.
SHE IS MINE FOREVER! MY PRIZE AND MY JOY!

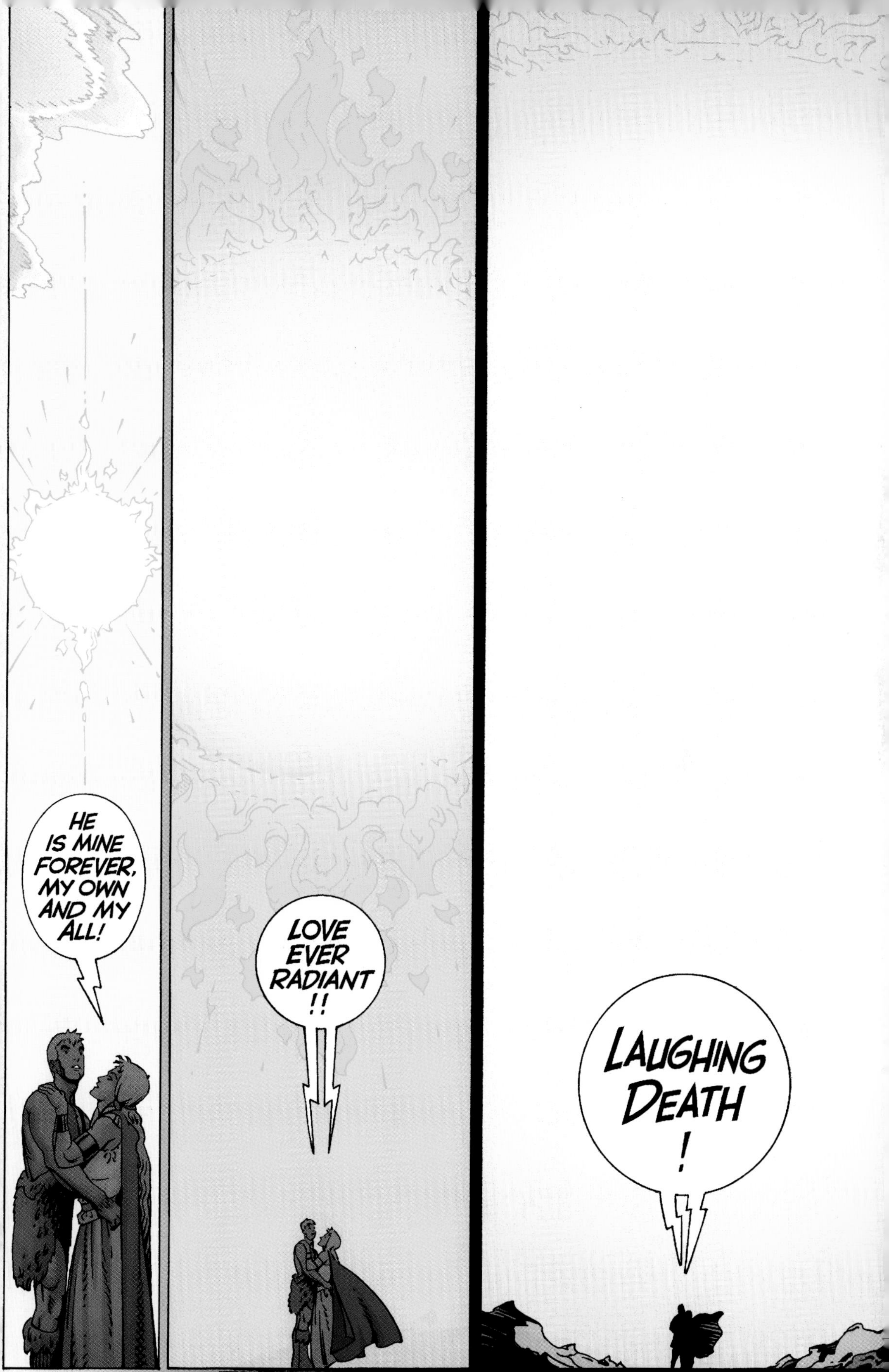
HE IS MINE FOREVER, MY OWN AND MY ALL!
LOVE EVER RADIANT !!
LAUGHING DEATH !

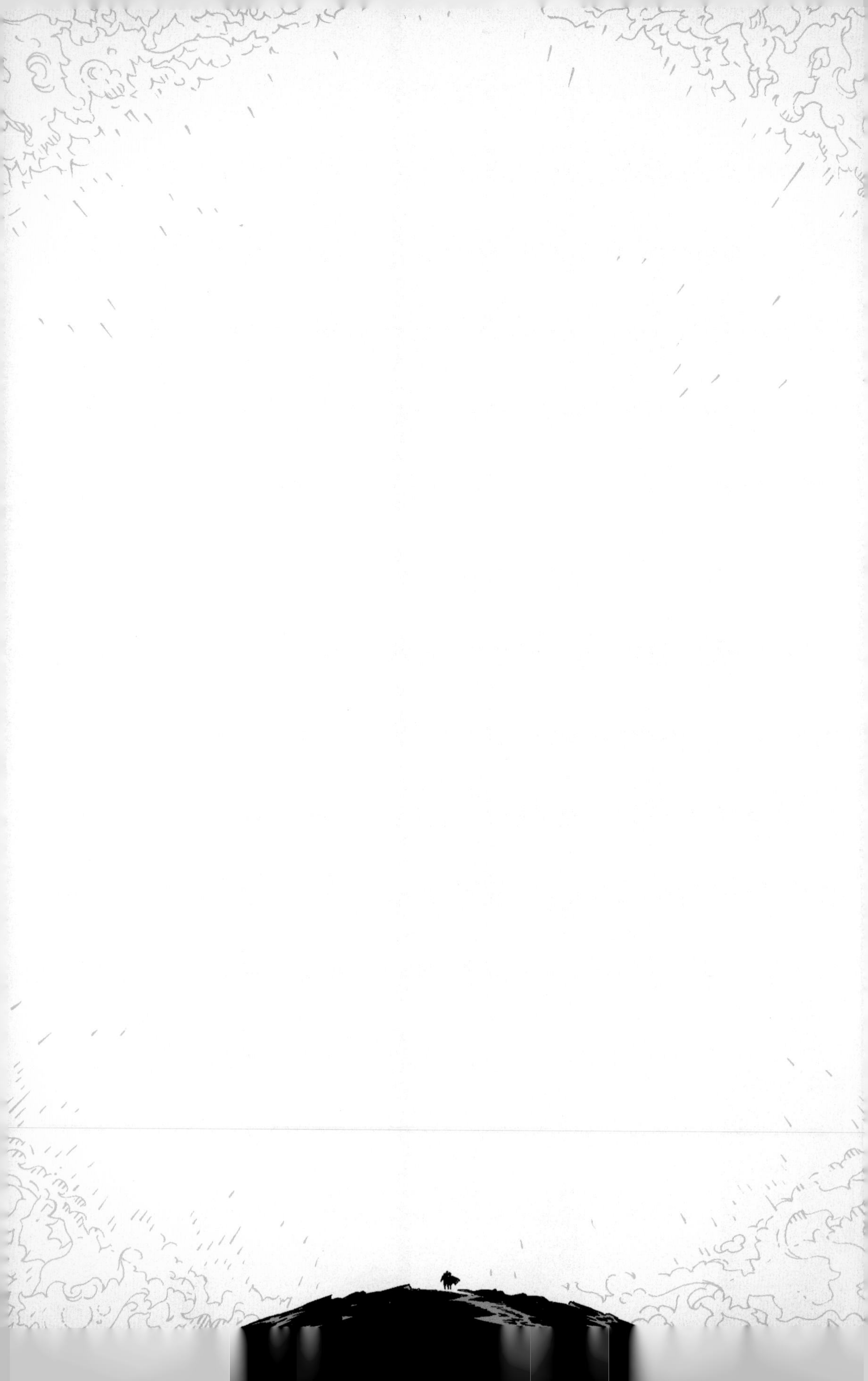

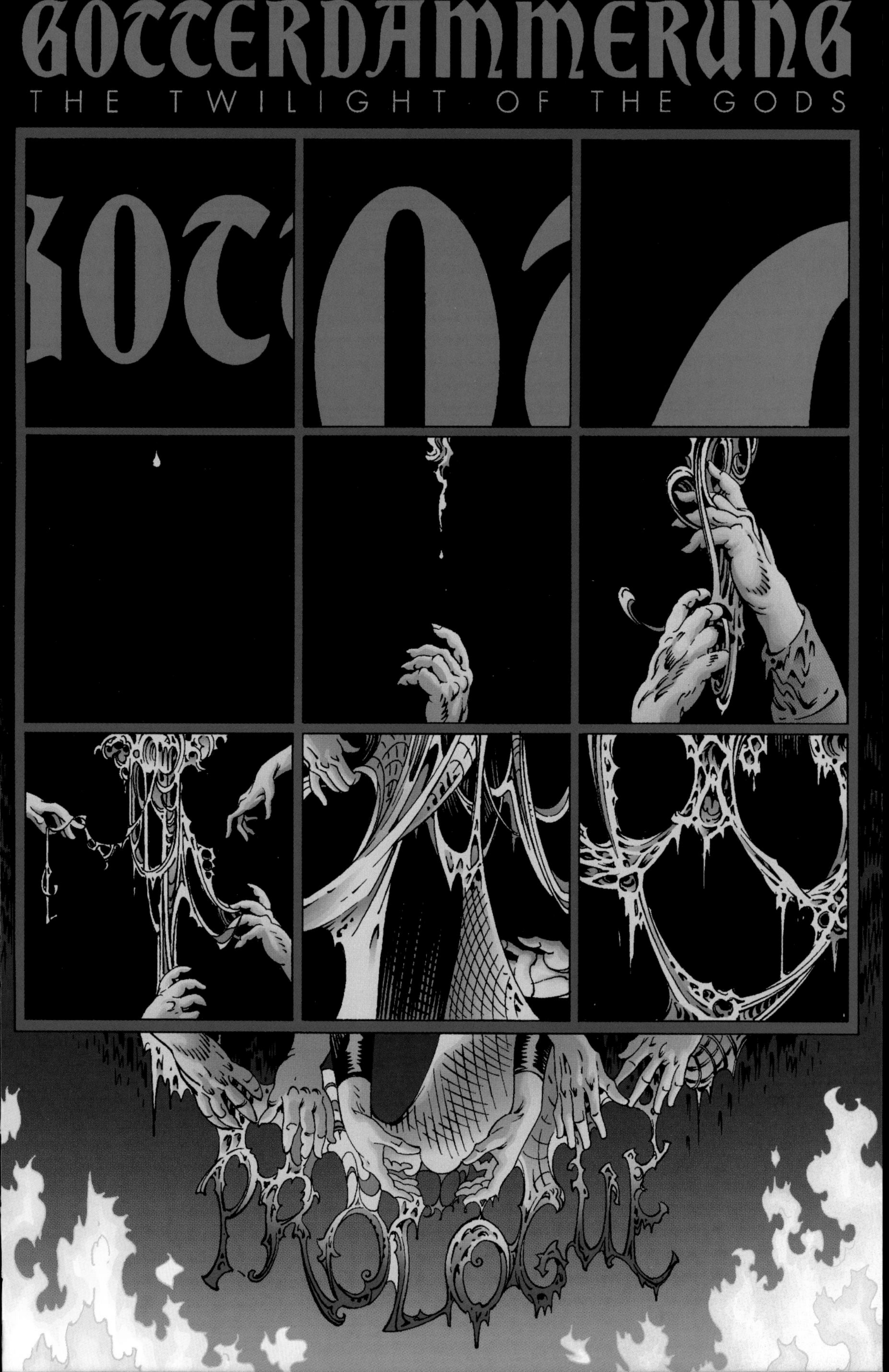
GOTTERDAMMERUNG
THE TWILIGHT OF THE GODS
PROLOGUE

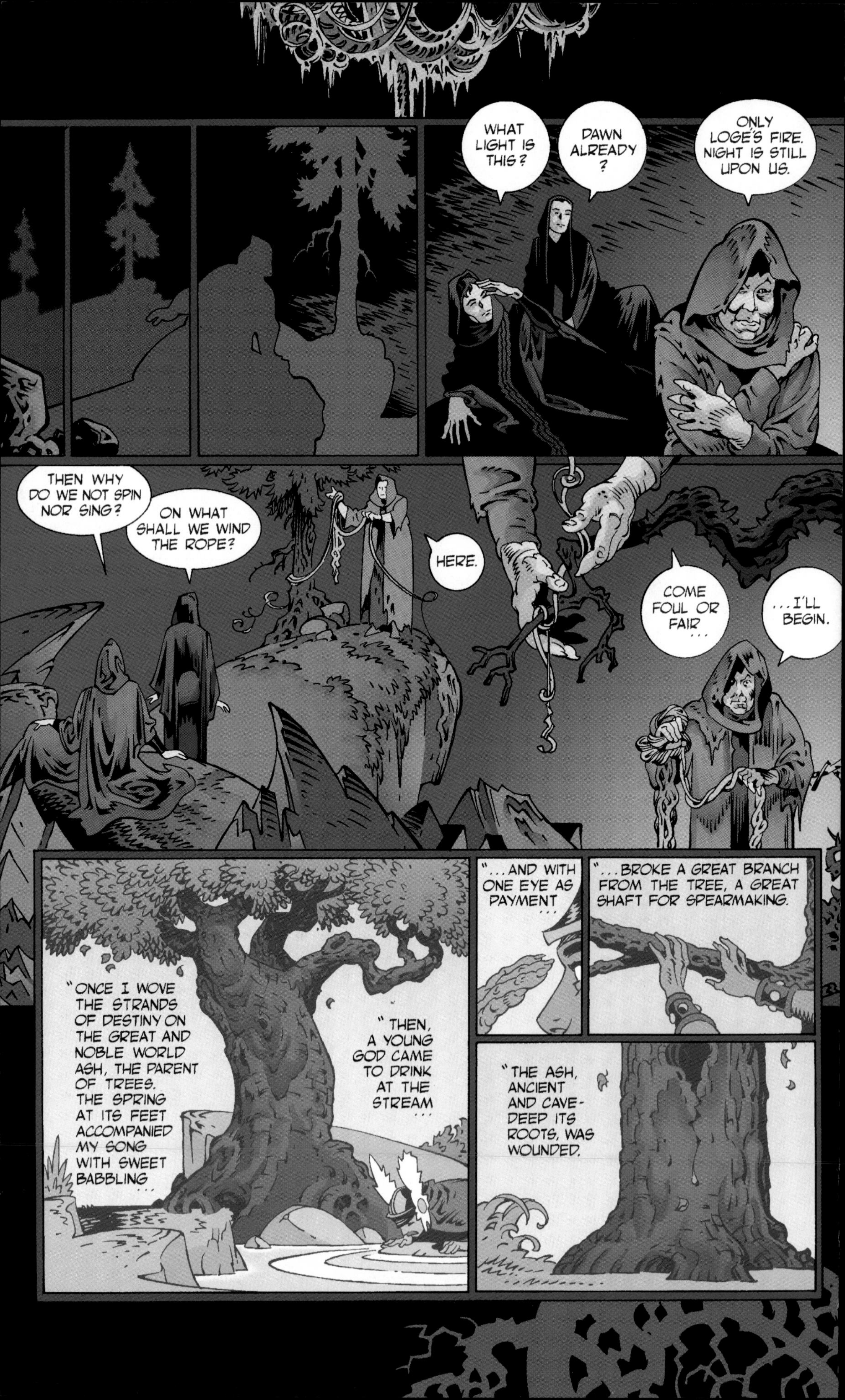
WHAT LIGHT IS THIS?
DAWN ALREADY?
ONLY LOGE'S FIRE. NIGHT IS STILL UPON US.
THEN WHY DO WE NOT SPIN NOR SING?
ON WHAT SHALL WE WIND THE ROPE?
HERE.
COME FOUL OR FAIR...
...I'LL BEGIN.
"ONCE I WOVE THE STRANDS OF DESTINY ON THE GREAT AND NOBLE WORLD ASH, THE PARENT OF TREES. THE SPRING AT ITS FEET ACCOMPANIED MY SONG WITH SWEET BABBLING...
"THEN, A YOUNG GOD CAME TO DRINK AT THE STREAM...
"...AND WITH ONE EYE AS PAYMENT...
"...BROKE A GREAT BRANCH FROM THE TREE, A GREAT SHAFT FOR SPEARMAKING.
"THE ASH, ANCIENT AND CAVE-DEEP ITS ROOTS, WAS WOUNDED.

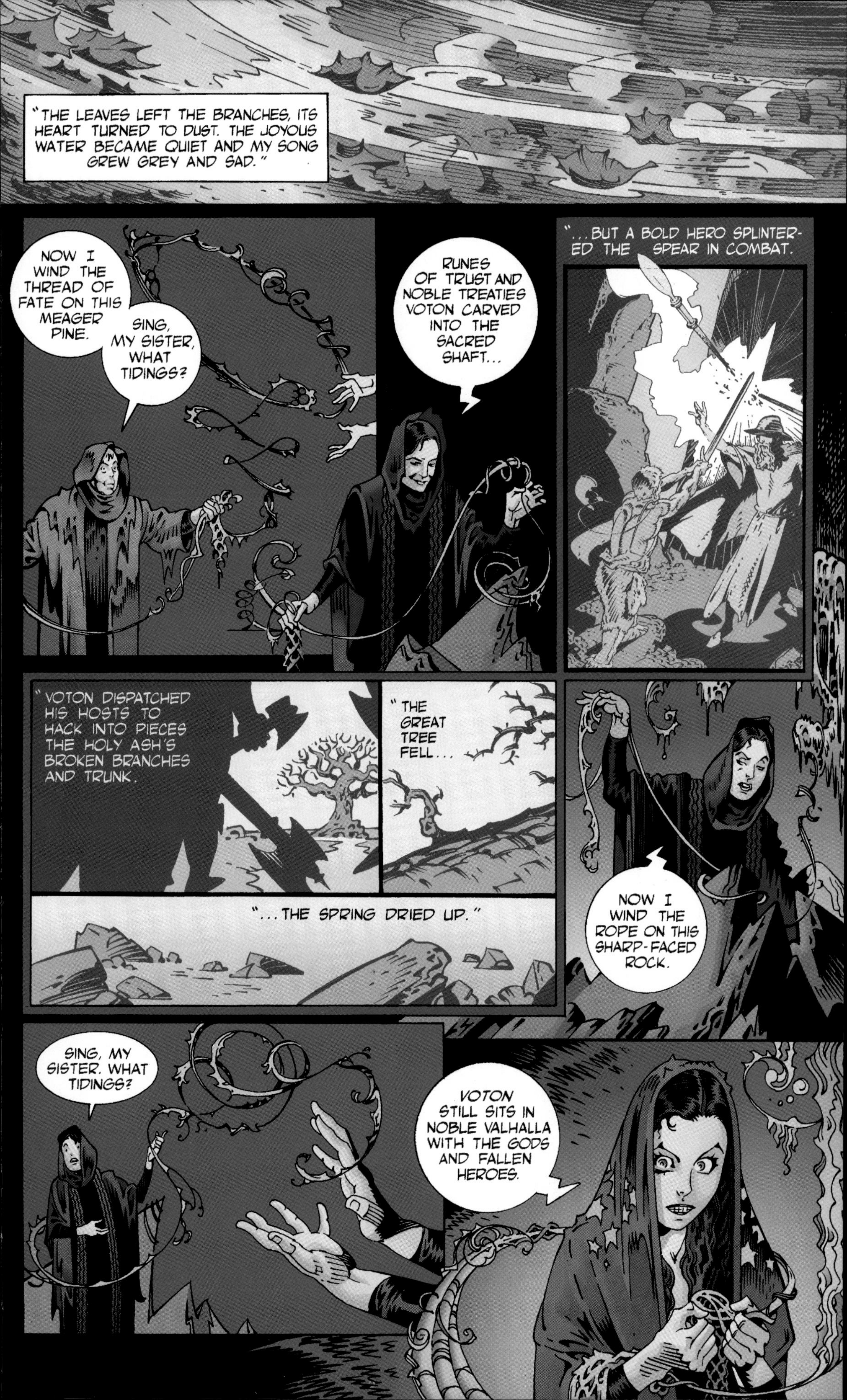
"THE LEAVES LEFT THE BRANCHES, ITS HEART TURNED TO DUST. THE JOYOUS WATER BECAME QUIET AND MY SONG GREW GREY AND SAD."
NOW I WIND THE THREAD OF FATE ON THIS MEAGER PINE.
SING, MY SISTER, WHAT TIDINGS?
RUNES OF TRUST AND NOBLE TREATIES VOTON CARVED INTO THE SACRED SHAFT...
"...BUT A BOLD HERO SPLINTERED THE SPEAR IN COMBAT.
"VOTON DISPATCHED HIS HOSTS TO HACK INTO PIECES THE HOLY ASH'S BROKEN BRANCHES AND TRUNK.
"THE GREAT TREE FELL...
"...THE SPRING DRIED UP."
NOW I WIND THE ROPE ON THIS SHARP-FACED ROCK.
SING, MY SISTER. WHAT TIDINGS?
VOTON STILL SITS IN NOBLE VALHALLA WITH THE GODS AND FALLEN HEROES.

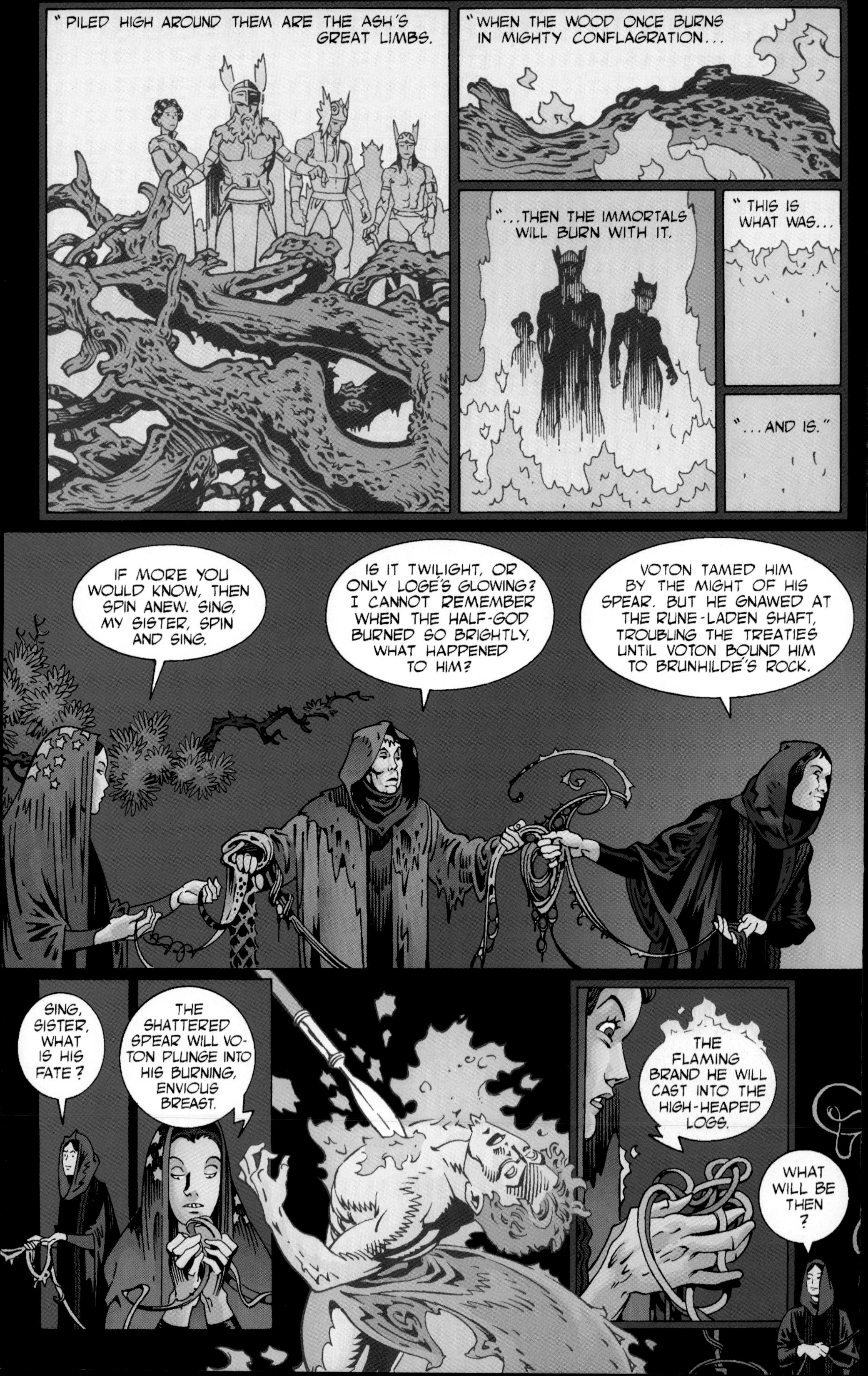
"PILED HIGH AROUND THEM ARE THE ASH'S GREAT LIMBS.
"WHEN THE WOOD ONCE BURNS IN MIGHTY CONFLAGRATION...
"...THEN THE IMMORTALS WILL BURN WITH IT.
"THIS IS WHAT WAS...
"...AND IS."
IF MORE YOU WOULD KNOW, THEN SPIN ANEW. SING, MY SISTER, SPIN AND SING.
IS IT TWILIGHT, OR ONLY LOGE'S GLOWING? I CANNOT REMEMBER WHEN THE HALF-GOD BURNED SO BRIGHTLY. WHAT HAPPENED TO HIM?
VOTON TAMED HIM BY THE MIGHT OF HIS SPEAR. BUT HE GNAWED AT THE RUNE-LADEN SHAFT, TROUBLING THE TREATIES UNTIL VOTON BOUND HIM TO BRUNHILDE'S ROCK.
SING, SISTER, WHAT IS HIS FATE?
THE SHATTERED SPEAR WILL VOTON PLUNGE INTO HIS BURNING, ENVIOUS BREAST.
THE FLAMING BRAND HE WILL CAST INTO THE HIGH-HEAPED LOGS.
WHAT WILL BE THEN?

NIGHT IS PASSING.

THE STRANDS ARE TANGLED.

AN IMAGE OF MADNESS MUDDLES MY MIND.

ALBERICH.

"...HE WHO ROBBED THE RHINE... WHAT OF HIM...?"

SISTER, WHAT OF ALBERICH?

SISTER?

THE RAGGED ROCK RIPS AT THE ROPE.

THE THREADS UNRAVEL...

"...THEY UNRAVEL AND WEAKEN."

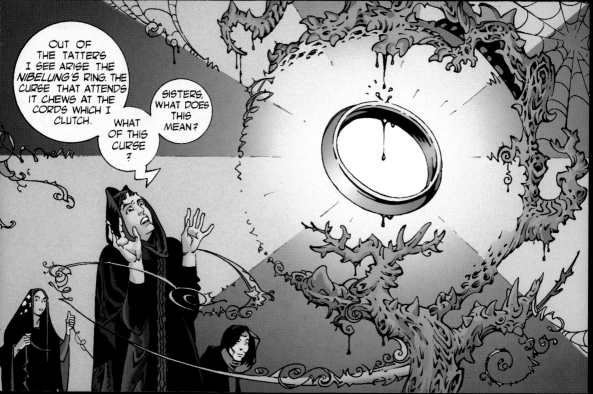

OUT OF THE TATTERS I SEE ARISE THE NIBELUNG'S RING. THE CURSE THAT ATTENDS IT CHEWS AT THE CORDS WHICH I CLUTCH.

WHAT OF THIS CURSE?

SISTERS, WHAT DOES THIS MEAN?

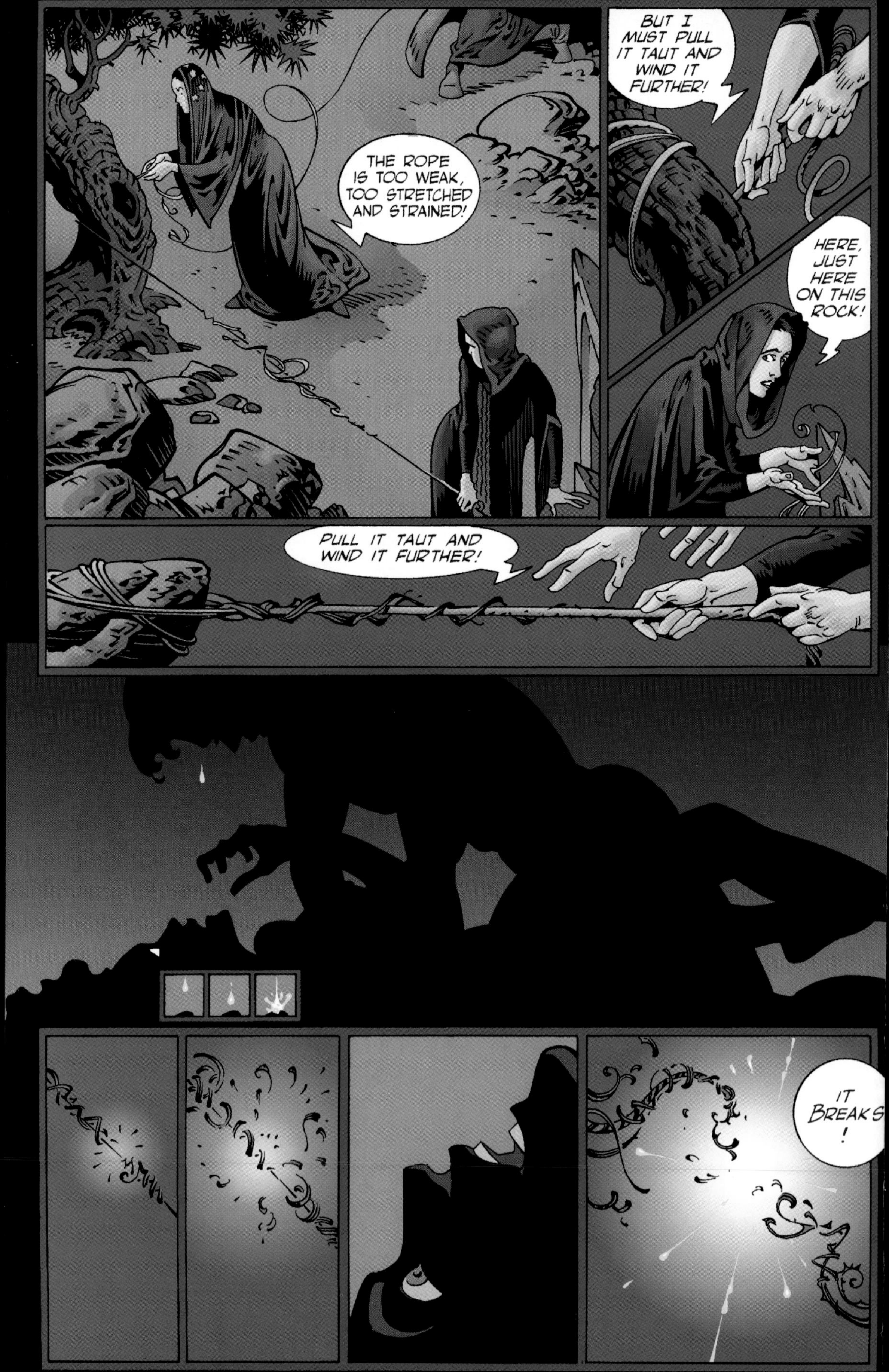

THE ROPE IS TOO WEAK, TOO STRETCHED AND STRAINED!
BUT I MUST PULL IT TAUT AND WIND IT FURTHER!
HERE, JUST HERE ON THIS ROCK!
PULL IT TAUT AND WIND IT FURTHER!
IT BREAKS!

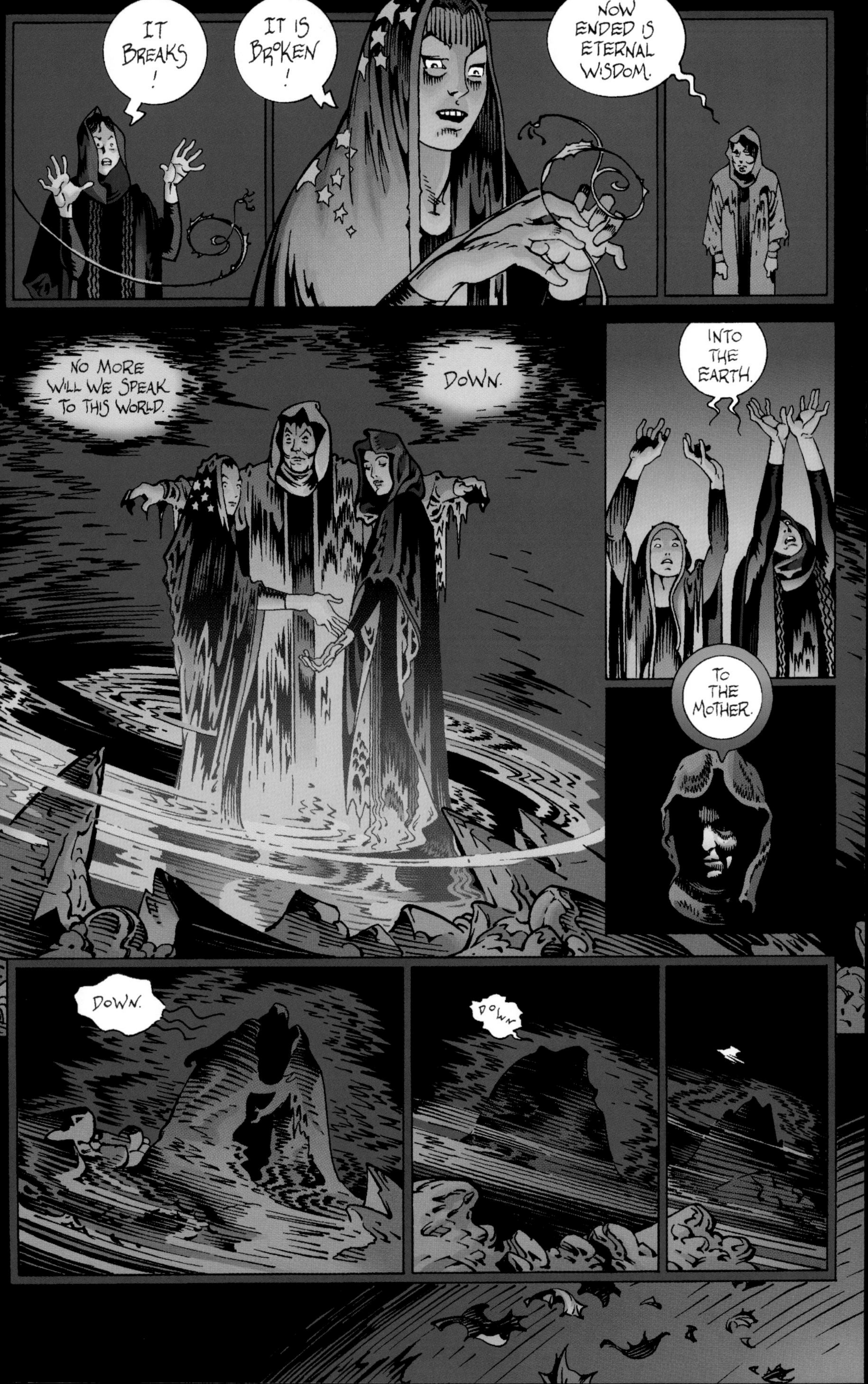
IT BREAKS!
IT IS BROKEN!
NOW ENDED IS ETERNAL WISDOM.
NO MORE WILL WE SPEAK TO THIS WORLD.
DOWN.
INTO THE EARTH.
TO THE MOTHER.
DOWN.
DOWN

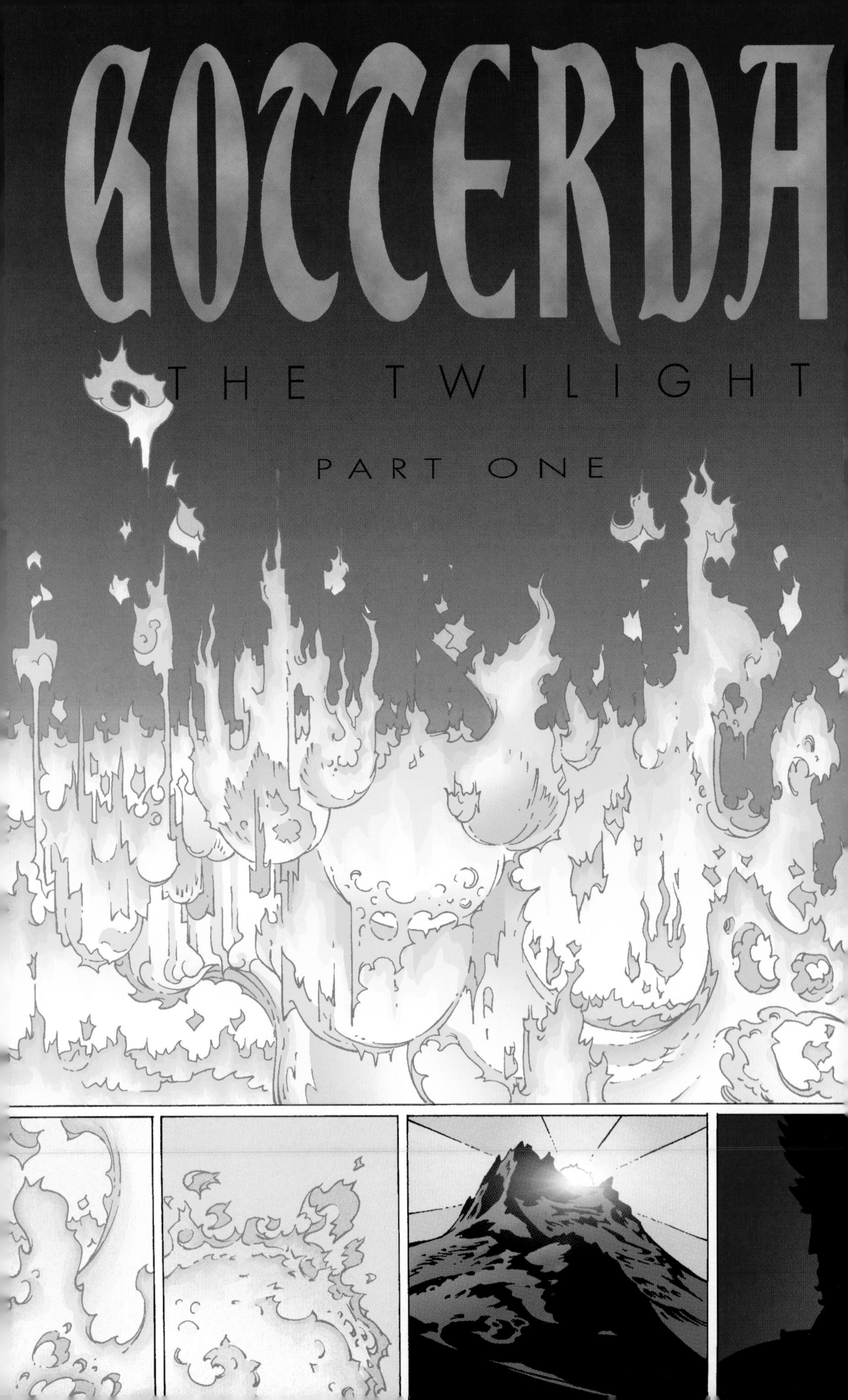
GOTTERDA
THE TWILIGHT
PART ONE

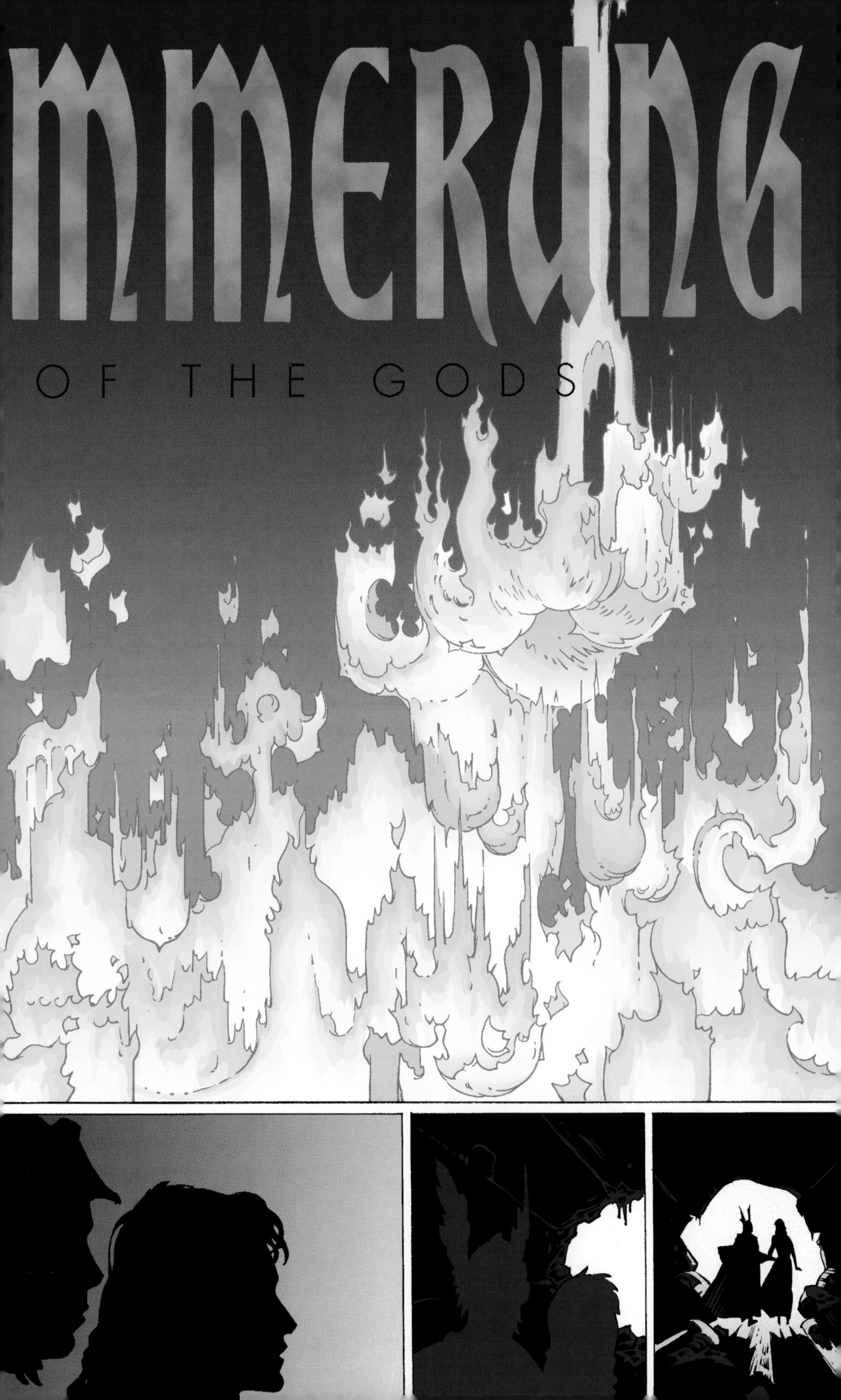
MMERUNG
OF THE GODS

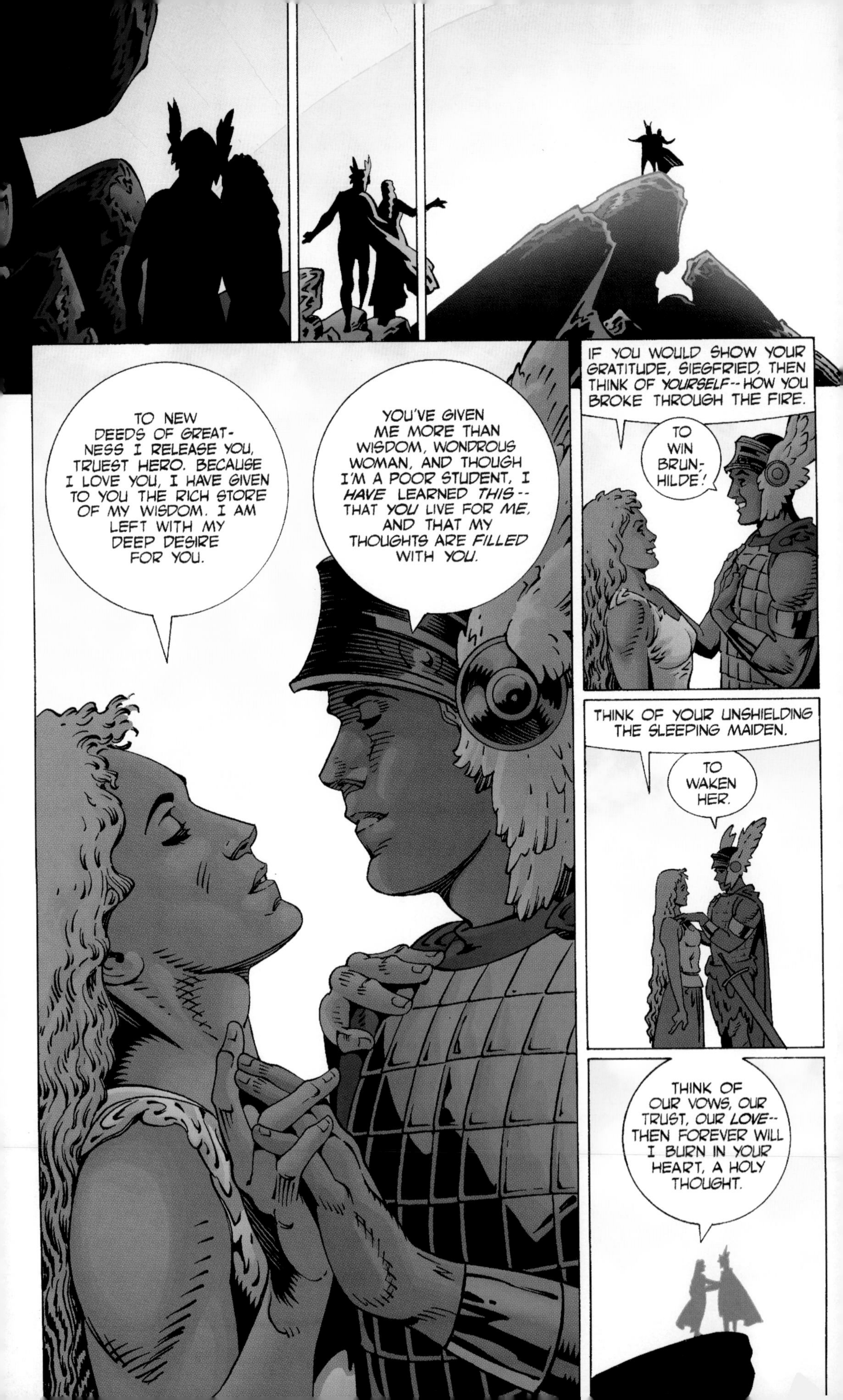
TO NEW DEEDS OF GREATNESS I RELEASE YOU, TRUEST HERO. BECAUSE I LOVE YOU, I HAVE GIVEN TO YOU THE RICH STORE OF MY WISDOM. I AM LEFT WITH MY DEEP DESIRE FOR YOU.
YOU'VE GIVEN ME MORE THAN WISDOM, WONDROUS WOMAN, AND THOUGH I'M A POOR STUDENT, I *HAVE* LEARNED *THIS*-- THAT *YOU* LIVE FOR *ME*, AND THAT MY THOUGHTS ARE *FILLED* WITH *YOU*.
IF YOU WOULD SHOW YOUR GRATITUDE, SIEGFRIED, THEN THINK OF *YOURSELF*-- HOW YOU BROKE THROUGH THE FIRE.
TO WIN BRUNHILDE!
THINK OF YOUR UNSHIELDING THE SLEEPING MAIDEN.
TO WAKEN HER.
THINK OF OUR VOWS, OUR TRUST, OUR *LOVE*-- THEN FOREVER WILL I BURN IN YOUR HEART, A HOLY THOUGHT.

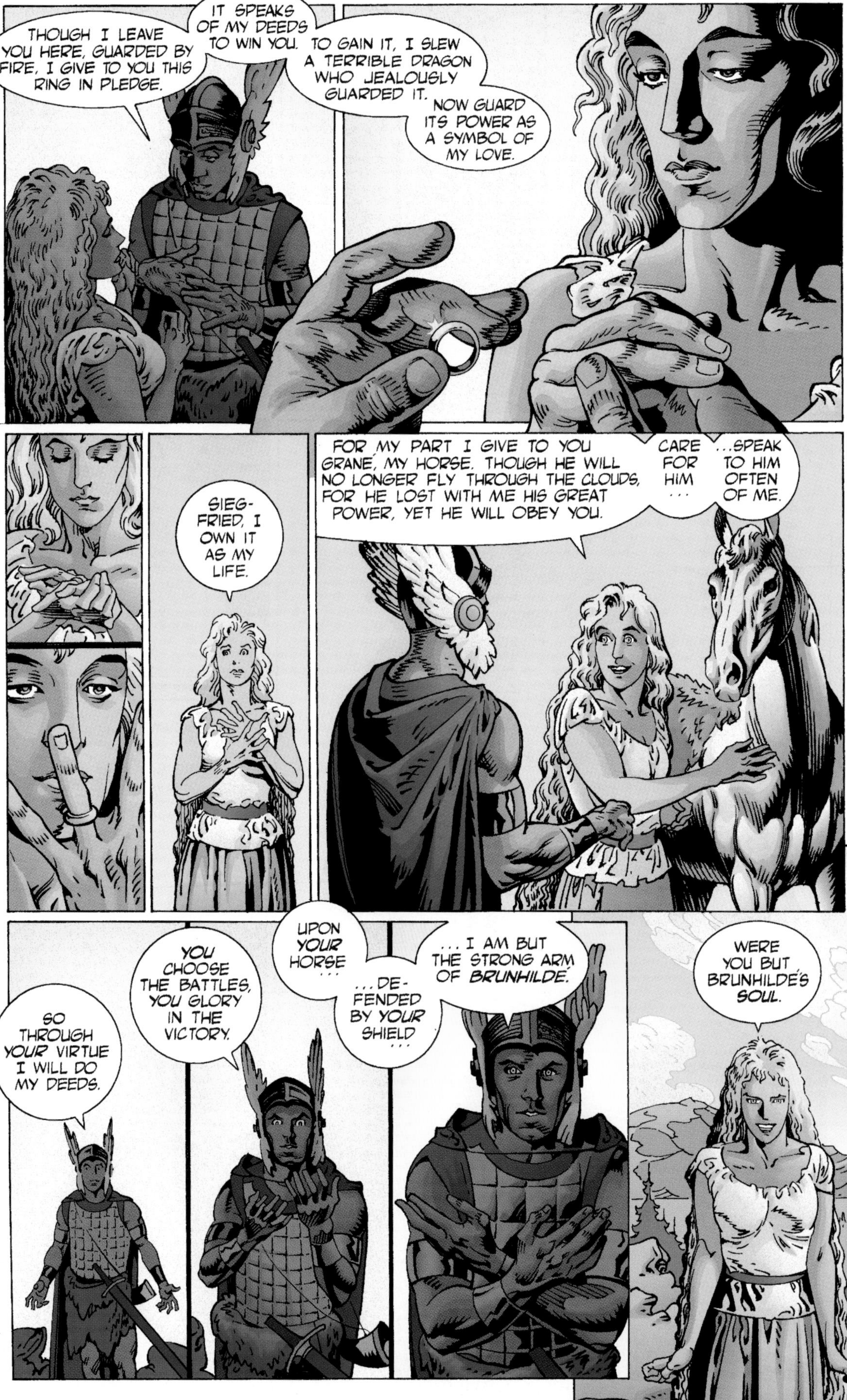
THOUGH I LEAVE YOU HERE, GUARDED BY FIRE, I GIVE TO YOU THIS RING IN PLEDGE.
IT SPEAKS OF MY DEEDS TO WIN YOU.
TO GAIN IT, I SLEW A TERRIBLE DRAGON WHO JEALOUSLY GUARDED IT.
NOW GUARD ITS POWER AS A SYMBOL OF MY LOVE.
SIEG-FRIED, I OWN IT AS MY LIFE.
FOR MY PART I GIVE TO YOU GRANE, MY HORSE. THOUGH HE WILL NO LONGER FLY THROUGH THE CLOUDS, FOR HE LOST WITH ME HIS GREAT POWER, YET HE WILL OBEY YOU.
CARE FOR HIM . . .
...SPEAK TO HIM OFTEN OF ME.
SO THROUGH *YOUR* VIRTUE I WILL DO MY DEEDS.
YOU CHOOSE THE BATTLES, *YOU* GLORY IN THE VICTORY.
UPON *YOUR* HORSE . . .
. . .DE-FENDED BY *YOUR* SHIELD . . .
. . . I AM BUT THE STRONG ARM OF *BRUNHILDE*.
WERE YOU BUT BRUNHILDE'S *SOUL*.

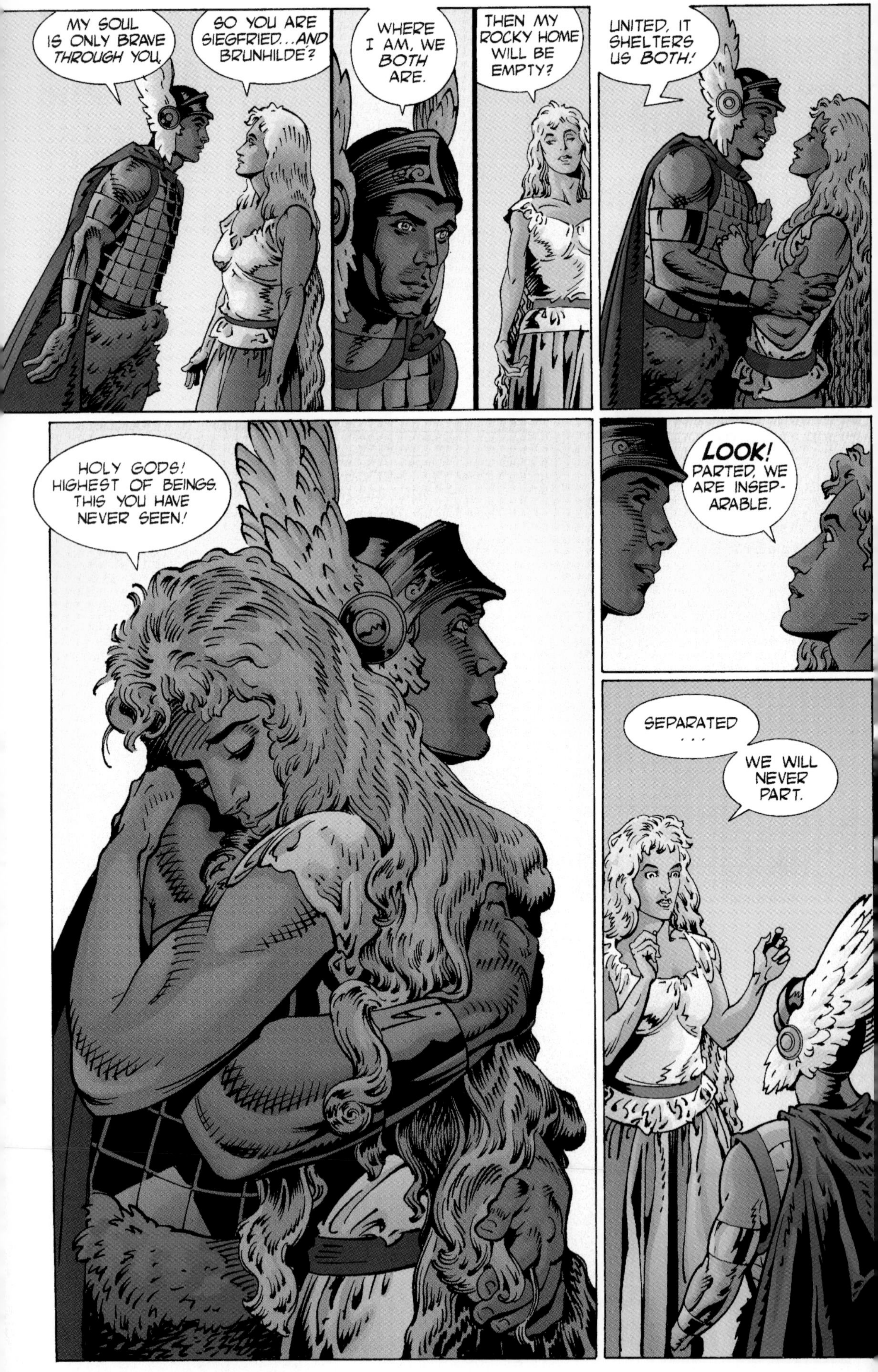

MY SOUL IS ONLY BRAVE *THROUGH YOU.*
SO YOU ARE SIEGFRIED...*AND* BRUNHILDE?
WHERE I AM, WE *BOTH* ARE.
THEN MY ROCKY HOME WILL BE EMPTY?
UNITED, IT SHELTERS US *BOTH!*
HOLY GODS! HIGHEST OF BEINGS. THIS YOU HAVE NEVER SEEN!
LOOK! PARTED, WE ARE INSEP-ARABLE.
SEPARATED . . .
WE WILL NEVER PART.

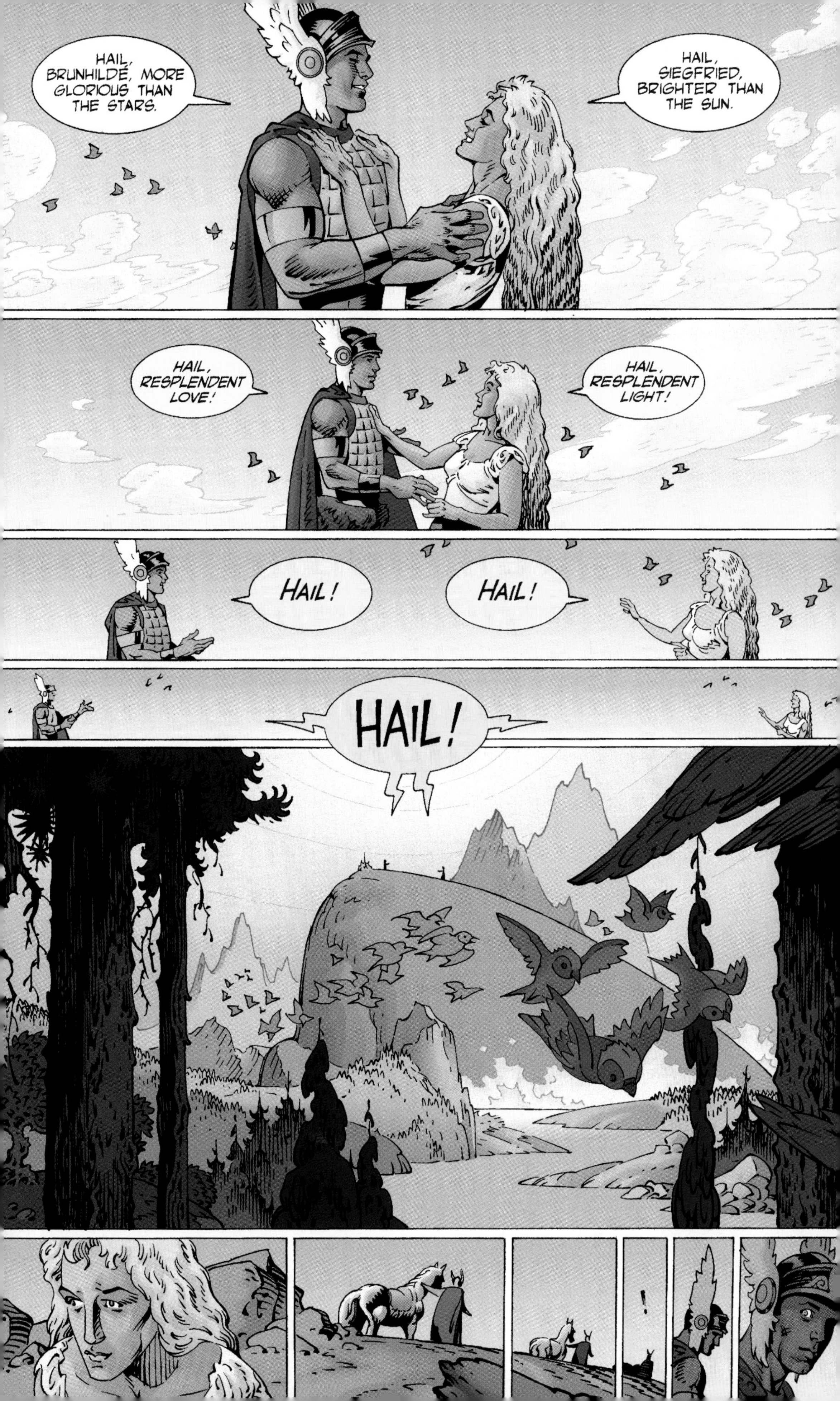
HAIL, BRUNHILDÉ, MORE GLORIOUS THAN THE STARS.
HAIL, SIEGFRIED, BRIGHTER THAN THE SUN.
HAIL, RESPLENDENT LOVE!
HAIL, RESPLENDENT LIGHT!
HAIL!
HAIL!
HAIL!
!

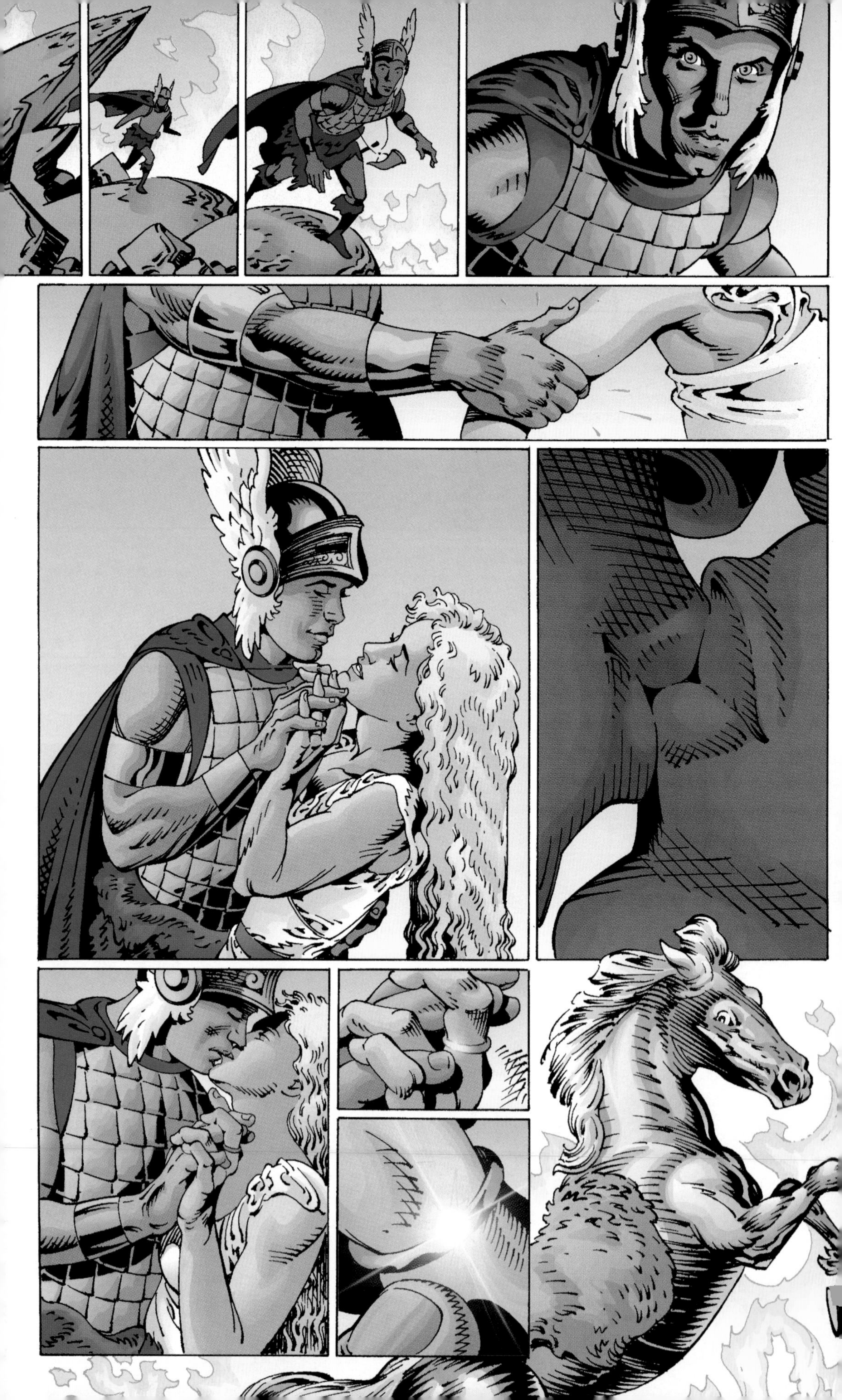

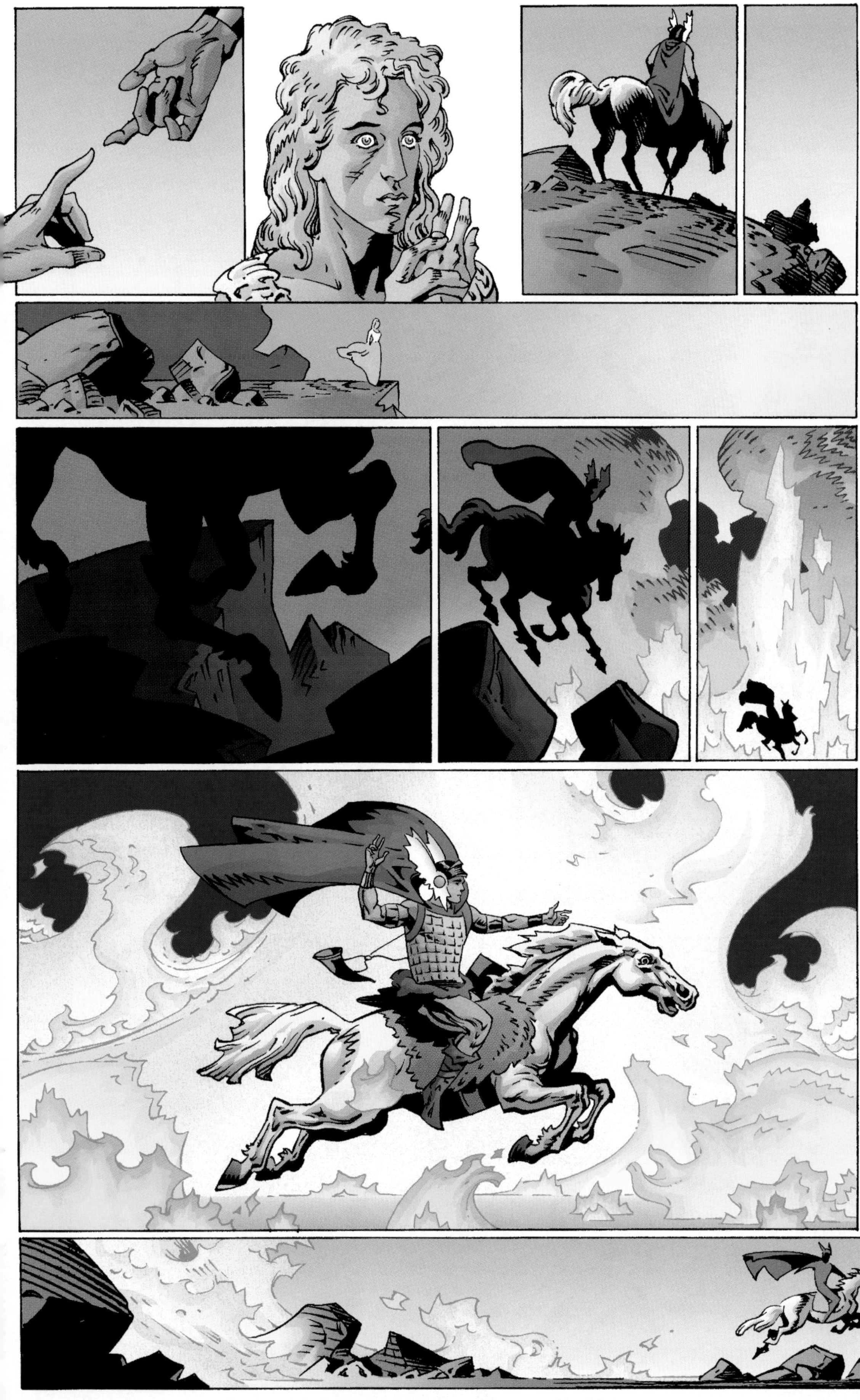

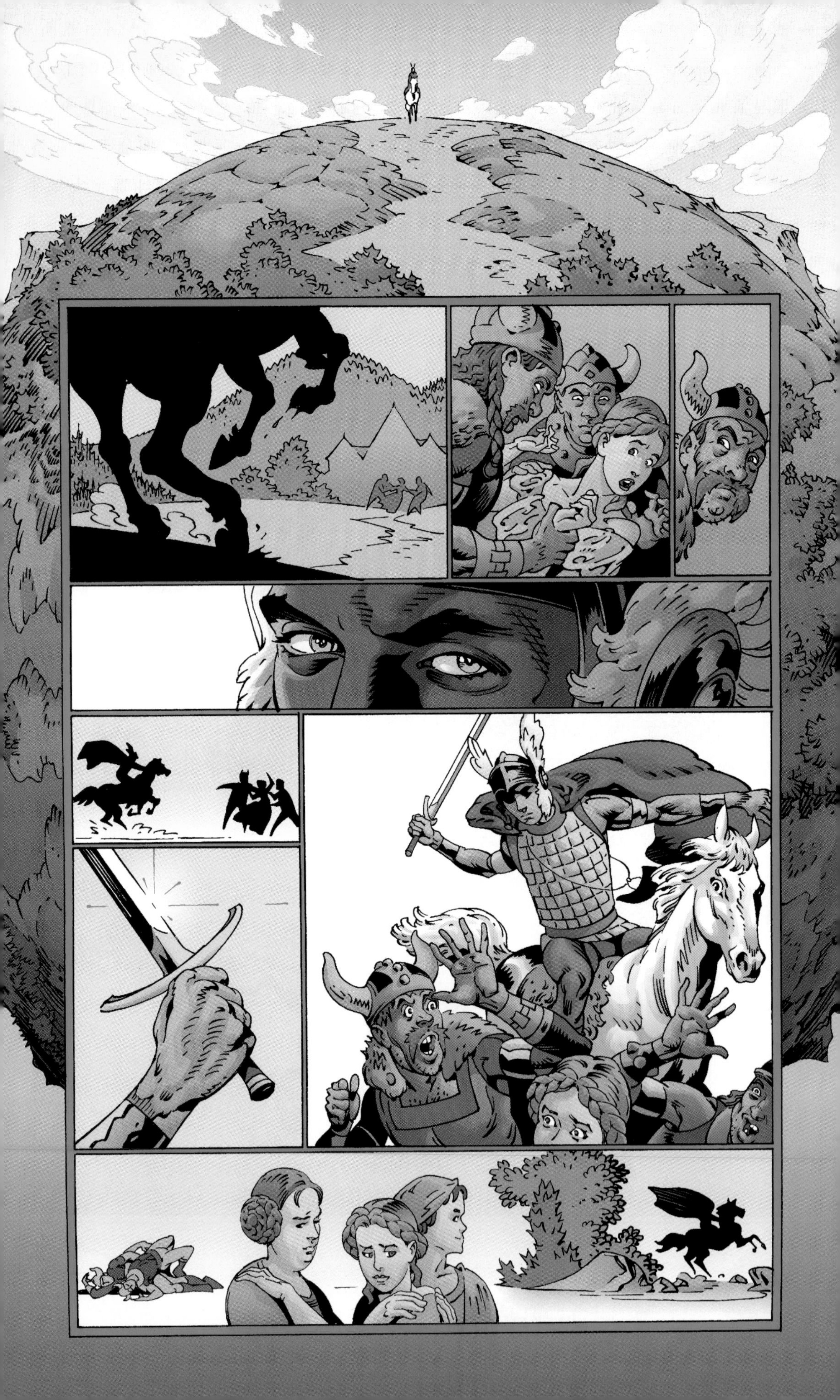

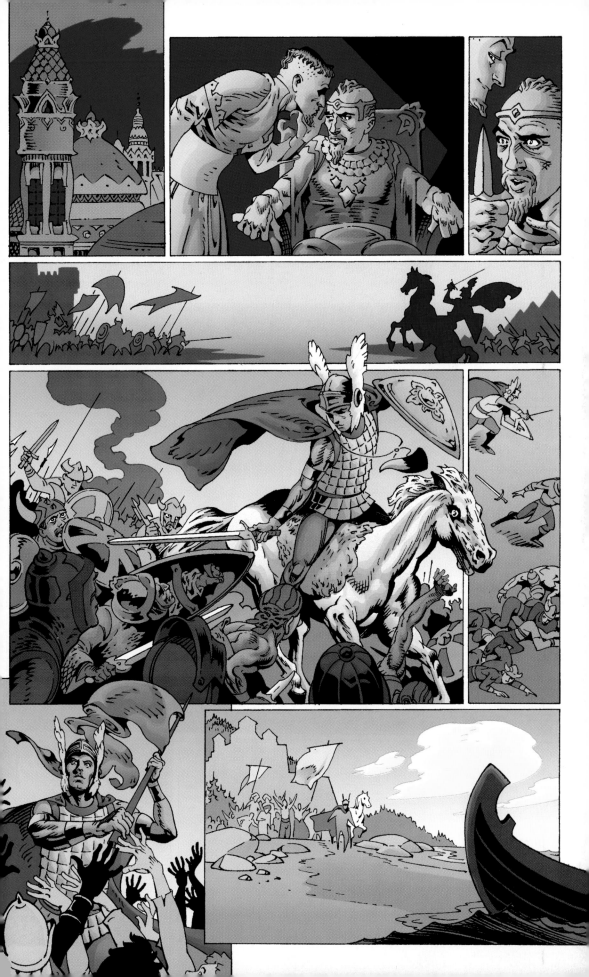

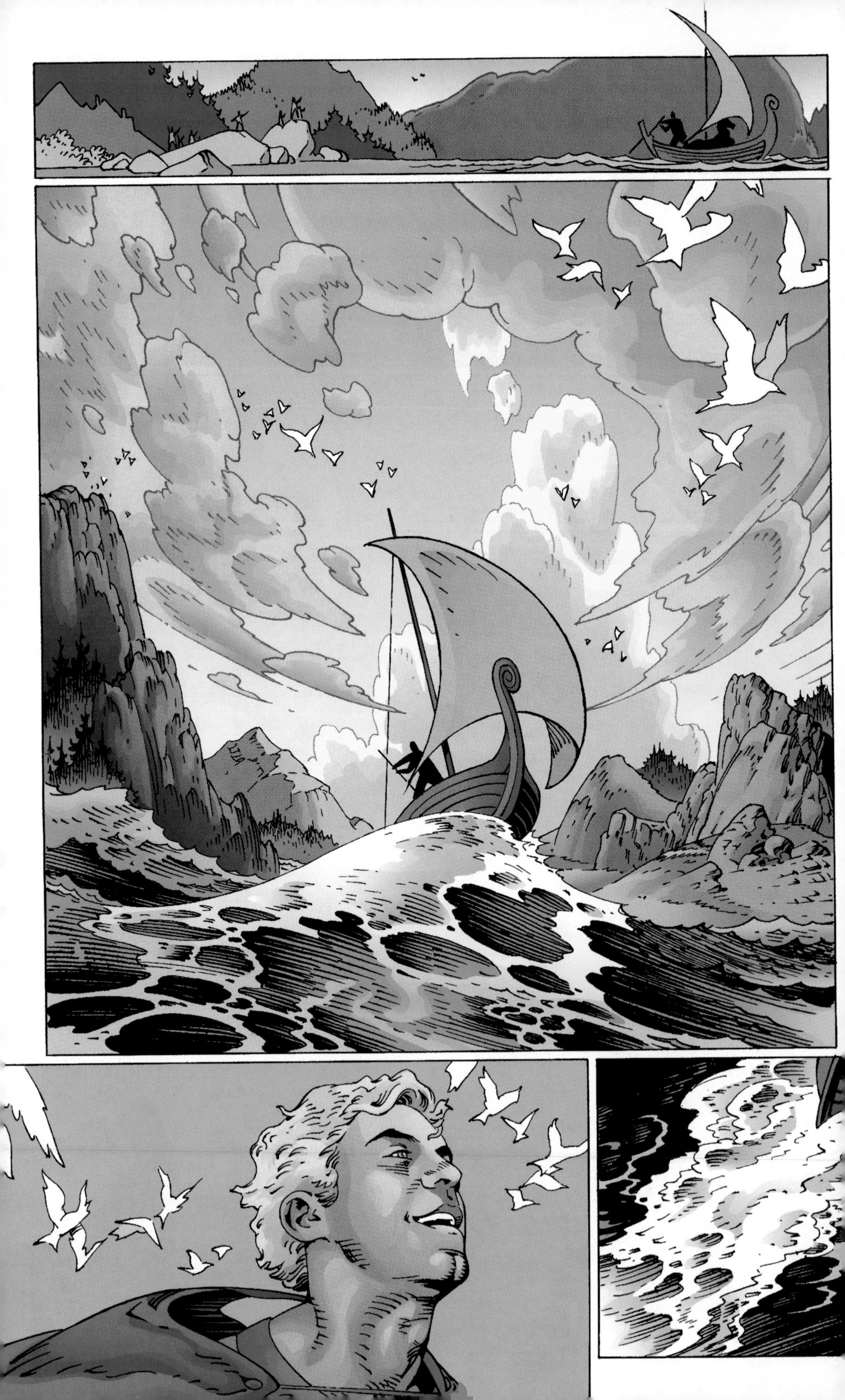

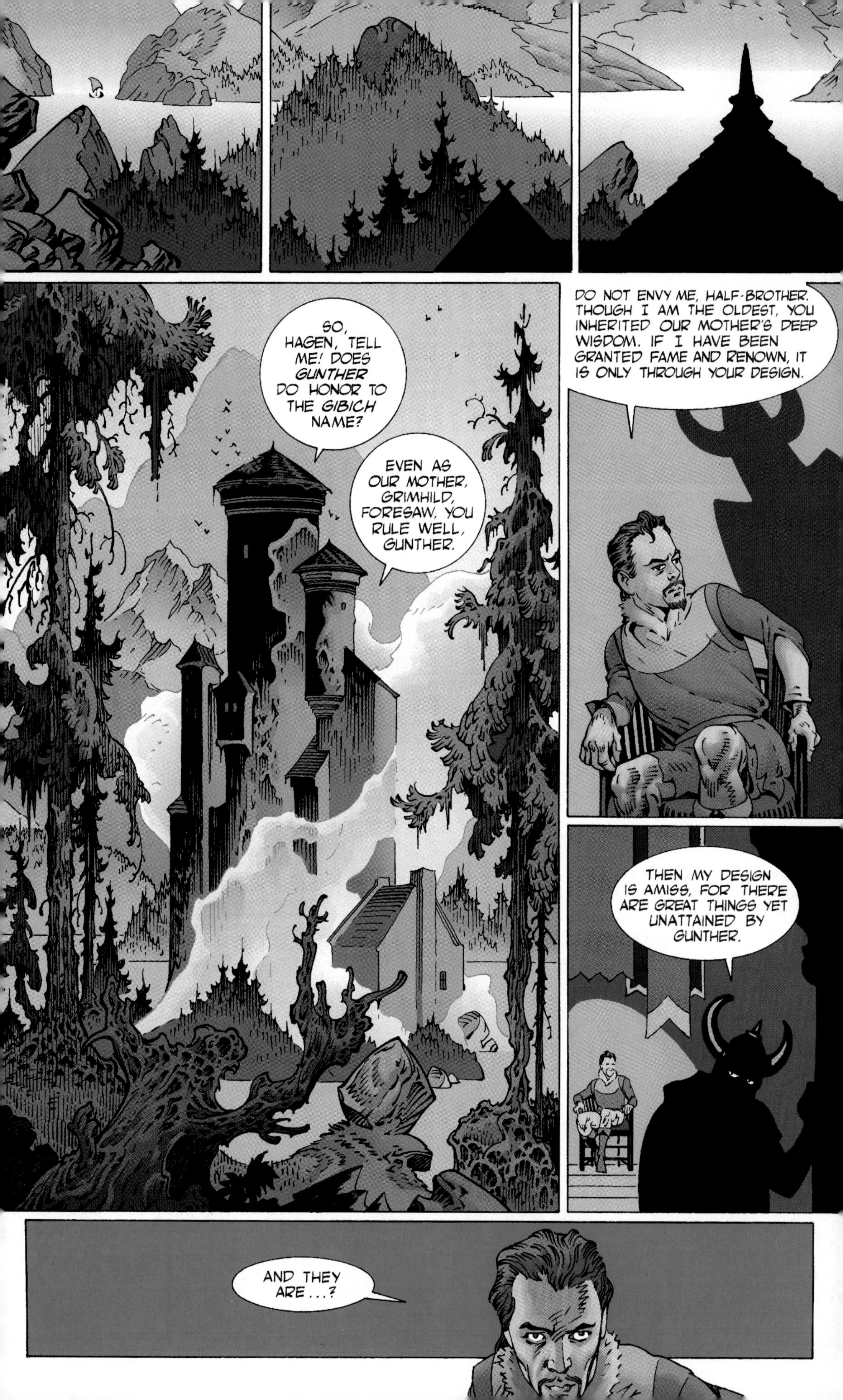
SO, HAGEN, TELL ME! DOES GUNTHER DO HONOR TO THE GIBICH NAME?
EVEN AS OUR MOTHER, GRIMHILD, FORESAW, YOU RULE WELL, GUNTHER.
DO NOT ENVY ME, HALF-BROTHER. THOUGH I AM THE OLDEST, YOU INHERITED OUR MOTHER'S DEEP WISDOM. IF I HAVE BEEN GRANTED FAME AND RENOWN, IT IS ONLY THROUGH YOUR DESIGN.
THEN MY DESIGN IS AMISS, FOR THERE ARE GREAT THINGS YET UNATTAINED BY GUNTHER.
AND THEY ARE...?

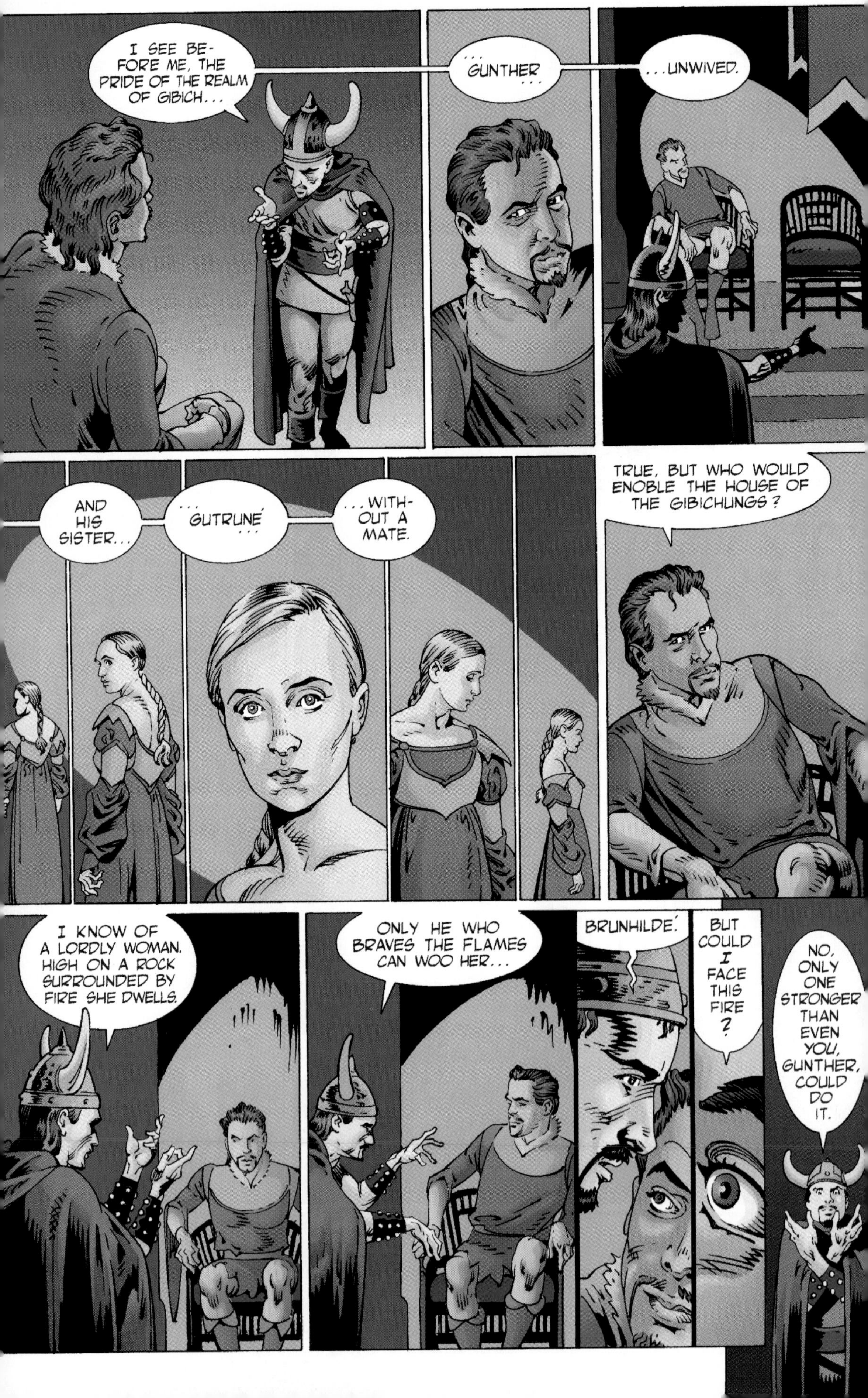
I SEE BE-FORE ME, THE PRIDE OF THE REALM OF GIBICH...
...GUNTHER...
...UNWIVED.
AND HIS SISTER...
...GUTRUNE...
...WITH-OUT A MATE.
TRUE, BUT WHO WOULD ENOBLE THE HOUSE OF THE GIBICHUNGS?
I KNOW OF A LORDLY WOMAN. HIGH ON A ROCK SURROUNDED BY FIRE SHE DWELLS.
ONLY HE WHO BRAVES THE FLAMES CAN WOO HER...
BRUNHILDE!
BUT COULD I FACE THIS FIRE?
NO, ONLY ONE STRONGER THAN EVEN YOU, GUNTHER, COULD DO IT.

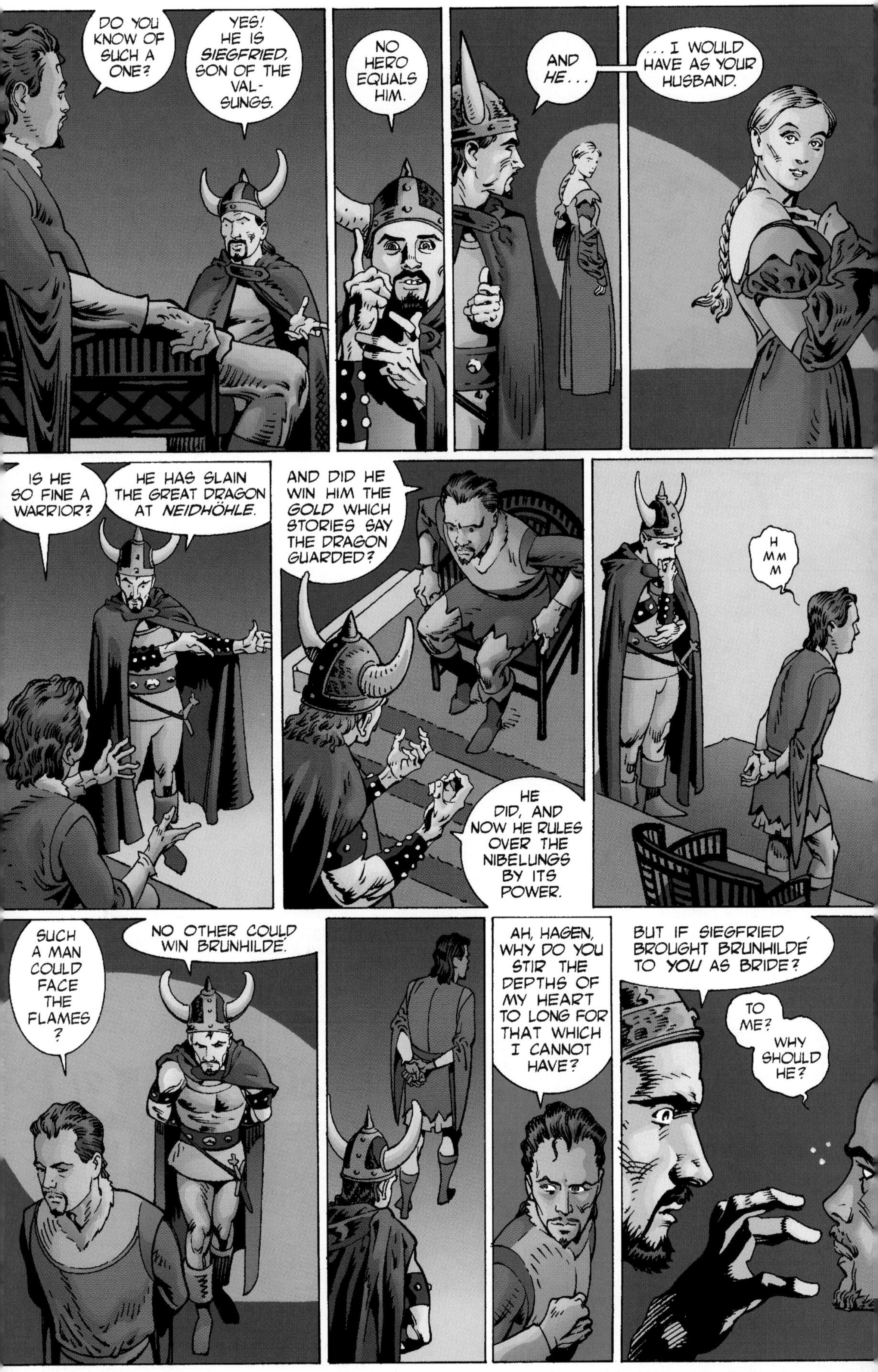
DO YOU KNOW OF SUCH A ONE?
YES! HE IS *SIEGFRIED*, SON OF THE VAL-SUNGS.
NO HERO EQUALS HIM.
AND *HE*...
...I WOULD HAVE AS YOUR HUSBAND.
IS HE SO FINE A WARRIOR?
HE HAS SLAIN THE GREAT DRAGON AT *NEIDHÖHLE*.
AND DID HE WIN HIM THE *GOLD* WHICH STORIES SAY THE DRAGON GUARDED?
HE DID, AND NOW HE RULES OVER THE NIBELUNGS BY ITS POWER.
H MMM M
SUCH A MAN COULD FACE THE FLAMES?
NO OTHER COULD WIN BRUNHILDE.
AH, HAGEN, WHY DO YOU STIR THE DEPTHS OF MY HEART TO LONG FOR THAT WHICH I CANNOT HAVE?
BUT IF SIEGFRIED BROUGHT BRUNHILDE TO *YOU* AS BRIDE?
TO ME? WHY SHOULD HE?

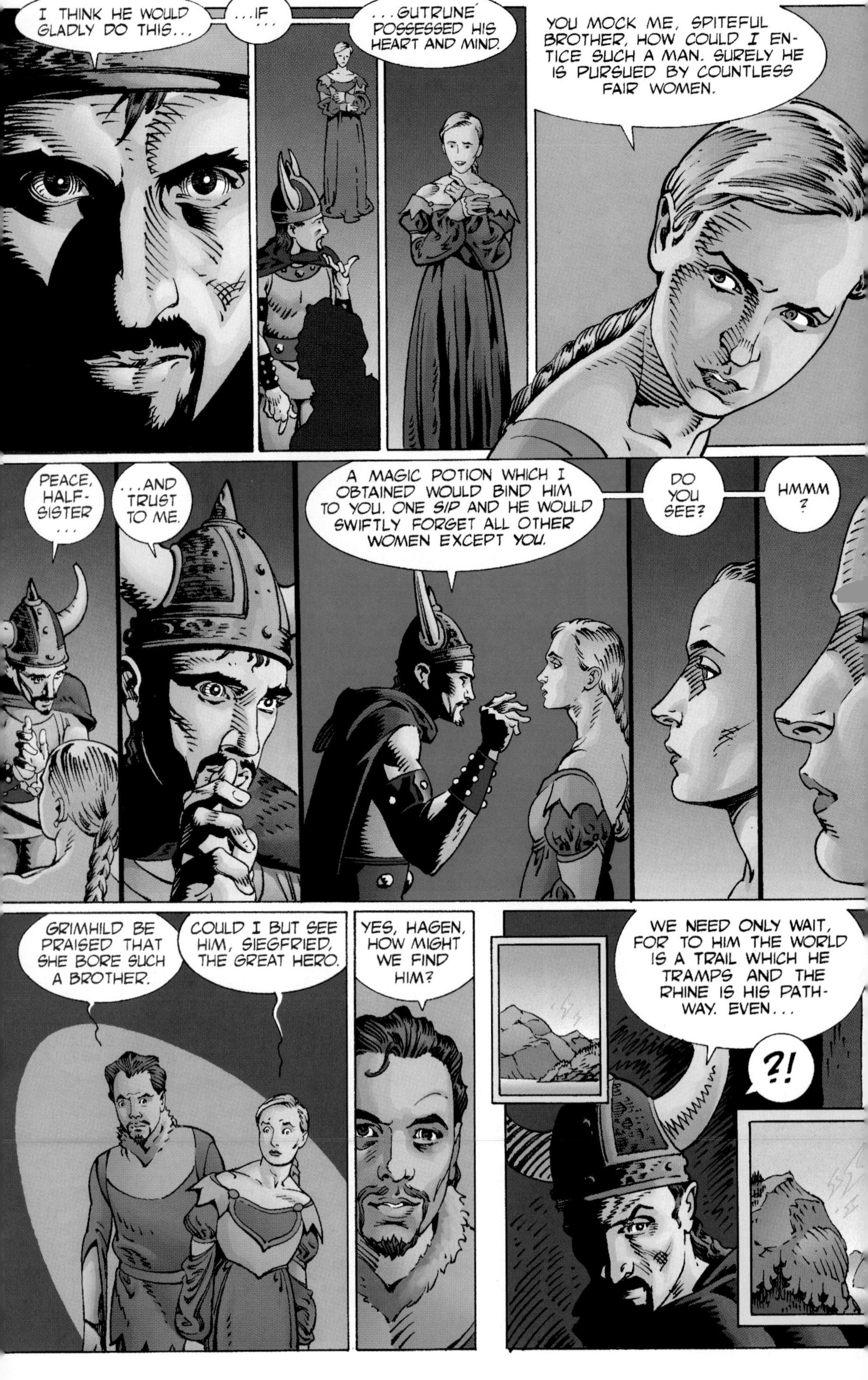
I THINK HE WOULD GLADLY DO THIS...
...IF ...
...GUTRUNE POSSESSED HIS HEART AND MIND.
YOU MOCK ME, SPITEFUL BROTHER, HOW COULD *I* ENTICE SUCH A MAN. SURELY HE IS PURSUED BY COUNTLESS FAIR WOMEN.
PEACE, HALF-SISTER ...
...AND TRUST TO ME.
A MAGIC POTION WHICH I OBTAINED WOULD BIND HIM TO YOU. ONE *SIP* AND HE WOULD SWIFTLY FORGET ALL OTHER WOMEN EXCEPT *YOU.*
DO YOU SEE?
HMMM ?
GRIMHILD BE PRAISED THAT SHE BORE SUCH A BROTHER.
COULD I BUT SEE HIM, SIEGFRIED, THE GREAT HERO.
YES, HAGEN, HOW MIGHT WE FIND HIM?
WE NEED ONLY WAIT, FOR TO HIM THE WORLD IS A TRAIL WHICH HE TRAMPS AND THE RHINE IS HIS PATHWAY. EVEN...
?!

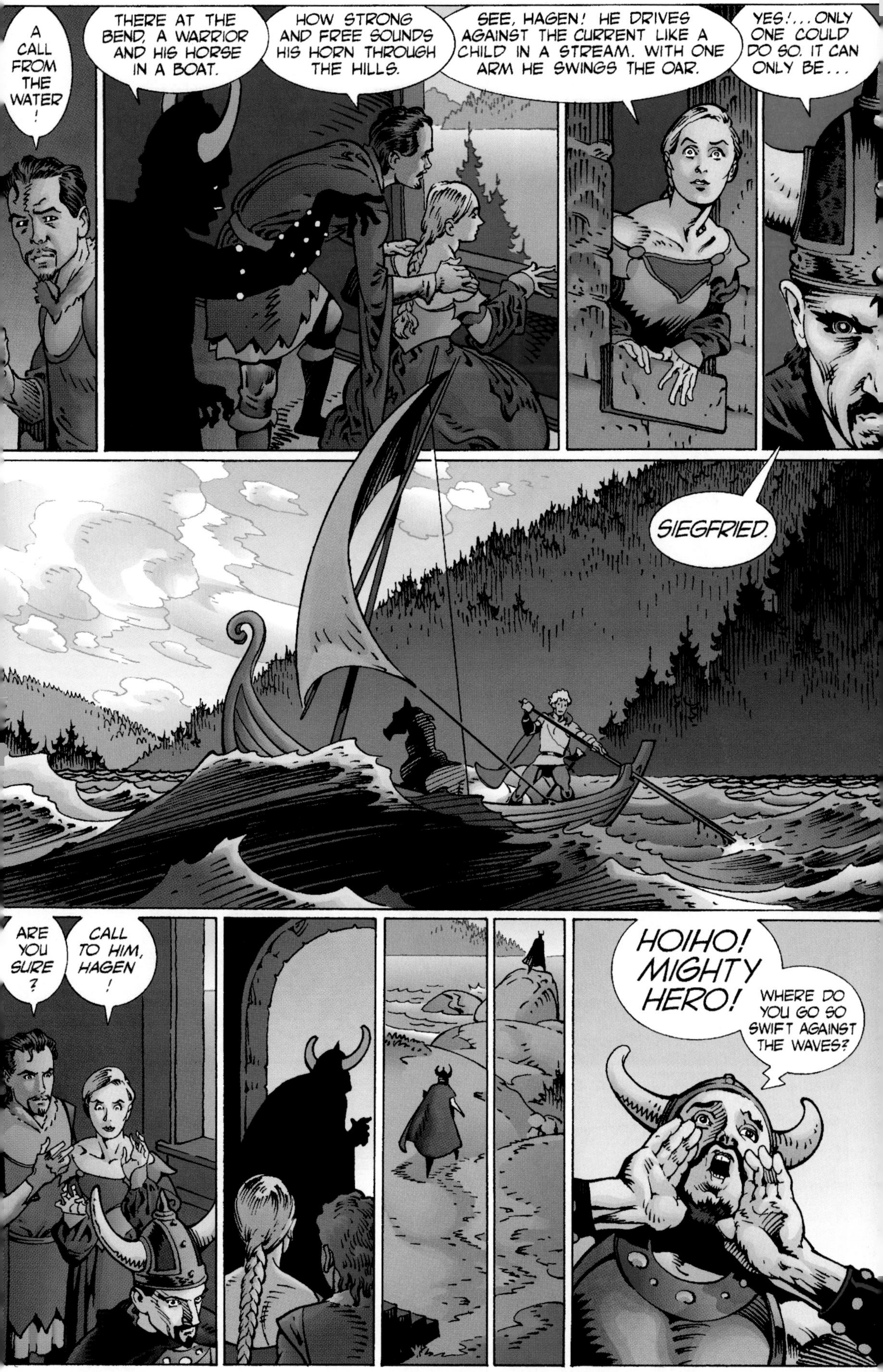
A CALL FROM THE WATER!
THERE AT THE BEND, A WARRIOR AND HIS HORSE IN A BOAT.
HOW STRONG AND FREE SOUNDS HIS HORN THROUGH THE HILLS.
SEE, HAGEN! HE DRIVES AGAINST THE CURRENT LIKE A CHILD IN A STREAM. WITH ONE ARM HE SWINGS THE OAR.
YES!...ONLY ONE COULD DO SO. IT CAN ONLY BE...
SIEGFRIED.
ARE YOU SURE?
CALL TO HIM, HAGEN!
HOIHO! MIGHTY HERO!
WHERE DO YOU GO SO SWIFT AGAINST THE WAVES?

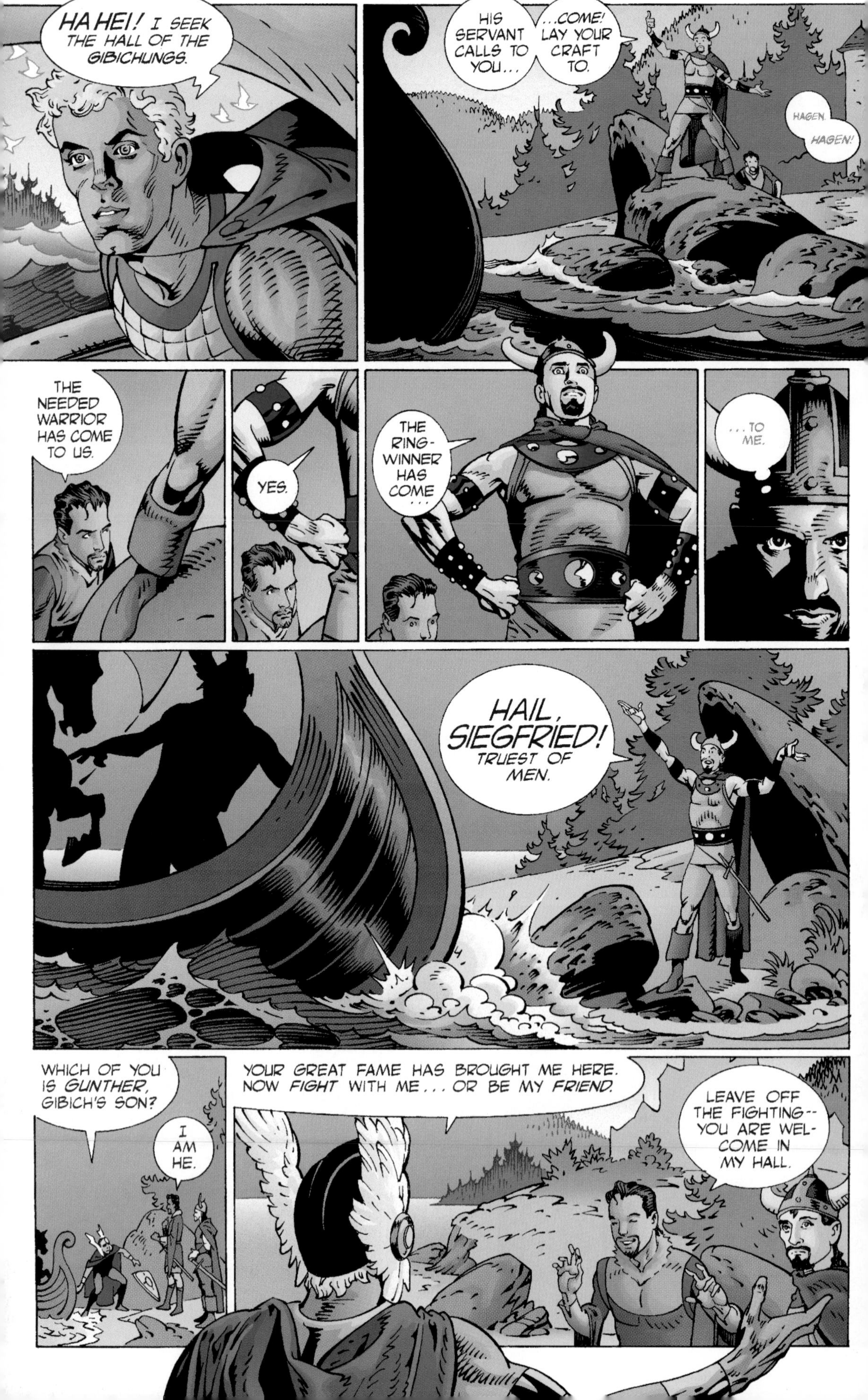
HA HEI! I SEEK THE HALL OF THE GIBICHUNGS.
HIS SERVANT CALLS TO YOU...
...COME! LAY YOUR CRAFT TO.
HAGEN.
HAGEN!
THE NEEDED WARRIOR HAS COME TO US.
YES.
THE RING-WINNER HAS COME...
...TO ME.
HAIL, SIEGFRIED! TRUEST OF MEN.
WHICH OF YOU IS GUNTHER, GIBICH'S SON?
I AM HE.
YOUR GREAT FAME HAS BROUGHT ME HERE. NOW FIGHT WITH ME... OR BE MY FRIEND.
LEAVE OFF THE FIGHTING-- YOU ARE WEL-COME IN MY HALL.

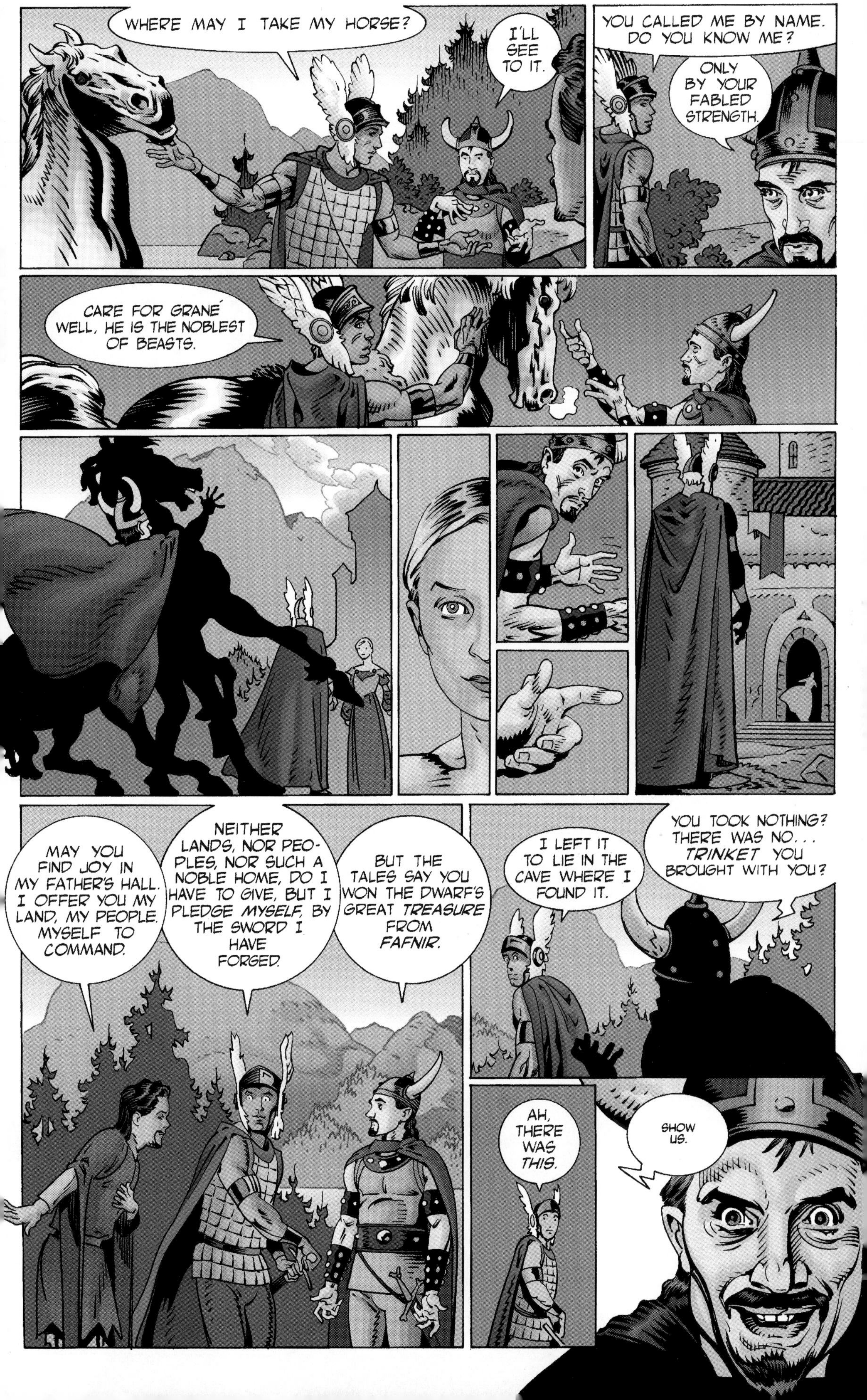

WHERE MAY I TAKE MY HORSE?
I'LL SEE TO IT.
YOU CALLED ME BY NAME. DO YOU KNOW ME?
ONLY BY YOUR FABLED STRENGTH.
CARE FOR GRANÉ WELL, HE IS THE NOBLEST OF BEASTS.
MAY YOU FIND JOY IN MY FATHER'S HALL. I OFFER YOU MY LAND, MY PEOPLE. MYSELF TO COMMAND.
NEITHER LANDS, NOR PEOPLES, NOR SUCH A NOBLE HOME, DO I HAVE TO GIVE, BUT I PLEDGE MYSELF, BY THE SWORD I HAVE FORGED.
BUT THE TALES SAY YOU WON THE DWARF'S GREAT TREASURE FROM FAFNIR.
I LEFT IT TO LIE IN THE CAVE WHERE I FOUND IT.
YOU TOOK NOTHING? THERE WAS NO... TRINKET YOU BROUGHT WITH YOU?
AH, THERE WAS THIS.
SHOW US.

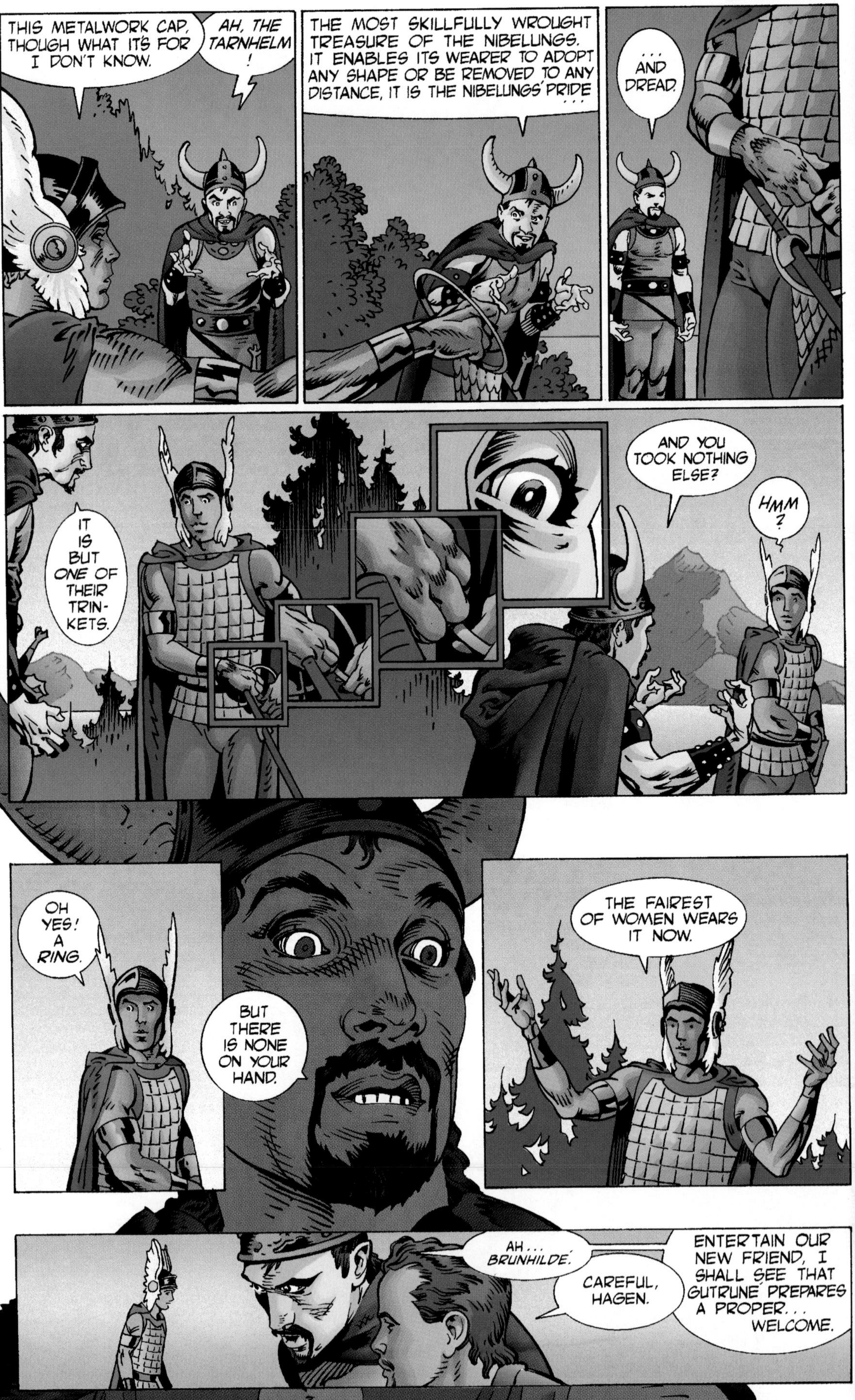
THIS METALWORK CAP, THOUGH WHAT IT'S FOR I DON'T KNOW.
AH, THE TARNHELM!
THE MOST SKILLFULLY WROUGHT TREASURE OF THE NIBELUNGS. IT ENABLES ITS WEARER TO ADOPT ANY SHAPE OR BE REMOVED TO ANY DISTANCE, IT IS THE NIBELUNGS' PRIDE . . .
. . . AND DREAD.
IT IS BUT ONE OF THEIR TRIN-KETS.
AND YOU TOOK NOTHING ELSE?
HMM?
OH YES! A RING.
BUT THERE IS NONE ON YOUR HAND.
THE FAIREST OF WOMEN WEARS IT NOW.
AH... BRUNHILDE.
CAREFUL, HAGEN.
ENTERTAIN OUR NEW FRIEND, I SHALL SEE THAT GUTRUNE PREPARES A PROPER... WELCOME.

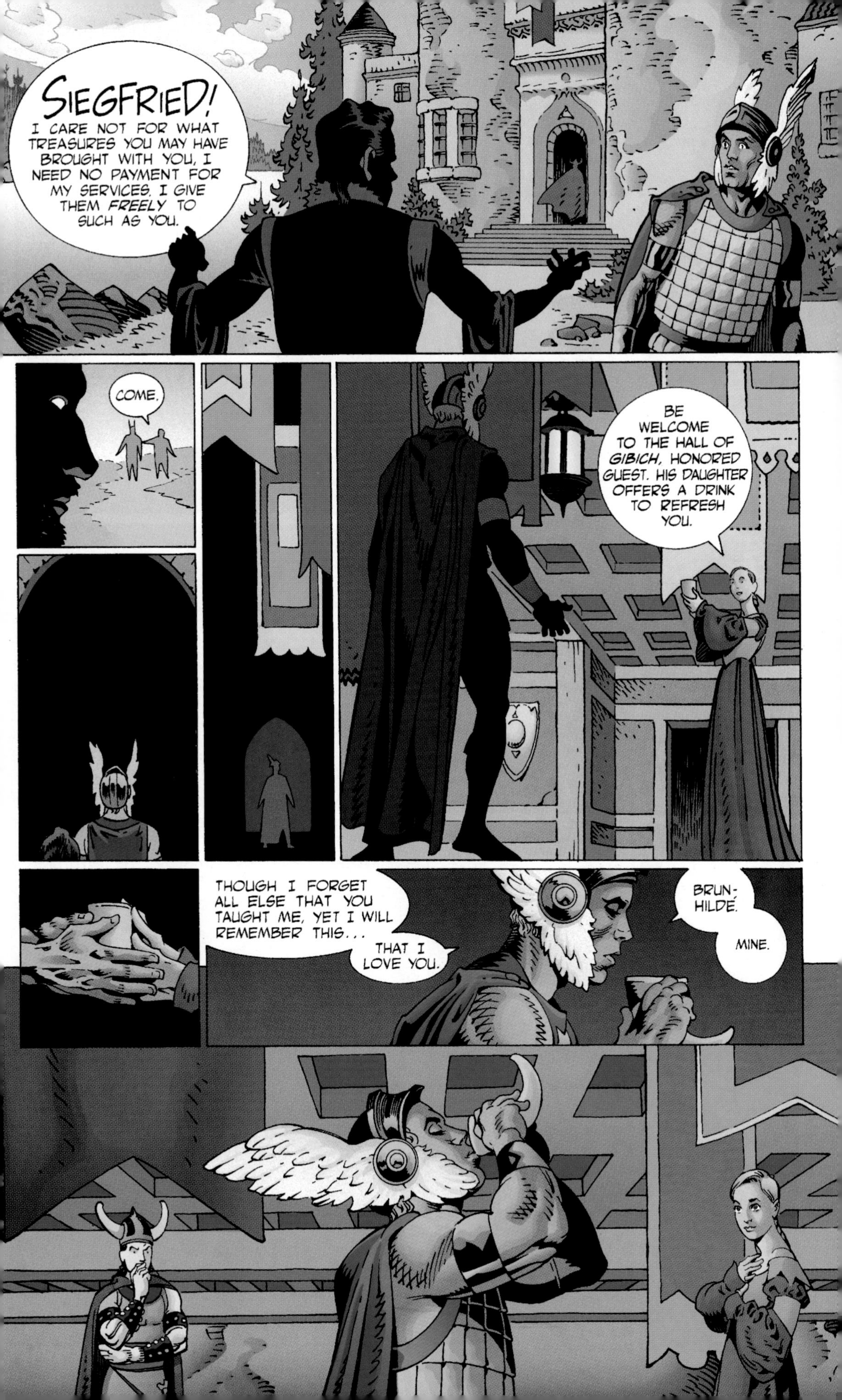
SIEGFRIED!
I CARE NOT FOR WHAT TREASURES YOU MAY HAVE BROUGHT WITH YOU, I NEED NO PAYMENT FOR MY SERVICES. I GIVE THEM *FREELY* TO SUCH AS YOU.
COME.
BE WELCOME TO THE HALL OF *GIBICH*, HONORED GUEST. HIS DAUGHTER OFFERS A DRINK TO REFRESH YOU.
THOUGH I FORGET ALL ELSE THAT YOU TAUGHT ME, YET I WILL REMEMBER THIS...
THAT I LOVE YOU.
BRUN-HILDE.
MINE.

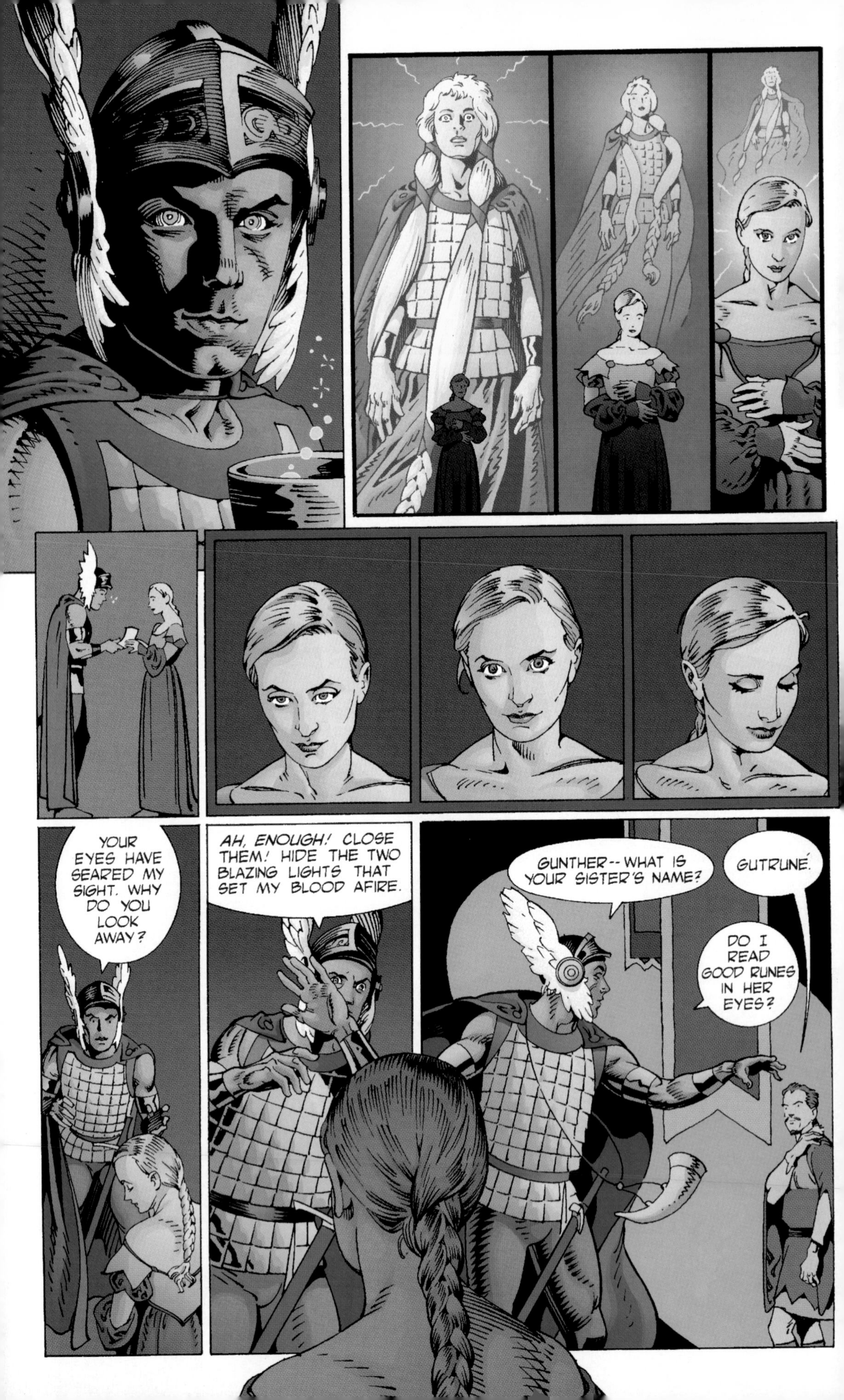
YOUR EYES HAVE SEARED MY SIGHT. WHY DO YOU LOOK AWAY?
AH, ENOUGH! CLOSE THEM! HIDE THE TWO BLAZING LIGHTS THAT SET MY BLOOD AFIRE.
GUNTHER-- WHAT IS YOUR SISTER'S NAME?
GUTRUNE.
DO I READ GOOD RUNES IN HER EYES?

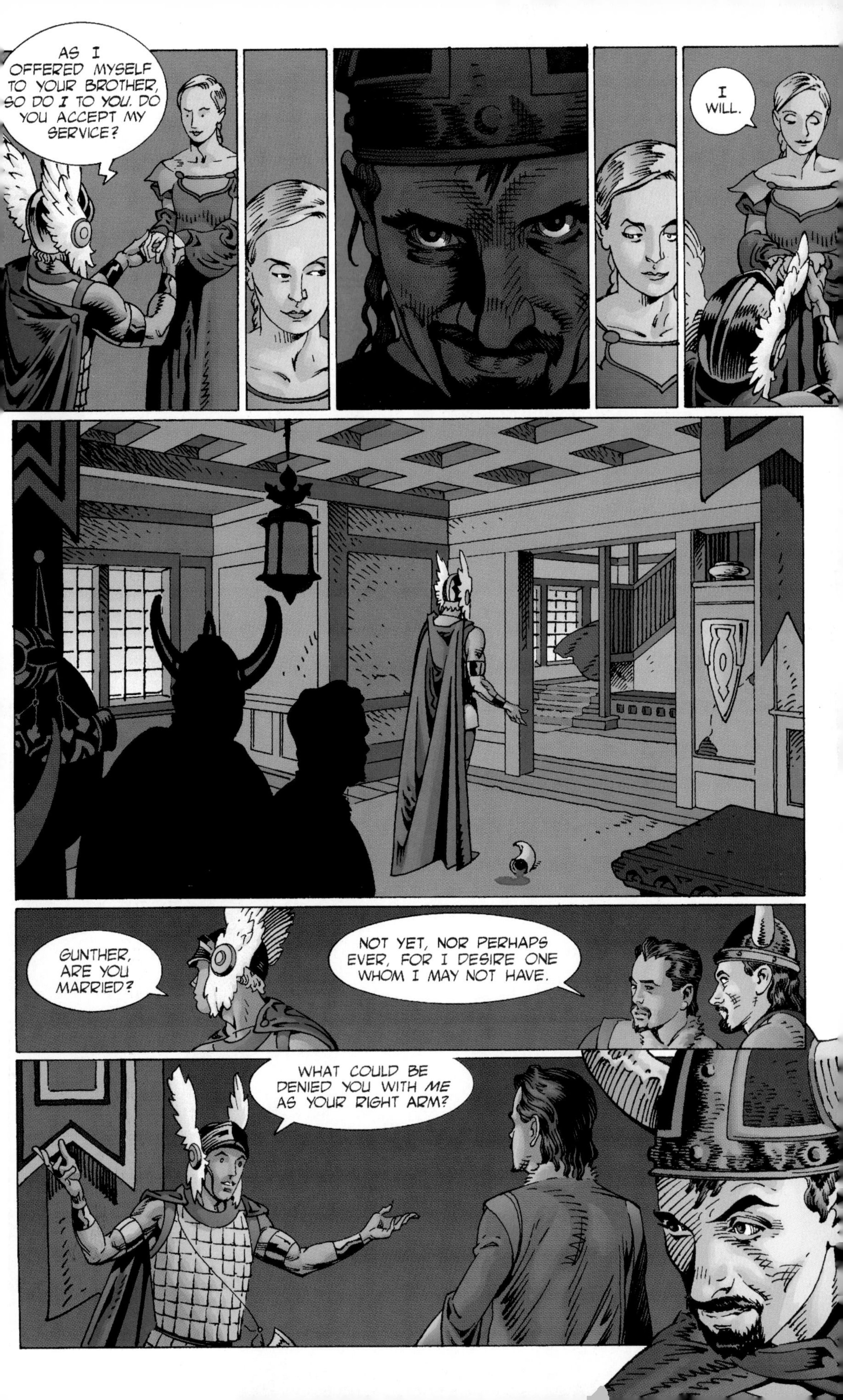
AS I OFFERED MYSELF TO YOUR BROTHER, SO DO *I* TO *YOU*. DO YOU ACCEPT MY SERVICE?
I WILL.
GUNTHER, ARE YOU MARRIED?
NOT YET, NOR PERHAPS EVER, FOR I DESIRE ONE WHOM I MAY NOT HAVE.
WHAT COULD BE DENIED YOU WITH *ME* AS YOUR RIGHT ARM?

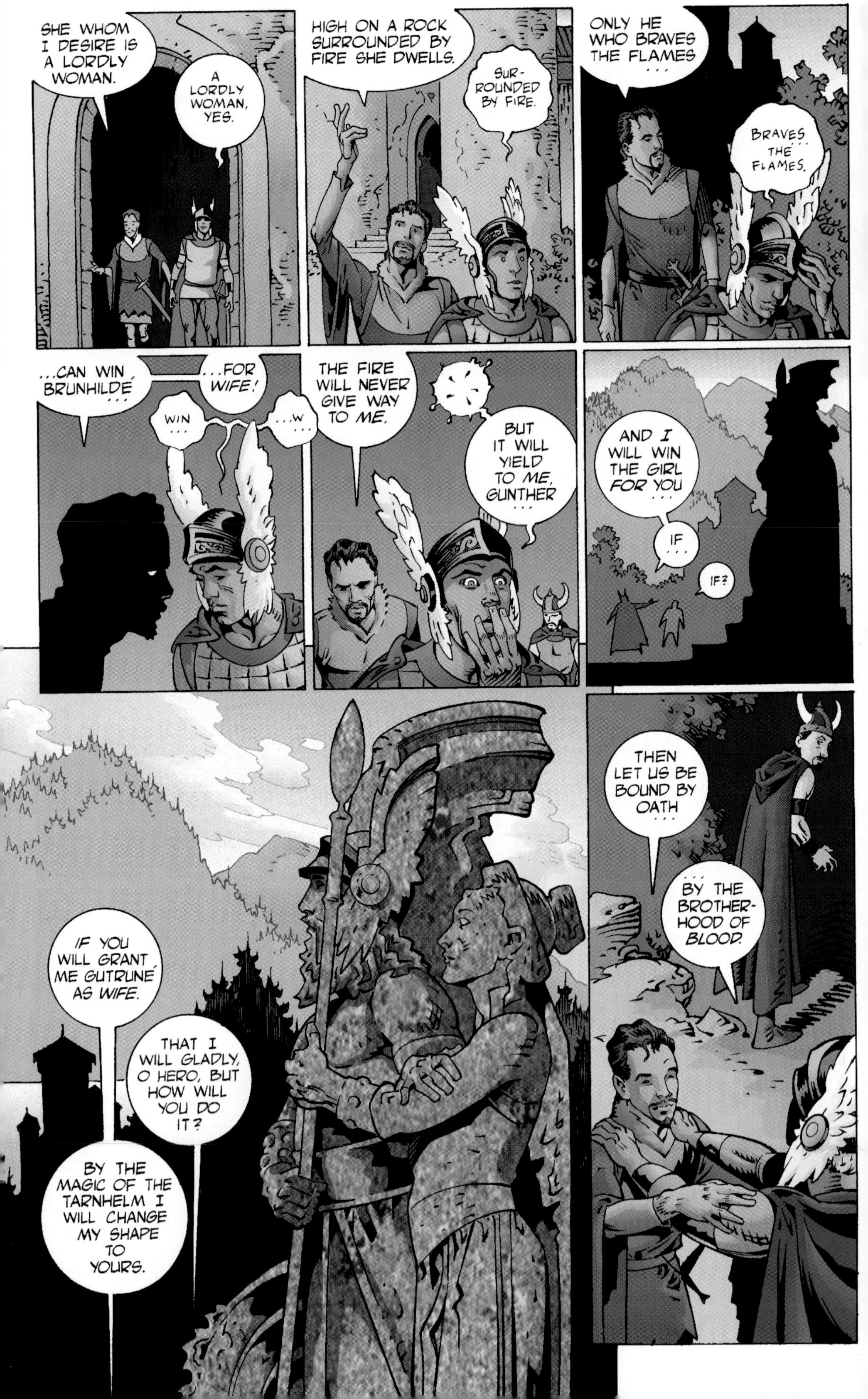
SHE WHOM I DESIRE IS A LORDLY WOMAN.
A LORDLY WOMAN, YES.
HIGH ON A ROCK SURROUNDED BY FIRE SHE DWELLS.
SUR-ROUNDED BY FIRE.
ONLY HE WHO BRAVES THE FLAMES . . .
BRAVES . . . THE FLAMES.
...CAN WIN BRUNHILDE . . .
...FOR WIFE!
WIN . . .
. . .W . . .
THE FIRE WILL NEVER GIVE WAY TO ME.
BUT IT WILL YIELD TO ME, GUNTHER . . .
AND I WILL WIN THE GIRL FOR YOU . . .
IF . . .
IF?
IF YOU WILL GRANT ME GUTRUNE AS WIFE.
THAT I WILL GLADLY, O HERO, BUT HOW WILL YOU DO IT?
BY THE MAGIC OF THE TARNHELM I WILL CHANGE MY SHAPE TO YOURS.
THEN LET US BE BOUND BY OATH . . .
. . . BY THE BROTHER-HOOD OF BLOOD.

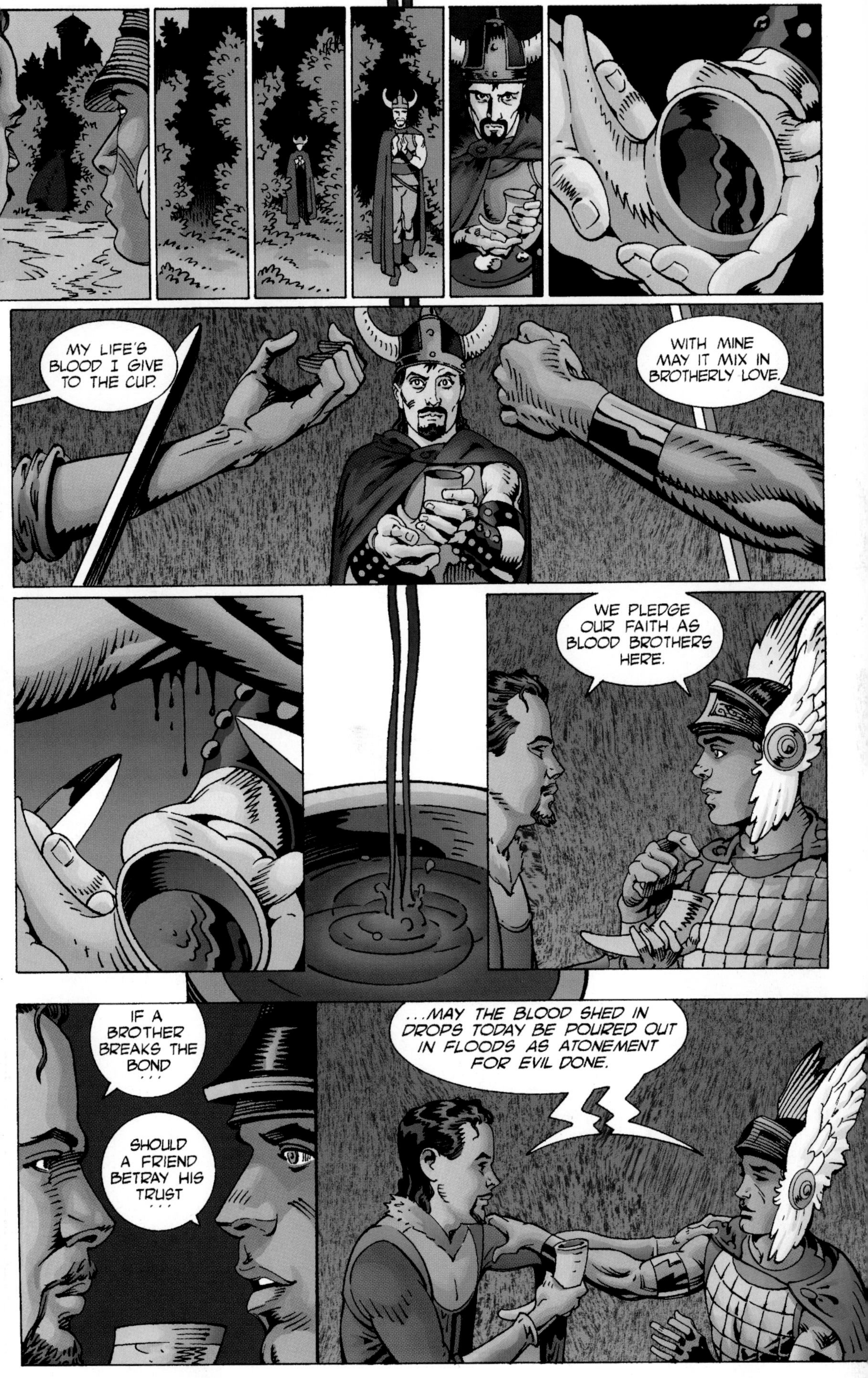
MY LIFE'S BLOOD I GIVE TO THE CUP.
WITH MINE MAY IT MIX IN BROTHERLY LOVE.
WE PLEDGE OUR FAITH AS BLOOD BROTHERS HERE.
IF A BROTHER BREAKS THE BOND . . .
SHOULD A FRIEND BETRAY HIS TRUST . . .
...MAY THE BLOOD SHED IN DROPS TODAY BE POURED OUT IN FLOODS AS ATONEMENT FOR EVIL DONE.

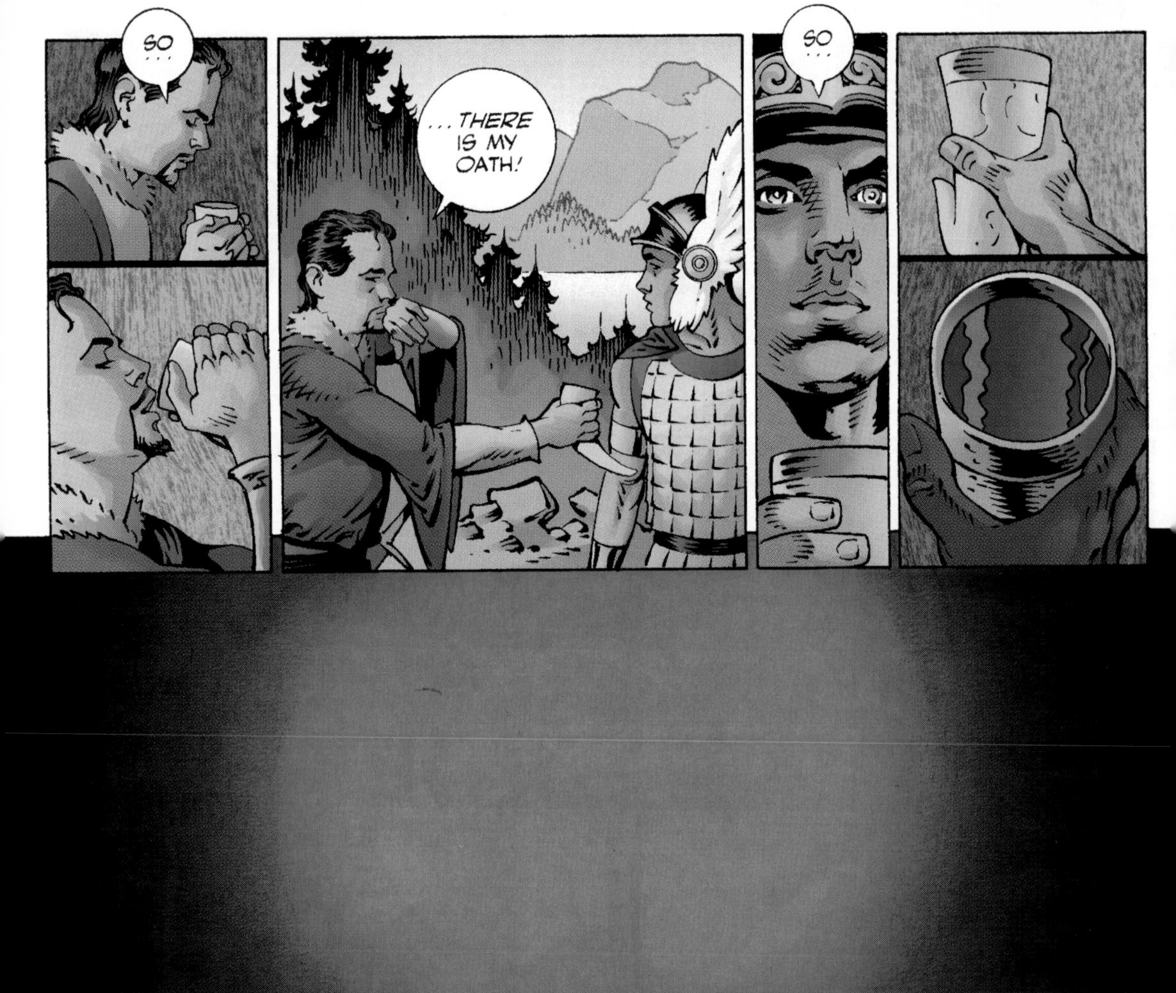

SO . . .
. . . THERE IS MY OATH!
SO . . .

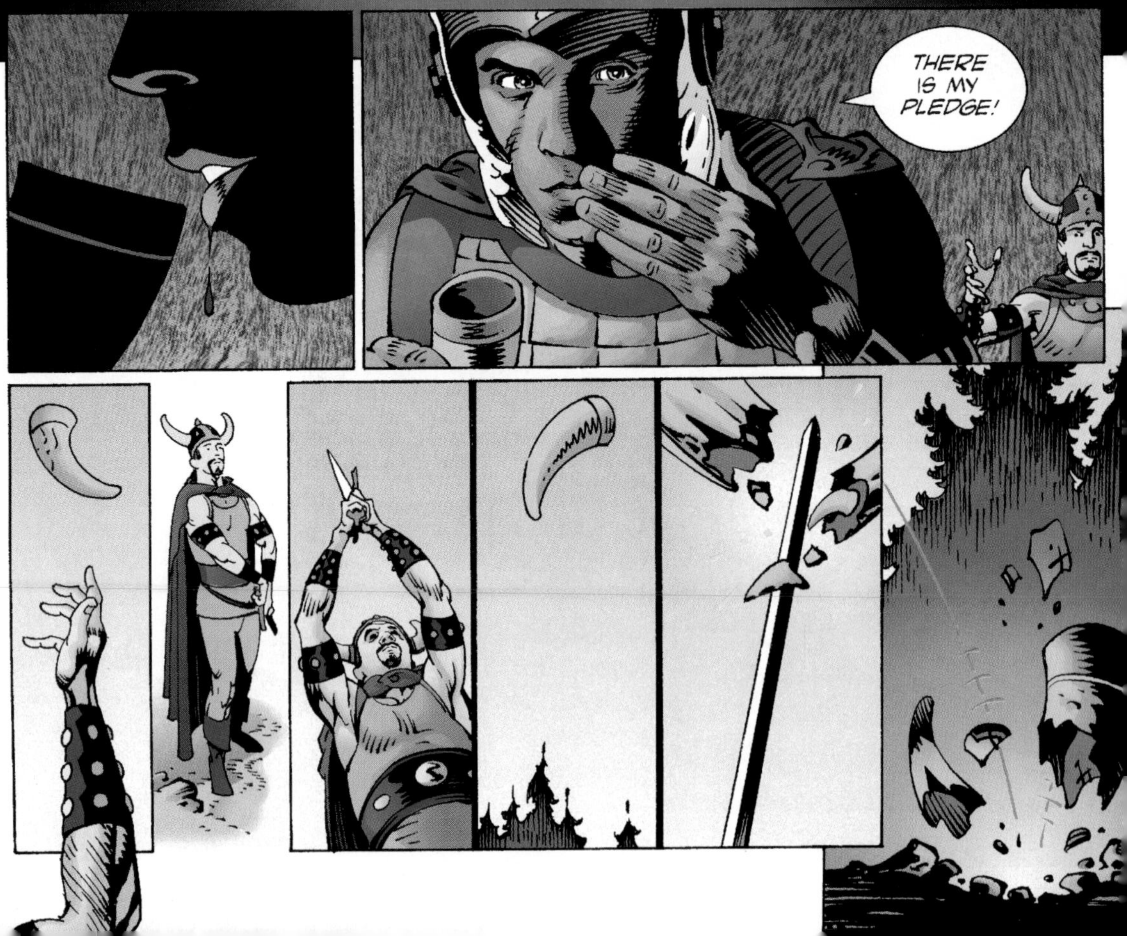

THERE IS MY PLEDGE!

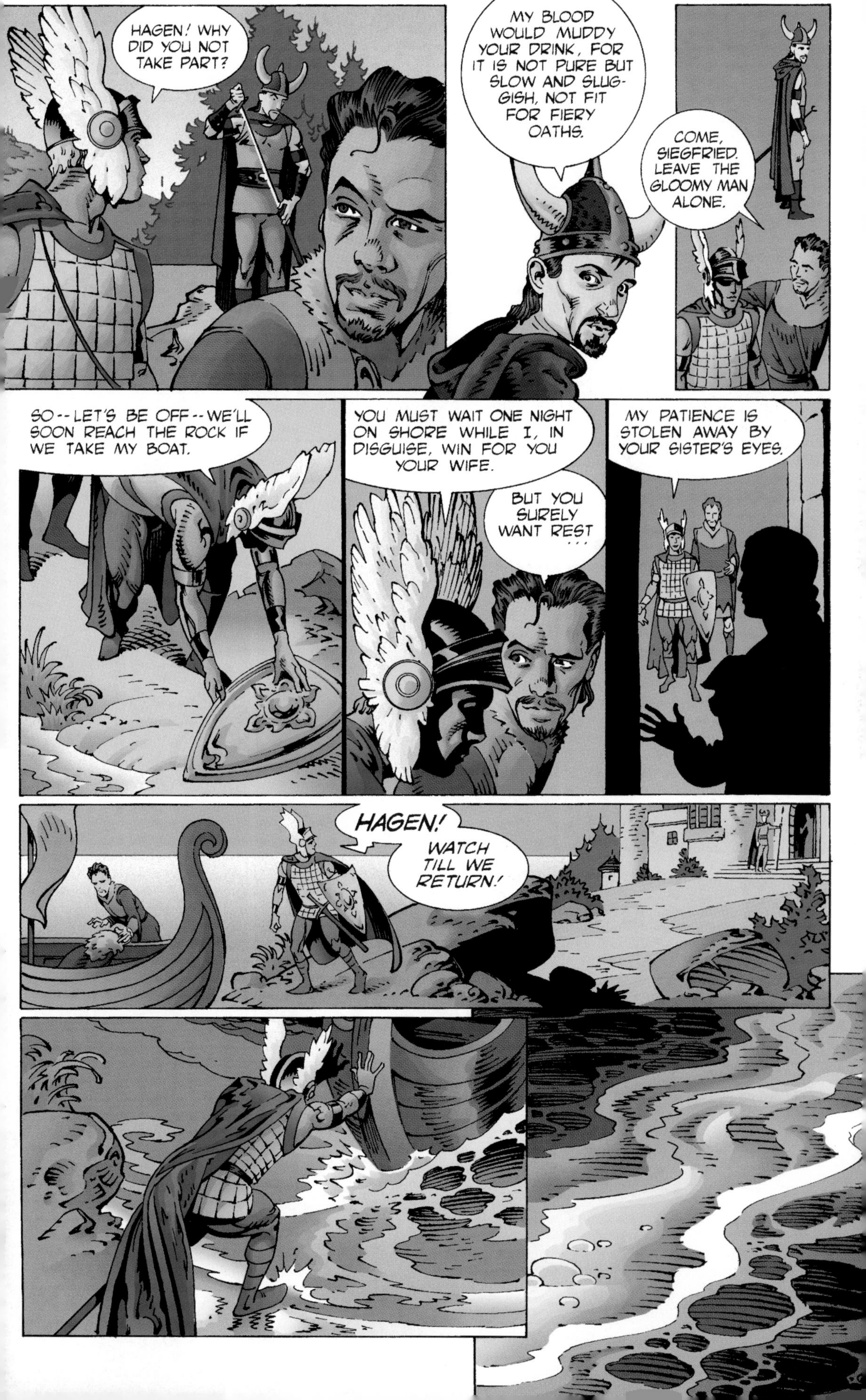
HAGEN! WHY DID YOU NOT TAKE PART?
MY BLOOD WOULD MUDDY YOUR DRINK, FOR IT IS NOT PURE BUT SLOW AND SLUGGISH, NOT FIT FOR FIERY OATHS.
COME, SIEGFRIED. LEAVE THE GLOOMY MAN ALONE.
SO--LET'S BE OFF--WE'LL SOON REACH THE ROCK IF WE TAKE MY BOAT.
YOU MUST WAIT ONE NIGHT ON SHORE WHILE I, IN DISGUISE, WIN FOR YOU YOUR WIFE.
BUT YOU SURELY WANT REST...
MY PATIENCE IS STOLEN AWAY BY YOUR SISTER'S EYES.
HAGEN!
WATCH TILL WE RETURN!

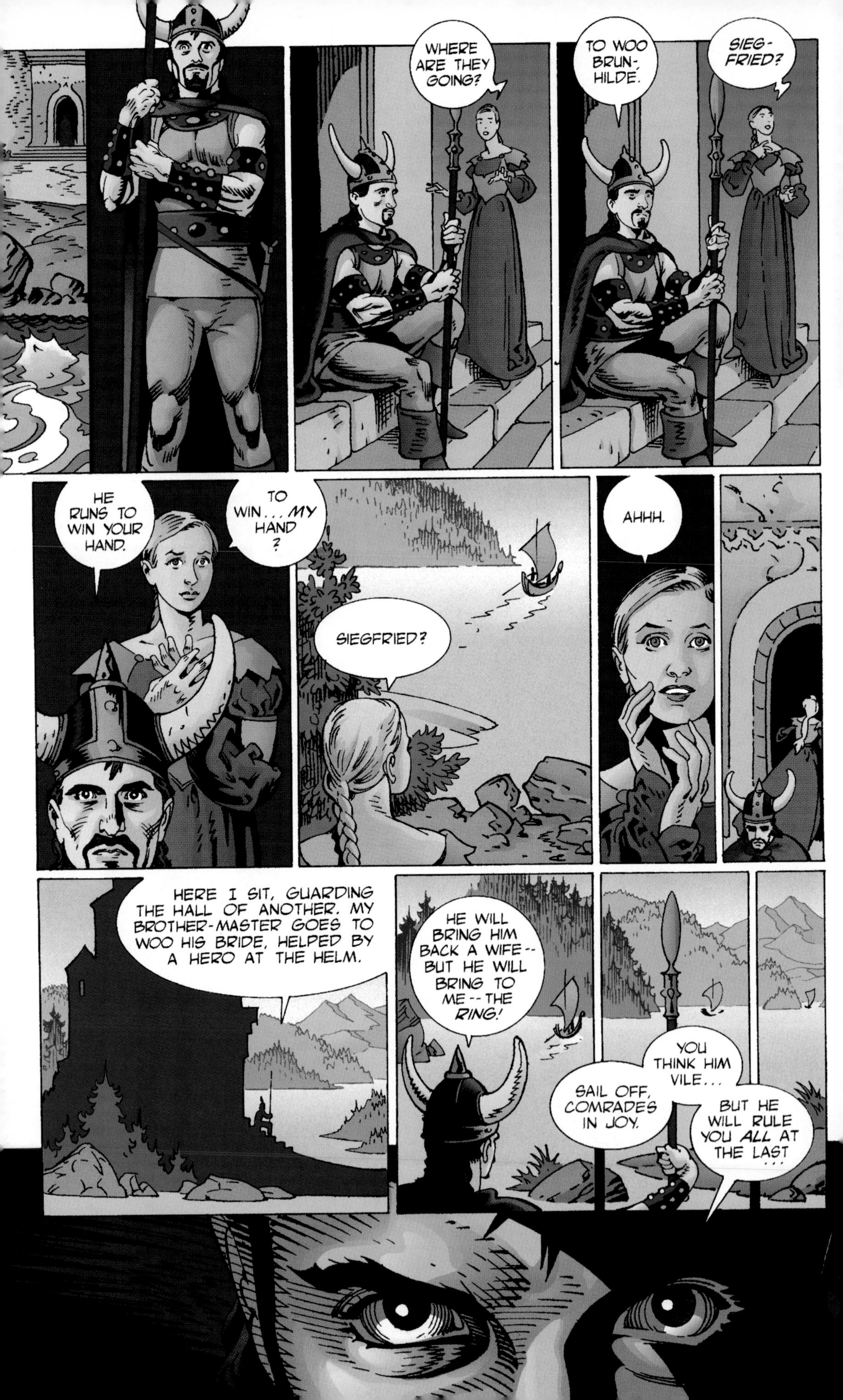
WHERE ARE THEY GOING?
TO WOO BRUN-HILDE.
SIEG-FRIED?
HE RUNS TO WIN YOUR HAND.
TO WIN... MY HAND?
SIEGFRIED?
AHHH.
HERE I SIT, GUARDING THE HALL OF ANOTHER. MY BROTHER-MASTER GOES TO WOO HIS BRIDE, HELPED BY A HERO AT THE HELM.
HE WILL BRING HIM BACK A WIFE-- BUT HE WILL BRING TO ME--THE RING!
SAIL OFF, COMRADES IN JOY.
YOU THINK HIM VILE...
BUT HE WILL RULE YOU ALL AT THE LAST...

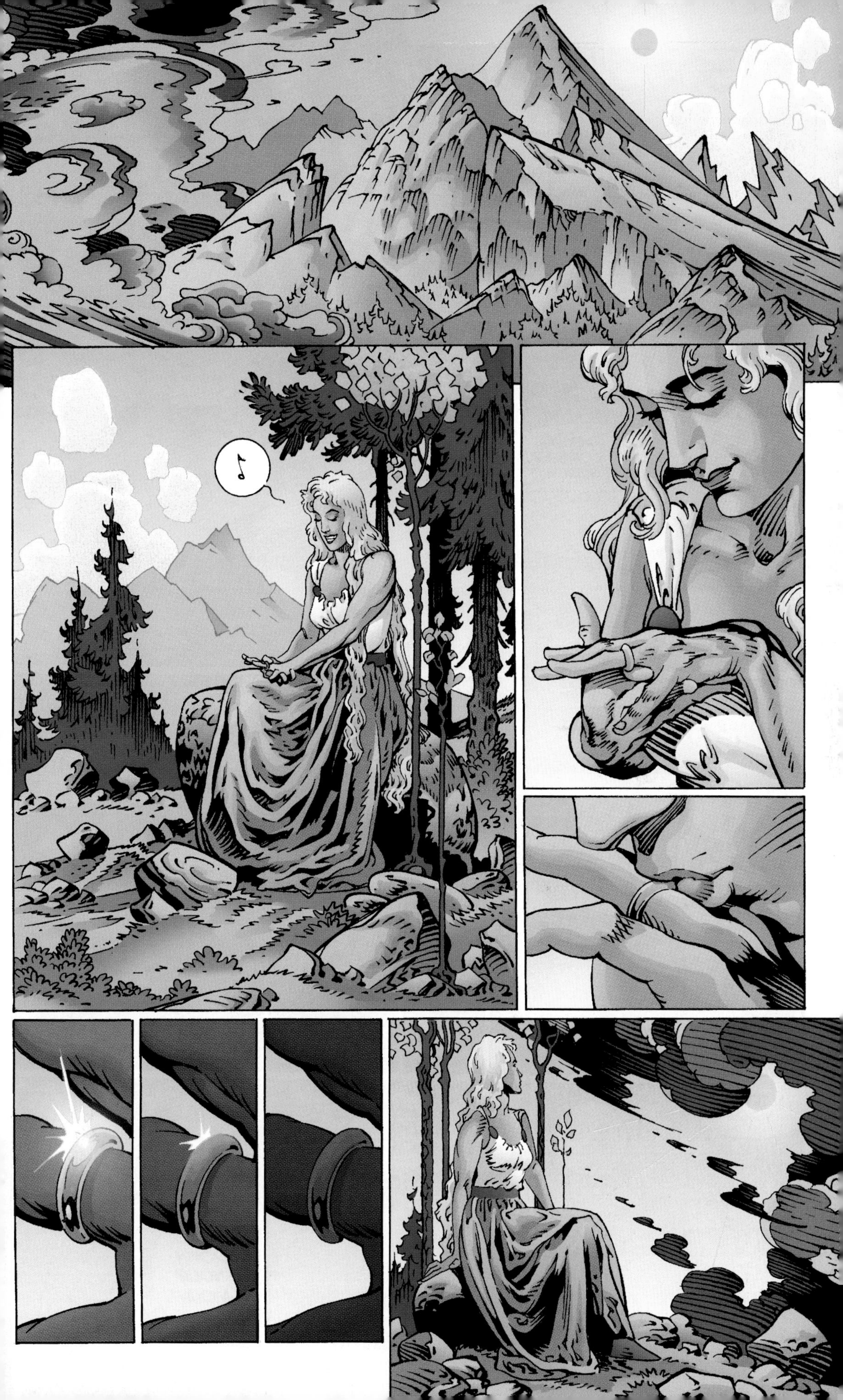

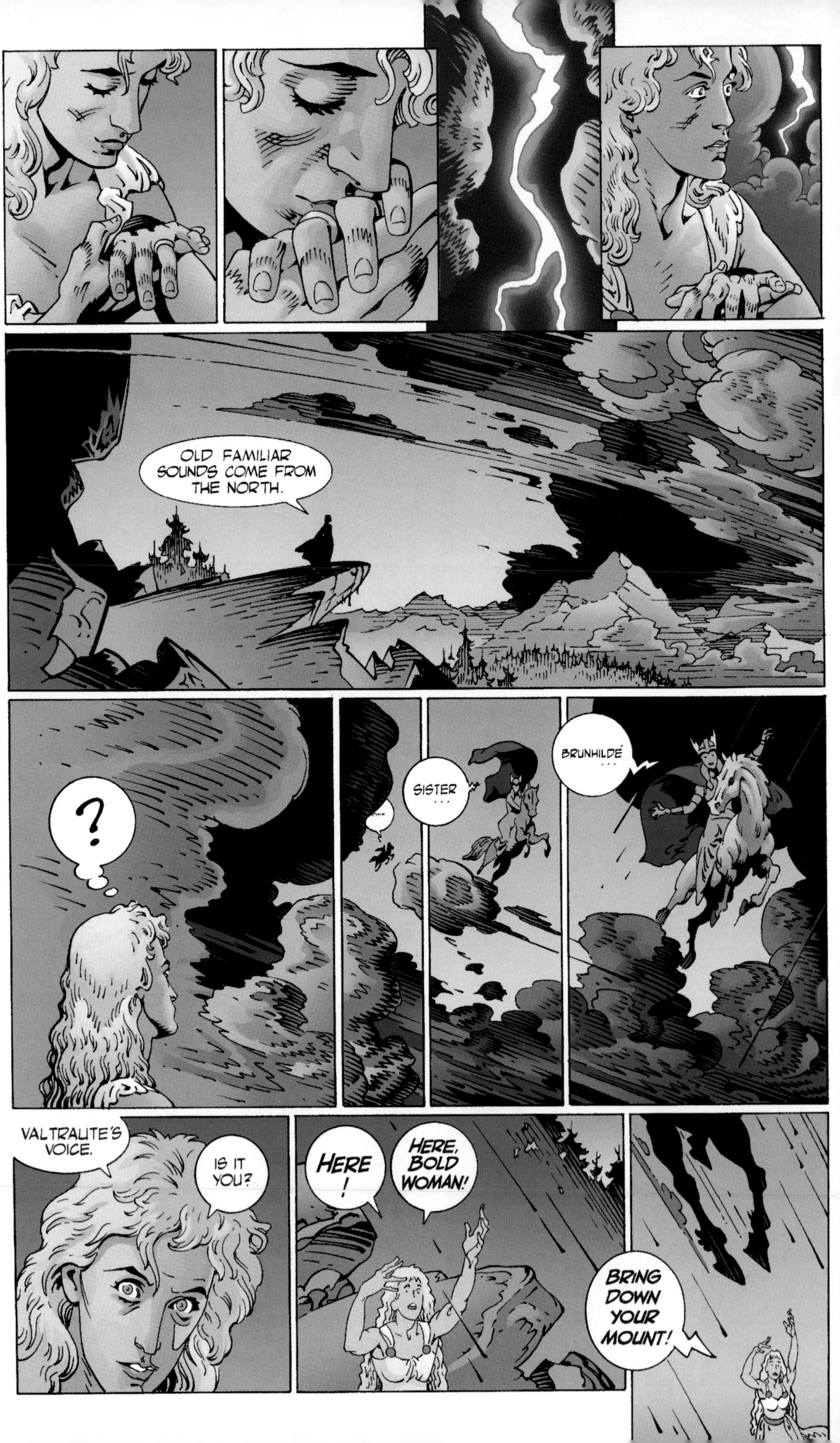
OLD FAMILIAR SOUNDS COME FROM THE NORTH.
?
SISTER . . .
BRUNHILDÉ . . .
VALTRAUTE'S VOICE.
IS IT YOU?
HERE!
HERE, BOLD WOMAN!
BRING DOWN YOUR MOUNT!

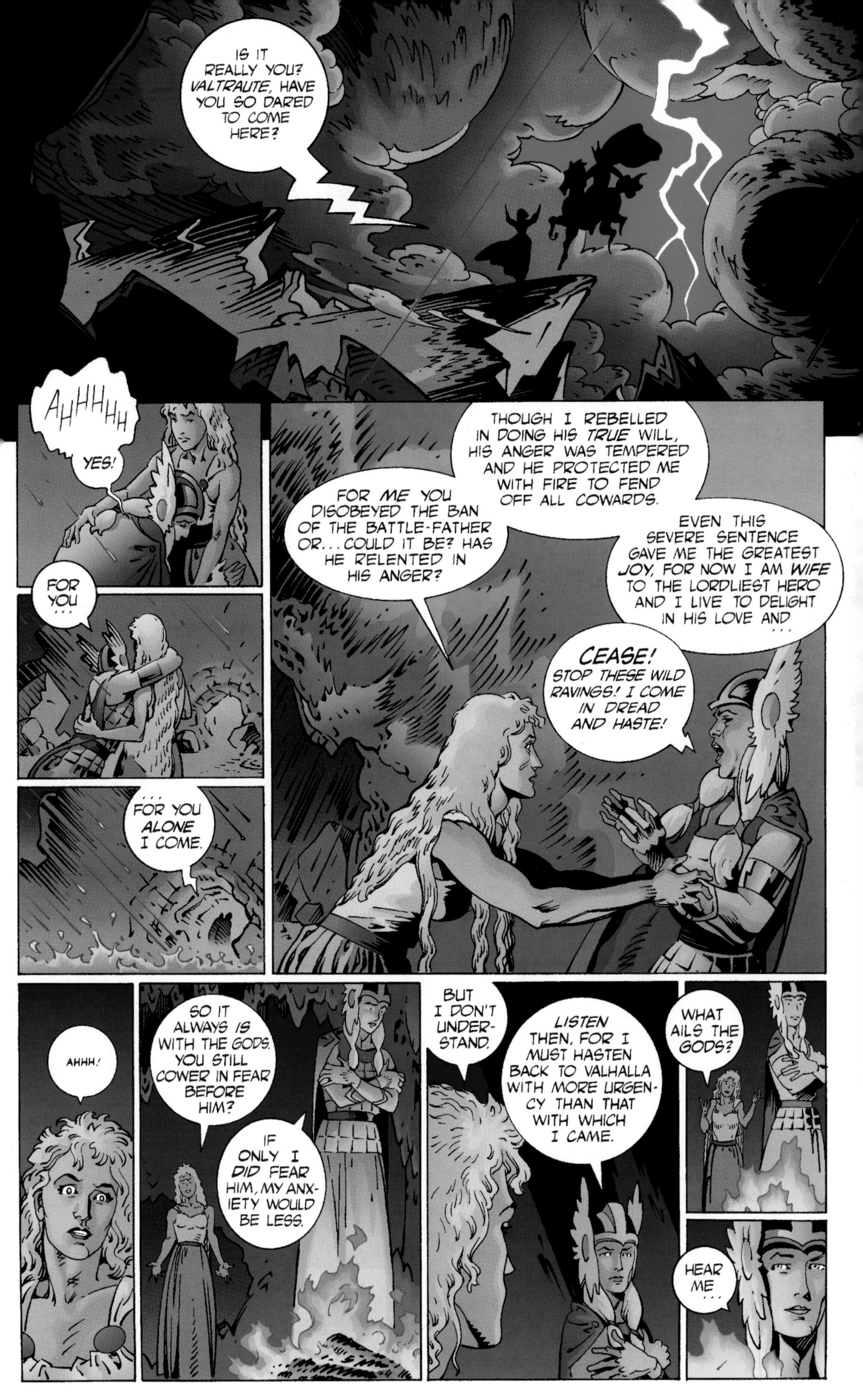
IS IT REALLY YOU? VALTRAUTE, HAVE YOU SO DARED TO COME HERE?
AHHHHH
YES!
FOR YOU . . .
. . . FOR YOU ALONE I COME.
FOR ME YOU DISOBEYED THE BAN OF THE BATTLE-FATHER OR... COULD IT BE? HAS HE RELENTED IN HIS ANGER?
THOUGH I REBELLED IN DOING HIS TRUE WILL, HIS ANGER WAS TEMPERED AND HE PROTECTED ME WITH FIRE TO FEND OFF ALL COWARDS.
EVEN THIS SEVERE SENTENCE GAVE ME THE GREATEST JOY, FOR NOW I AM WIFE TO THE LORDLIEST HERO AND I LIVE TO DELIGHT IN HIS LOVE AND . . .
CEASE! STOP THESE WILD RAVINGS! I COME IN DREAD AND HASTE!
AHHH!
SO IT ALWAYS IS WITH THE GODS. YOU STILL COWER IN FEAR BEFORE HIM?
IF ONLY I DID FEAR HIM, MY ANXIETY WOULD BE LESS.
BUT I DON'T UNDERSTAND.
LISTEN THEN, FOR I MUST HASTEN BACK TO VALHALLA WITH MORE URGENCY THAN THAT WITH WHICH I CAME.
WHAT AILS THE GODS?
HEAR ME . . .

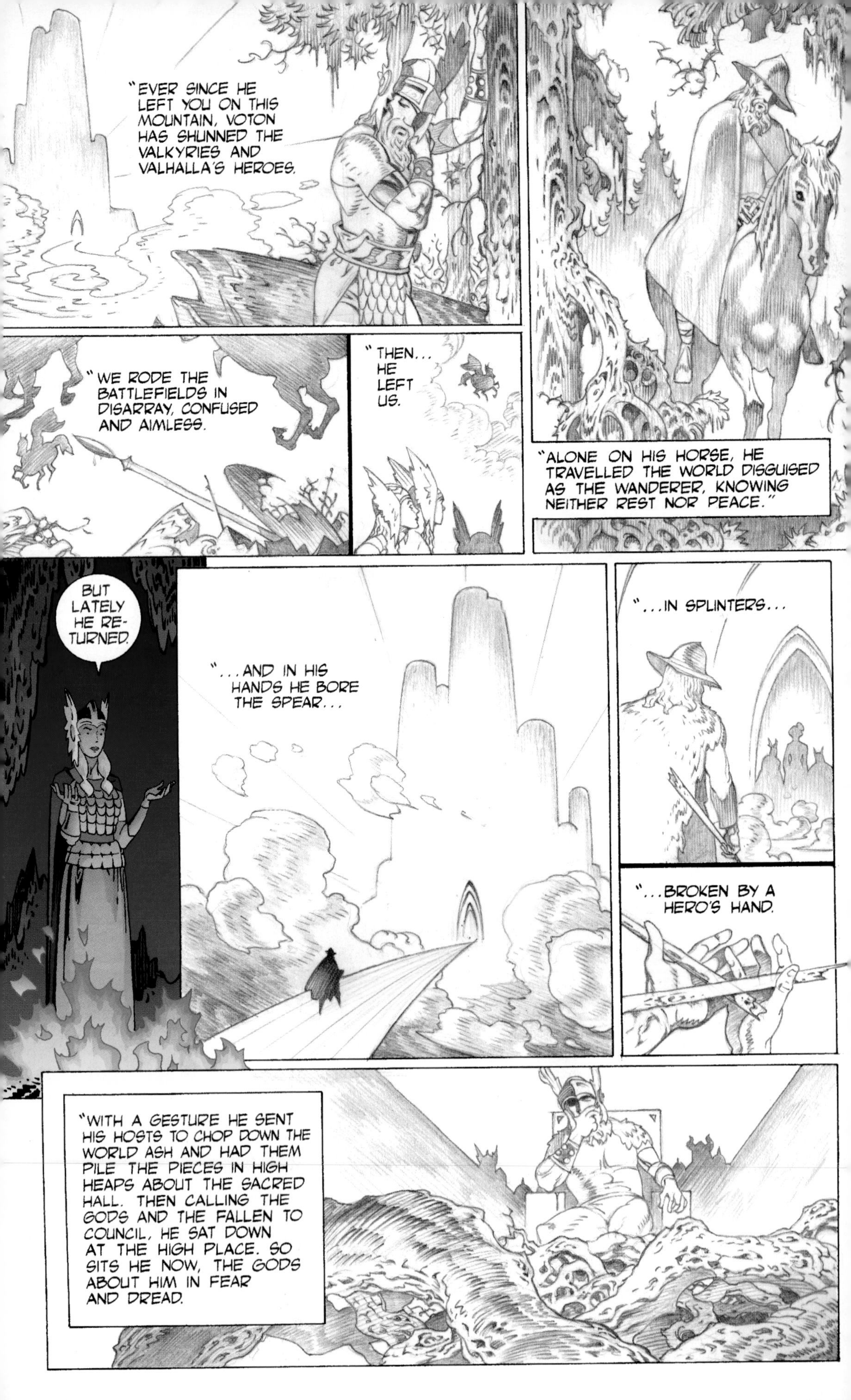
"EVER SINCE HE LEFT YOU ON THIS MOUNTAIN, VOTON HAS SHUNNED THE VALKYRIES AND VALHALLA'S HEROES.
"WE RODE THE BATTLEFIELDS IN DISARRAY, CONFUSED AND AIMLESS.
"THEN... HE LEFT US.
"ALONE ON HIS HORSE, HE TRAVELLED THE WORLD DISGUISED AS THE WANDERER, KNOWING NEITHER REST NOR PEACE."
BUT LATELY HE RE-TURNED.
"...AND IN HIS HANDS HE BORE THE SPEAR...
"...IN SPLINTERS...
"...BROKEN BY A HERO'S HAND.
"WITH A GESTURE HE SENT HIS HOSTS TO CHOP DOWN THE WORLD ASH AND HAD THEM PILE THE PIECES IN HIGH HEAPS ABOUT THE SACRED HALL. THEN CALLING THE GODS AND THE FALLEN TO COUNCIL, HE SAT DOWN AT THE HIGH PLACE. SO SITS HE NOW, THE GODS ABOUT HIM IN FEAR AND DREAD.

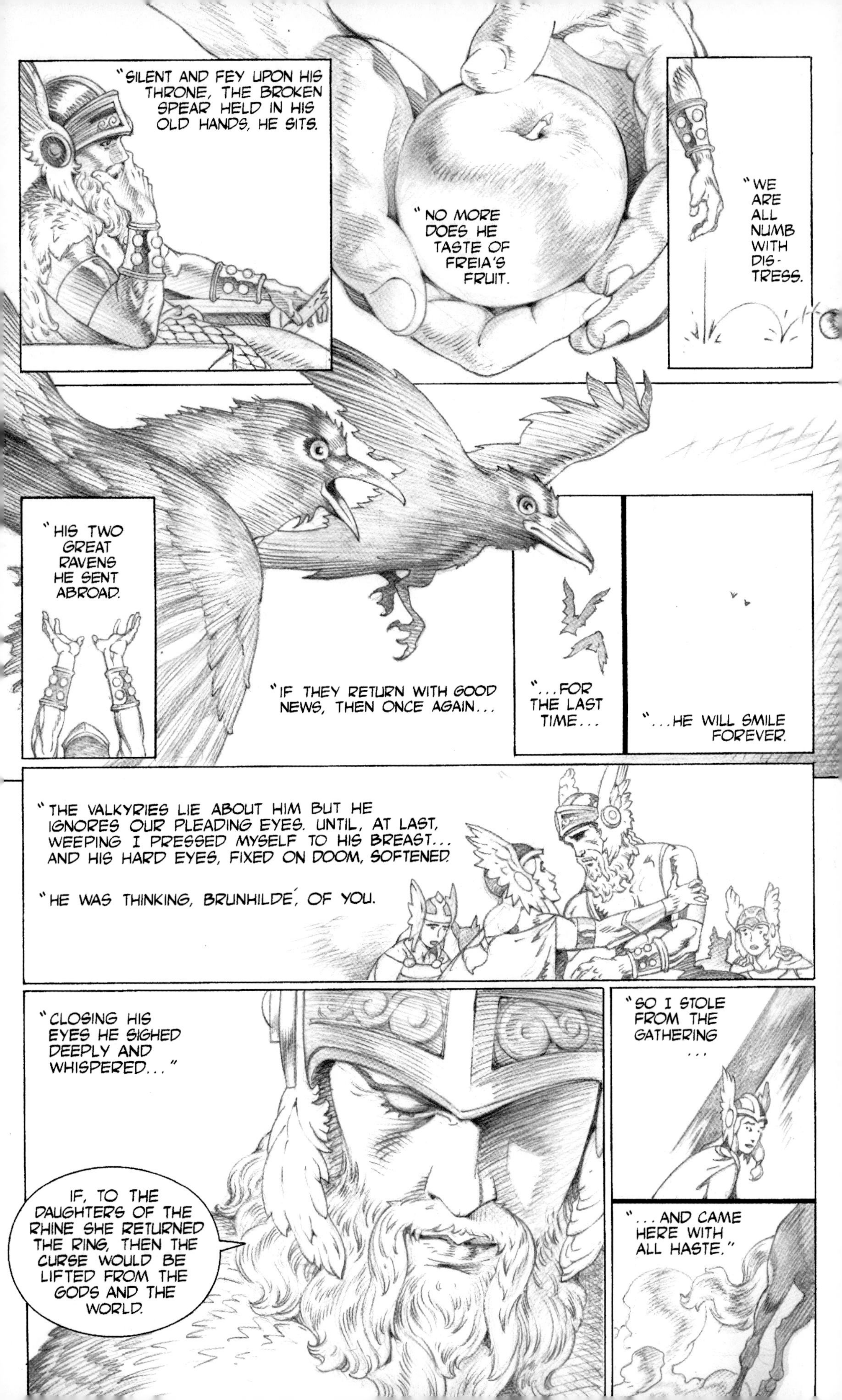
"SILENT AND FEY UPON HIS THRONE, THE BROKEN SPEAR HELD IN HIS OLD HANDS, HE SITS.
"NO MORE DOES HE TASTE OF FREIA'S FRUIT.
"WE ARE ALL NUMB WITH DIS-TRESS.
"HIS TWO GREAT RAVENS HE SENT ABROAD.
"IF THEY RETURN WITH GOOD NEWS, THEN ONCE AGAIN...
"...FOR THE LAST TIME...
"...HE WILL SMILE FOREVER.
"THE VALKYRIES LIE ABOUT HIM BUT HE IGNORES OUR PLEADING EYES. UNTIL, AT LAST, WEEPING I PRESSED MYSELF TO HIS BREAST... AND HIS HARD EYES, FIXED ON DOOM, SOFTENED.
"HE WAS THINKING, BRUNHILDE, OF YOU.
"CLOSING HIS EYES HE SIGHED DEEPLY AND WHISPERED..."
IF, TO THE DAUGHTERS OF THE RHINE SHE RETURNED THE RING, THEN THE CURSE WOULD BE LIFTED FROM THE GODS AND THE WORLD.
"SO I STOLE FROM THE GATHERING ...
"...AND CAME HERE WITH ALL HASTE."

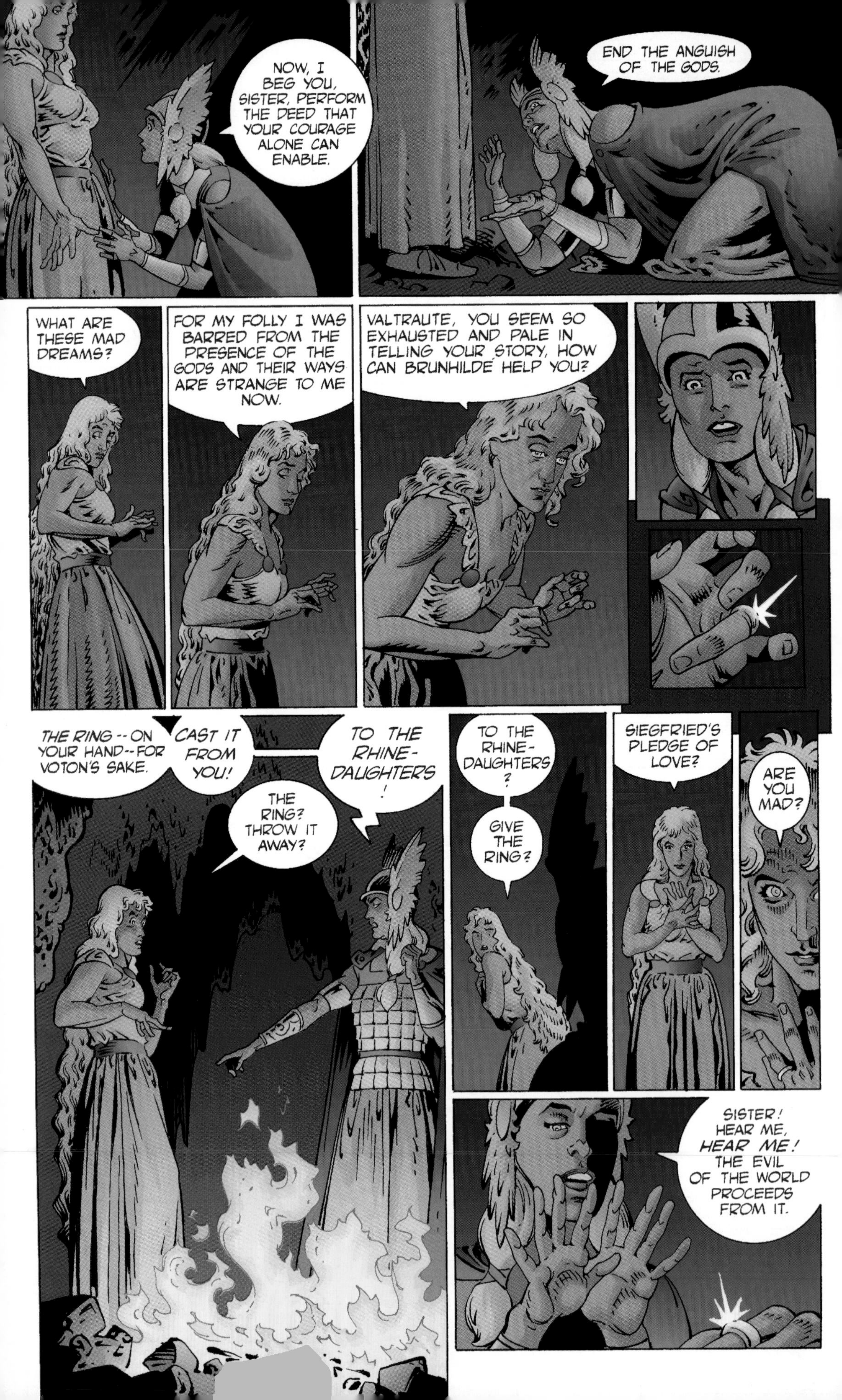

NOW, I BEG YOU, SISTER, PERFORM THE DEED THAT YOUR COURAGE ALONE CAN ENABLE.
END THE ANGUISH OF THE GODS.
WHAT ARE THESE MAD DREAMS?
FOR MY FOLLY I WAS BARRED FROM THE PRESENCE OF THE GODS AND THEIR WAYS ARE STRANGE TO ME NOW.
VALTRAUTE, YOU SEEM SO EXHAUSTED AND PALE IN TELLING YOUR STORY, HOW CAN BRUNHILDE HELP YOU?
THE RING -- ON YOUR HAND -- FOR VOTON'S SAKE.
CAST IT FROM YOU!
THE RING? THROW IT AWAY?
TO THE RHINE-DAUGHTERS!
TO THE RHINE-DAUGHTERS?
GIVE THE RING?
SIEGFRIED'S PLEDGE OF LOVE?
ARE YOU MAD?
SISTER! HEAR ME, HEAR ME! THE EVIL OF THE WORLD PROCEEDS FROM IT.

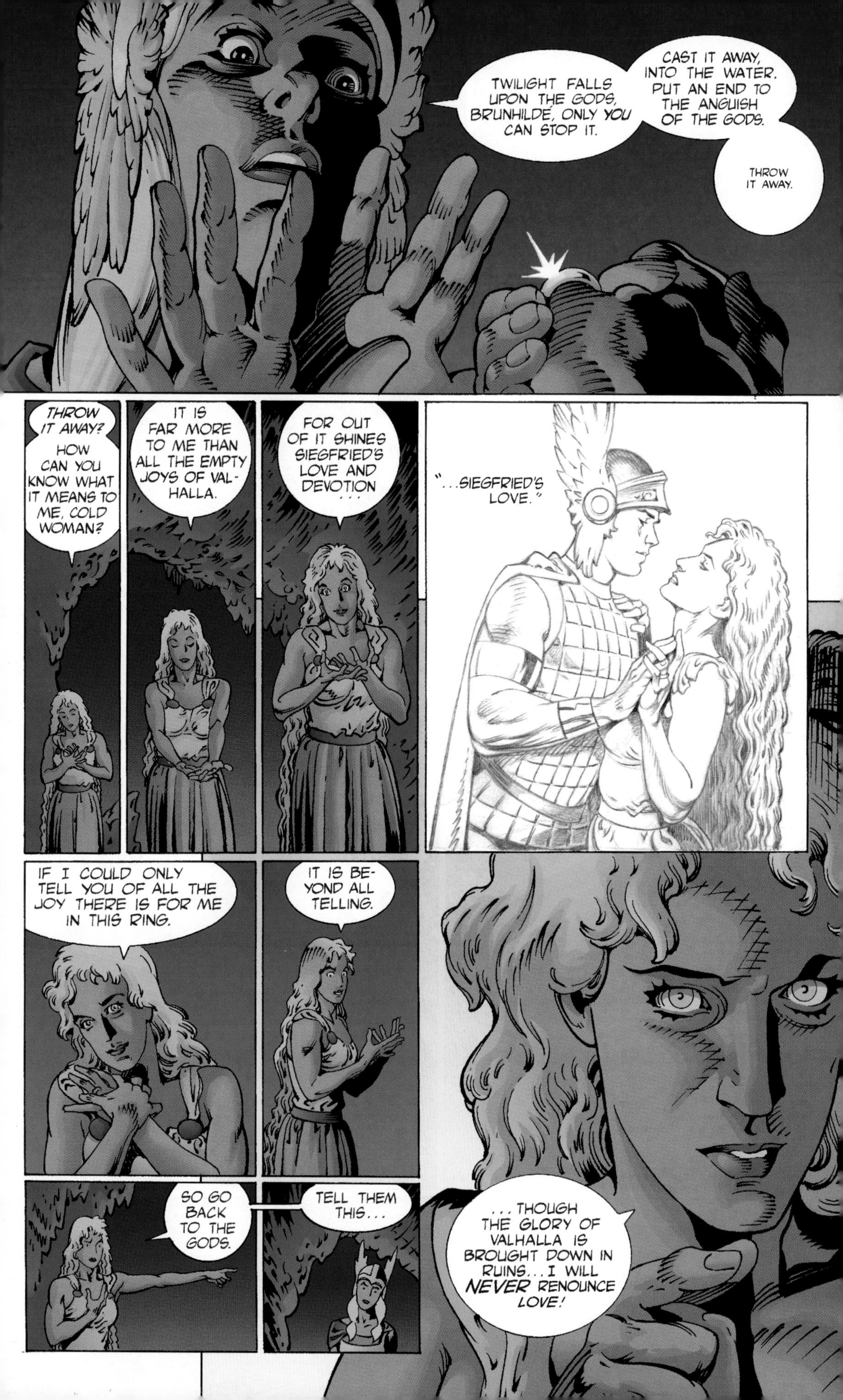
TWILIGHT FALLS UPON THE GODS, BRUNHILDE, ONLY YOU CAN STOP IT.
CAST IT AWAY, INTO THE WATER. PUT AN END TO THE ANGUISH OF THE GODS.
THROW IT AWAY.
THROW IT AWAY? HOW CAN YOU KNOW WHAT IT MEANS TO ME, COLD WOMAN?
IT IS FAR MORE TO ME THAN ALL THE EMPTY JOYS OF VAL-HALLA.
FOR OUT OF IT SHINES SIEGFRIED'S LOVE AND DEVOTION . . .
". . . SIEGFRIED'S LOVE."
IF I COULD ONLY TELL YOU OF ALL THE JOY THERE IS FOR ME IN THIS RING.
IT IS BE-YOND ALL TELLING.
SO GO BACK TO THE GODS.
TELL THEM THIS . . .
. . . THOUGH THE GLORY OF VALHALLA IS BROUGHT DOWN IN RUINS . . . I WILL NEVER RENOUNCE LOVE!

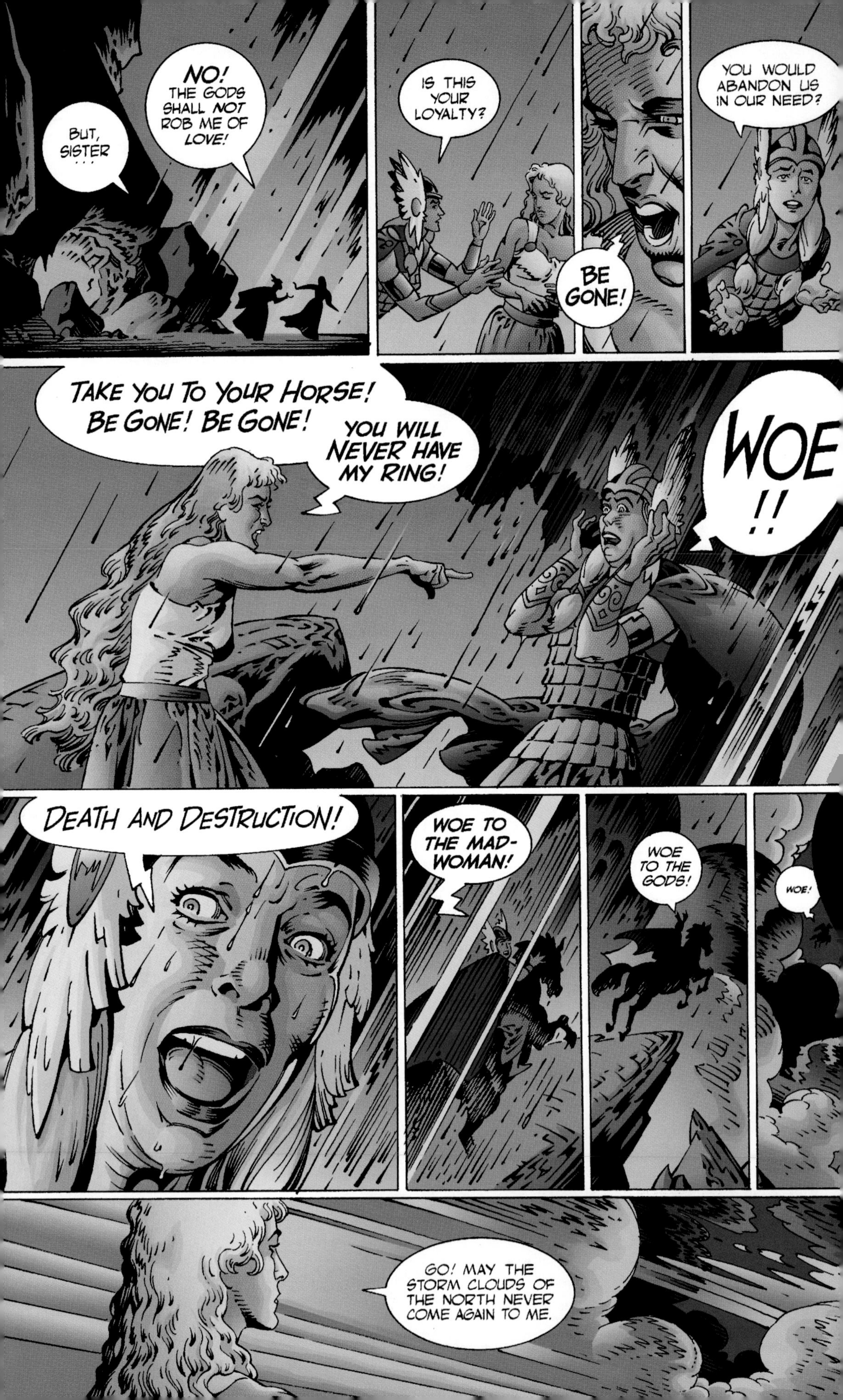

BUT, SISTER . . .
NO! THE GODS SHALL NOT ROB ME OF LOVE!
IS THIS YOUR LOYALTY?
BE GONE!
YOU WOULD ABANDON US IN OUR NEED?
TAKE YOU TO YOUR HORSE! BE GONE! BE GONE!
YOU WILL NEVER HAVE MY RING!
WOE !!
DEATH AND DESTRUCTION!
WOE TO THE MAD-WOMAN!
WOE TO THE GODS!
WOE!
GO! MAY THE STORM CLOUDS OF THE NORTH NEVER COME AGAIN TO ME.

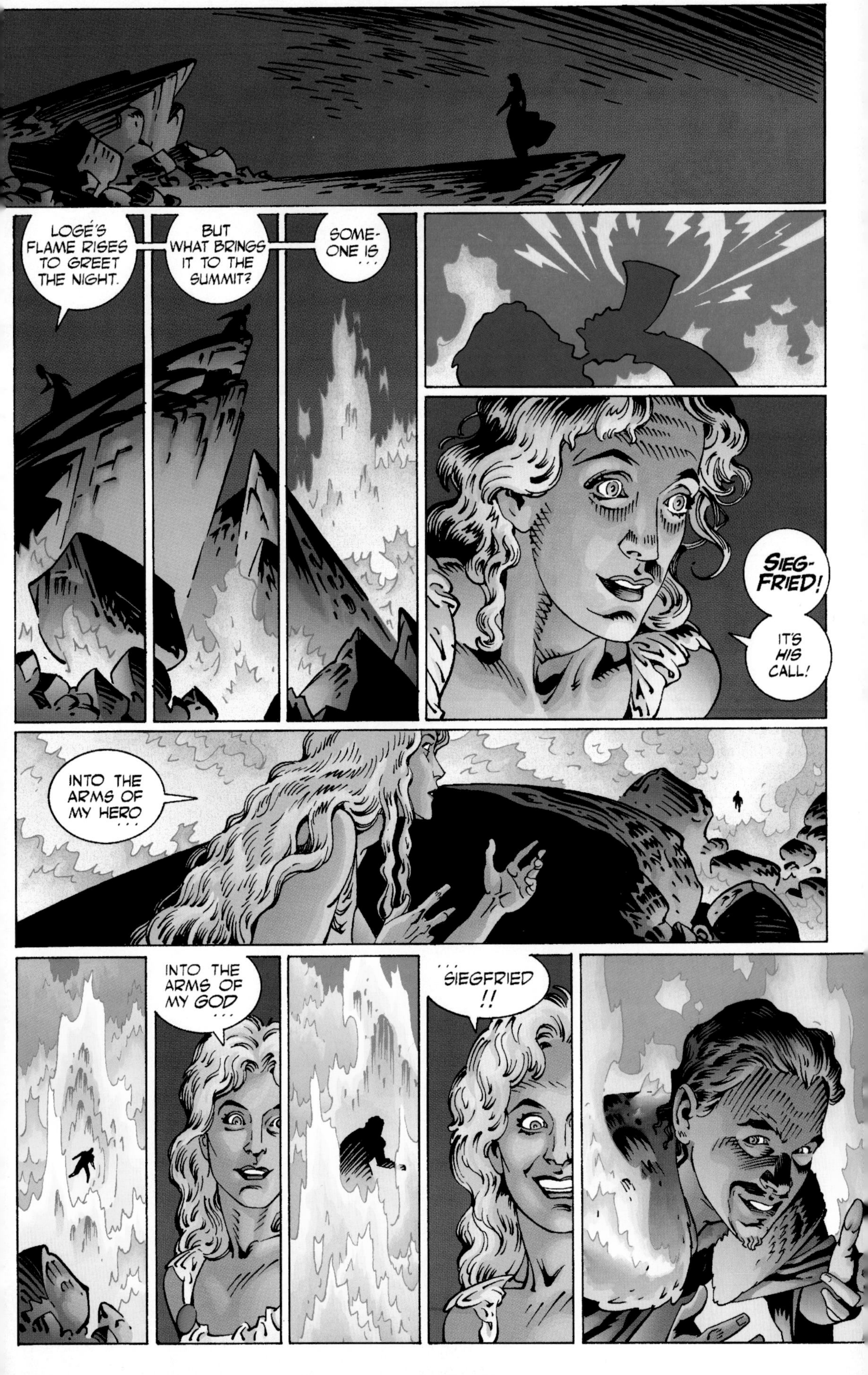

LOGÉ'S FLAME RISES TO GREET THE NIGHT.
BUT WHAT BRINGS IT TO THE SUMMIT?
SOME-ONE IS . . .
SIEG-FRIED!
IT'S HIS CALL!
INTO THE ARMS OF MY HERO . . .
INTO THE ARMS OF MY GOD . . .
. . . SIEGFRIED !!

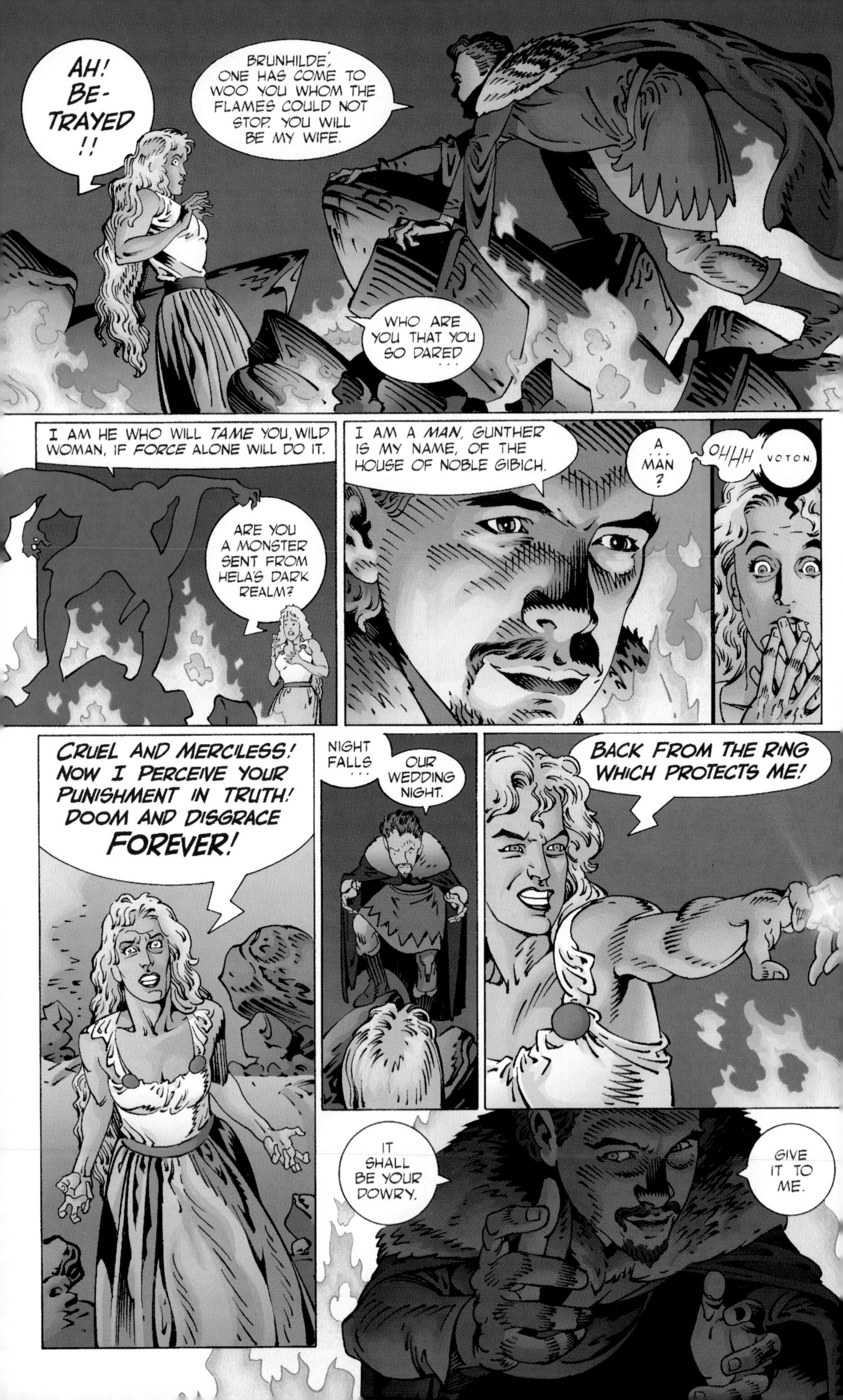
AH! BE-TRAYED !!
BRUNHILDE, ONE HAS COME TO WOO YOU WHOM THE FLAMES COULD NOT STOP. YOU WILL BE MY WIFE.
WHO ARE YOU THAT YOU SO DARED . . .
I AM HE WHO WILL TAME YOU, WILD WOMAN, IF FORCE ALONE WILL DO IT.
ARE YOU A MONSTER SENT FROM HELA'S DARK REALM?
I AM A MAN, GUNTHER IS MY NAME, OF THE HOUSE OF NOBLE GIBICH.
A . . . MAN ?
OHHH VOTON.
CRUEL AND MERCILESS! NOW I PERCEIVE YOUR PUNISHMENT IN TRUTH! DOOM AND DISGRACE FOREVER!
NIGHT FALLS . . .
OUR WEDDING NIGHT.
BACK FROM THE RING WHICH PROTECTS ME!
IT SHALL BE YOUR DOWRY.
GIVE IT TO ME.

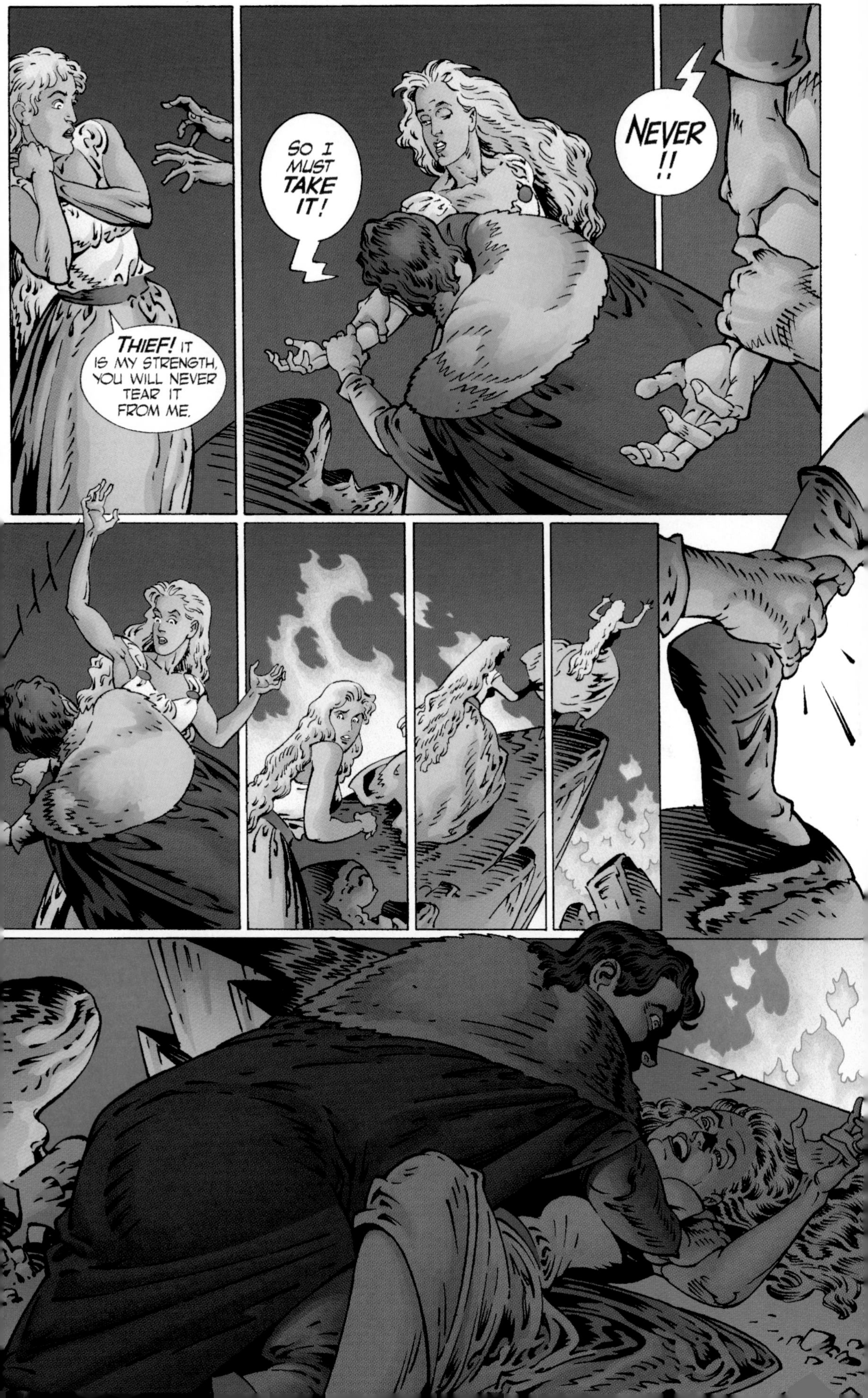
THIEF! IT IS MY STRENGTH, YOU WILL NEVER TEAR IT FROM ME.
SO I MUST TAKE IT!
NEVER !!

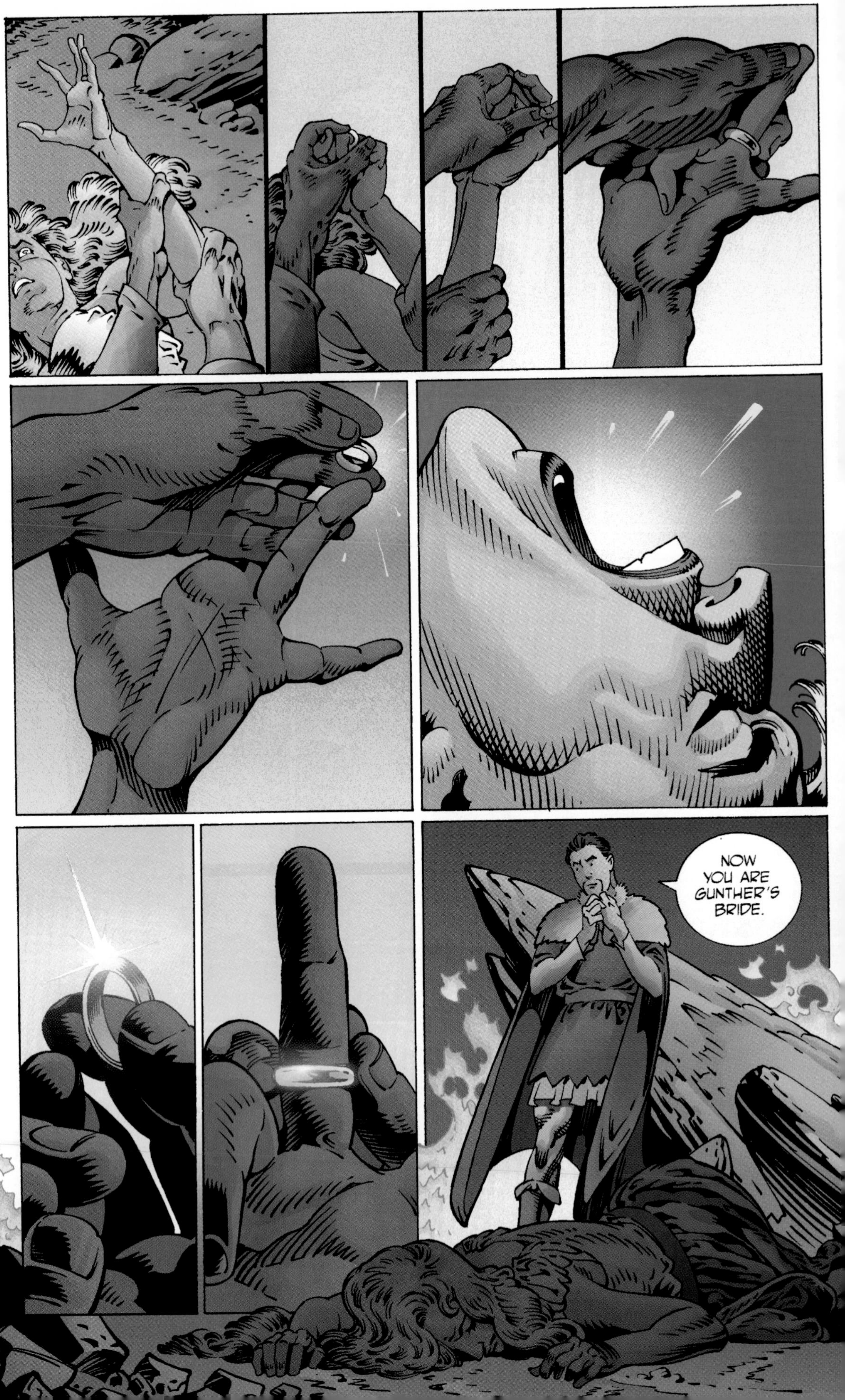
NOW YOU ARE GUNTHER'S BRIDE.

COME . . .

WE WILL BE WED IN YOUR CAVE.

?

WHAT STRENGTH COULD HAVE...

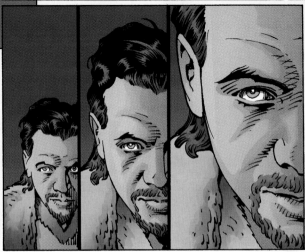

WHAT STRENGTH?

GO!

BUILD THE FIRE AND WAIT FOR ME.

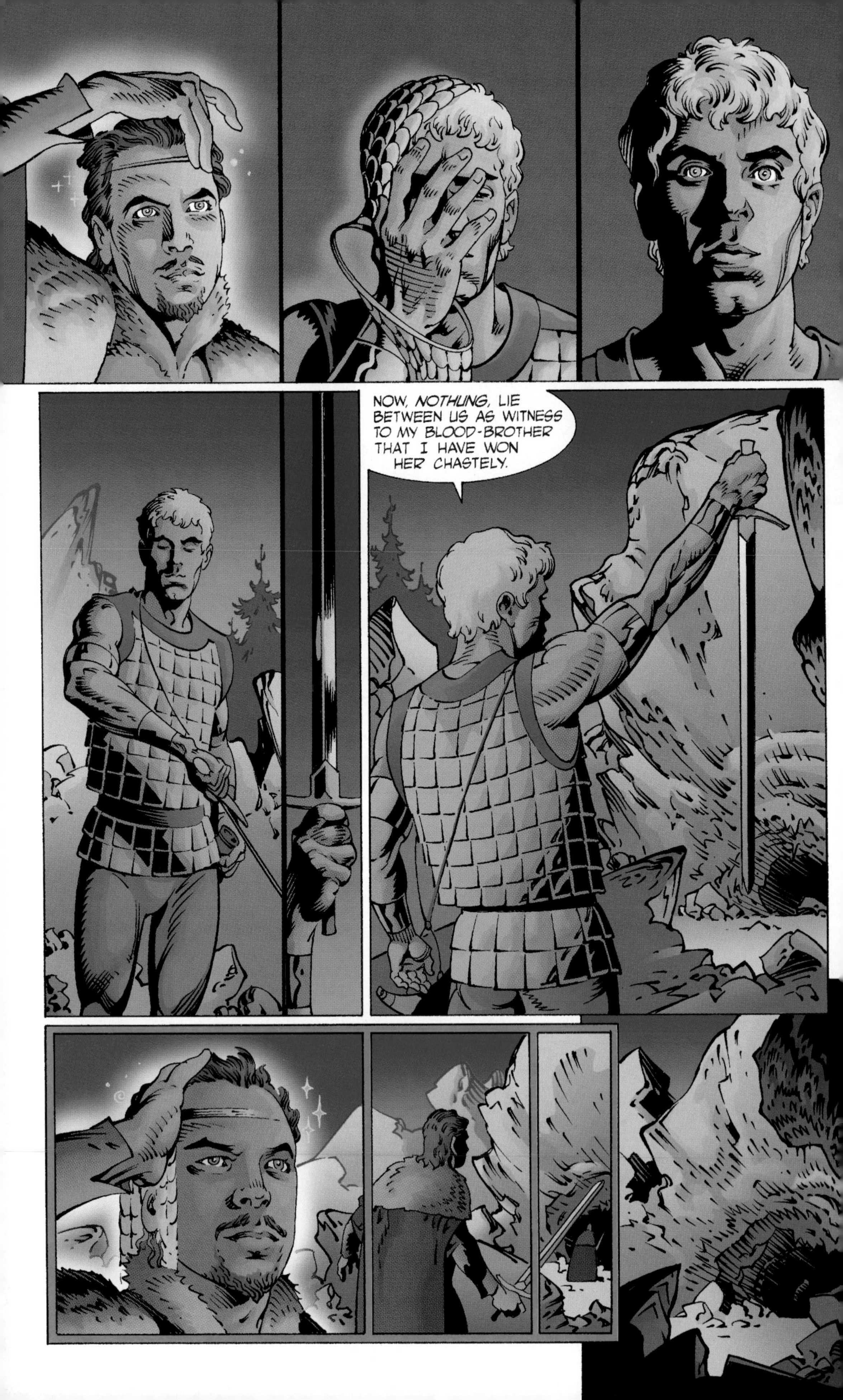
NOW, *NOTHUNG*, LIE BETWEEN US AS WITNESS TO MY BLOOD-BROTHER THAT I HAVE WON HER CHASTELY.

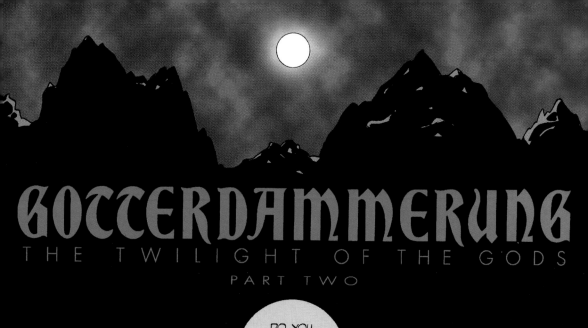

GOTTERDAMMERUNG

THE TWILIGHT OF THE GODS

PART TWO

DO YOU SLEEP, HAGEN, MY SON, AND HEAR NOT HIM WHOM REST AND SLEEP BETRAYED?

I HEAR YOU, EVIL DWARF, WHAT WORDS DO YOU SPEAK IN MY SLEEP?

HAVE THE COURAGE OF THE ONE WHO GAVE YOU BIRTH.

I HAVE IT, BUT I THANK HER NOT. SHE WHO WAS ENTICED BY YOU ALSO GAVE ME OLD AGE IN MY YOUTH.

I AM PALE AND BLOOD-LESS, HATING THOSE WHO ARE HAPPY, DEVOID OF JOY.

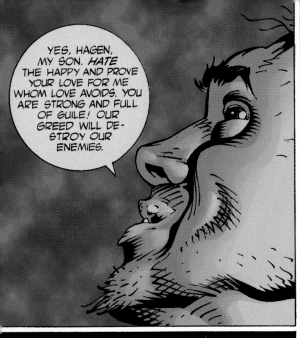

YES, HAGEN, MY SON. *HATE* THE HAPPY AND PROVE YOUR LOVE FOR ME WHOM LOVE AVOIDS. YOU ARE STRONG AND FULL OF GUILE! OUR GREED WILL DESTROY OUR ENEMIES.

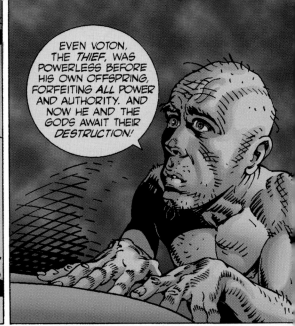

EVEN VOTON, THE *THIEF*, WAS POWERLESS BEFORE HIS OWN OFFSPRING, FORFEITING *ALL* POWER AND AUTHORITY. AND NOW HE AND THE GODS AWAIT THEIR *DESTRUCTION!*

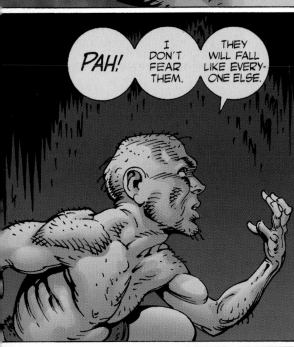

PAH! I DON'T FEAR THEM. THEY WILL FALL LIKE EVERYONE ELSE.

DO YOU *SLEEP*, HAGEN, MY SON?

THE POWER OF THE GODS... WHO INHERITS IT?

I.... *YOU!* WE WILL GAIN THE WHOLE WORLD IF YOU ARE TRUE AND SHARE MY WRATH.

WHEN THE *VALSUNG*, WHO KILLED FAFNIR AND GAINED THE *RING*, SHATTERED VOTON'S SPEAR, VOTON'S POWER WAS BROKEN. THOUGH HEAVEN AND EARTH ARE NOW IN SIEGFRIED'S POWER, MY CURSE DOESN'T TOUCH HIM AS LONG AS HE DOES NOT *USE* THAT POWER.

HIS ONLY JOY IS LOVE, WITH WHICH HE THROWS HIS LIFE AWAY. WE MUST ELIMINATE HIM, THAT ALONE IS *NEEDFUL.*

DO YOU SLEEP, HAGEN, MY SON?

HE ALREADY RUSHES TO HIS DESTRUCTION AT MY COMMAND.

BUT THE RING, *THAT* WE MUST HAVE.

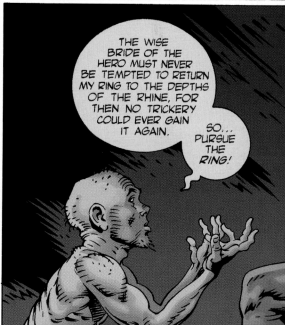

THE WISE BRIDE OF THE HERO MUST NEVER BE TEMPTED TO RETURN MY RING TO THE DEPTHS OF THE RHINE, FOR THEN NO TRICKERY COULD EVER GAIN IT AGAIN.

SO... PURSUE THE RING!

FOR THIS I BEGOT YOU.

I GROW WEAK, BUT I HAVE PLANTED IN *YOU* ALL MY VILE HATRED AND VENGEANCE SO THAT FOR *ME* YOU WILL WIN THE RING AND DEFY THE VALSUNG AND GREAT VOTON.

SWEAR IT...

HAGEN... MY SON!

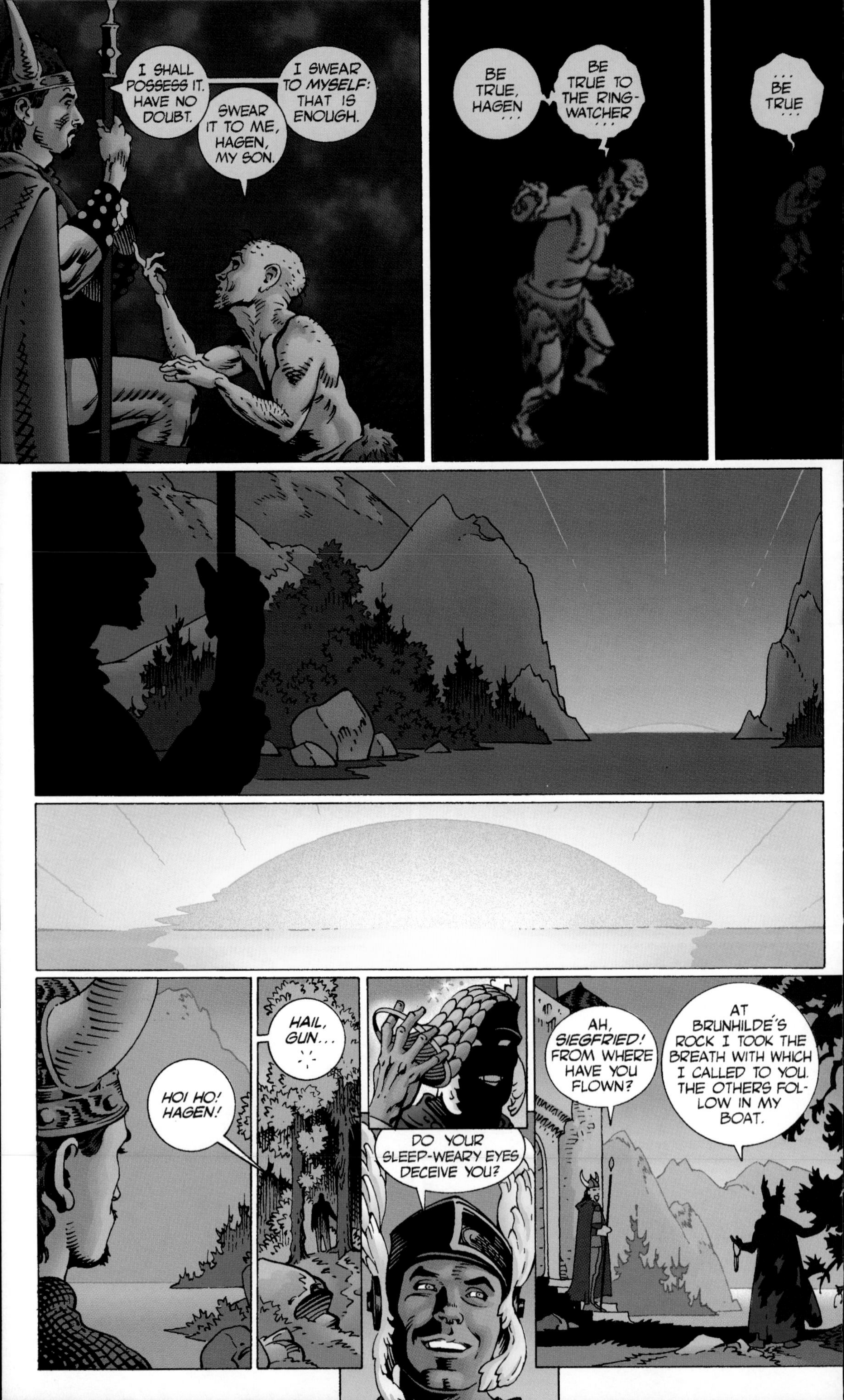
I SHALL POSSESS IT. HAVE NO DOUBT.
SWEAR IT TO ME, HAGEN, MY SON.
I SWEAR TO *MYSELF*: THAT IS ENOUGH.
BE TRUE, HAGEN . . .
BE TRUE TO THE RING-WATCHER . . .
. . . BE TRUE . . .
HOI HO! HAGEN!
HAIL, GUN . . .
DO YOUR SLEEP-WEARY EYES DECEIVE YOU?
AH, *SIEGFRIED!* FROM WHERE HAVE YOU FLOWN?
AT BRUNHILDE'S ROCK I TOOK THE BREATH WITH WHICH I CALLED TO YOU. THE OTHERS FOLLOW IN MY BOAT.

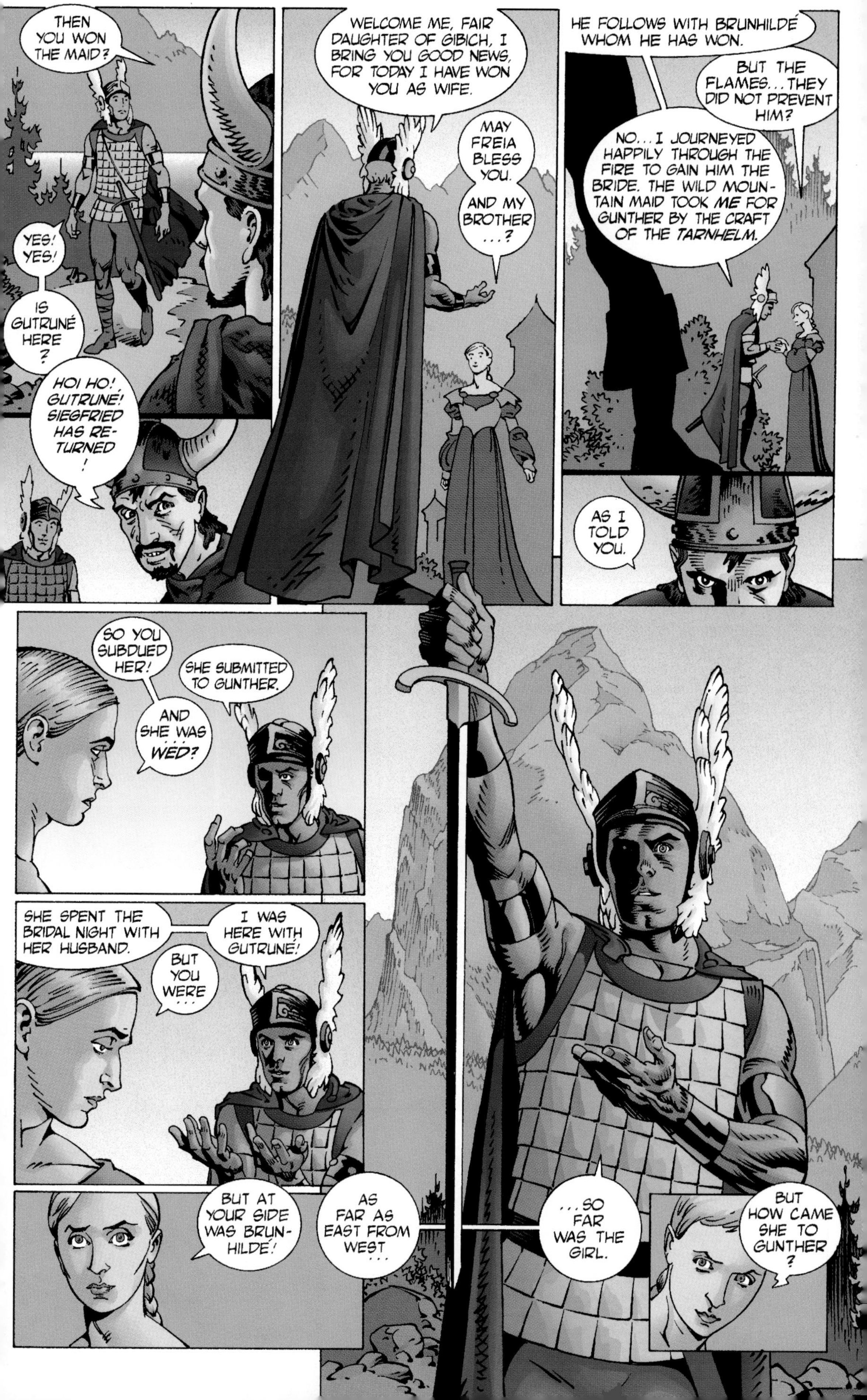
THEN YOU WON THE MAID?
YES! YES!
IS GUTRUNÉ HERE?
HOI HO! GUTRUNE! SIEGFRIED HAS RETURNED!
WELCOME ME, FAIR DAUGHTER OF GIBICH, I BRING YOU GOOD NEWS, FOR TODAY I HAVE WON YOU AS WIFE.
MAY FREIA BLESS YOU.
AND MY BROTHER . . . ?
HE FOLLOWS WITH BRUNHILDÉ WHOM HE HAS WON.
BUT THE FLAMES... THEY DID NOT PREVENT HIM?
NO... I JOURNEYED HAPPILY THROUGH THE FIRE TO GAIN HIM THE BRIDE. THE WILD MOUNTAIN MAID TOOK ME FOR GUNTHER BY THE CRAFT OF THE TARNHELM.
AS I TOLD YOU.
SO YOU SUBDUED HER!
SHE SUBMITTED TO GUNTHER.
AND SHE WAS . . . WED?
SHE SPENT THE BRIDAL NIGHT WITH HER HUSBAND.
BUT YOU WERE . . .
I WAS HERE WITH GUTRUNE!
BUT AT YOUR SIDE WAS BRUNHILDÉ!
AS FAR AS EAST FROM WEST . . .
. . . SO FAR WAS THE GIRL.
BUT HOW CAME SHE TO GUNTHER?

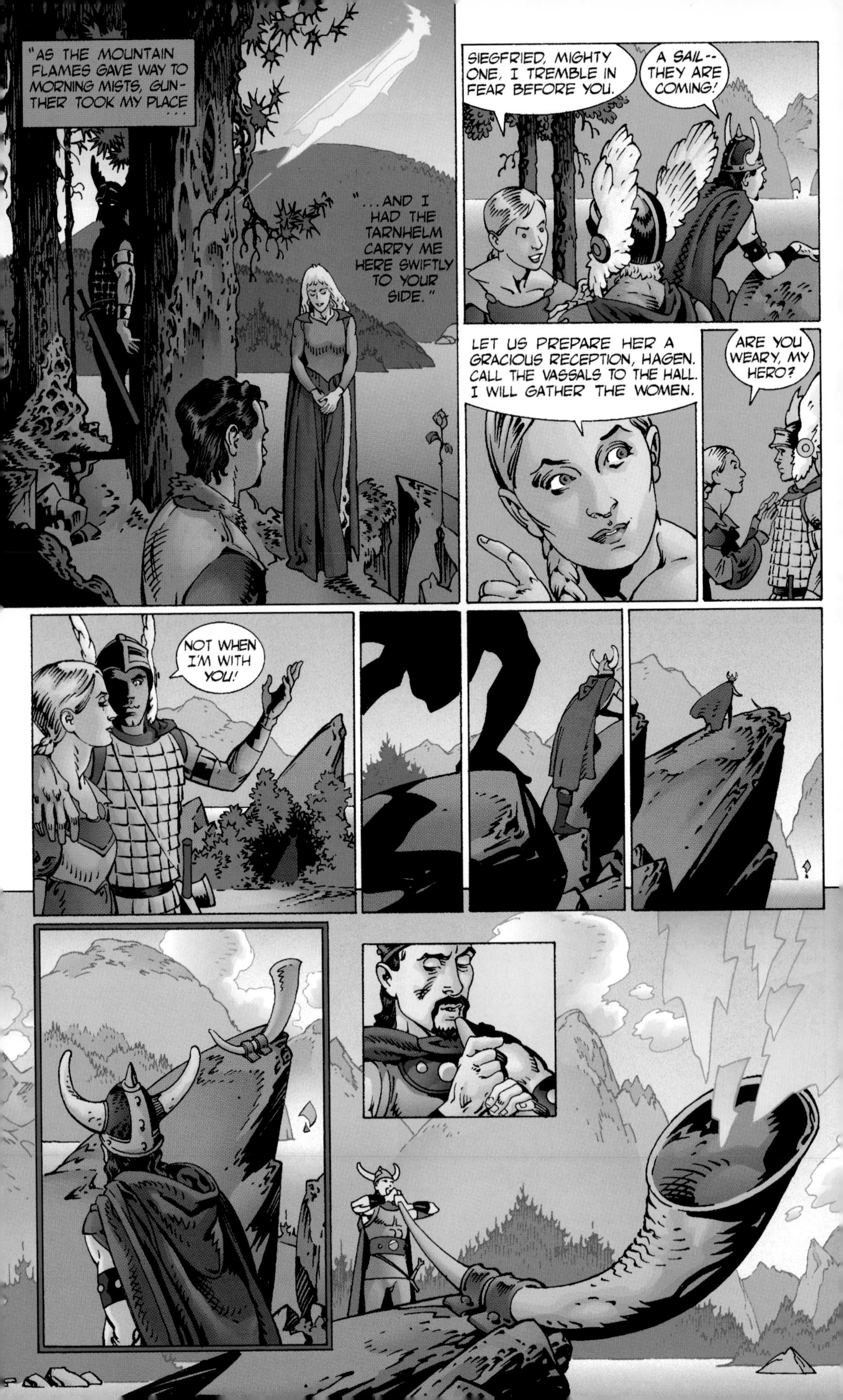
"AS THE MOUNTAIN FLAMES GAVE WAY TO MORNING MISTS, GUNTHER TOOK MY PLACE . . .
". . . AND I HAD THE TARNHELM CARRY ME HERE SWIFTLY TO YOUR SIDE."
SIEGFRIED, MIGHTY ONE, I TREMBLE IN FEAR BEFORE YOU.
A SAIL -- THEY ARE COMING!
LET US PREPARE HER A GRACIOUS RECEPTION, HAGEN. CALL THE VASSALS TO THE HALL. I WILL GATHER THE WOMEN.
ARE YOU WEARY, MY HERO?
NOT WHEN I'M WITH YOU!

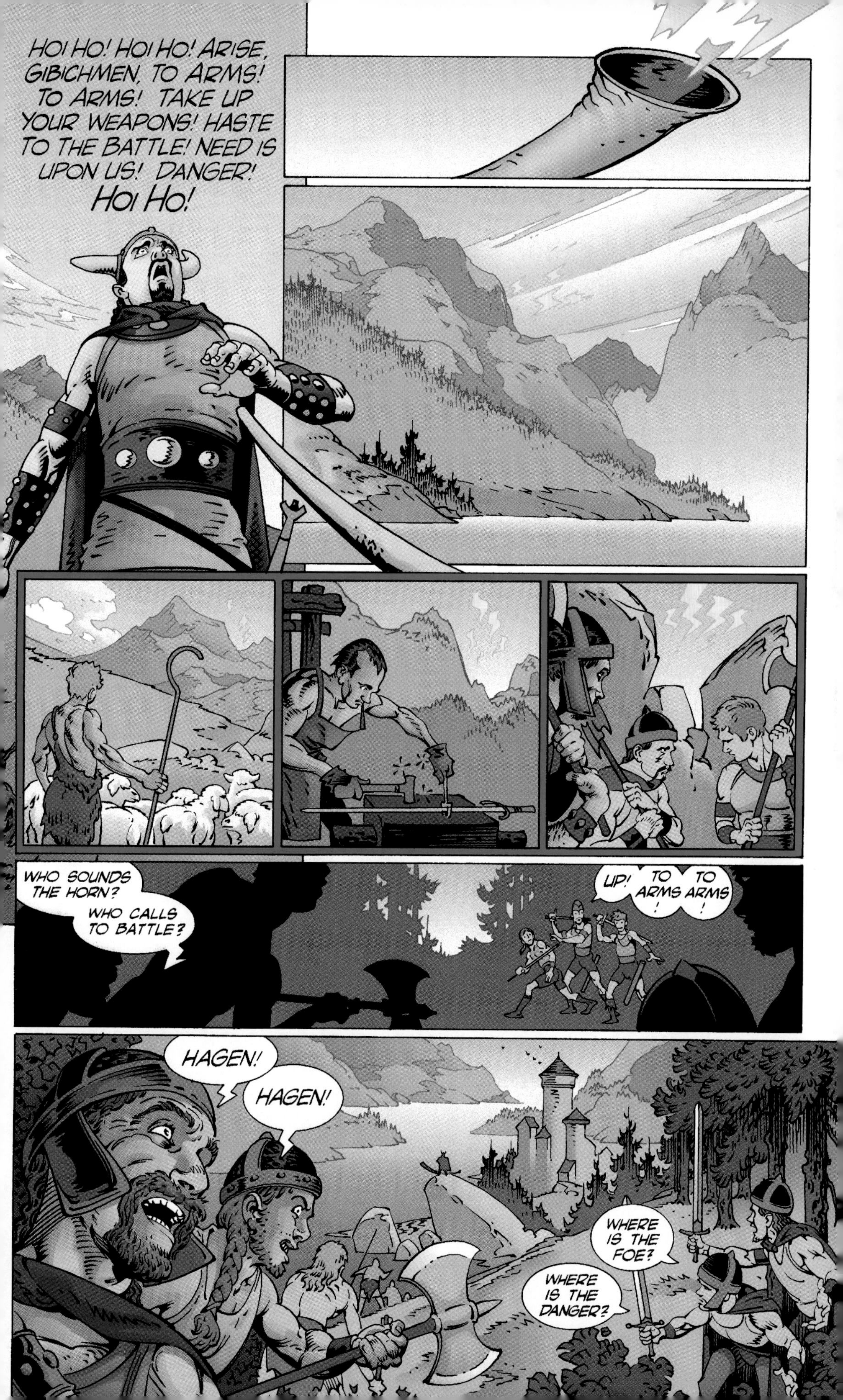
HOI HO! HOI HO! ARISE, GIBICHMEN, TO ARMS! TO ARMS! TAKE UP YOUR WEAPONS! HASTE TO THE BATTLE! NEED IS UPON US! DANGER! HOI HO!
WHO SOUNDS THE HORN?
WHO CALLS TO BATTLE?
UP!
TO ARMS!
TO ARMS!
HAGEN!
HAGEN!
WHERE IS THE FOE?
WHERE IS THE DANGER?

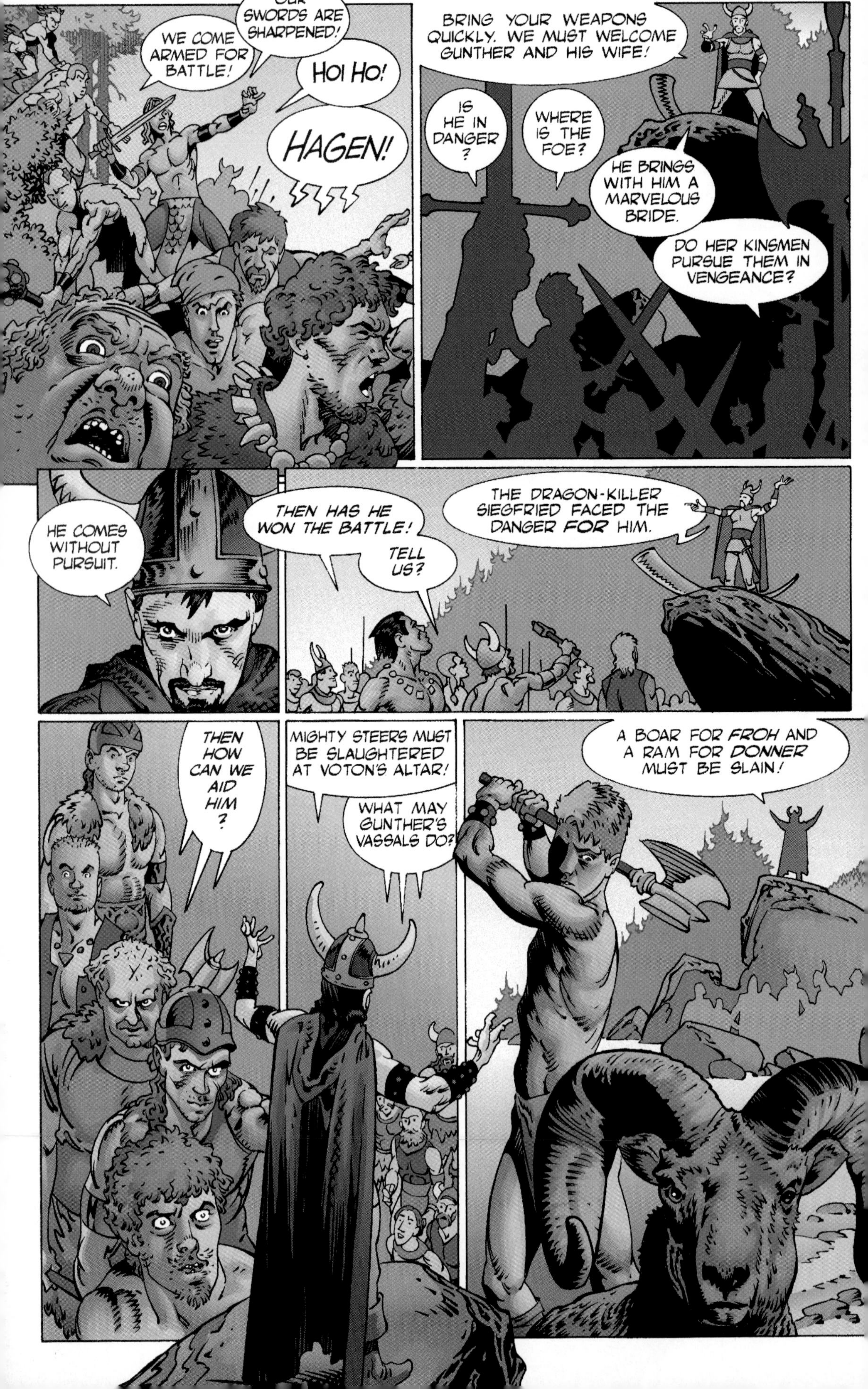
WE COME ARMED FOR BATTLE!
OUR SWORDS ARE SHARPENED!
HOI HO!
HAGEN!
BRING YOUR WEAPONS QUICKLY. WE MUST WELCOME GUNTHER AND HIS WIFE!
IS HE IN DANGER?
WHERE IS THE FOE?
HE BRINGS WITH HIM A MARVELOUS BRIDE.
DO HER KINSMEN PURSUE THEM IN VENGEANCE?
HE COMES WITHOUT PURSUIT.
THEN HAS HE WON THE BATTLE!
TELL US?
THE DRAGON-KILLER SIEGFRIED FACED THE DANGER FOR HIM.
THEN HOW CAN WE AID HIM?
MIGHTY STEERS MUST BE SLAUGHTERED AT VOTON'S ALTAR!
WHAT MAY GUNTHER'S VASSALS DO?
A BOAR FOR FROH AND A RAM FOR DONNER MUST BE SLAIN!

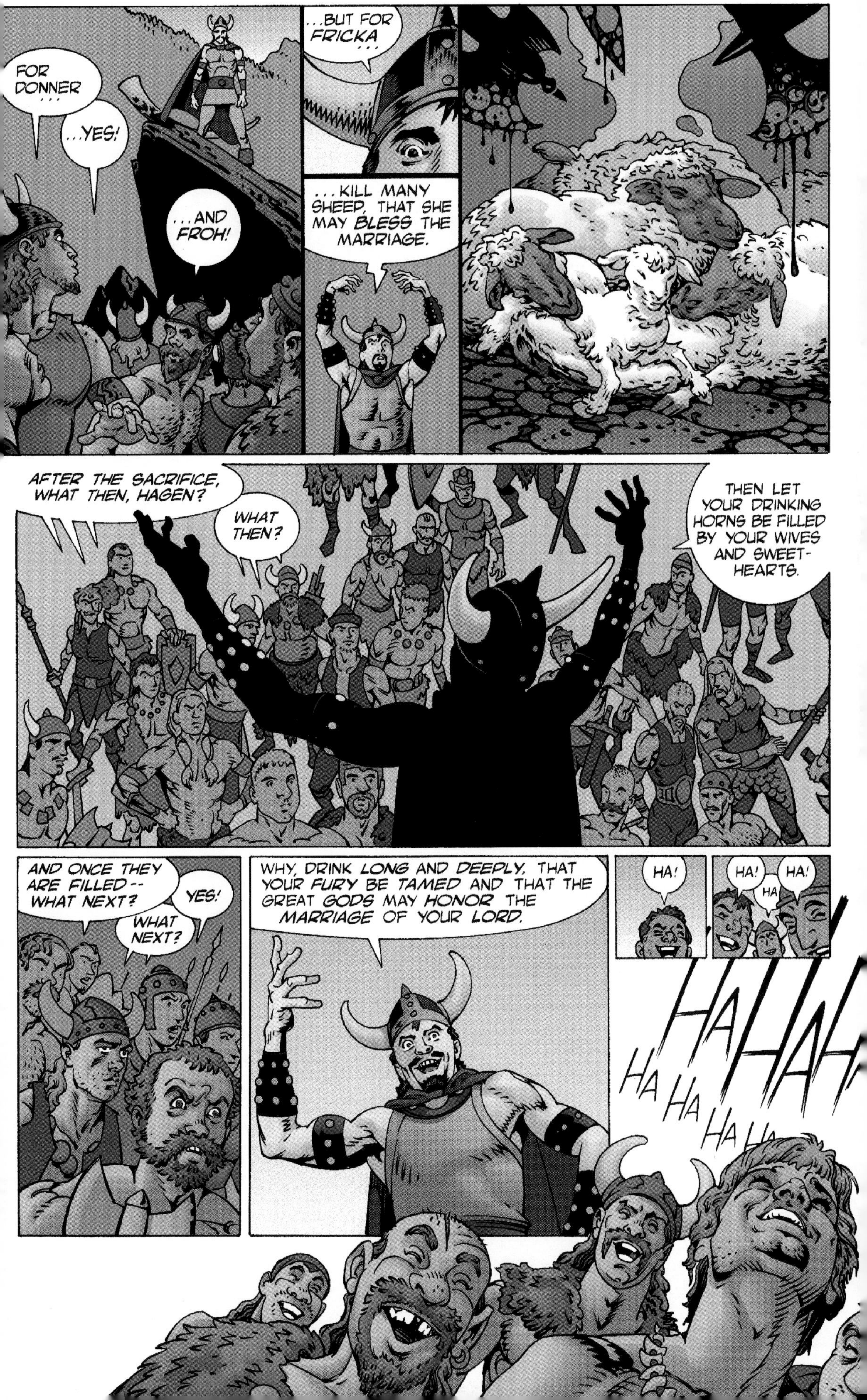

FOR DONNER . . .
. . . YES!
. . . AND FROH!
. . . BUT FOR FRICKA . . .
. . . KILL MANY SHEEP, THAT SHE MAY BLESS THE MARRIAGE.
AFTER THE SACRIFICE, WHAT THEN, HAGEN?
WHAT THEN?
THEN LET YOUR DRINKING HORNS BE FILLED BY YOUR WIVES AND SWEET-HEARTS.
AND ONCE THEY ARE FILLED -- WHAT NEXT?
YES!
WHAT NEXT?
WHY, DRINK LONG AND DEEPLY, THAT YOUR FURY BE TAMED AND THAT THE GREAT GODS MAY HONOR THE MARRIAGE OF YOUR LORD.
HA!
HA!
HA
HA!
HAHAH
HA HA HA HA

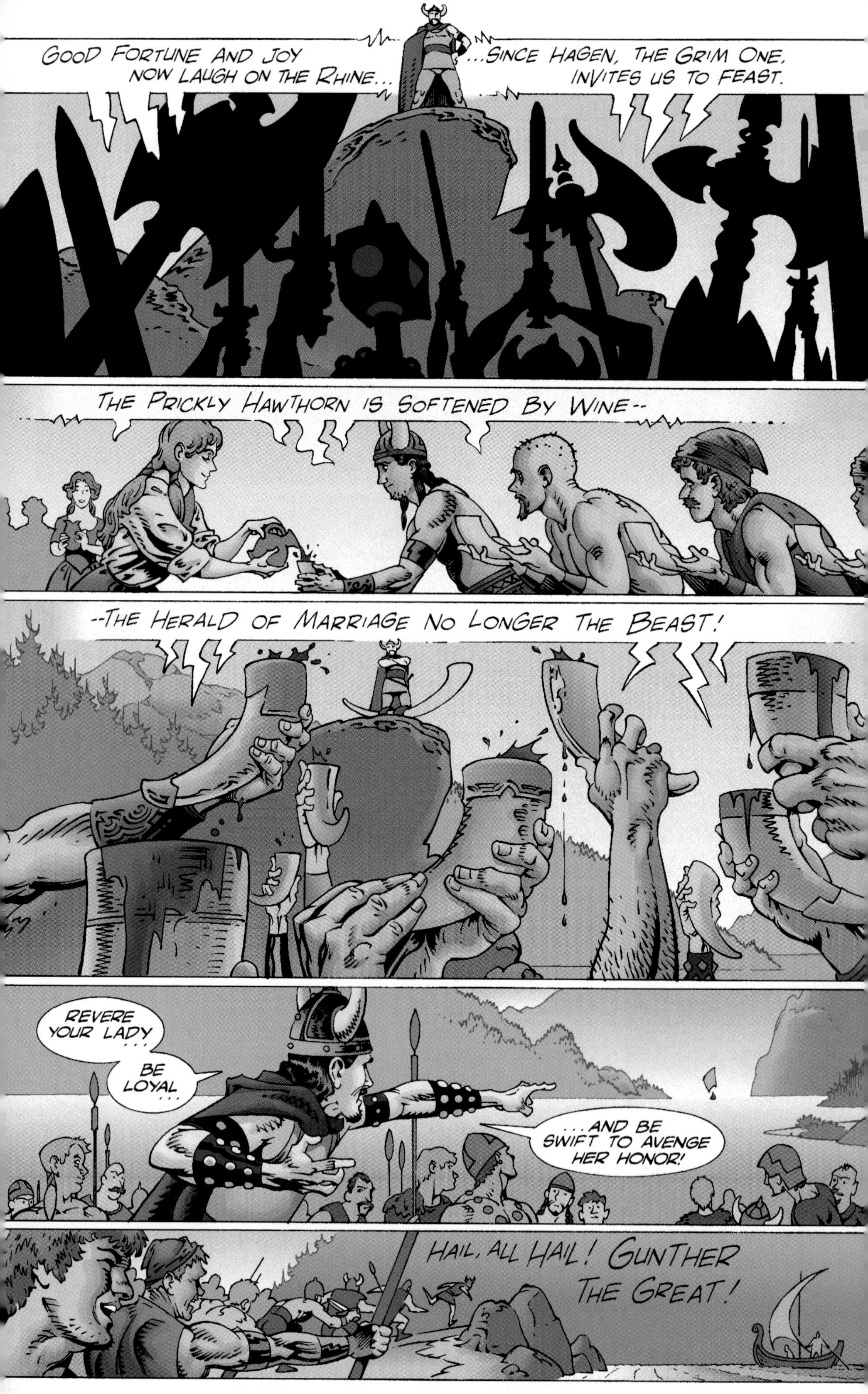
GOOD FORTUNE AND JOY NOW LAUGH ON THE RHINE...
...SINCE HAGEN, THE GRIM ONE, INVITES US TO FEAST.
THE PRICKLY HAWTHORN IS SOFTENED BY WINE--
--THE HERALD OF MARRIAGE NO LONGER THE BEAST!
REVERE YOUR LADY...
BE LOYAL...
...AND BE SWIFT TO AVENGE HER HONOR!
HAIL, ALL HAIL! GUNTHER THE GREAT!

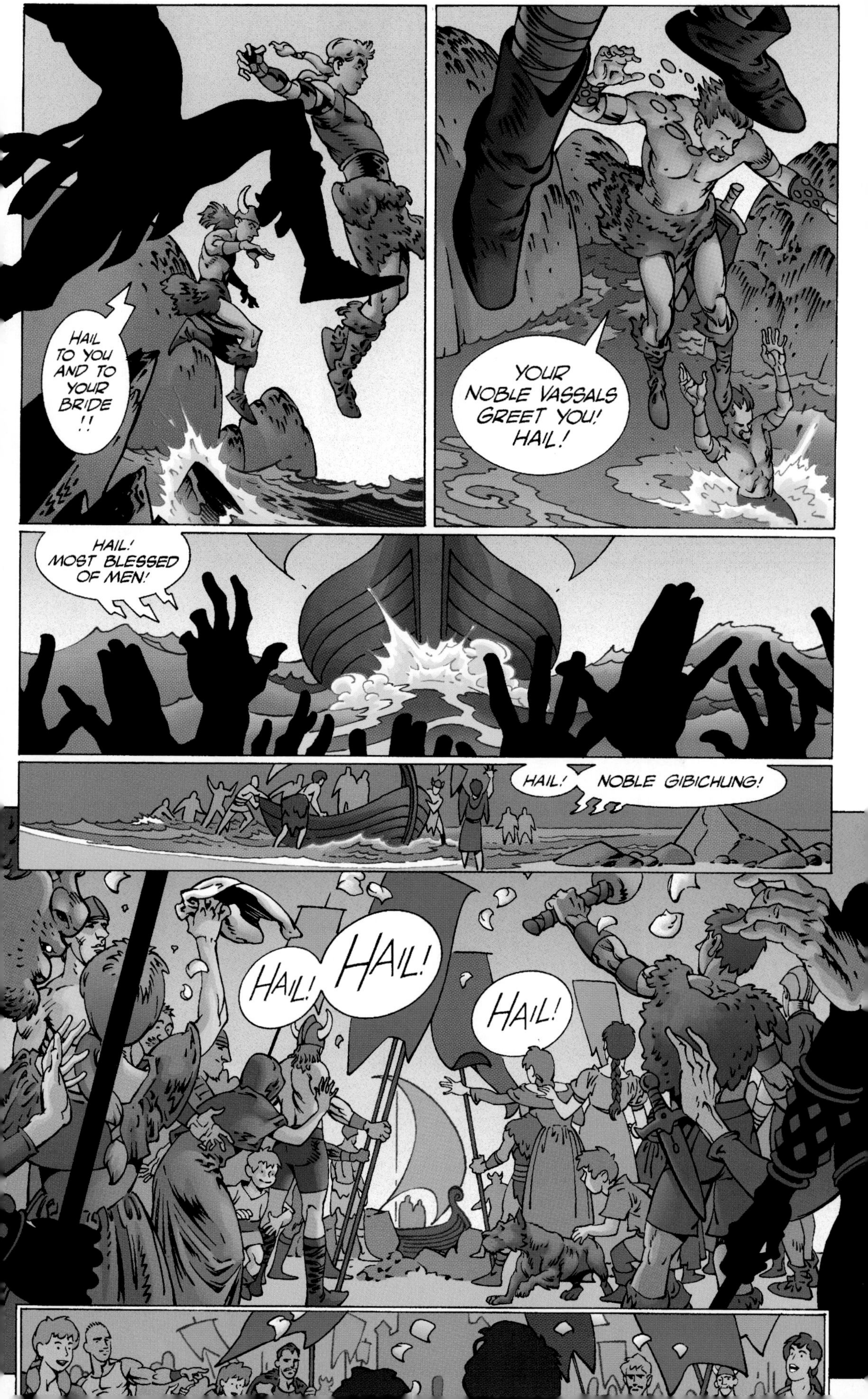
HAIL TO YOU AND TO YOUR BRIDE !!
YOUR NOBLE VASSALS GREET YOU! HAIL!
HAIL! MOST BLESSED OF MEN!
HAIL!
NOBLE GIBICHUNG!
HAIL!
HAIL!
HAIL!

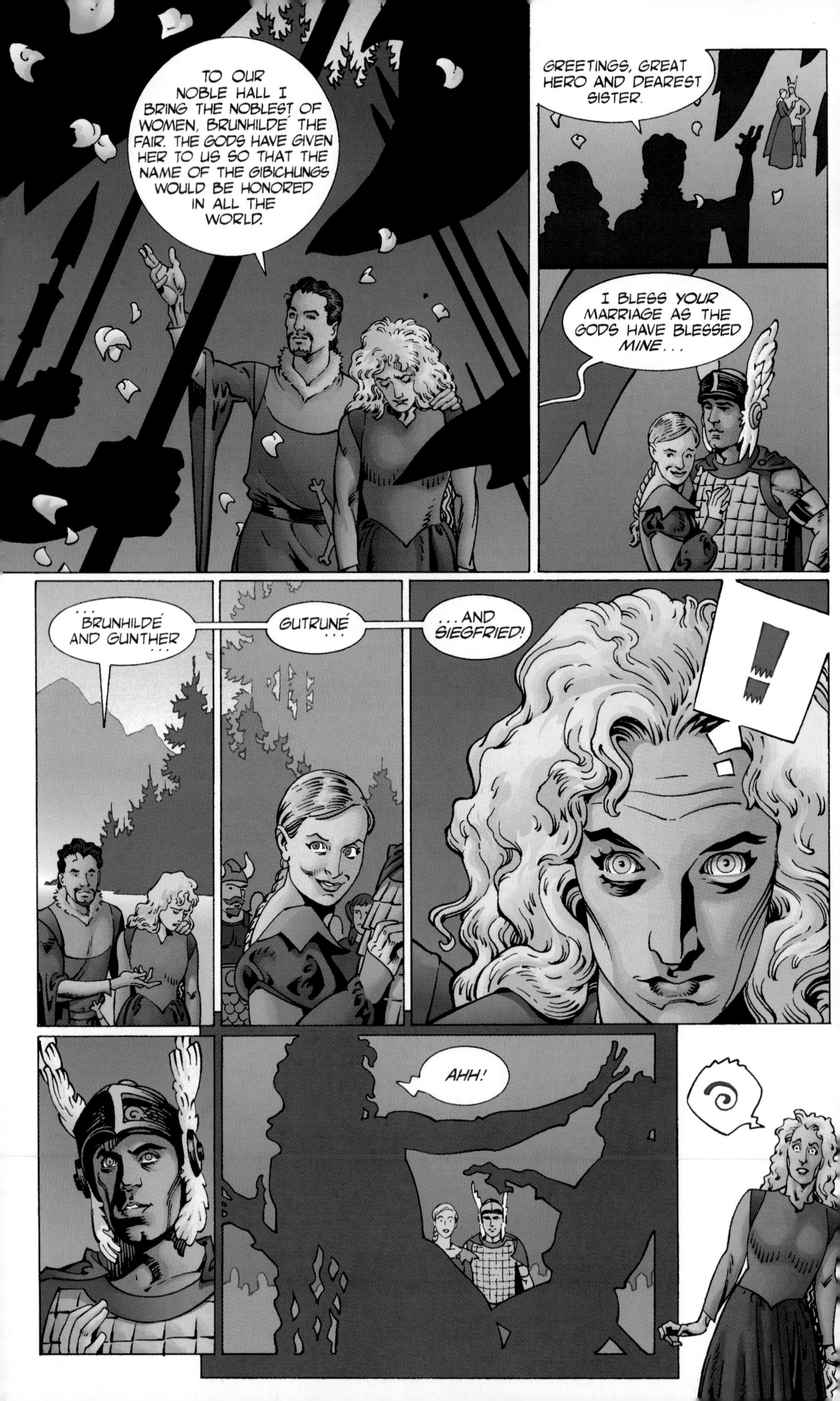

TO OUR NOBLE HALL I BRING THE NOBLEST OF WOMEN, BRUNHILDE THE FAIR. THE GODS HAVE GIVEN HER TO US SO THAT THE NAME OF THE GIBICHUNGS WOULD BE HONORED IN ALL THE WORLD.
GREETINGS, GREAT HERO AND DEAREST SISTER.
I BLESS *YOUR* MARRIAGE AS THE GODS HAVE BLESSED *MINE*...
...BRUNHILDE AND GUNTHER...
GUTRUNE...
...AND *SIEGFRIED!*
!
AHH!

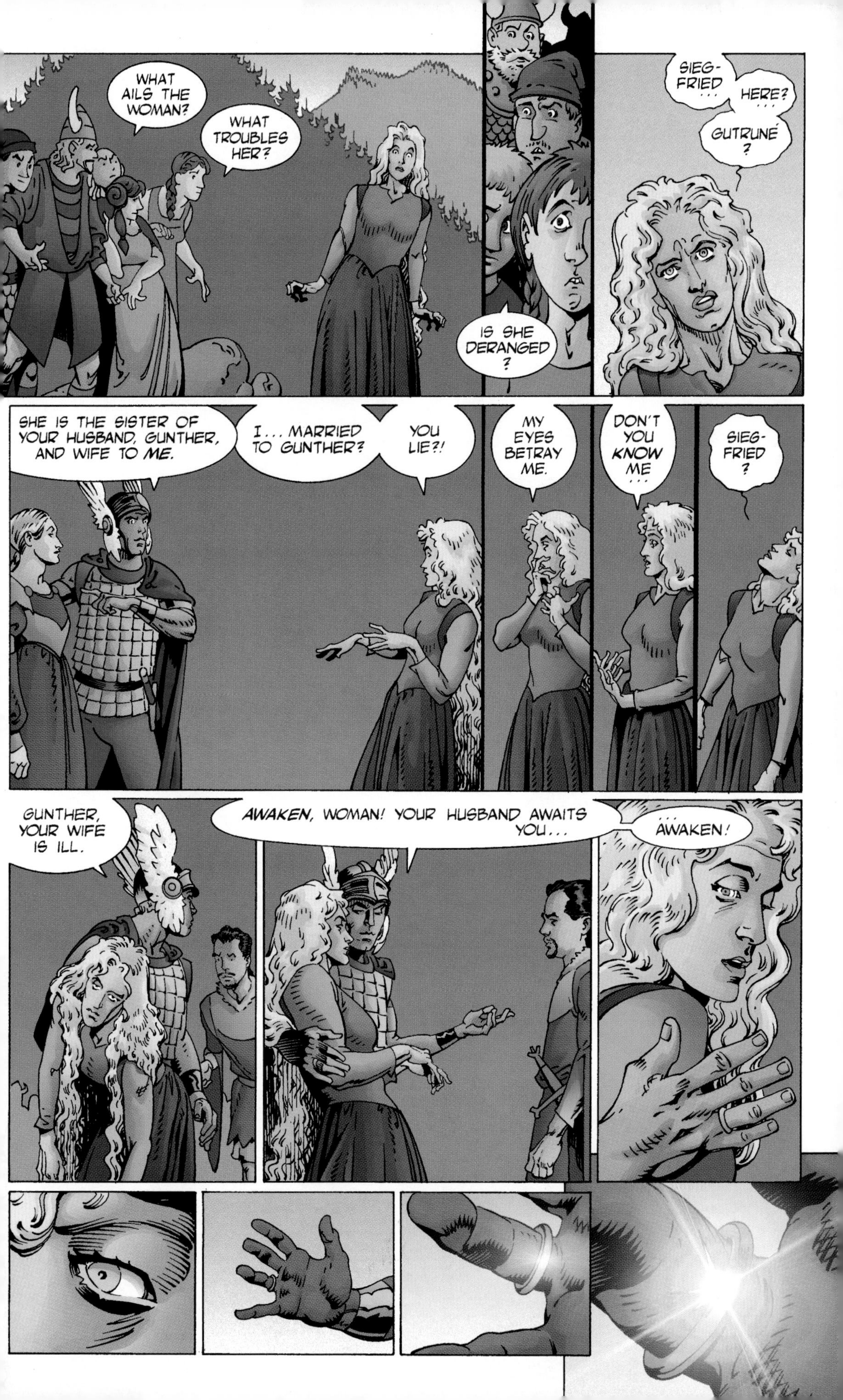
WHAT AILS THE WOMAN?
WHAT TROUBLES HER?
IS SHE DERANGED?
SIEG-FRIED . . .
HERE? . . .
GUTRUNE?
SHE IS THE SISTER OF YOUR HUSBAND, GUNTHER, AND WIFE TO ME.
I . . . MARRIED TO GUNTHER?
YOU LIE?!
MY EYES BETRAY ME.
DON'T YOU KNOW ME . . .
SIEG-FRIED?
GUNTHER, YOUR WIFE IS ILL.
AWAKEN, WOMAN! YOUR HUSBAND AWAITS YOU . . .
. . . AWAKEN!

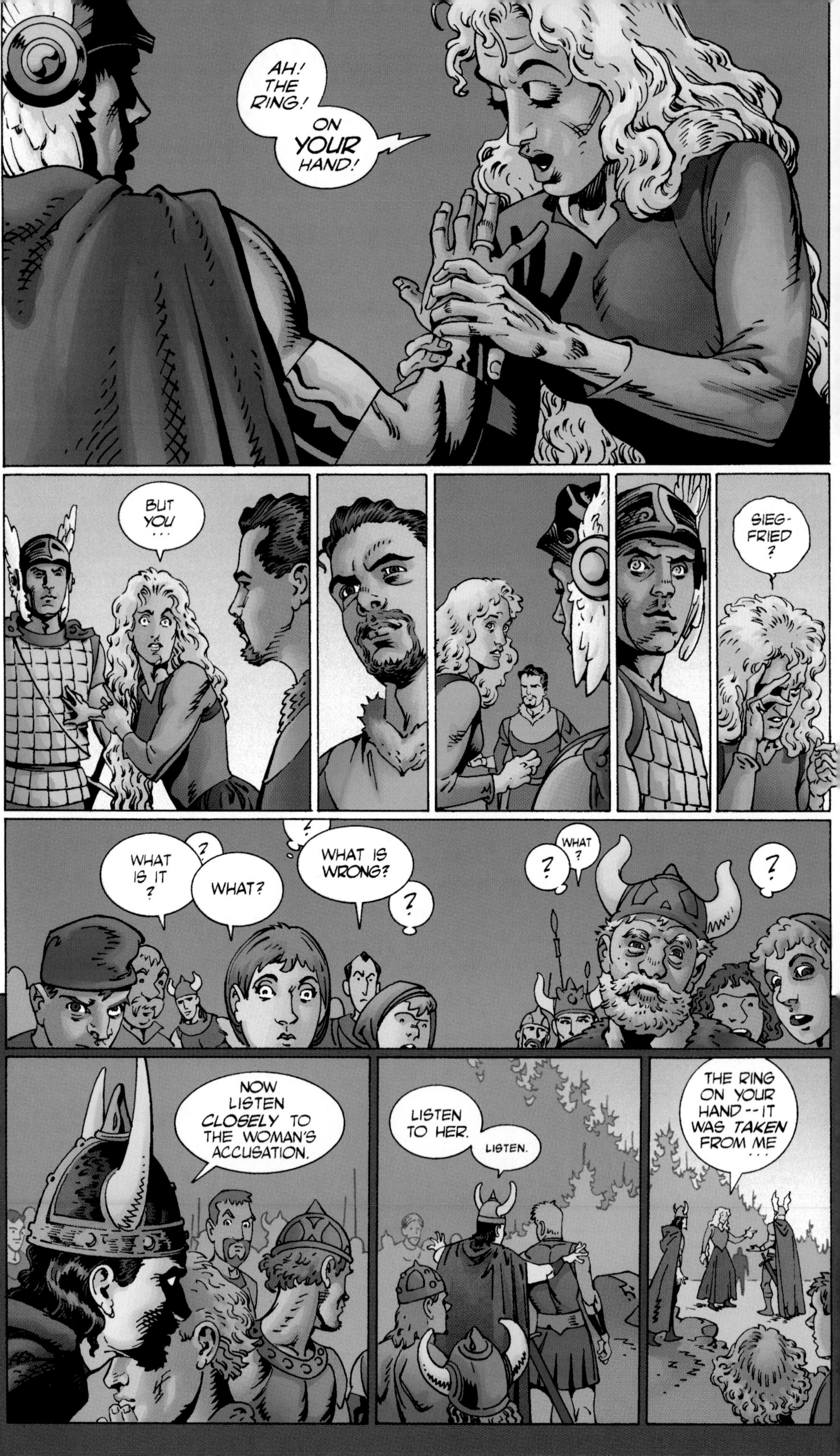
AH! THE RING!
ON YOUR HAND!
BUT YOU . . .
SIEG-FRIED ?
WHAT IS IT ?
?
WHAT?
?
WHAT IS WRONG?
?
?
WHAT ?
?
?
NOW LISTEN CLOSELY TO THE WOMAN'S ACCUSATION.
LISTEN TO HER.
LISTEN.
THE RING ON YOUR HAND -- IT WAS TAKEN FROM ME . . .

...BY *THIS MAN!*

BUT *HOW* DID IT COME TO *YOU?*

GUNTHER GAVE ME NO RING.

BUT GUNTHER, *YOU* TOOK IT FROM *ME* ON OUR BRIDAL NIGHT. YOU MUST DEMAND THE RETURN OF YOUR *POSSESSION.*

THE MAN GOT NO RING FROM *ME.*

YET *YOU* KNOW OF IT?

WHERE IS THE RING YOU WRESTED FROM MY HAND? *SPEAK!* HOW CAME IT TO...

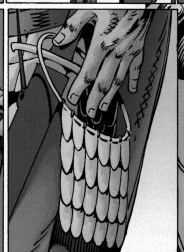

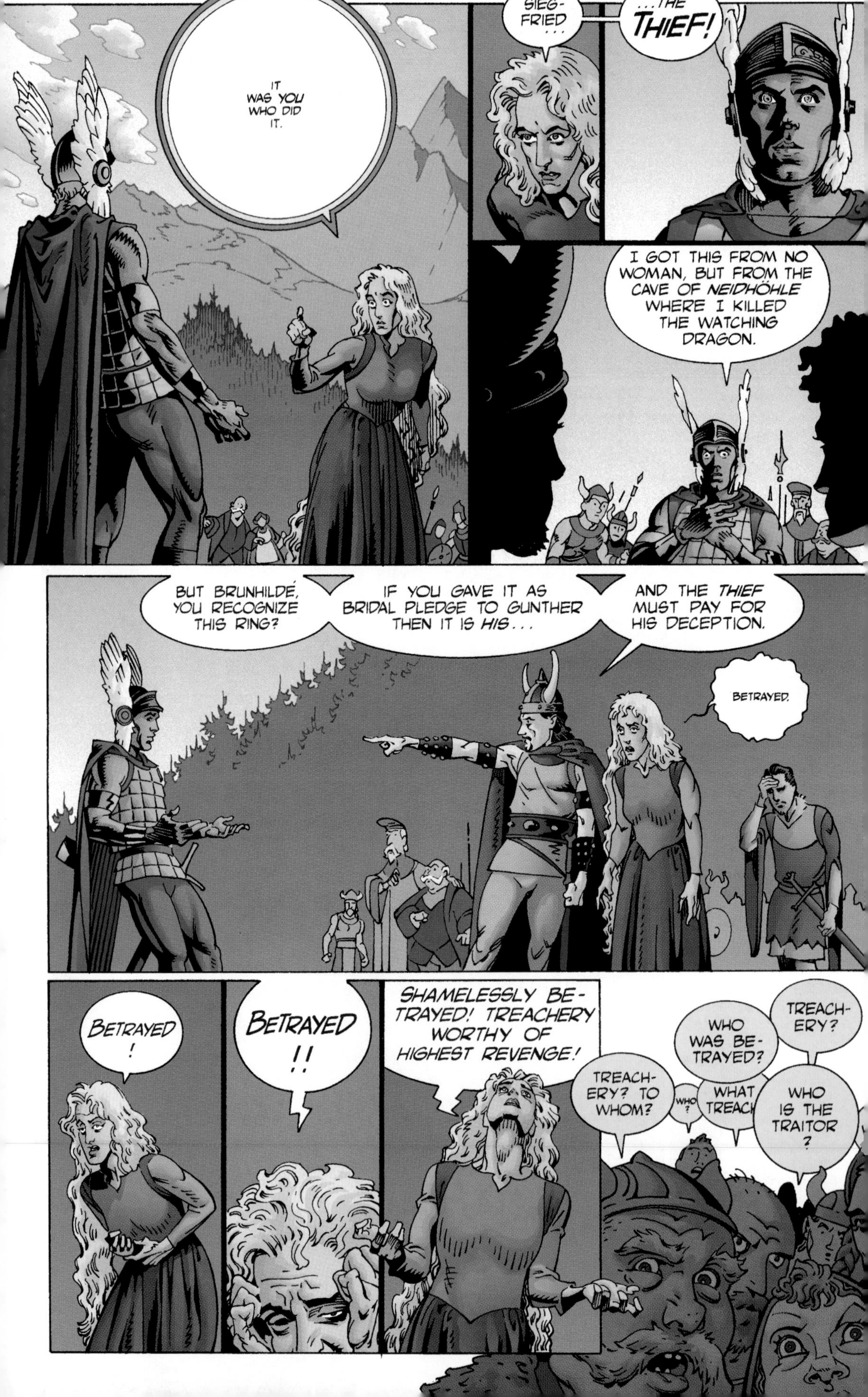

IT WAS YOU WHO DID IT.
SIEG-FRIED . . .
. . . THE THIEF!
I GOT THIS FROM NO WOMAN, BUT FROM THE CAVE OF NEIDHÖHLE WHERE I KILLED THE WATCHING DRAGON.
BUT BRUNHILDÉ, YOU RECOGNIZE THIS RING?
IF YOU GAVE IT AS BRIDAL PLEDGE TO GUNTHER THEN IT IS HIS . . .
AND THE THIEF MUST PAY FOR HIS DECEPTION.
BETRAYED.
BETRAYED!
BETRAYED!!
SHAMELESSLY BE-TRAYED! TREACHERY WORTHY OF HIGHEST REVENGE!
TREACH-ERY? TO WHOM?
WHO?
WHO WAS BE-TRAYED?
WHAT TREACH
TREACH-ERY?
WHO IS THE TRAITOR?

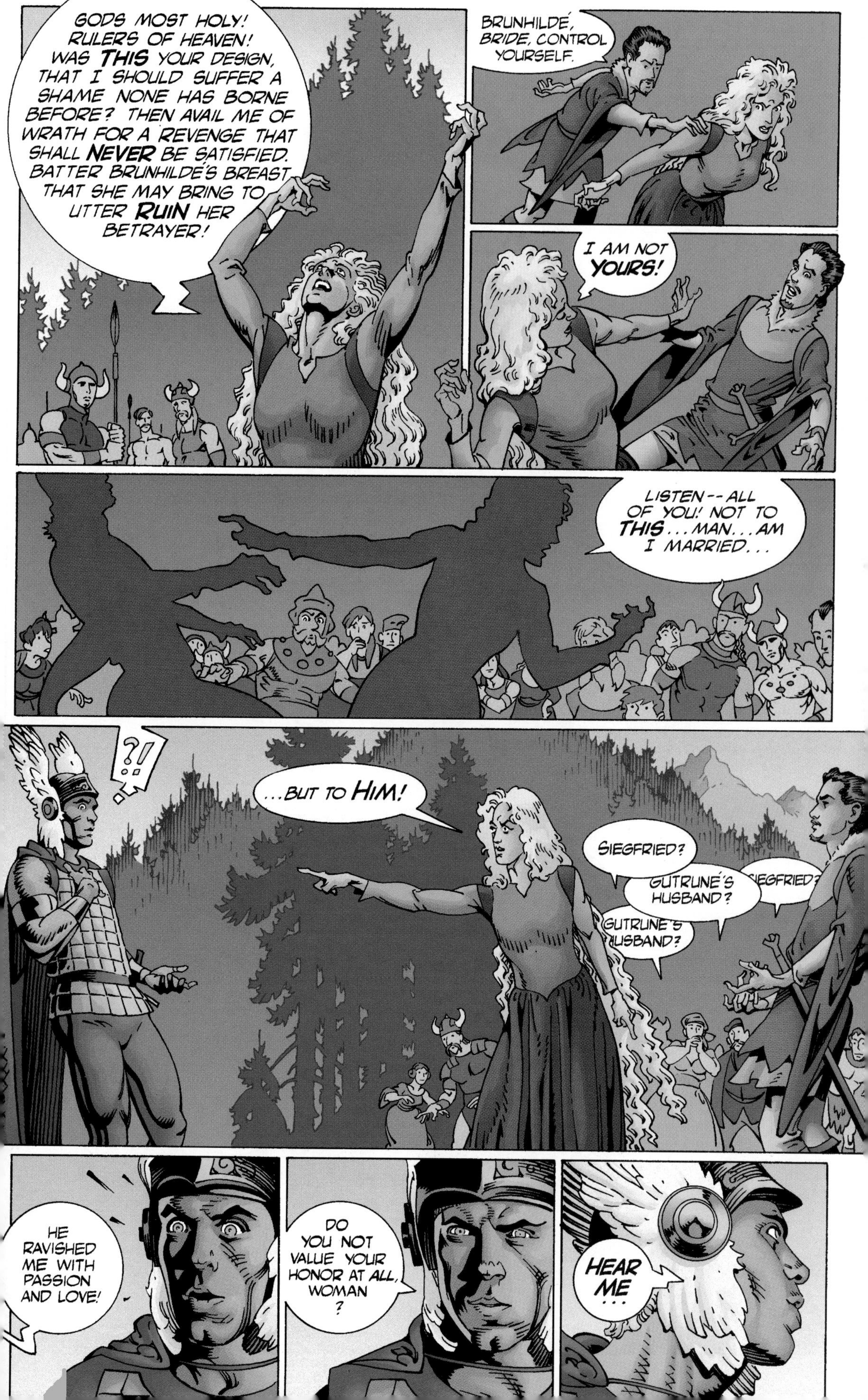
GODS MOST HOLY! RULERS OF HEAVEN! WAS THIS YOUR DESIGN, THAT I SHOULD SUFFER A SHAME NONE HAS BORNE BEFORE? THEN AVAIL ME OF WRATH FOR A REVENGE THAT SHALL NEVER BE SATISFIED. BATTER BRUNHILDE'S BREAST THAT SHE MAY BRING TO UTTER RUIN HER BETRAYER!
BRUNHILDE, BRIDE, CONTROL YOURSELF.
I AM NOT YOURS!
LISTEN--ALL OF YOU! NOT TO THIS...MAN...AM I MARRIED...
?!
...BUT TO HIM!
SIEGFRIED?
GUTRUNE'S HUSBAND?
SIEGFRIED?
GUTRUNE'S HUSBAND?
HE RAVISHED ME WITH PASSION AND LOVE!
DO YOU NOT VALUE YOUR HONOR AT ALL, WOMAN?
HEAR ME...

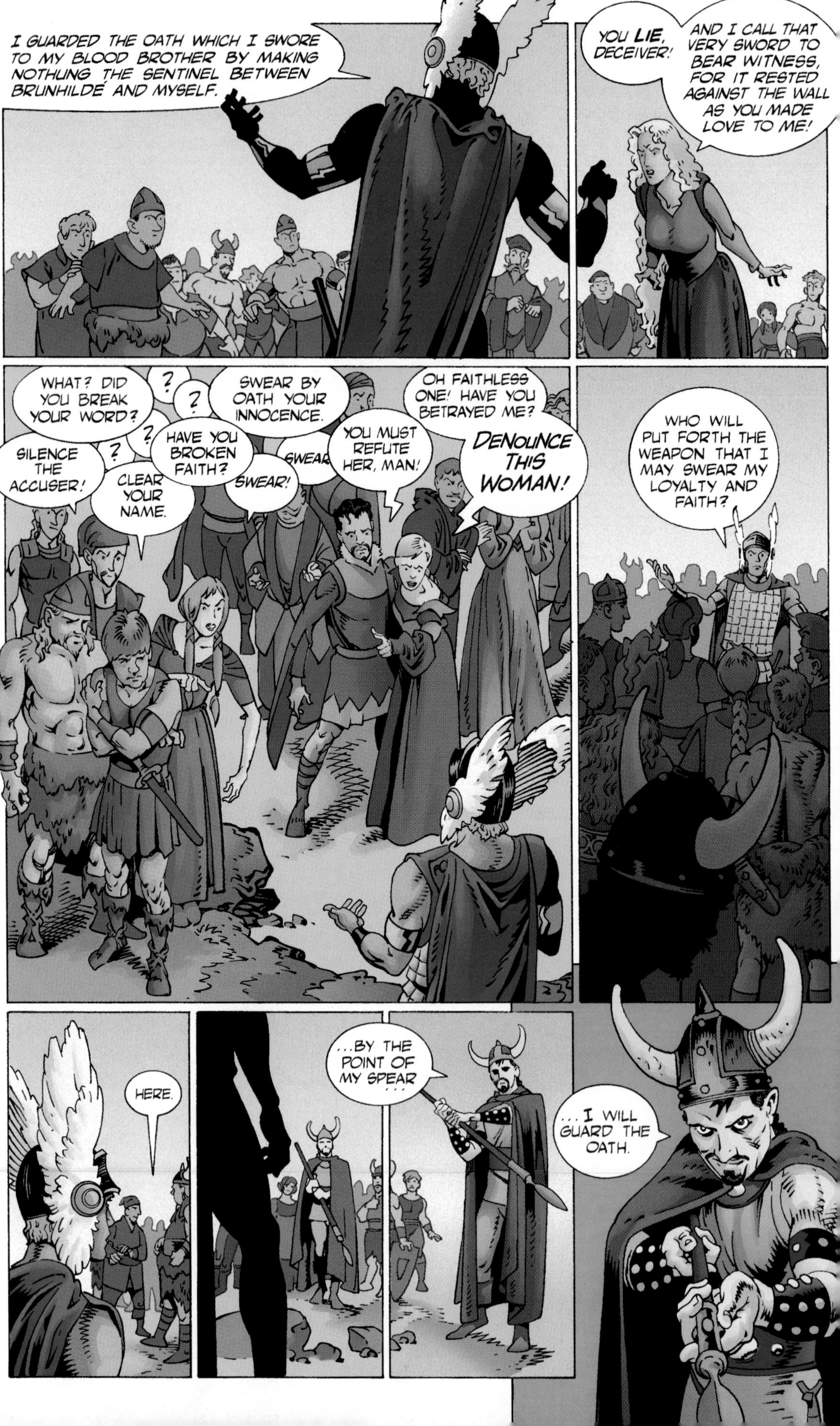

I GUARDED THE OATH WHICH I SWORE TO MY BLOOD BROTHER BY MAKING NOTHUNG THE SENTINEL BETWEEN BRUNHILDE AND MYSELF.
YOU LIE, DECEIVER!
AND I CALL THAT VERY SWORD TO BEAR WITNESS, FOR IT RESTED AGAINST THE WALL AS YOU MADE LOVE TO ME!
WHAT? DID YOU BREAK YOUR WORD?
?
?
?
?
SILENCE THE ACCUSER!
CLEAR YOUR NAME.
HAVE YOU BROKEN FAITH?
SWEAR BY OATH YOUR INNOCENCE.
SWEAR!
SWEAR
YOU MUST REFUTE HER, MAN!
OH FAITHLESS ONE! HAVE YOU BETRAYED ME?
DENOUNCE THIS WOMAN!
WHO WILL PUT FORTH THE WEAPON THAT I MAY SWEAR MY LOYALTY AND FAITH?
HERE.
...BY THE POINT OF MY SPEAR ...
... I WILL GUARD THE OATH.

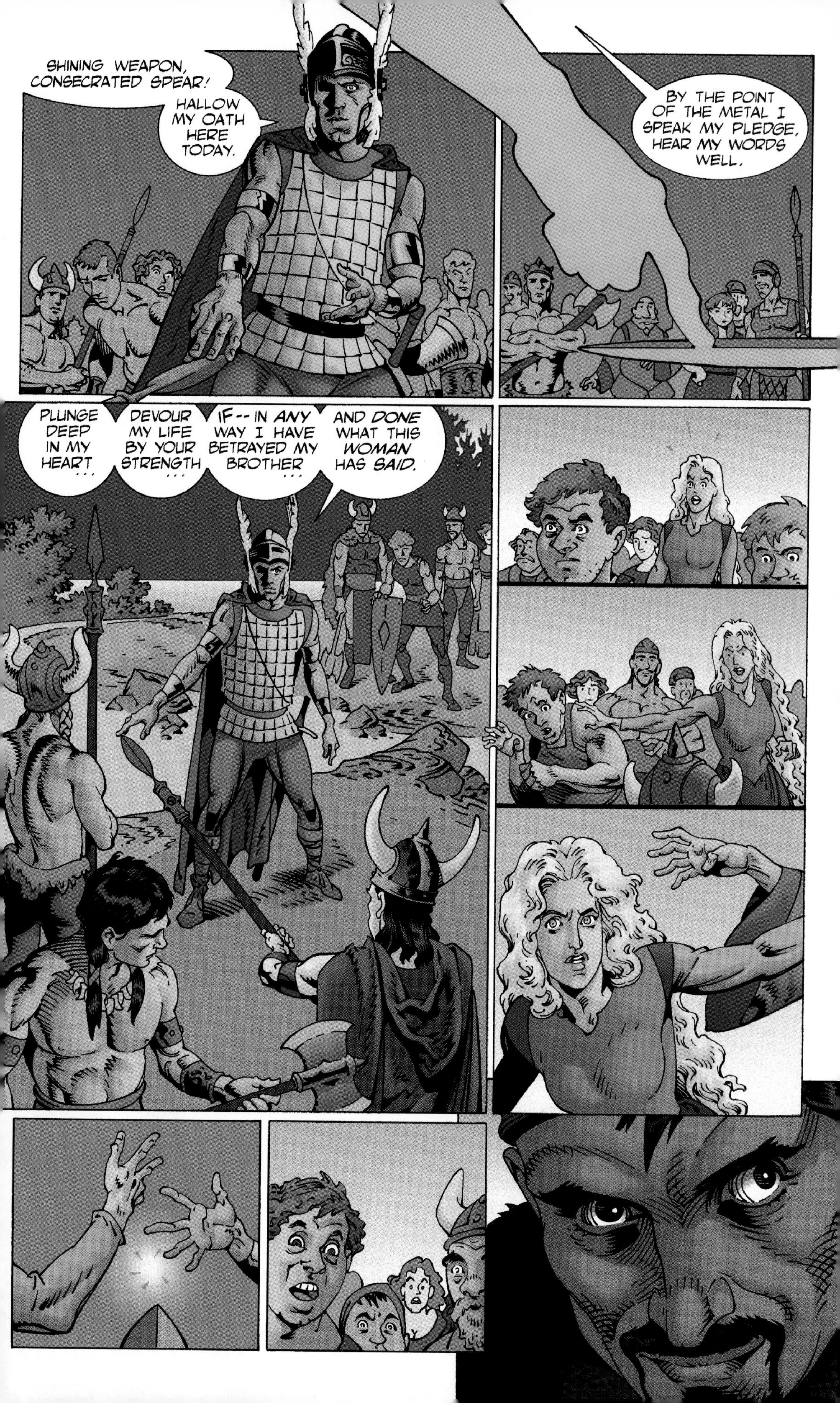
SHINING WEAPON, CONSECRATED SPEAR!
HALLOW MY OATH HERE TODAY.
BY THE POINT OF THE METAL I SPEAK MY PLEDGE, HEAR MY WORDS WELL.
PLUNGE DEEP IN MY HEART ...
DEVOUR MY LIFE BY YOUR STRENGTH ...
IF-- IN ANY WAY I HAVE BETRAYED MY BROTHER ...
AND DONE WHAT THIS WOMAN HAS SAID.

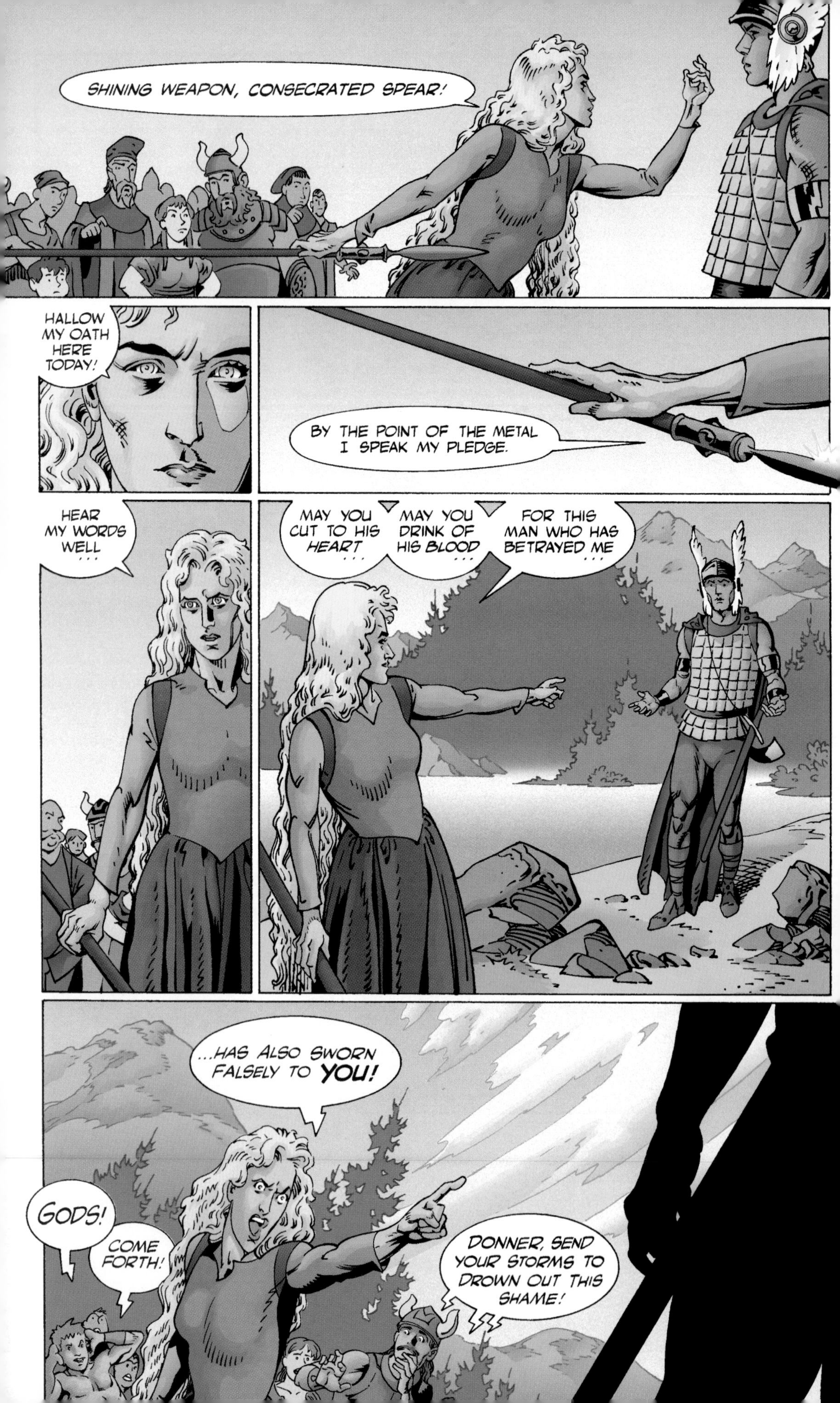
SHINING WEAPON, CONSECRATED SPEAR!
HALLOW MY OATH HERE TODAY!
BY THE POINT OF THE METAL I SPEAK MY PLEDGE.
HEAR MY WORDS WELL . . .
MAY YOU CUT TO HIS HEART . . .
MAY YOU DRINK OF HIS BLOOD . . .
FOR THIS MAN WHO HAS BETRAYED ME . . .
...HAS ALSO SWORN FALSELY TO YOU!
GODS!
COME FORTH!
DONNER, SEND YOUR STORMS TO DROWN OUT THIS SHAME!

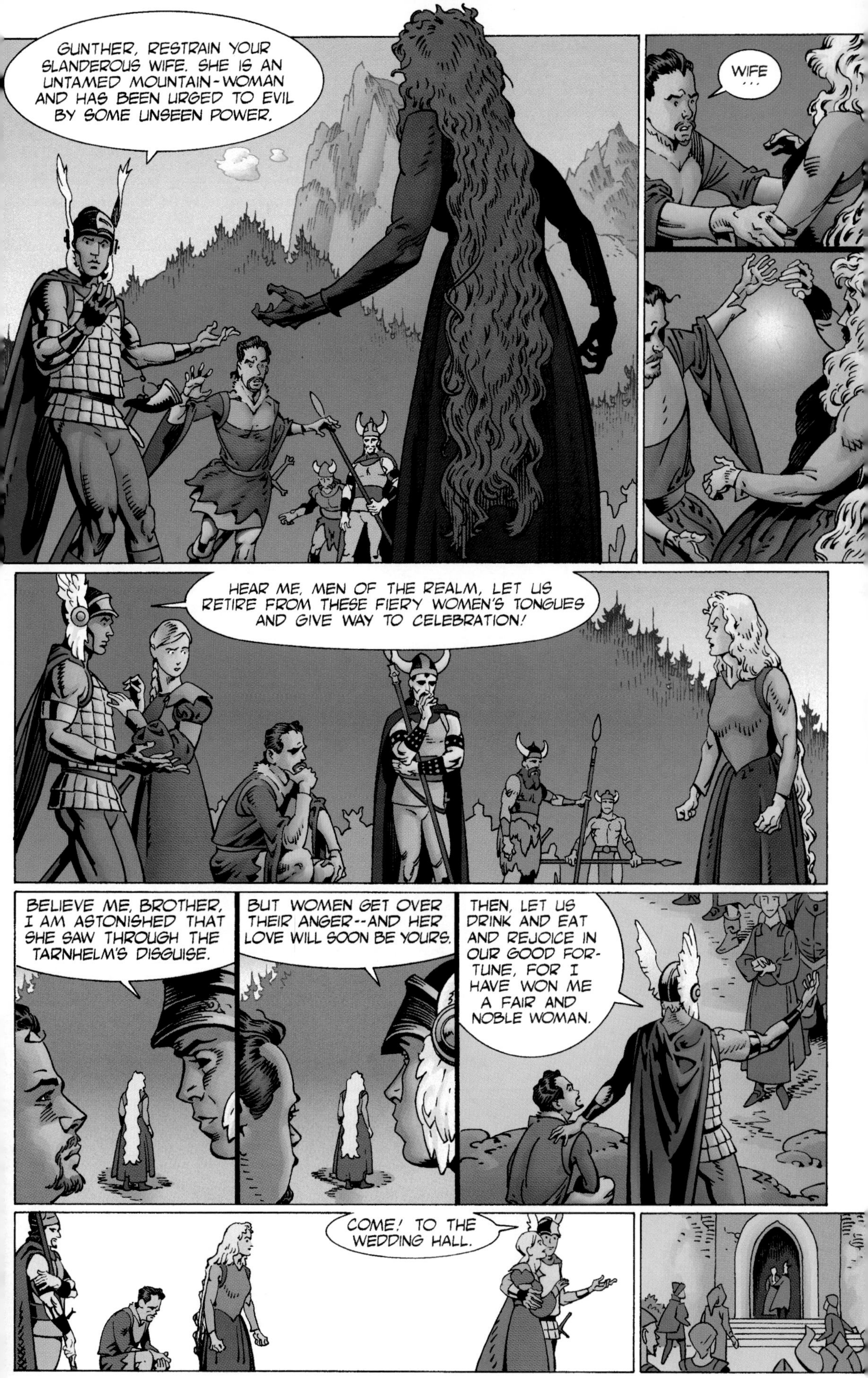
GUNTHER, RESTRAIN YOUR SLANDEROUS WIFE. SHE IS AN UNTAMED MOUNTAIN-WOMAN AND HAS BEEN URGED TO EVIL BY SOME UNSEEN POWER.
WIFE . . .
HEAR ME, MEN OF THE REALM, LET US RETIRE FROM THESE FIERY WOMEN'S TONGUES AND GIVE WAY TO CELEBRATION!
BELIEVE ME, BROTHER, I AM ASTONISHED THAT SHE SAW THROUGH THE TARNHELM'S DISGUISE.
BUT WOMEN GET OVER THEIR ANGER--AND HER LOVE WILL SOON BE YOURS.
THEN, LET US DRINK AND EAT AND REJOICE IN OUR GOOD FORTUNE, FOR I HAVE WON ME A FAIR AND NOBLE WOMAN.
COME! TO THE WEDDING HALL.

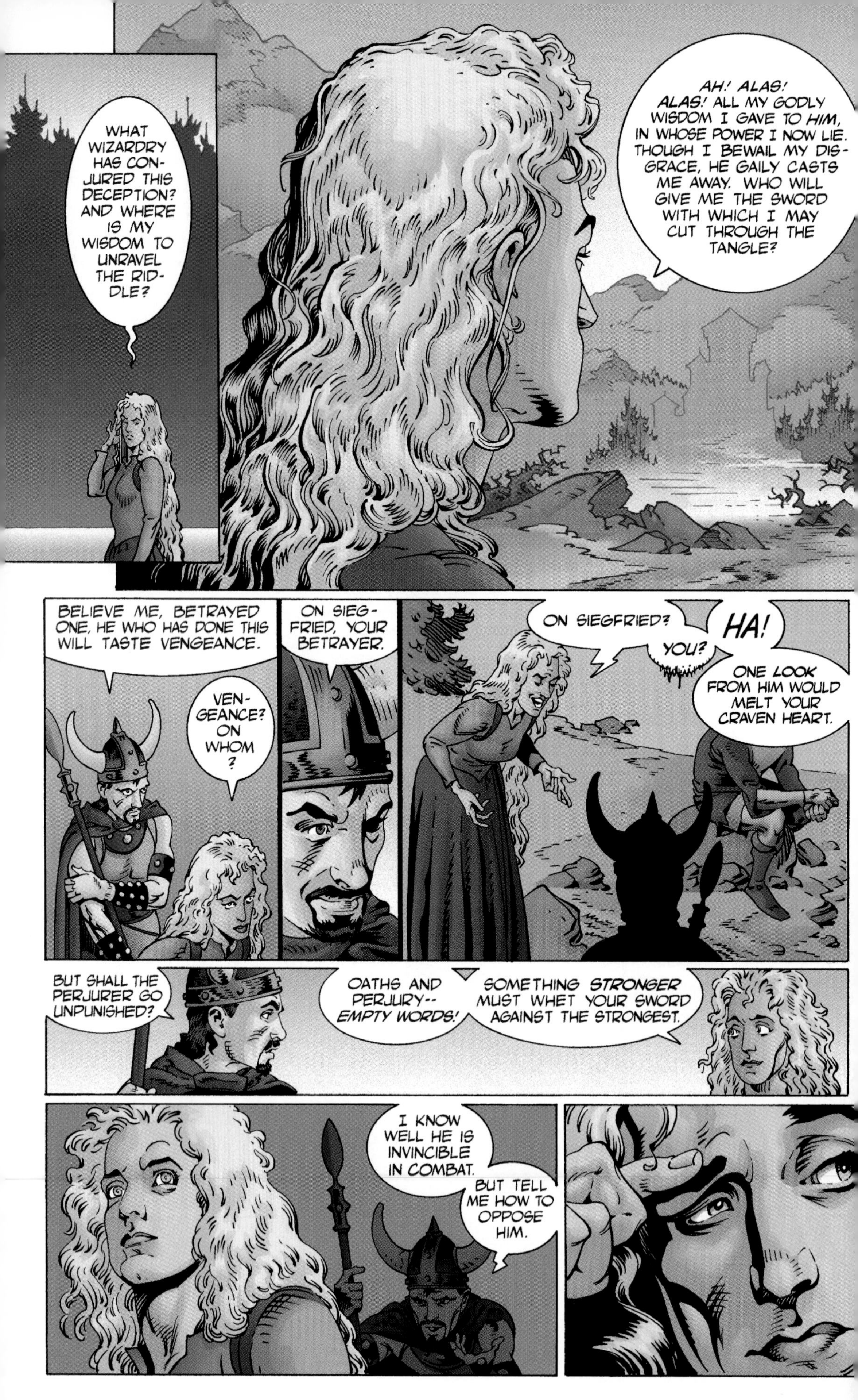
WHAT WIZARDRY HAS CONJURED THIS DECEPTION? AND WHERE IS MY WISDOM TO UNRAVEL THE RIDDLE?
AH! ALAS! ALAS! ALL MY GODLY WISDOM I GAVE TO HIM, IN WHOSE POWER I NOW LIE. THOUGH I BEWAIL MY DISGRACE, HE GAILY CASTS ME AWAY. WHO WILL GIVE ME THE SWORD WITH WHICH I MAY CUT THROUGH THE TANGLE?
BELIEVE ME, BETRAYED ONE, HE WHO HAS DONE THIS WILL TASTE VENGEANCE.
VENGEANCE? ON WHOM?
ON SIEGFRIED, YOUR BETRAYER.
ON SIEGFRIED?
YOU?
HA!
ONE LOOK FROM HIM WOULD MELT YOUR CRAVEN HEART.
BUT SHALL THE PERJURER GO UNPUNISHED?
OATHS AND PERJURY-- EMPTY WORDS!
SOMETHING STRONGER MUST WHET YOUR SWORD AGAINST THE STRONGEST.
I KNOW WELL HE IS INVINCIBLE IN COMBAT.
BUT TELL ME HOW TO OPPOSE HIM.

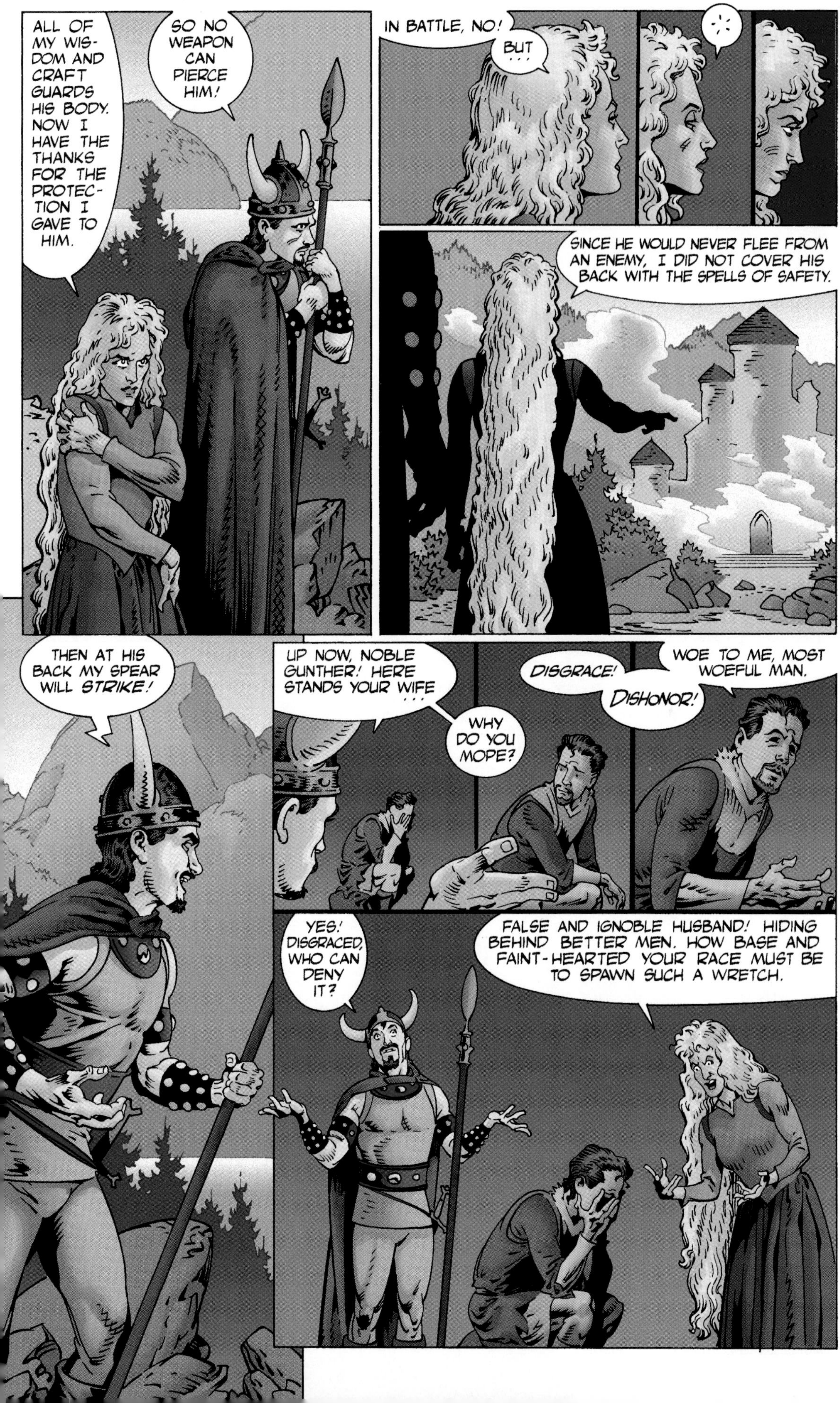

ALL OF MY WISDOM AND CRAFT GUARDS HIS BODY. NOW I HAVE THE THANKS FOR THE PROTECTION I GAVE TO HIM.
SO NO WEAPON CAN PIERCE HIM!
IN BATTLE, NO!
BUT . . .
. . .
SINCE HE WOULD NEVER FLEE FROM AN ENEMY, I DID NOT COVER HIS BACK WITH THE SPELLS OF SAFETY.
THEN AT HIS BACK MY SPEAR WILL STRIKE!
UP NOW, NOBLE GUNTHER! HERE STANDS YOUR WIFE . . .
WHY DO YOU MOPE?
DISGRACE!
DISHONOR!
WOE TO ME, MOST WOEFUL MAN.
YES! DISGRACED, WHO CAN DENY IT?
FALSE AND IGNOBLE HUSBAND! HIDING BEHIND BETTER MEN. HOW BASE AND FAINT-HEARTED YOUR RACE MUST BE TO SPAWN SUCH A WRETCH.

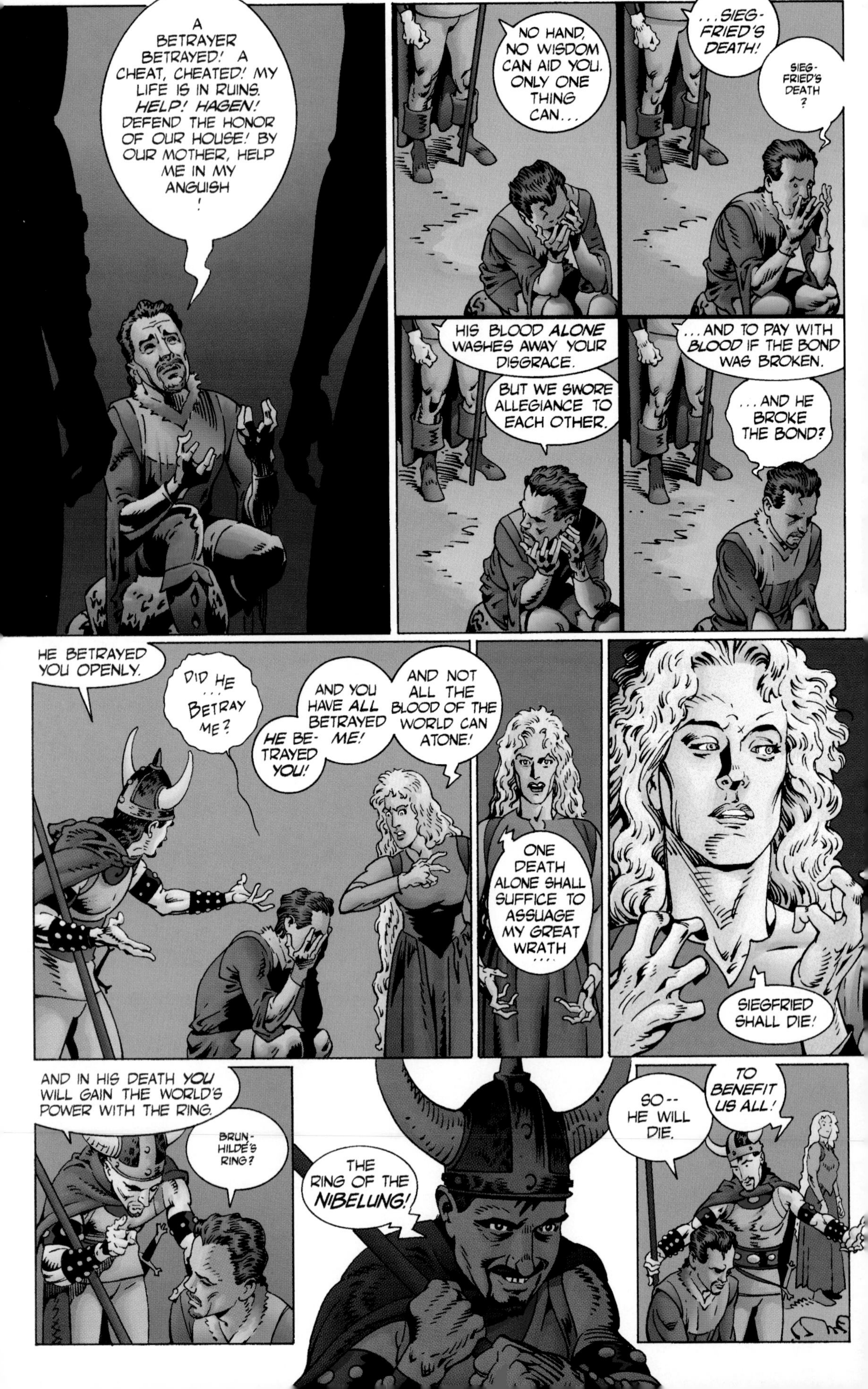
A BETRAYER BETRAYED! A CHEAT, CHEATED! MY LIFE IS IN RUINS. HELP! HAGEN! DEFEND THE HONOR OF OUR HOUSE! BY OUR MOTHER, HELP ME IN MY ANGUISH!
NO HAND, NO WISDOM CAN AID YOU. ONLY ONE THING CAN...
...SIEG-FRIED'S DEATH!
SIEG-FRIED'S DEATH?
HIS BLOOD ALONE WASHES AWAY YOUR DISGRACE.
BUT WE SWORE ALLEGIANCE TO EACH OTHER.
...AND TO PAY WITH BLOOD IF THE BOND WAS BROKEN.
...AND HE BROKE THE BOND?
HE BETRAYED YOU OPENLY.
DID HE ... BETRAY ME?
AND YOU HAVE ALL BETRAYED ME!
HE BE-TRAYED YOU!
AND NOT ALL THE BLOOD OF THE WORLD CAN ATONE!
ONE DEATH ALONE SHALL SUFFICE TO ASSUAGE MY GREAT WRATH...
SIEGFRIED SHALL DIE!
AND IN HIS DEATH YOU WILL GAIN THE WORLD'S POWER WITH THE RING.
BRUN-HILDE'S RING?
THE RING OF THE NIBELUNG!
SO-- HE WILL DIE.
TO BENEFIT US ALL!

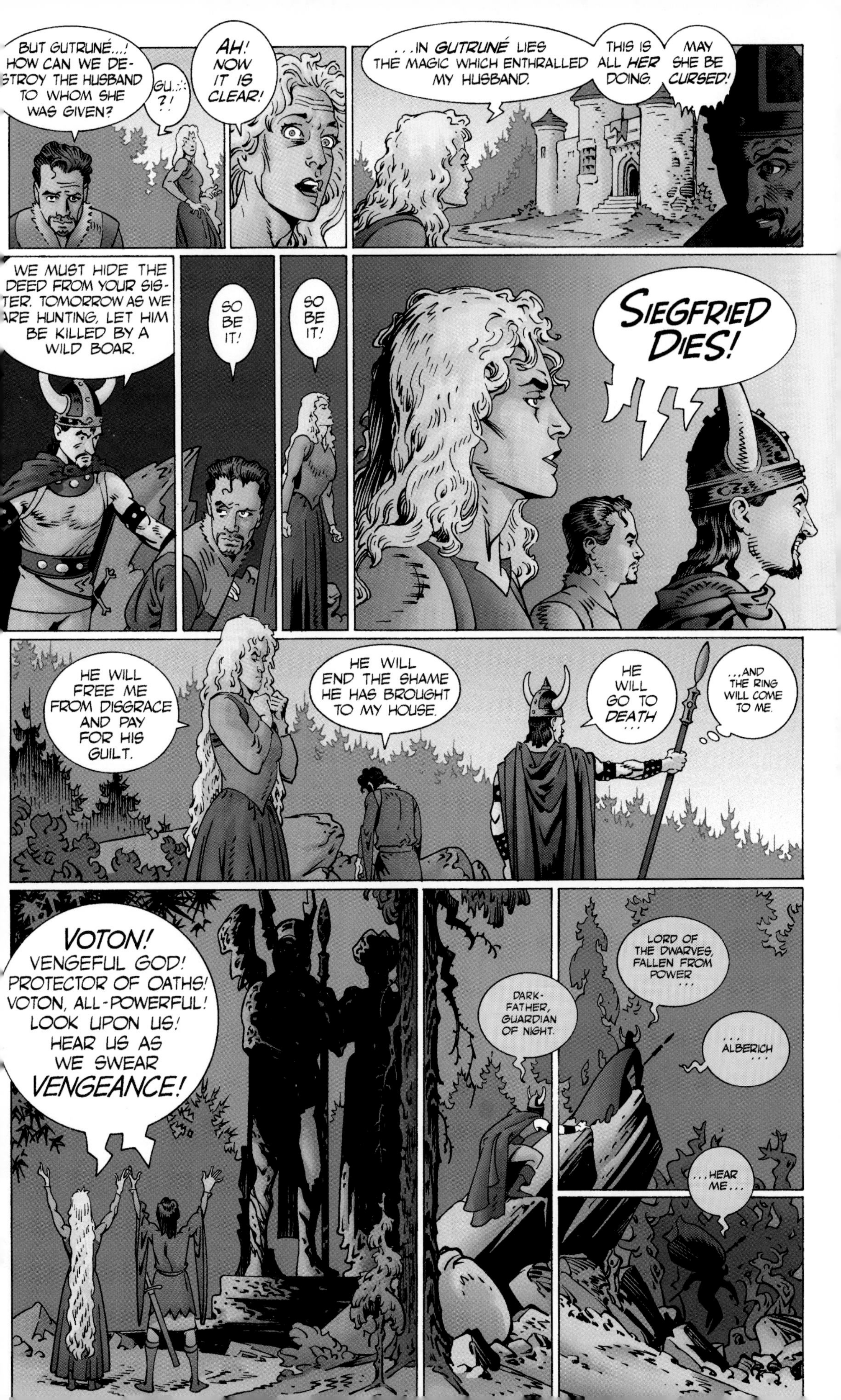

BUT GUTRUNÉ...! HOW CAN WE DESTROY THE HUSBAND TO WHOM SHE WAS GIVEN?
GU...?!
AH! NOW IT IS CLEAR!
...IN GUTRUNÉ LIES THE MAGIC WHICH ENTHRALLED MY HUSBAND.
THIS IS ALL HER DOING.
MAY SHE BE CURSED!
WE MUST HIDE THE DEED FROM YOUR SISTER. TOMORROW AS WE ARE HUNTING, LET HIM BE KILLED BY A WILD BOAR.
SO BE IT!
SO BE IT!
SIEGFRIED DIES!
HE WILL FREE ME FROM DISGRACE AND PAY FOR HIS GUILT.
HE WILL END THE SHAME HE HAS BROUGHT TO MY HOUSE.
HE WILL GO TO DEATH...
...AND THE RING WILL COME TO ME.
VOTON! VENGEFUL GOD! PROTECTOR OF OATHS! VOTON, ALL-POWERFUL! LOOK UPON US! HEAR US AS WE SWEAR VENGEANCE!
DARK-FATHER, GUARDIAN OF NIGHT.
LORD OF THE DWARVES, FALLEN FROM POWER...
...ALBERICH...
...HEAR ME...

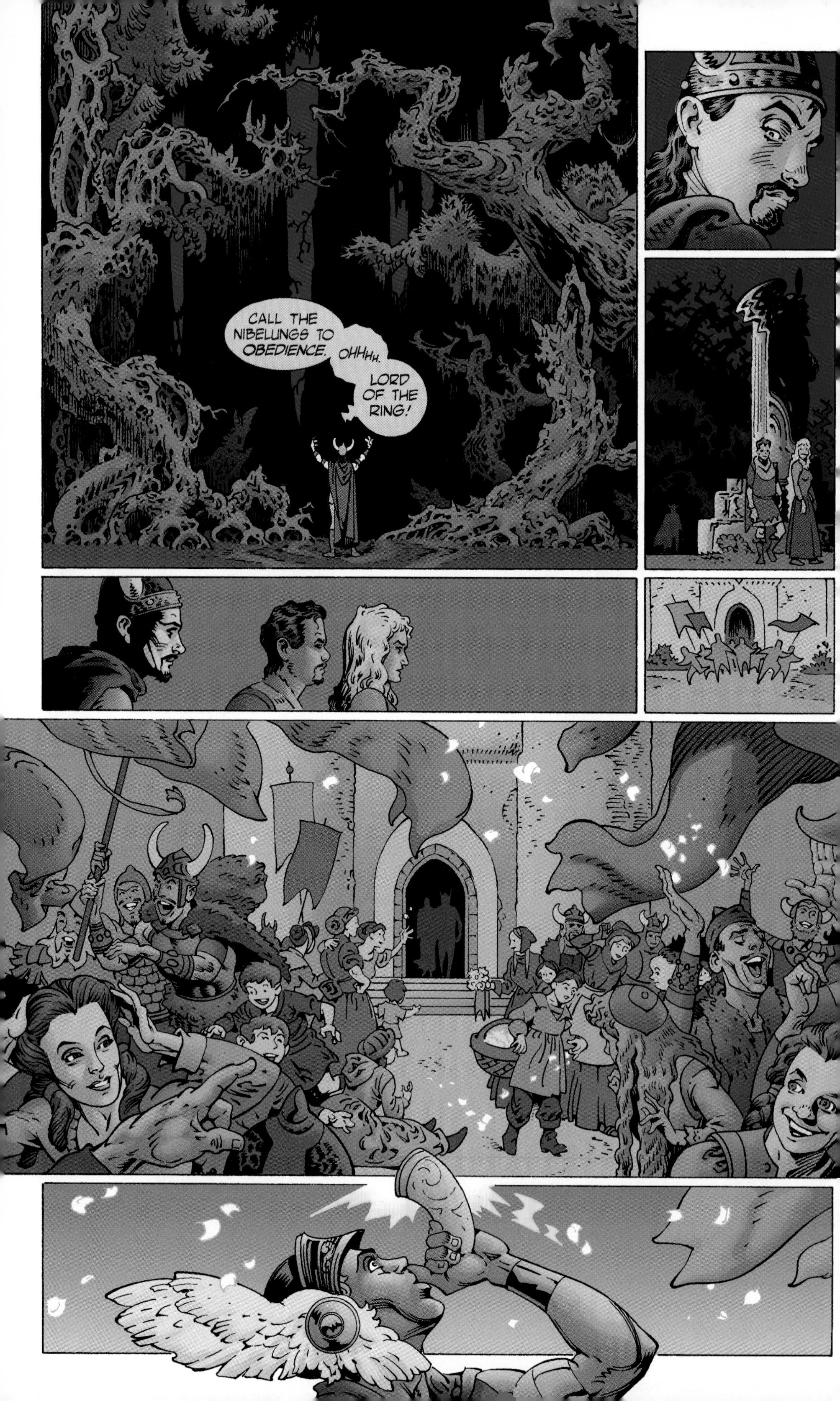
CALL THE NIBELUNGS TO OBEDIENCE. OHHHH.
LORD OF THE RING!

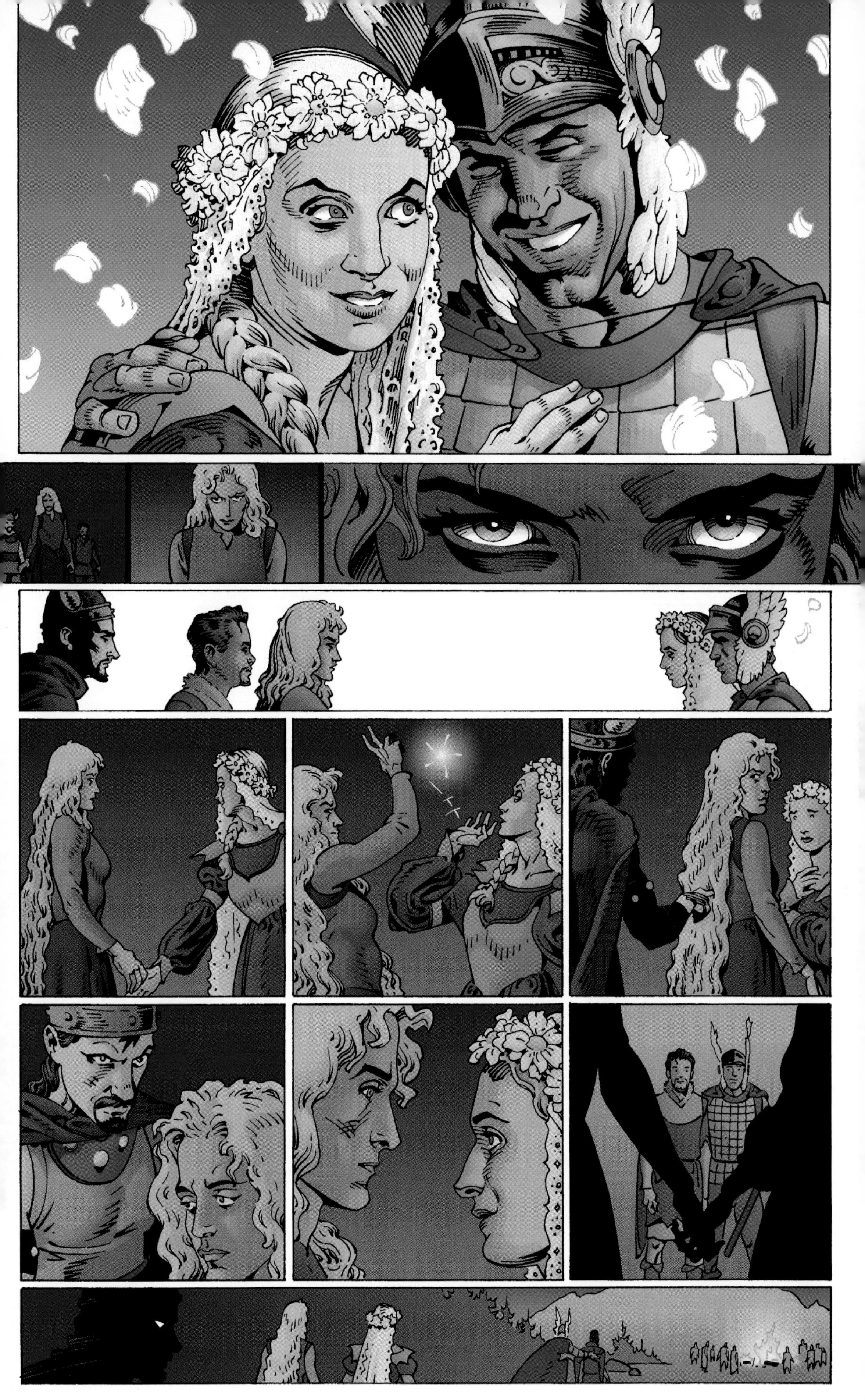

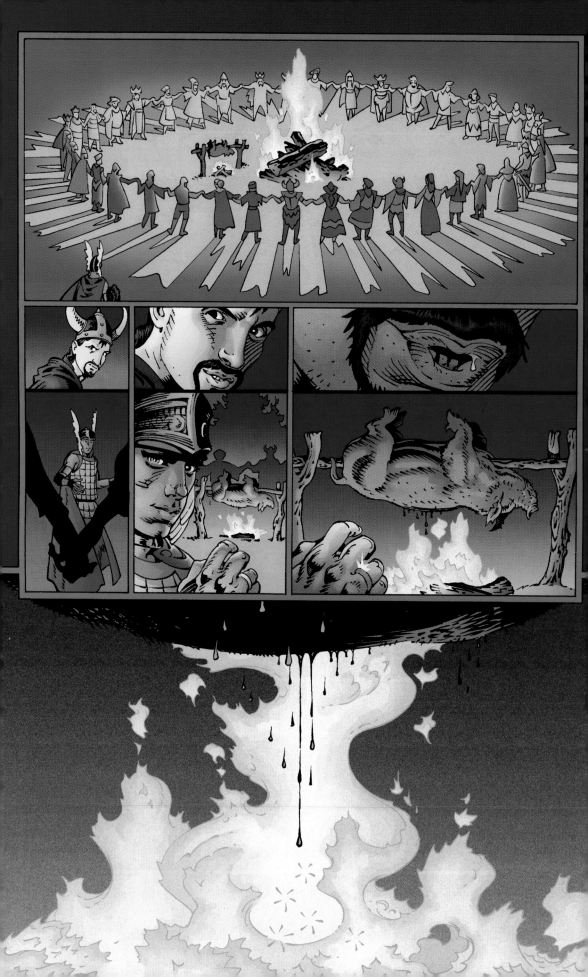

GOTTERDAMMERUNG

THE TWILIGHT OF THE GODS

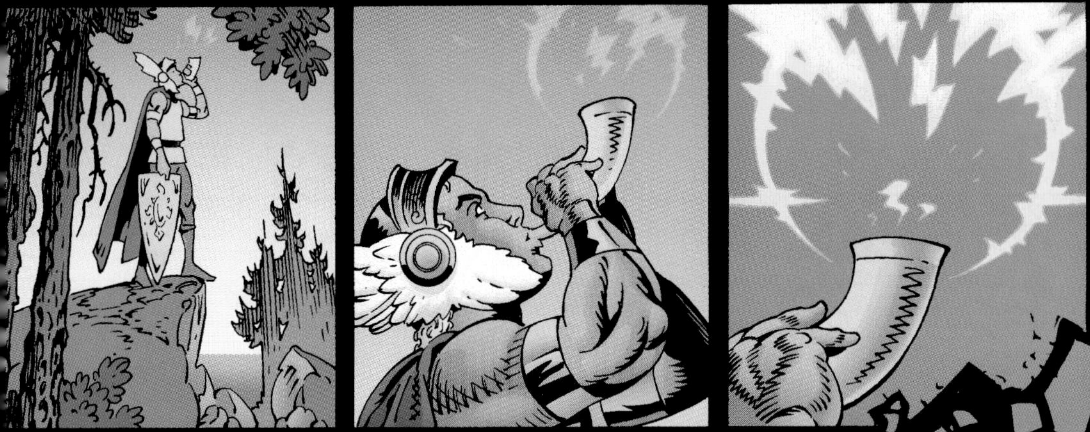

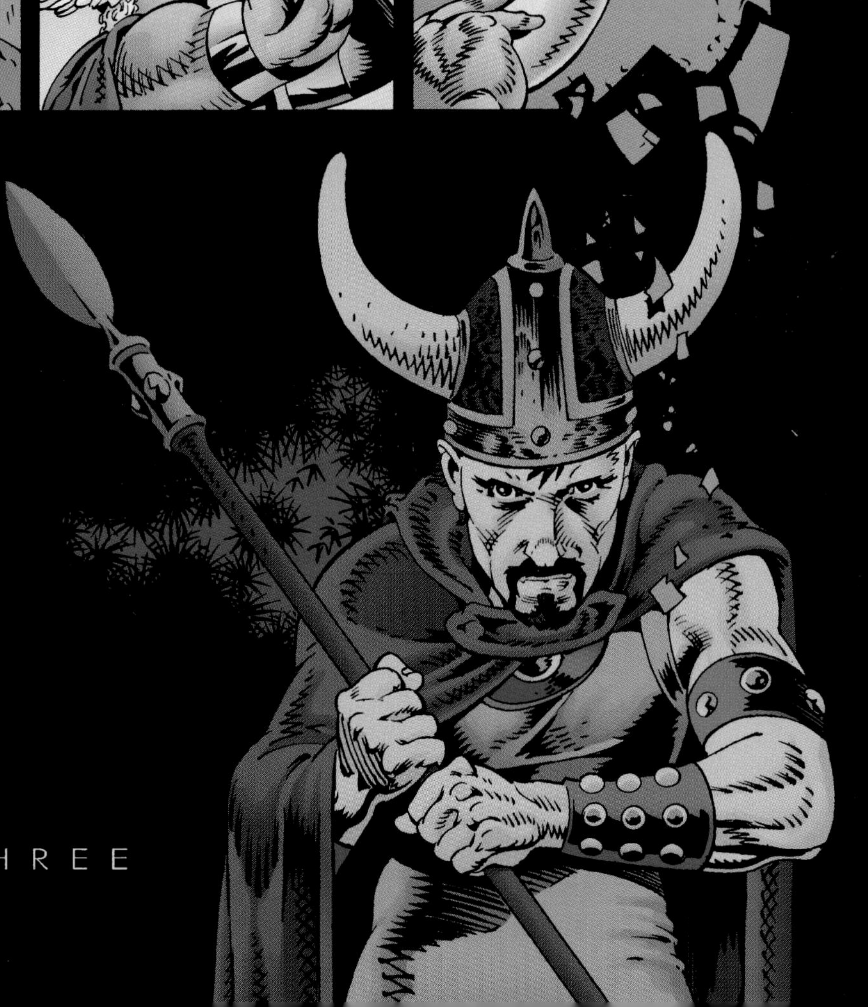

PART THREE

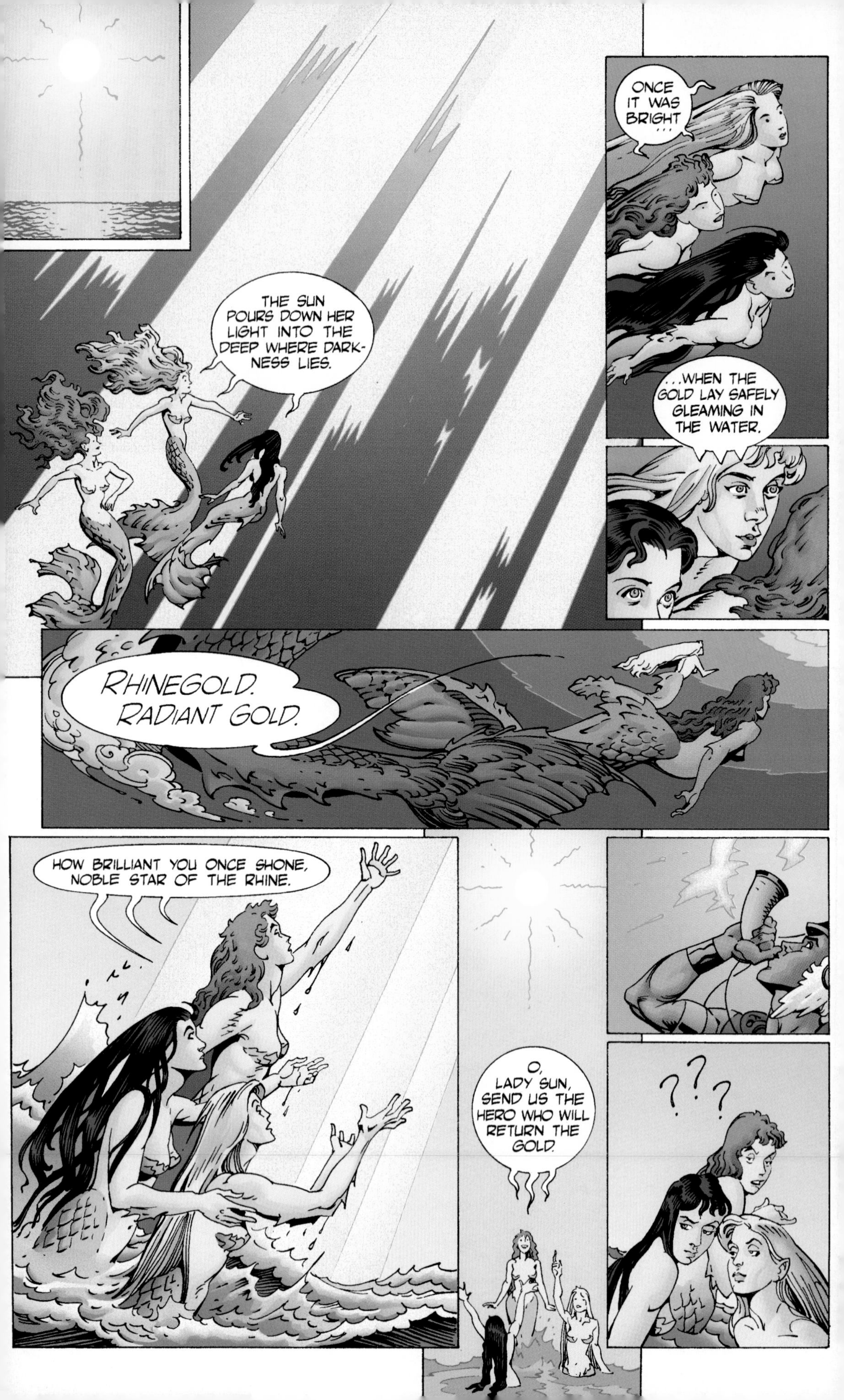
THE SUN POURS DOWN HER LIGHT INTO THE DEEP WHERE DARKNESS LIES.
ONCE IT WAS BRIGHT . . .
. . .WHEN THE GOLD LAY SAFELY GLEAMING IN THE WATER.
RHINEGOLD. RADIANT GOLD.
HOW BRILLIANT YOU ONCE SHONE, NOBLE STAR OF THE RHINE.
O, LADY SUN, SEND US THE HERO WHO WILL RETURN THE GOLD.
? ? ?

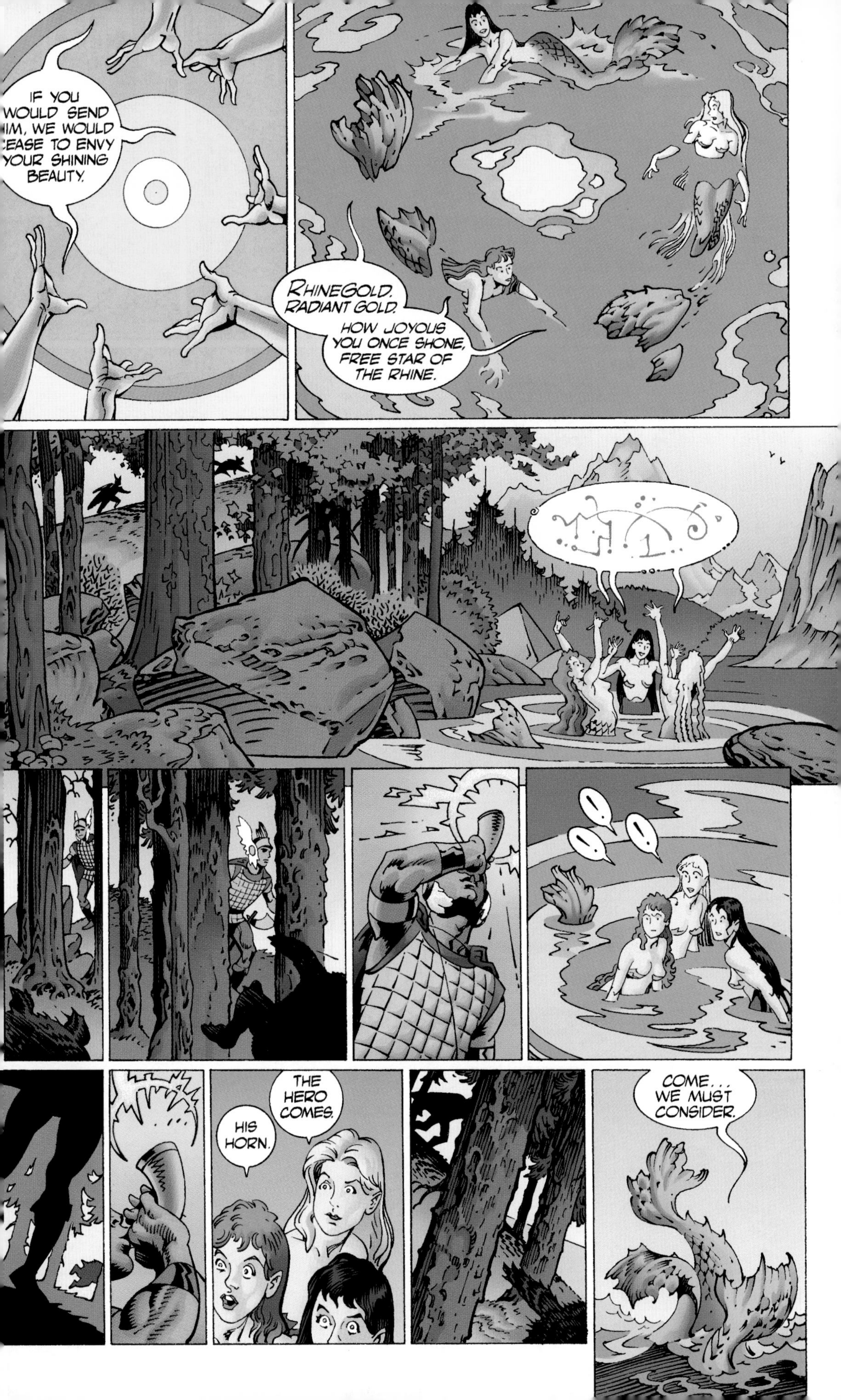
IF YOU WOULD SEND HIM, WE WOULD CEASE TO ENVY YOUR SHINING BEAUTY.
RHINEGOLD. RADIANT GOLD.
HOW JOYOUS YOU ONCE SHONE, FREE STAR OF THE RHINE.
!
!
!
THE HERO COMES.
HIS HORN.
COME... WE MUST CONSIDER.

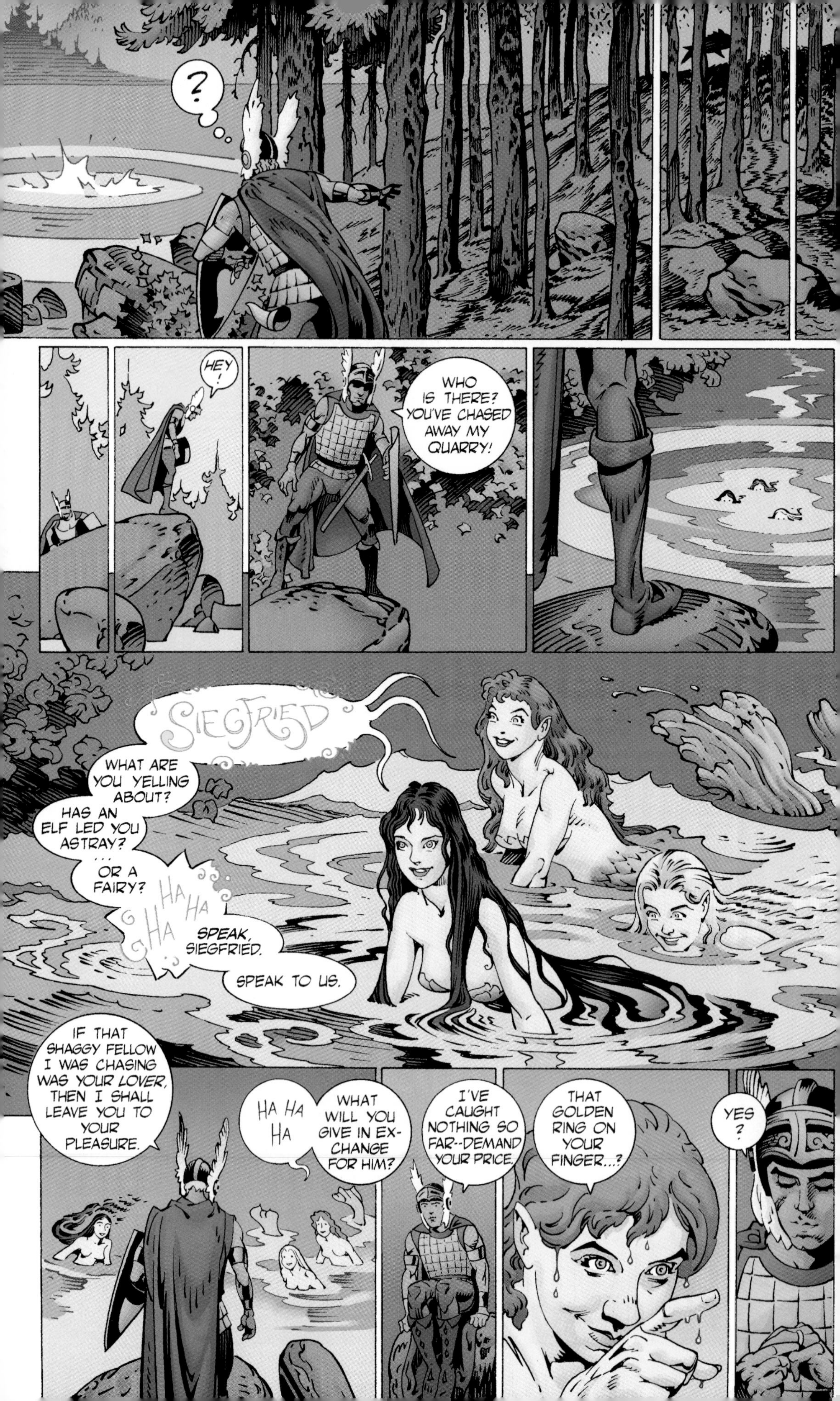
?
HEY!
WHO IS THERE? YOU'VE CHASED AWAY MY QUARRY!
SIEGFRIED
WHAT ARE YOU YELLING ABOUT?
HAS AN ELF LED YOU ASTRAY?
... OR A FAIRY?
HA HA HA HA
SPEAK, SIEGFRIED.
SPEAK TO US.
IF THAT SHAGGY FELLOW I WAS CHASING WAS YOUR *LOVER*, THEN I SHALL LEAVE YOU TO YOUR PLEASURE.
HA HA HA
WHAT WILL YOU GIVE IN EX-CHANGE FOR HIM?
I'VE CAUGHT NOTHING SO FAR--DEMAND YOUR PRICE.
THAT GOLDEN RING ON YOUR FINGER...?
YES?

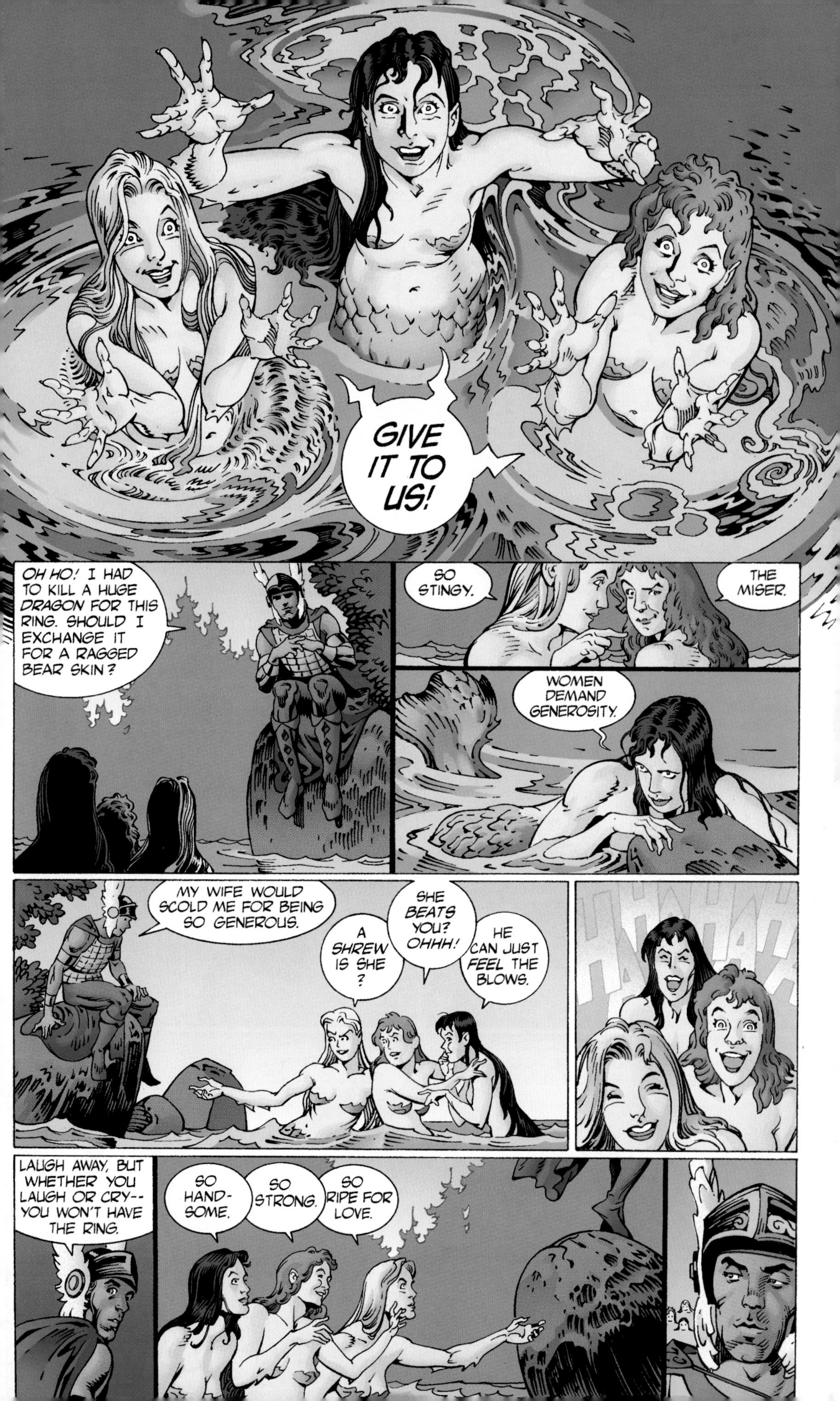

GIVE IT TO US!
OH HO! I HAD TO KILL A HUGE DRAGON FOR THIS RING. SHOULD I EXCHANGE IT FOR A RAGGED BEAR SKIN?
SO STINGY.
THE MISER.
WOMEN DEMAND GENEROSITY.
MY WIFE WOULD SCOLD ME FOR BEING SO GENEROUS.
A SHREW IS SHE?
SHE BEATS YOU? OHHH!
HE CAN JUST FEEL THE BLOWS.
HAHAHA
LAUGH AWAY, BUT WHETHER YOU LAUGH OR CRY-- YOU WON'T HAVE THE RING.
SO HAND-SOME.
SO STRONG.
SO RIPE FOR LOVE.

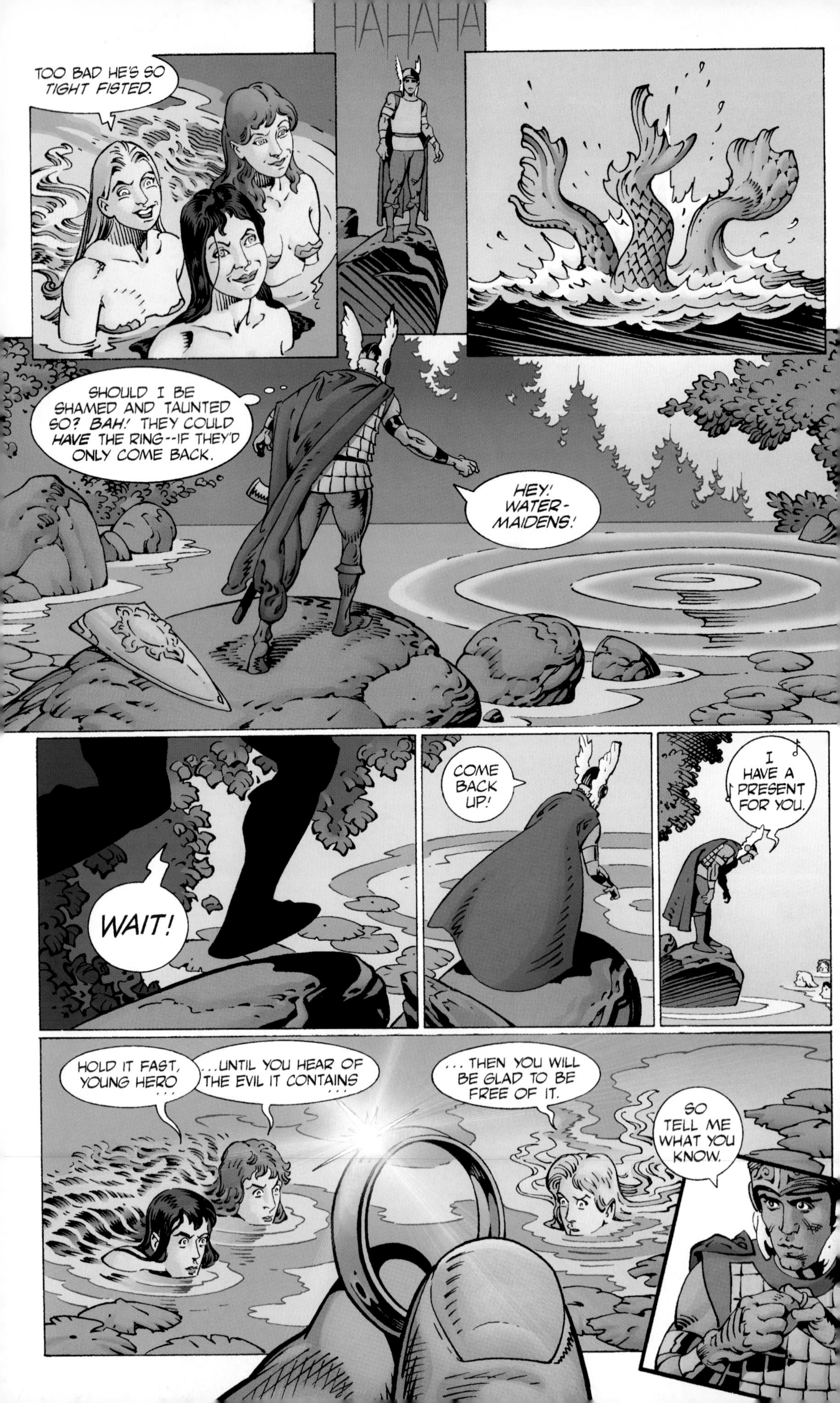
HAHAHA!
TOO BAD HE'S SO TIGHT FISTED.
SHOULD I BE SHAMED AND TAUNTED SO? BAH! THEY COULD HAVE THE RING--IF THEY'D ONLY COME BACK.
HEY! WATER-MAIDENS!
WAIT!
COME BACK UP!
I HAVE A PRESENT FOR YOU.
HOLD IT FAST, YOUNG HERO . . .
. . .UNTIL YOU HEAR OF THE EVIL IT CONTAINS . . .
. . . THEN YOU WILL BE GLAD TO BE FREE OF IT.
SO TELL ME WHAT YOU KNOW.

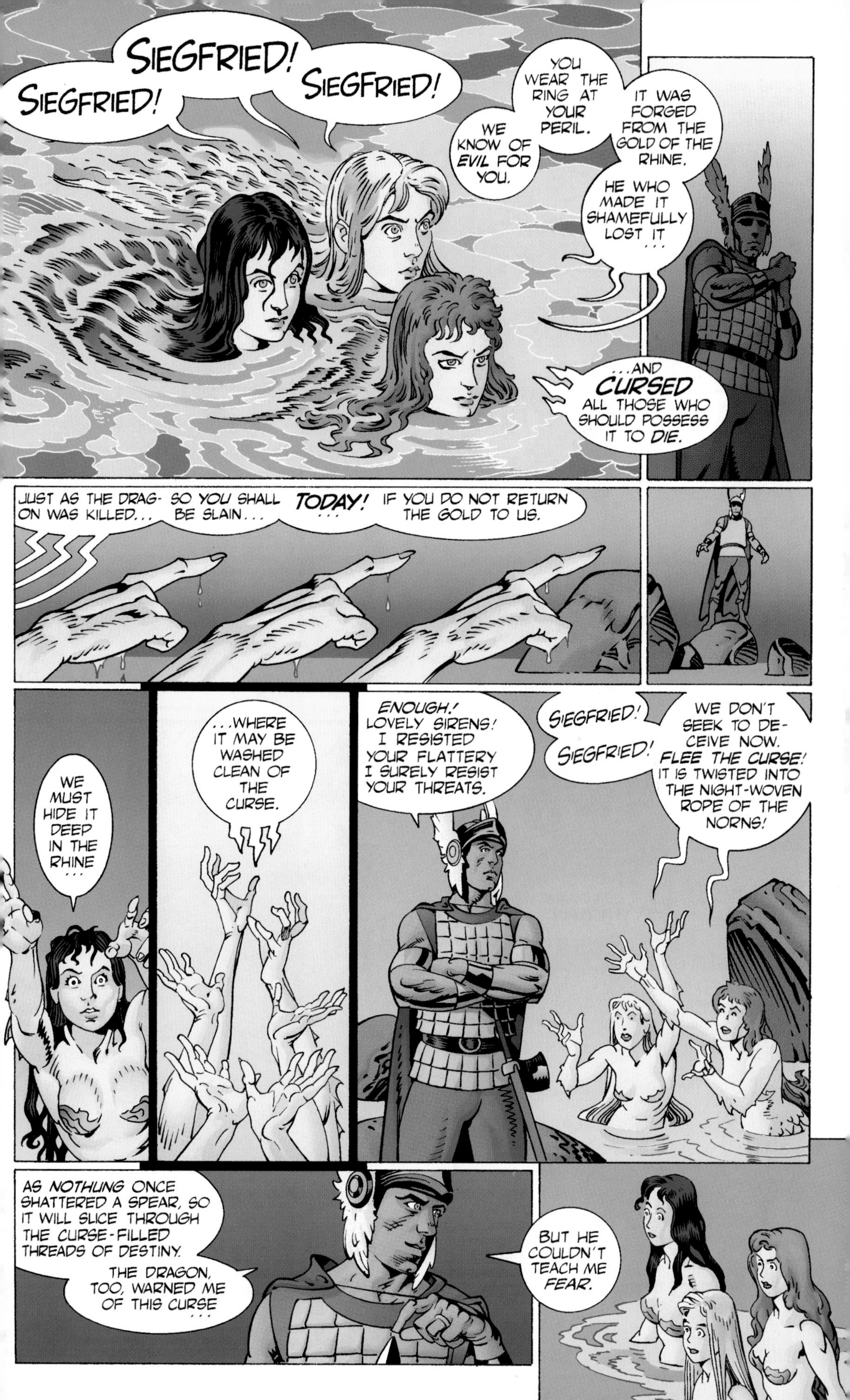
SIEGFRIED!
SIEGFRIED!
SIEGFRIED!
WE KNOW OF EVIL FOR YOU.
YOU WEAR THE RING AT YOUR PERIL.
IT WAS FORGED FROM THE GOLD OF THE RHINE.
HE WHO MADE IT SHAMEFULLY LOST IT . . .
. . .AND CURSED ALL THOSE WHO SHOULD POSSESS IT TO DIE.
JUST AS THE DRAG-ON WAS KILLED...
SO YOU SHALL BE SLAIN...
TODAY! . . .
IF YOU DO NOT RETURN THE GOLD TO US.
WE MUST HIDE IT DEEP IN THE RHINE . . .
. . .WHERE IT MAY BE WASHED CLEAN OF THE CURSE.
ENOUGH! LOVELY SIRENS! I RESISTED YOUR FLATTERY I SURELY RESIST YOUR THREATS.
SIEGFRIED!
SIEGFRIED!
WE DON'T SEEK TO DE-CEIVE NOW. FLEE THE CURSE! IT IS TWISTED INTO THE NIGHT-WOVEN ROPE OF THE NORNS!
AS NOTHUNG ONCE SHATTERED A SPEAR, SO IT WILL SLICE THROUGH THE CURSE-FILLED THREADS OF DESTINY.
THE DRAGON, TOO, WARNED ME OF THIS CURSE . . .
BUT HE COULDN'T TEACH ME FEAR.

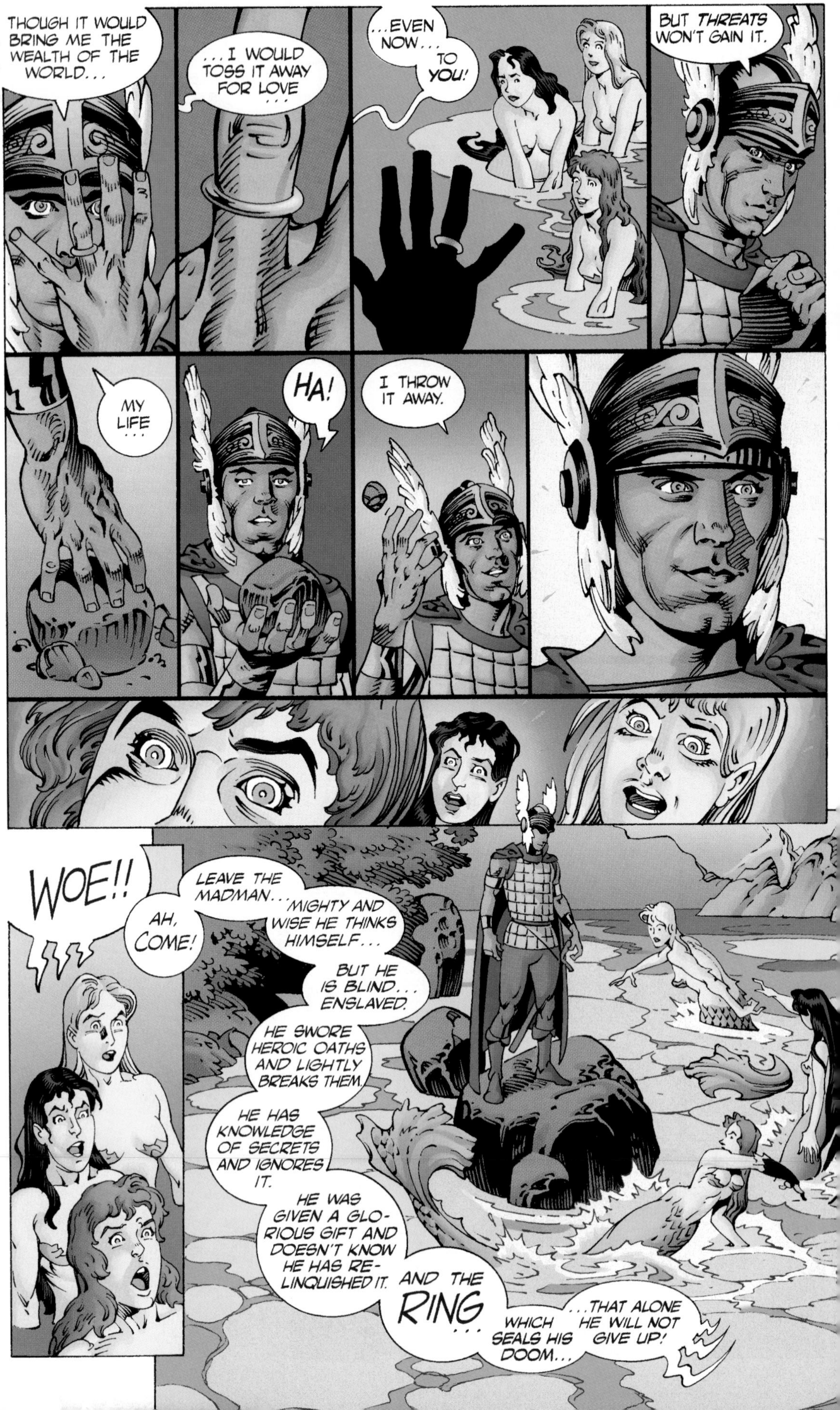
THOUGH IT WOULD BRING ME THE WEALTH OF THE WORLD...
...I WOULD TOSS IT AWAY FOR LOVE ...
...EVEN NOW... TO YOU!
BUT THREATS WON'T GAIN IT.
MY LIFE ...
HA!
I THROW IT AWAY.
WOE!!
AH, COME!
LEAVE THE MADMAN...
MIGHTY AND WISE HE THINKS HIMSELF...
BUT HE IS BLIND... ENSLAVED.
HE SWORE HEROIC OATHS AND LIGHTLY BREAKS THEM.
HE HAS KNOWLEDGE OF SECRETS AND IGNORES IT.
HE WAS GIVEN A GLO-RIOUS GIFT AND DOESN'T KNOW HE HAS RE-LINQUISHED IT.
AND THE RING...
WHICH SEALS HIS DOOM...
...THAT ALONE HE WILL NOT GIVE UP!

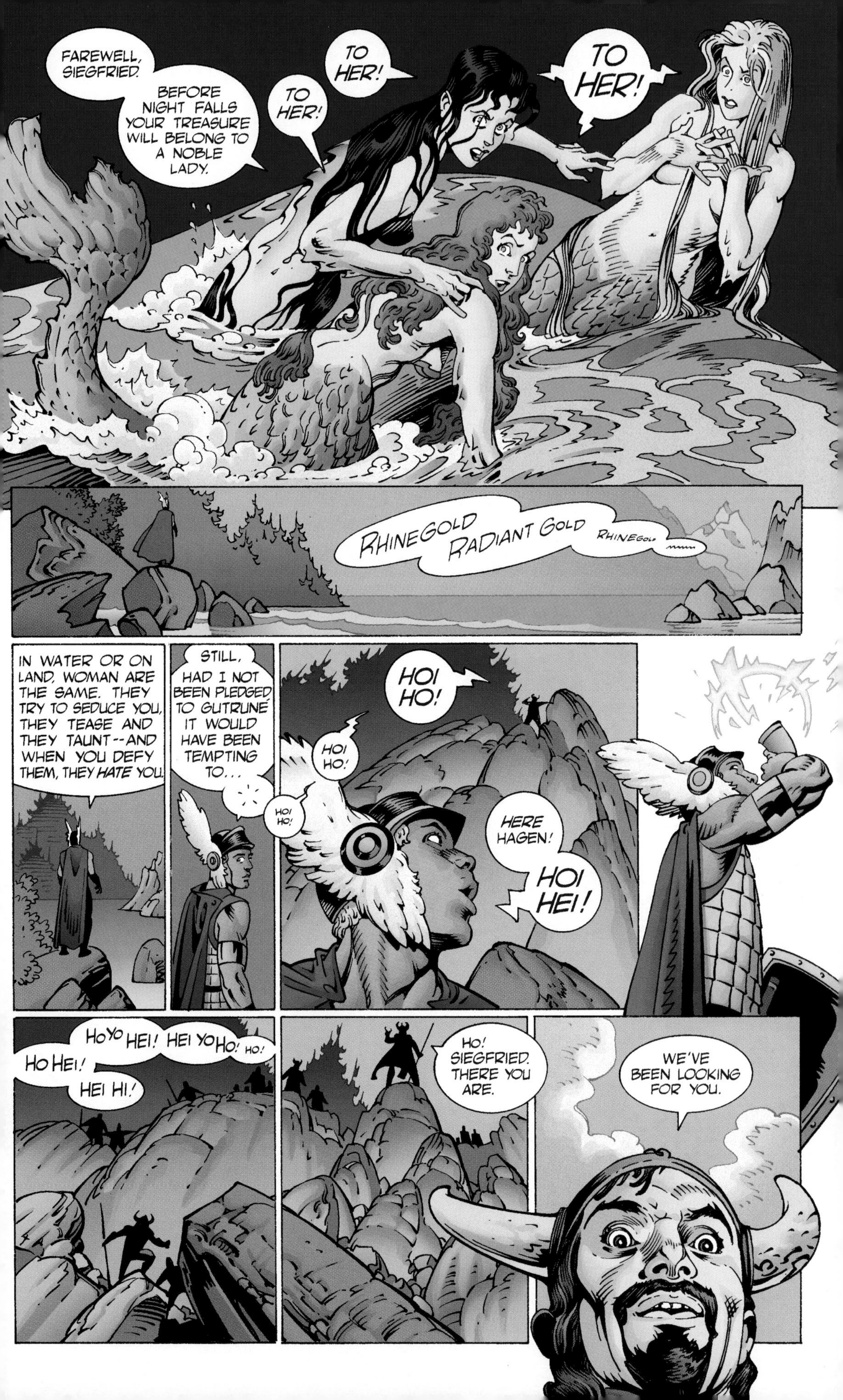
FAREWELL, SIEGFRIED.
BEFORE NIGHT FALLS YOUR TREASURE WILL BELONG TO A NOBLE LADY.
TO HER!
TO HER!
TO HER!
RHINEGOLD RADIANT GOLD RHINEGOLD
IN WATER OR ON LAND, WOMAN ARE THE SAME. THEY TRY TO SEDUCE YOU, THEY TEASE AND THEY TAUNT--AND WHEN YOU DEFY THEM, THEY HATE YOU.
STILL, HAD I NOT BEEN PLEDGED TO GUTRUNE IT WOULD HAVE BEEN TEMPTING TO...
HOI HO!
HOI HO!
HOI HO!
HERE HAGEN!
HOI HEI!
HO YO HEI! HEI YO HO! HO!
HO HEI!
HEI HI!
HO! SIEGFRIED. THERE YOU ARE.
WE'VE BEEN LOOKING FOR YOU.

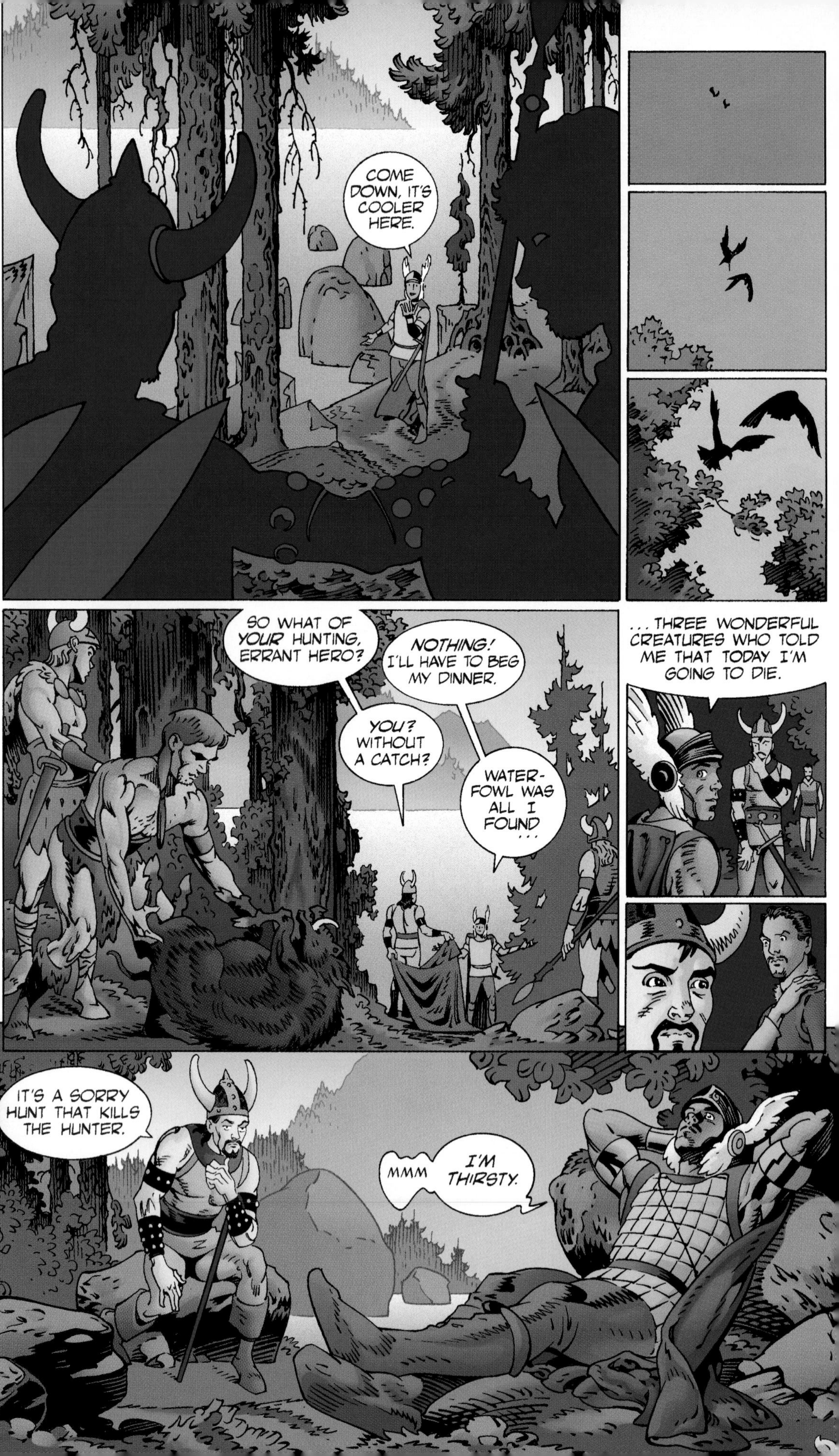
COME DOWN, IT'S COOLER HERE.
SO WHAT OF YOUR HUNTING, ERRANT HERO?
NOTHING! I'LL HAVE TO BEG MY DINNER.
YOU? WITHOUT A CATCH?
WATER-FOWL WAS ALL I FOUND . . .
. . . THREE WONDERFUL CREATURES WHO TOLD ME THAT TODAY I'M GOING TO DIE.
IT'S A SORRY HUNT THAT KILLS THE HUNTER.
MMM
I'M THIRSTY.

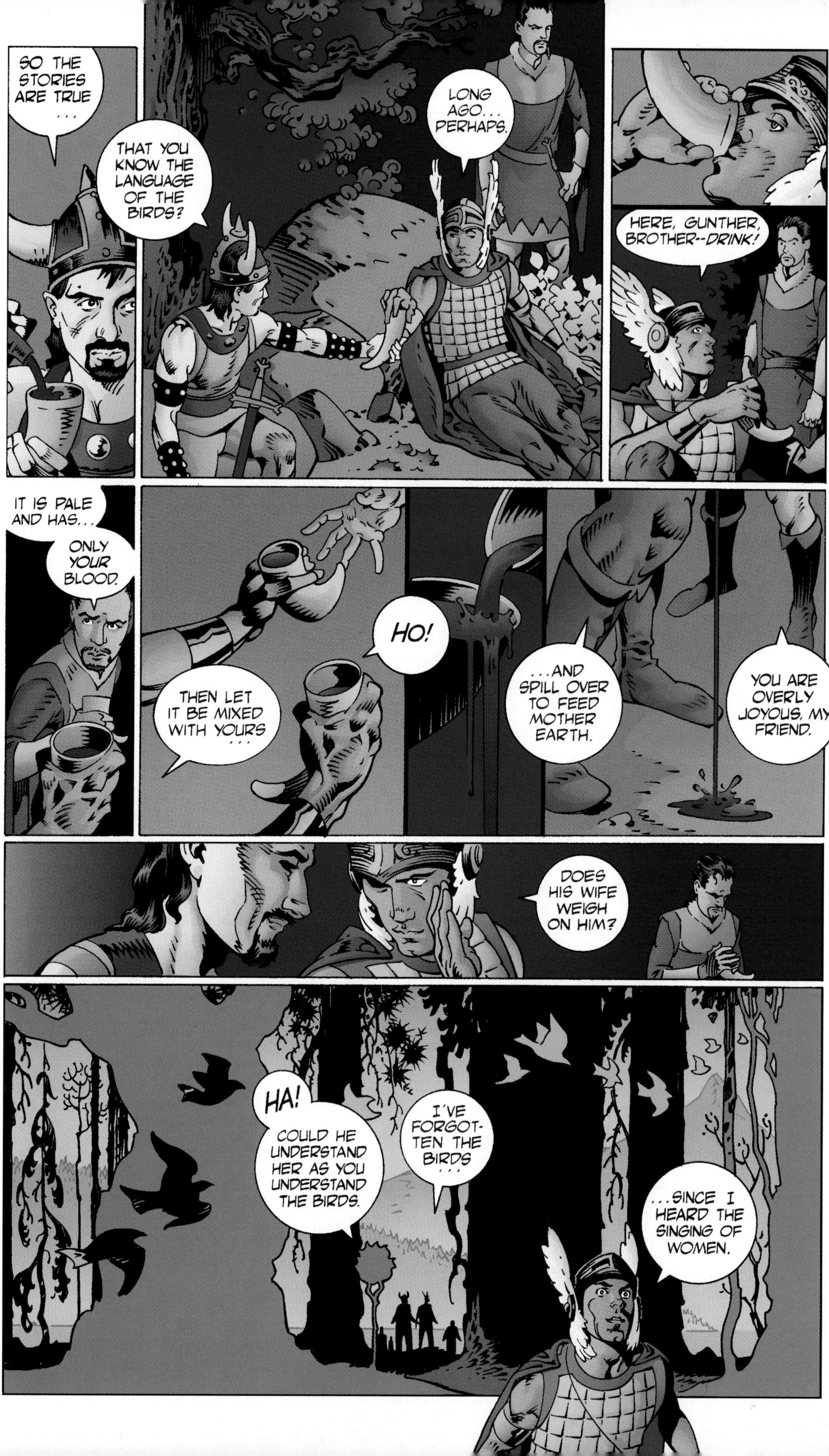
SO THE STORIES ARE TRUE . . .
THAT YOU KNOW THE LANGUAGE OF THE BIRDS?
LONG AGO. . . PERHAPS.
HERE, GUNTHER, BROTHER--*DRINK!*
IT IS PALE AND HAS. . .
ONLY *YOUR* BLOOD.
THEN LET IT BE MIXED WITH YOURS . . .
HO!
. . .AND SPILL OVER TO FEED MOTHER EARTH.
YOU ARE OVERLY JOYOUS, MY FRIEND.
DOES HIS WIFE WEIGH ON HIM?
HA!
COULD HE UNDERSTAND HER AS YOU UNDERSTAND THE BIRDS.
I'VE FORGOT-TEN THE BIRDS . . .
. . .SINCE I HEARD THE SINGING OF WOMEN.

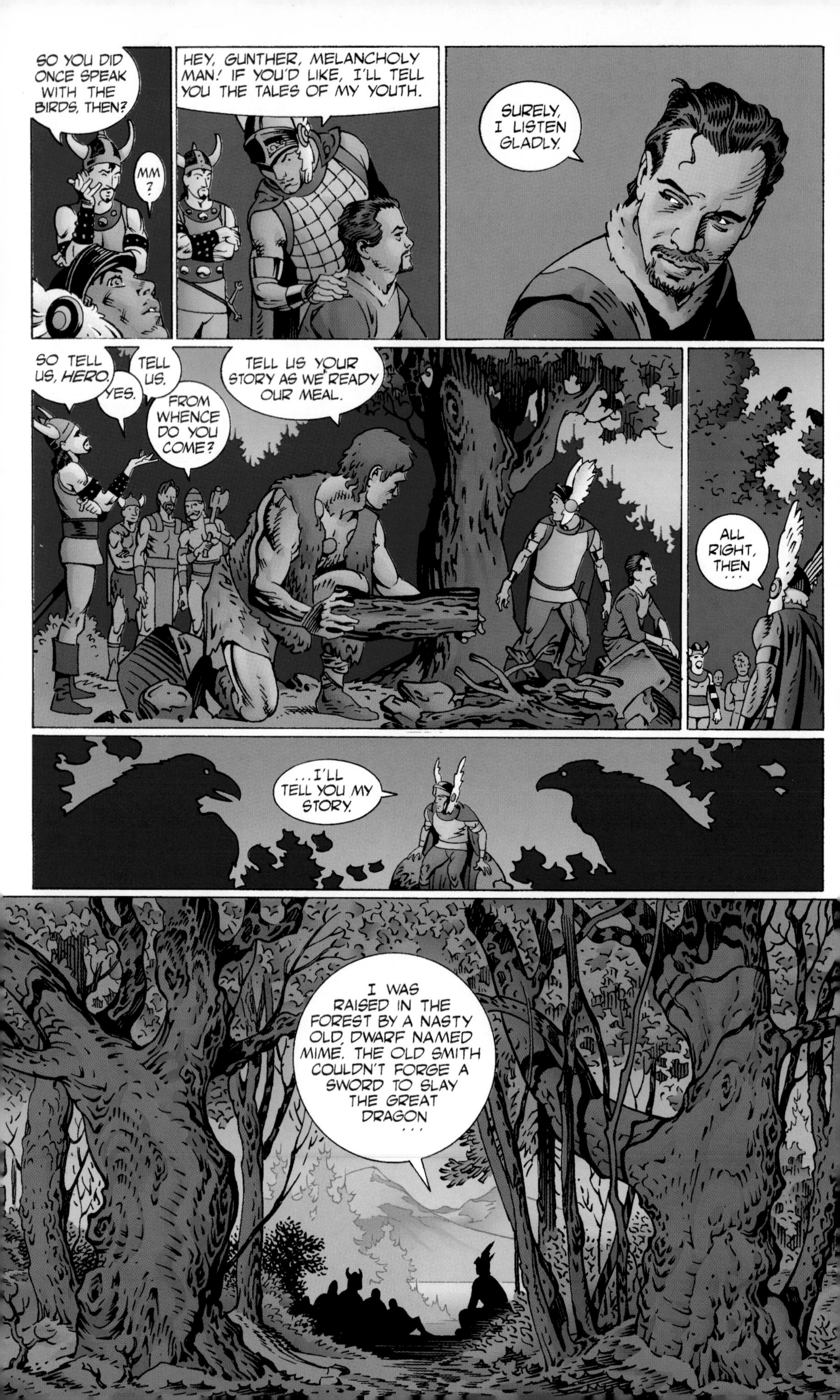

SO YOU DID ONCE SPEAK WITH THE BIRDS, THEN?
MM?
HEY, GUNTHER, MELANCHOLY MAN! IF YOU'D LIKE, I'LL TELL YOU THE TALES OF MY YOUTH.
SURELY, I LISTEN GLADLY.
SO TELL US, *HERO*.
YES.
TELL US.
FROM WHENCE DO YOU COME?
TELL US YOUR STORY AS WE READY OUR MEAL.
ALL RIGHT, THEN . . .
. . . I'LL TELL YOU MY STORY.
I WAS RAISED IN THE FOREST BY A NASTY OLD DWARF NAMED MIME. THE OLD SMITH COULDN'T FORGE A SWORD TO SLAY THE GREAT DRAGON . . .

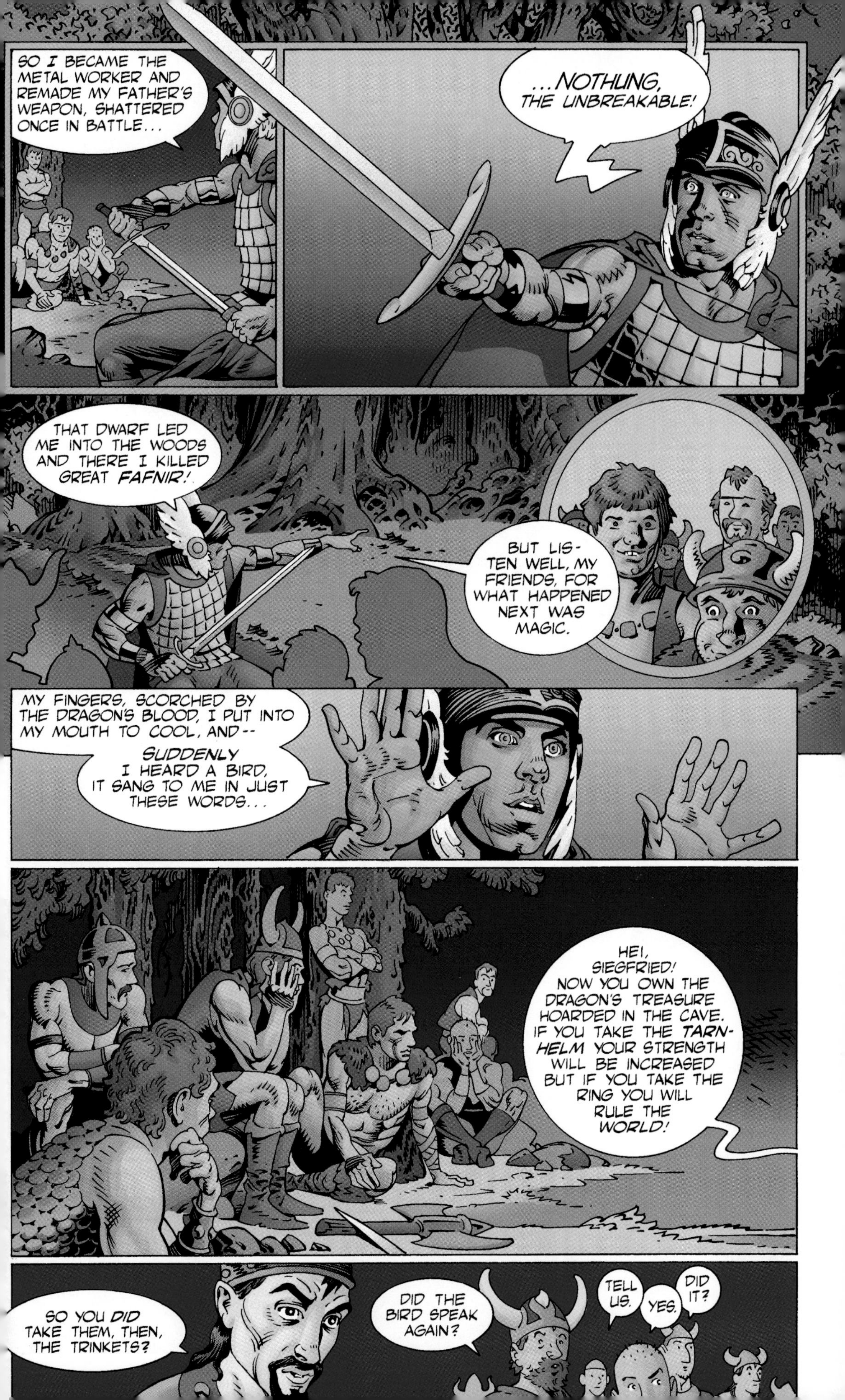
SO I BECAME THE METAL WORKER AND REMADE MY FATHER'S WEAPON, SHATTERED ONCE IN BATTLE...
...NOTHUNG, THE UNBREAKABLE!
THAT DWARF LED ME INTO THE WOODS AND THERE I KILLED GREAT FAFNIR!
BUT LISTEN WELL, MY FRIENDS, FOR WHAT HAPPENED NEXT WAS MAGIC.
MY FINGERS, SCORCHED BY THE DRAGON'S BLOOD, I PUT INTO MY MOUTH TO COOL, AND--
SUDDENLY I HEARD A BIRD, IT SANG TO ME IN JUST THESE WORDS...
HEI, SIEGFRIED! NOW YOU OWN THE DRAGON'S TREASURE HOARDED IN THE CAVE. IF YOU TAKE THE TARNHELM YOUR STRENGTH WILL BE INCREASED BUT IF YOU TAKE THE RING YOU WILL RULE THE WORLD!
SO YOU DID TAKE THEM, THEN, THE TRINKETS?
DID THE BIRD SPEAK AGAIN?
TELL US.
YES.
DID IT?

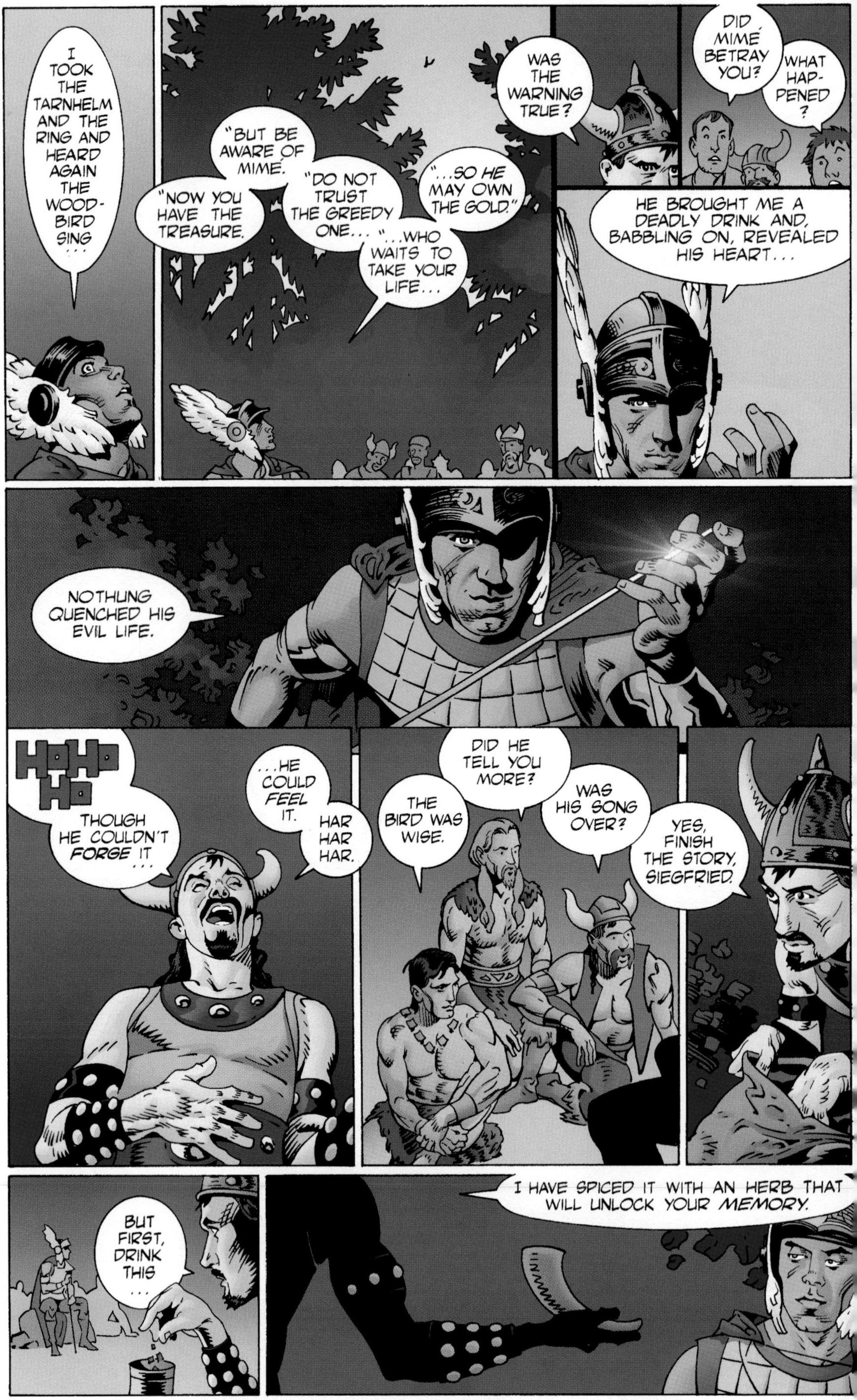
I TOOK THE TARNHELM AND THE RING AND HEARD AGAIN THE WOOD-BIRD SING . . .
"NOW YOU HAVE THE TREASURE.
"BUT BE AWARE OF MIME.
"DO NOT TRUST THE GREEDY ONE. . .
". . .WHO WAITS TO TAKE YOUR LIFE. . .
". . .SO HE MAY OWN THE GOLD."
WAS THE WARNING TRUE?
DID MIME BETRAY YOU?
WHAT HAP-PENED?
HE BROUGHT ME A DEADLY DRINK AND, BABBLING ON, REVEALED HIS HEART. . .
NOTHUNG QUENCHED HIS EVIL LIFE.
HO HO HO
THOUGH HE COULDN'T FORGE IT . . .
. . .HE COULD FEEL IT.
HAR HAR HAR.
THE BIRD WAS WISE.
DID HE TELL YOU MORE?
WAS HIS SONG OVER?
YES, FINISH THE STORY, SIEGFRIED.
BUT FIRST, DRINK THIS . . .
I HAVE SPICED IT WITH AN HERB THAT WILL UNLOCK YOUR MEMORY.

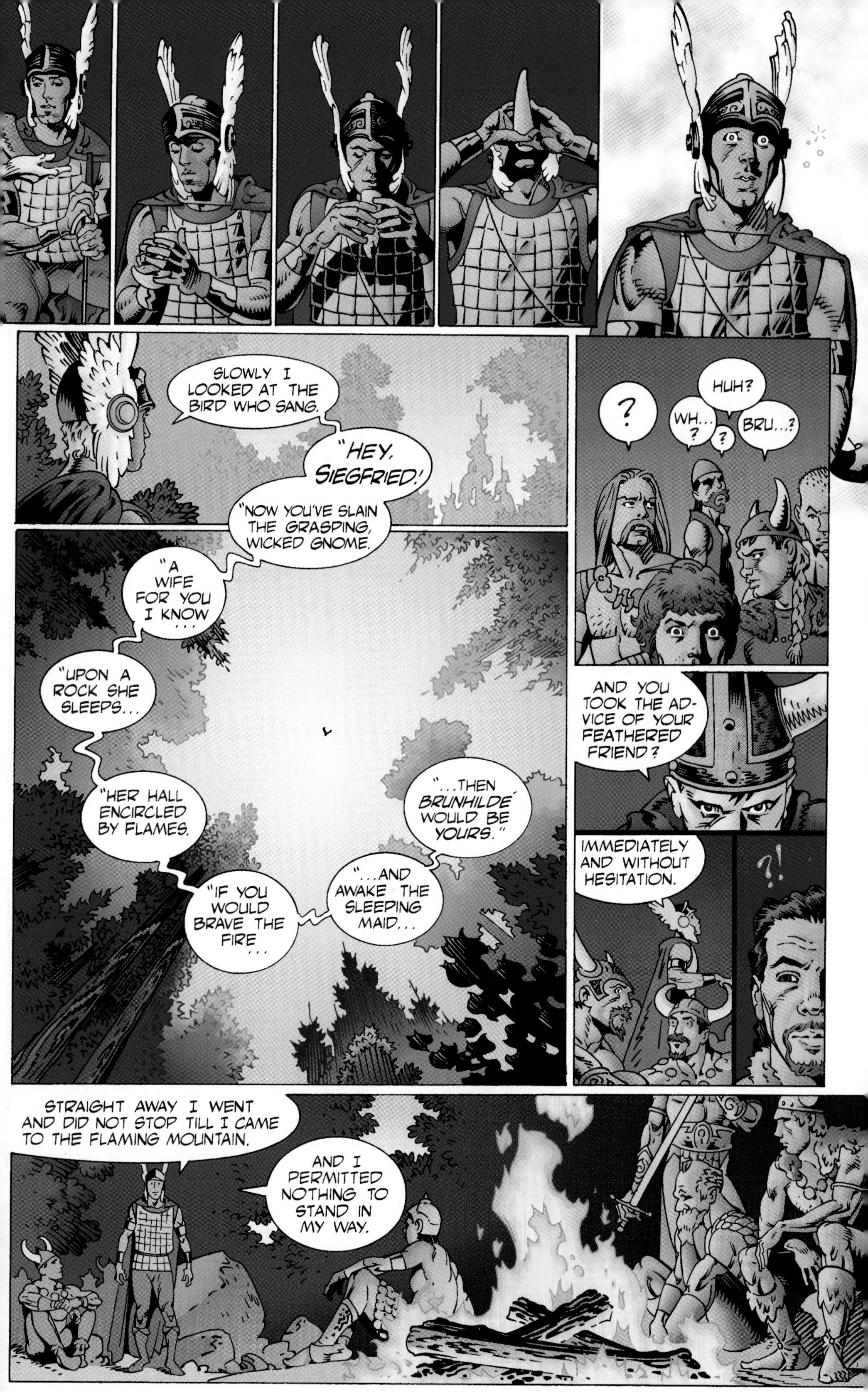

SLOWLY I LOOKED AT THE BIRD WHO SANG.
"HEY, SIEGFRIED!
"NOW YOU'VE SLAIN THE GRASPING, WICKED GNOME.
"A WIFE FOR YOU I KNOW . . .
"UPON A ROCK SHE SLEEPS...
"HER HALL ENCIRCLED BY FLAMES.
"IF YOU WOULD BRAVE THE FIRE . . .
"...AND AWAKE THE SLEEPING MAID...
"...THEN BRUNHILDE WOULD BE YOURS."
?
HUH?
WH...?
?
BRU...?
AND YOU TOOK THE ADVICE OF YOUR FEATHERED FRIEND?
IMMEDIATELY AND WITHOUT HESITATION.
?!
STRAIGHT AWAY I WENT AND DID NOT STOP TILL I CAME TO THE FLAMING MOUNTAIN.
AND I PERMITTED NOTHING TO STAND IN MY WAY.

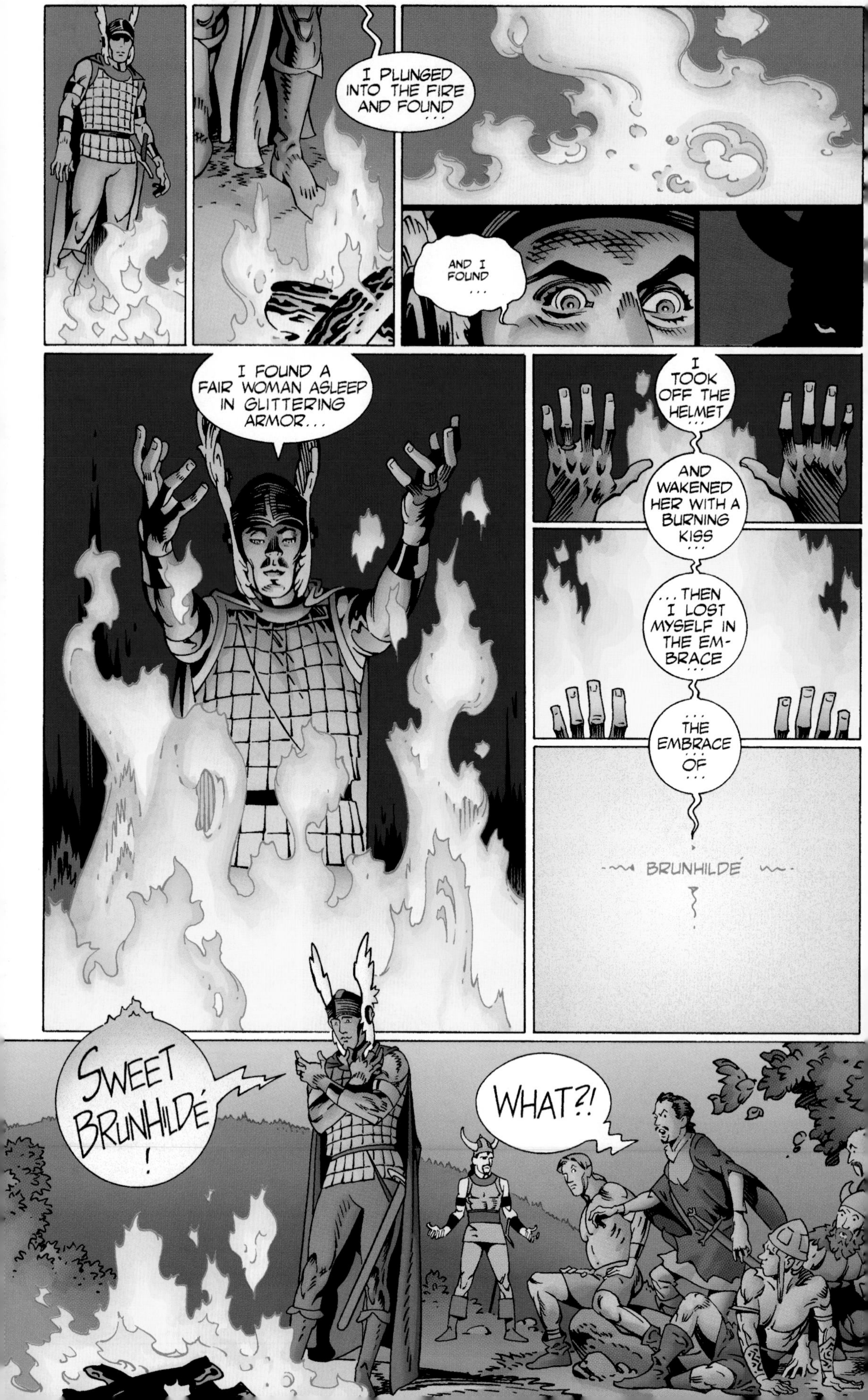
I PLUNGED INTO THE FIRE AND FOUND . . .
AND I FOUND . . .
I FOUND A FAIR WOMAN ASLEEP IN GLITTERING ARMOR . . .
I TOOK OFF THE HELMET . . .
AND WAKENED HER WITH A BURNING KISS . . .
. . . THEN I LOST MYSELF IN THE EM- BRACE . . .
. . . THE EMBRACE . . . OF . . .
BRUNHILDÉ
SWEET BRUNHILDÉ !
WHAT?!

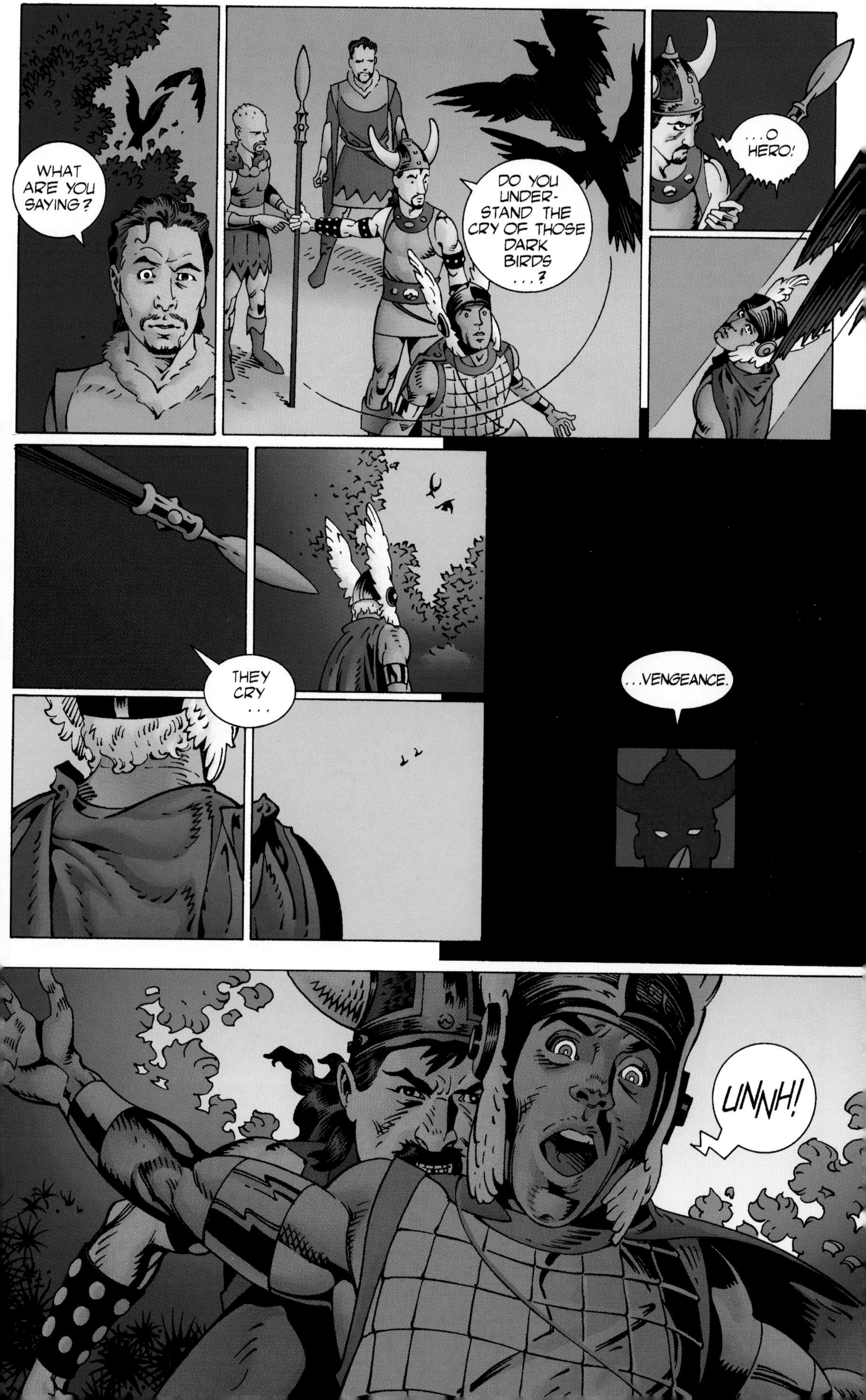
WHAT ARE YOU SAYING?
DO YOU UNDER-STAND THE CRY OF THOSE DARK BIRDS . . .?
. . .O HERO!
THEY CRY . . .
. . .VENGEANCE.
UNNH!

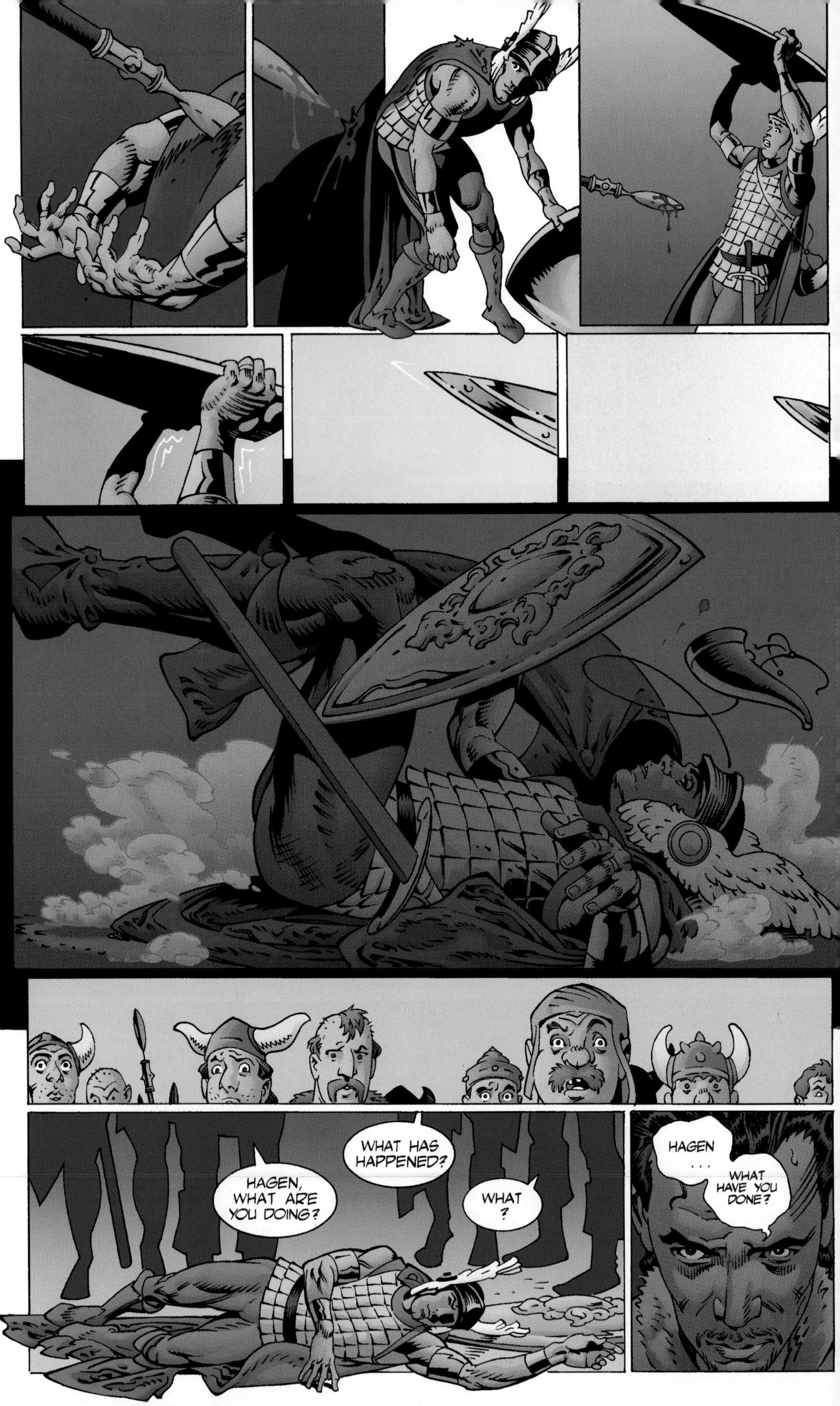
HAGEN, WHAT ARE YOU DOING?
WHAT HAS HAPPENED?
WHAT ?
HAGEN . . .
WHAT HAVE YOU DONE?

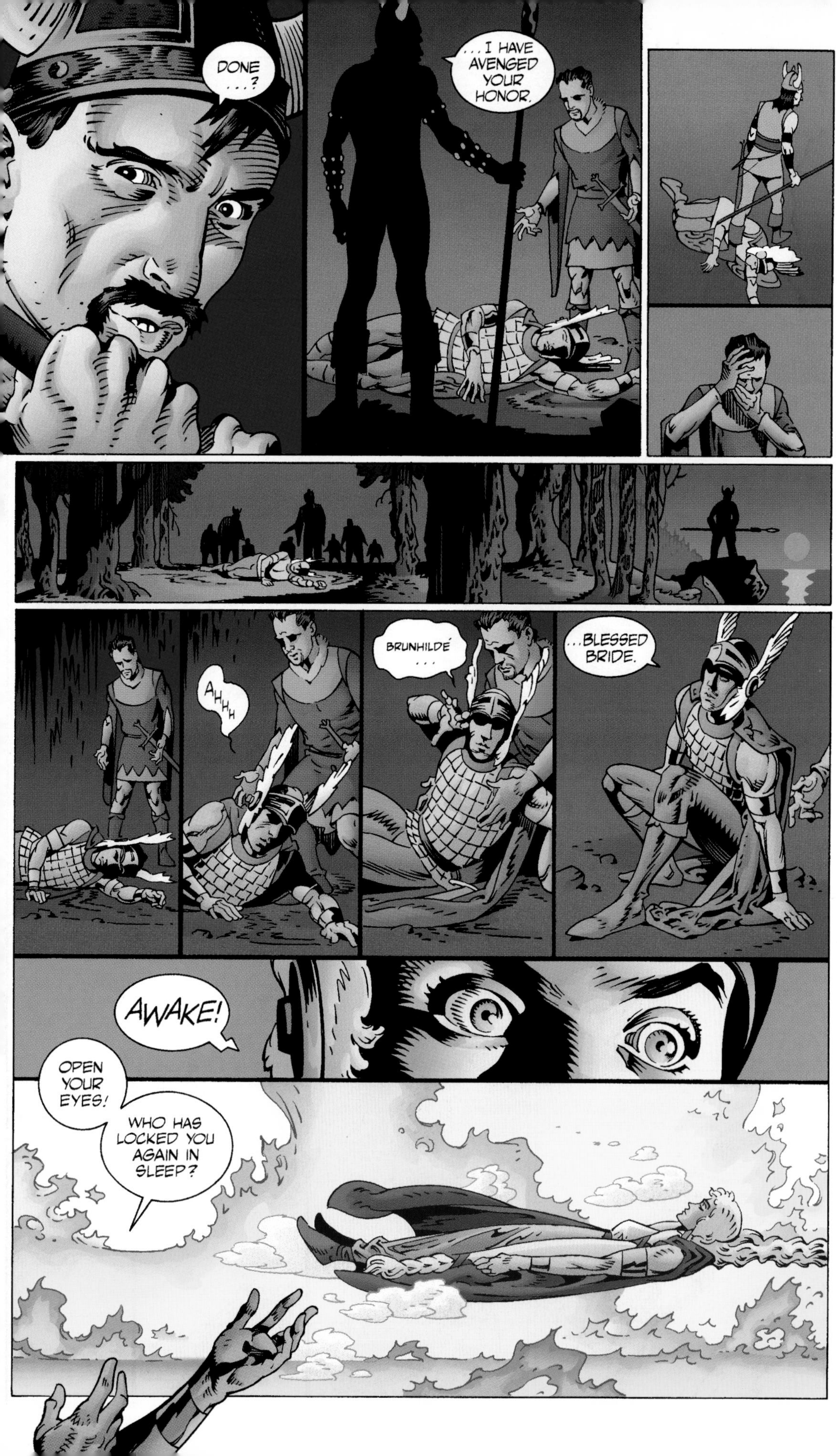
DONE ...?
...I HAVE AVENGED YOUR HONOR.
AHHH
BRUNHILDE ...
...BLESSED BRIDE.
AWAKE!
OPEN YOUR EYES!
WHO HAS LOCKED YOU AGAIN IN SLEEP?

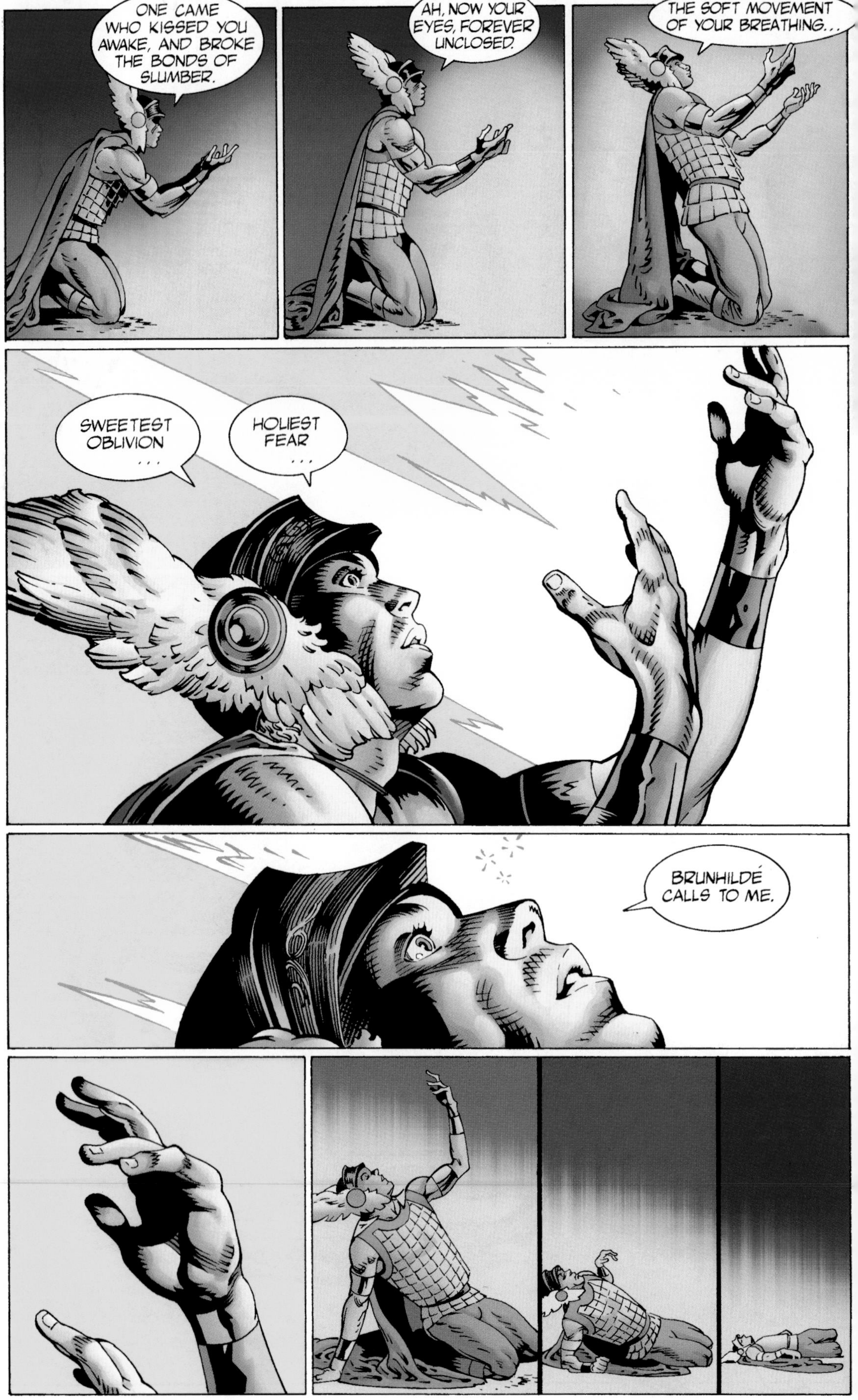
ONE CAME WHO KISSED YOU AWAKE, AND BROKE THE BONDS OF SLUMBER.
AH, NOW YOUR EYES, FOREVER UNCLOSED.
THE SOFT MOVEMENT OF YOUR BREATHING...
SWEETEST OBLIVION ...
HOLIEST FEAR ...
BRUNHILDÉ CALLS TO ME.

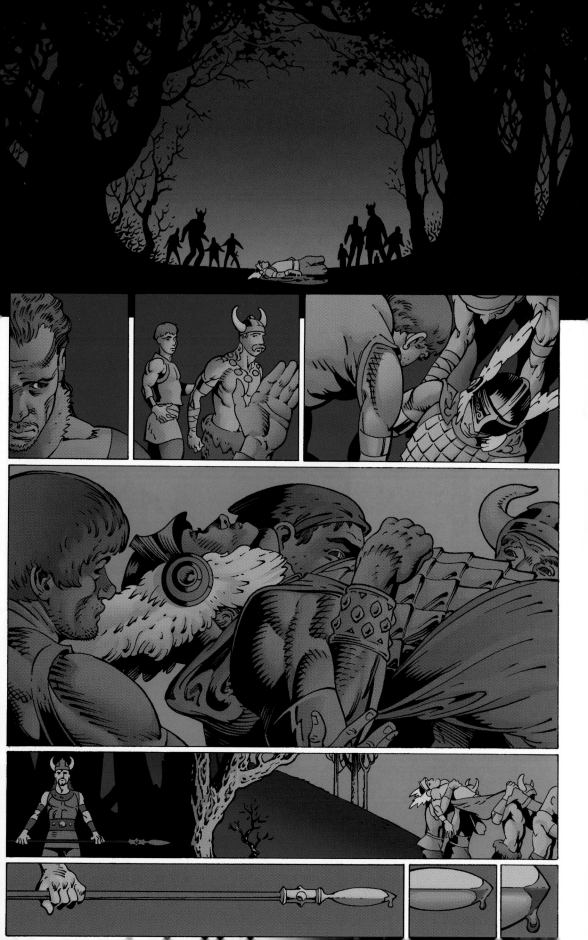

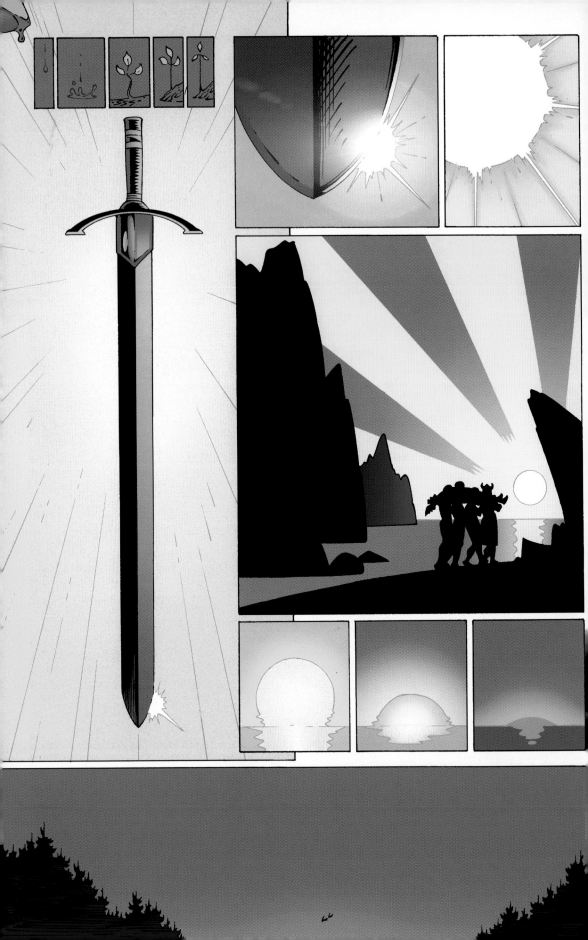

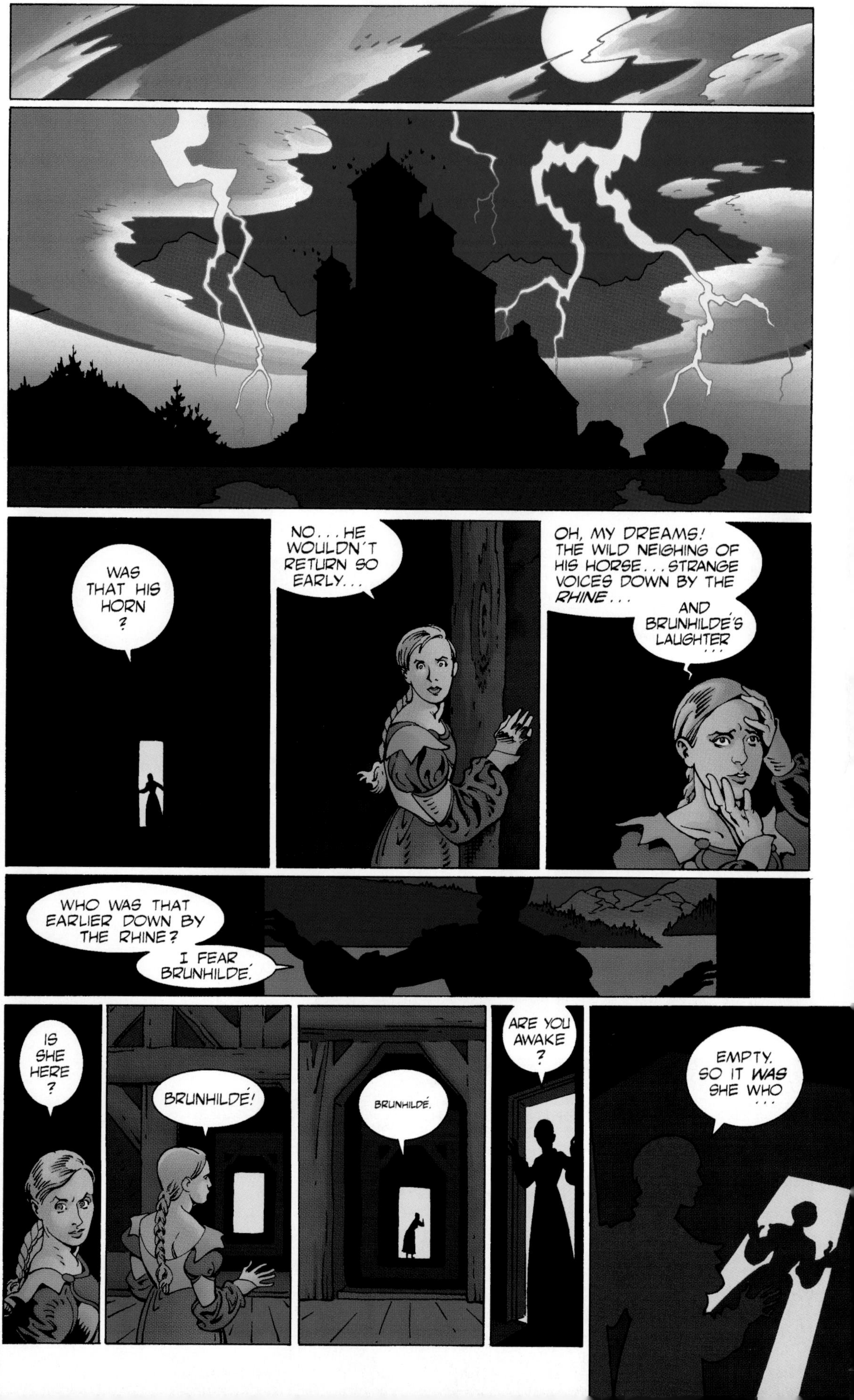
WAS THAT HIS HORN ?
NO . . . HE WOULDN'T RETURN SO EARLY . . .
OH, MY DREAMS! THE WILD NEIGHING OF HIS HORSE . . . STRANGE VOICES DOWN BY THE *RHINE* . . .
AND BRUNHILDE'S LAUGHTER . . .
WHO WAS THAT EARLIER DOWN BY THE RHINE?
I FEAR BRUNHILDE.
IS SHE HERE ?
BRUNHILDE!
BRUNHILDE.
ARE YOU AWAKE ?
EMPTY. SO IT *WAS* SHE WHO . . .

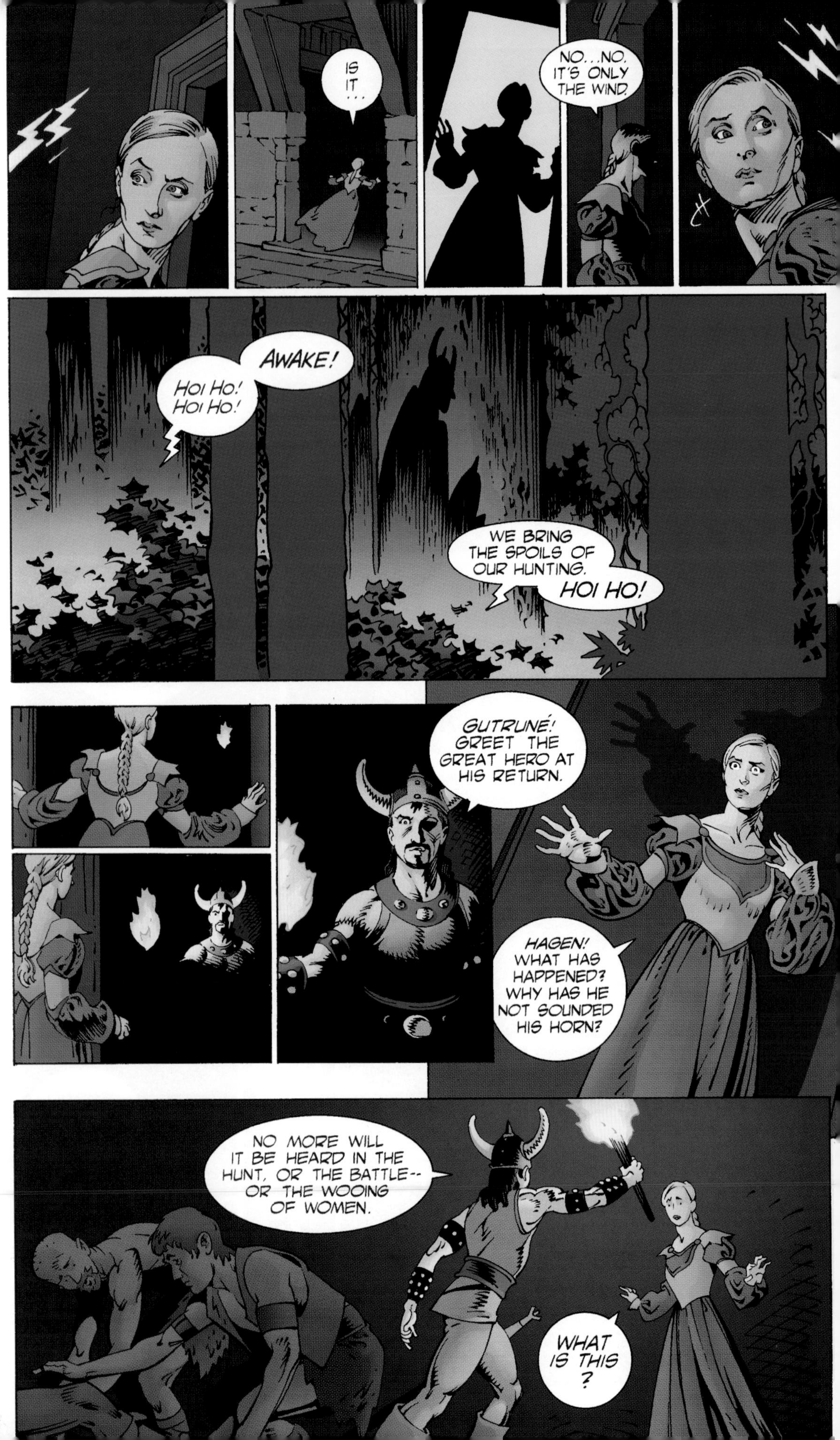
IS IT . . .
NO...NO. IT'S ONLY THE WIND.
HOI HO! HOI HO!
AWAKE!
WE BRING THE SPOILS OF OUR HUNTING. HOI HO!
GUTRUNE! GREET THE GREAT HERO AT HIS RETURN.
HAGEN! WHAT HAS HAPPENED? WHY HAS HE NOT SOUNDED HIS HORN?
NO MORE WILL IT BE HEARD IN THE HUNT, OR THE BATTLE-- OR THE WOOING OF WOMEN.
WHAT IS THIS ?

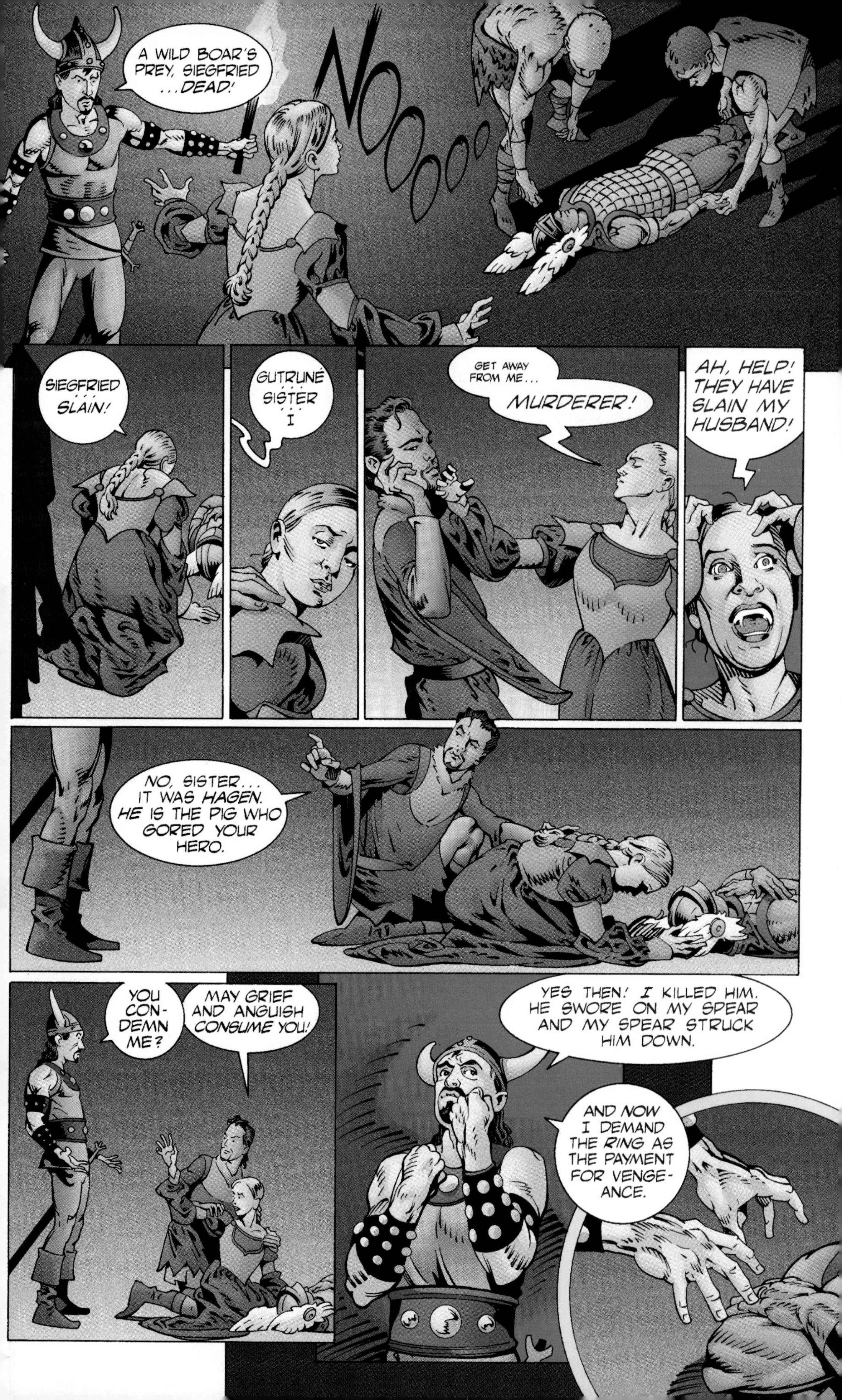
A WILD BOAR'S PREY, SIEGFRIED ...DEAD!
NOOOOO
SIEGFRIED ... SLAIN!
GUTRUNE SISTER ... I
GET AWAY FROM ME... MURDERER!
AH, HELP! THEY HAVE SLAIN MY HUSBAND!
NO, SISTER... IT WAS HAGEN. HE IS THE PIG WHO GORED YOUR HERO.
YOU CONDEMN ME?
MAY GRIEF AND ANGUISH CONSUME YOU!
YES THEN! I KILLED HIM. HE SWORE ON MY SPEAR AND MY SPEAR STRUCK HIM DOWN.
AND NOW I DEMAND THE RING AS THE PAYMENT FOR VENGEANCE.

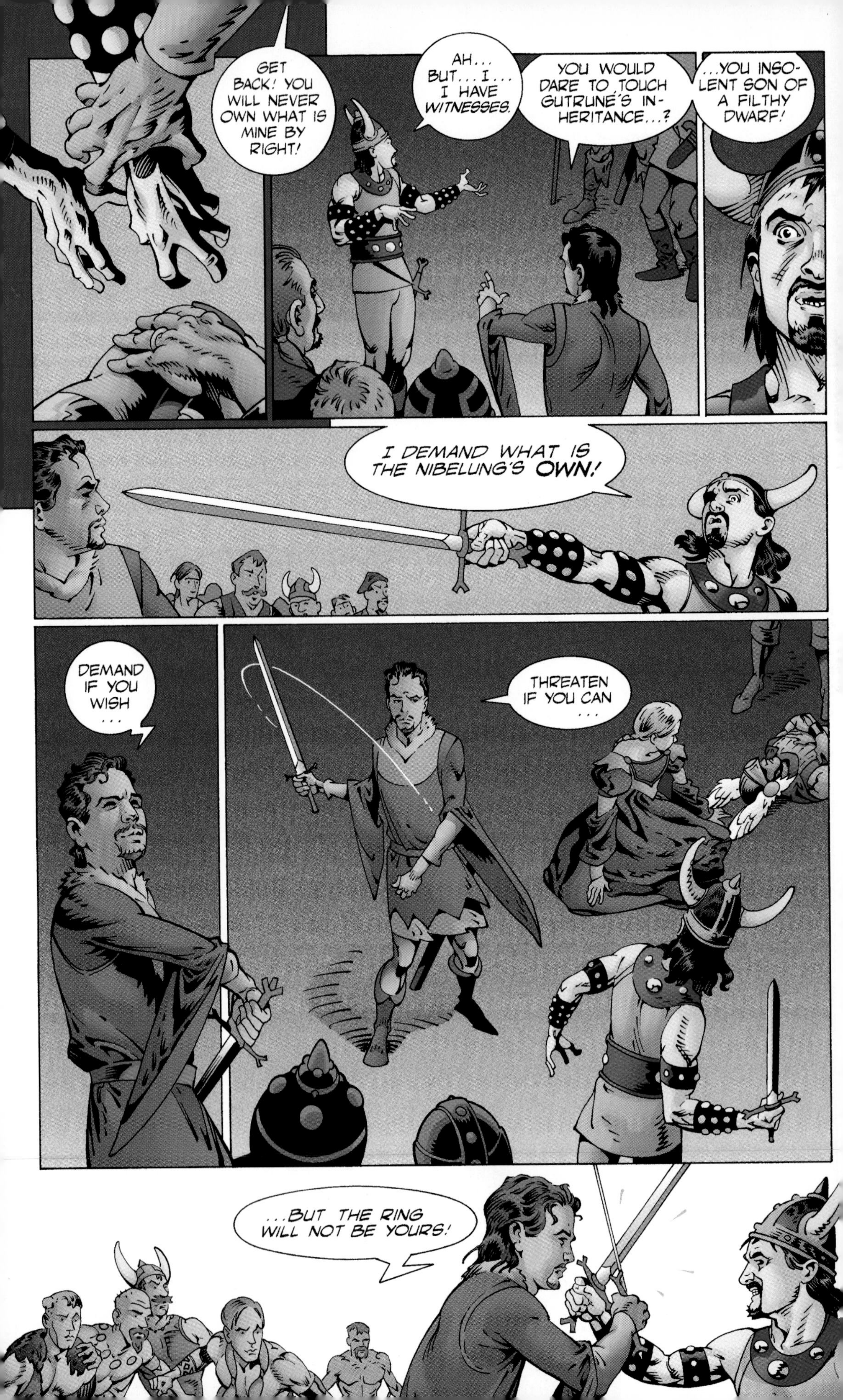
GET BACK! YOU WILL NEVER OWN WHAT IS MINE BY RIGHT!
AH... BUT... I... I HAVE WITNESSES.
YOU WOULD DARE TO TOUCH GUTRUNE'S IN-HERITANCE...?
...YOU INSO-LENT SON OF A FILTHY DWARF!
I DEMAND WHAT IS THE NIBELUNG'S OWN!
DEMAND IF YOU WISH...
THREATEN IF YOU CAN...
...BUT THE RING WILL NOT BE YOURS!

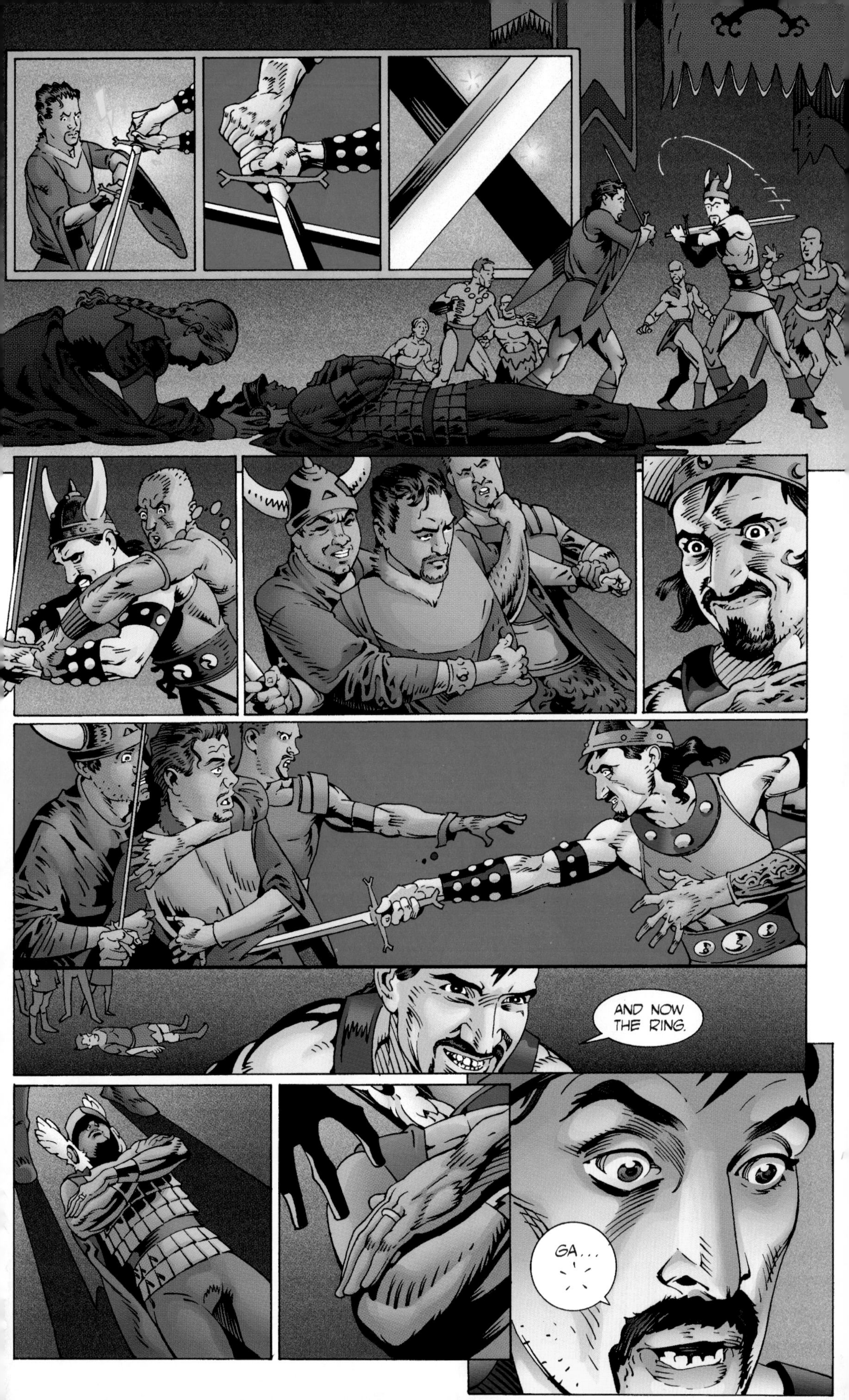
AND NOW THE RING.
GA...

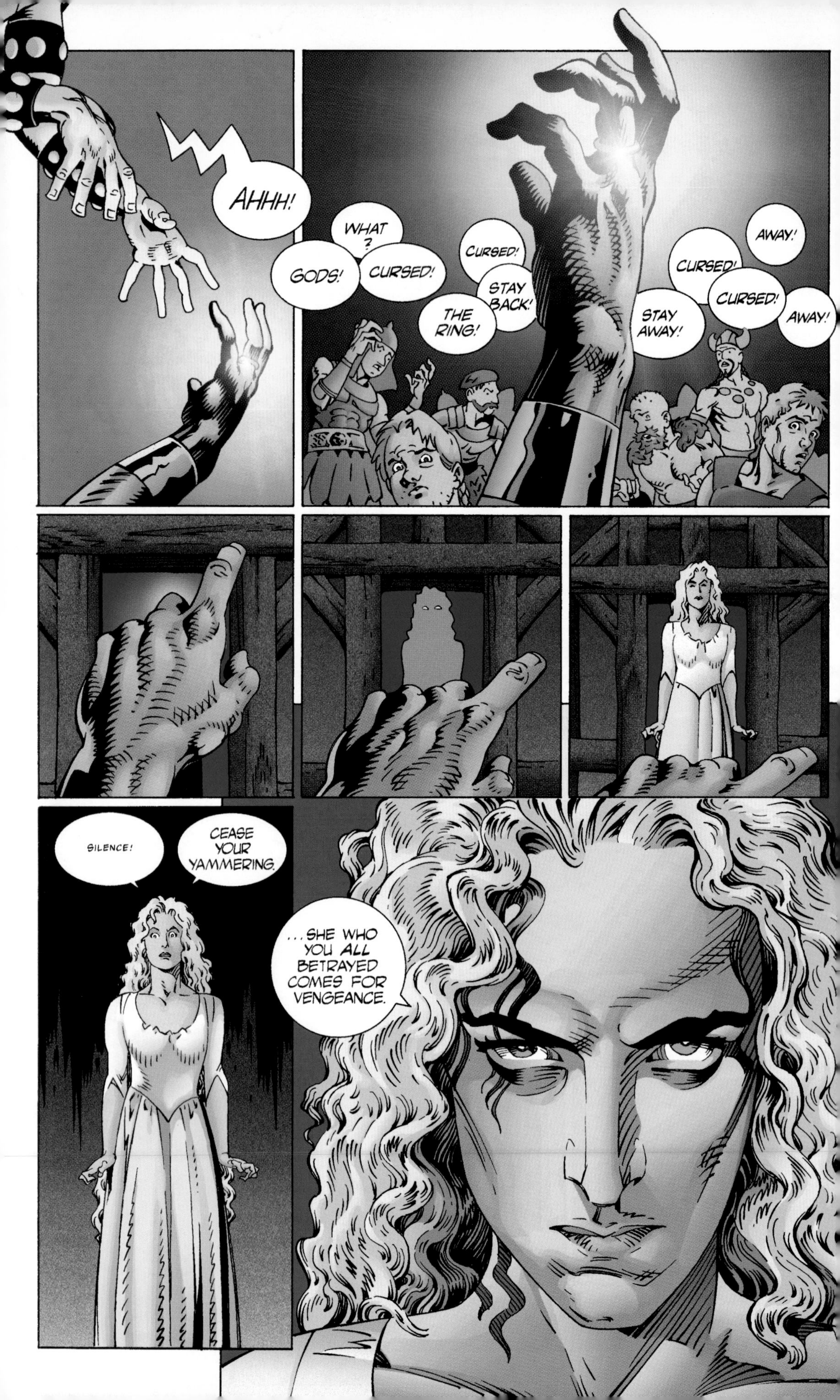
AHHH!
WHAT ?
GODS!
CURSED!
CURSED!
STAY BACK!
THE RING!
STAY AWAY!
CURSED!
AWAY!
CURSED!
AWAY!
SILENCE!
CEASE YOUR YAMMERING.
...SHE WHO YOU ALL BETRAYED COMES FOR VENGEANCE.

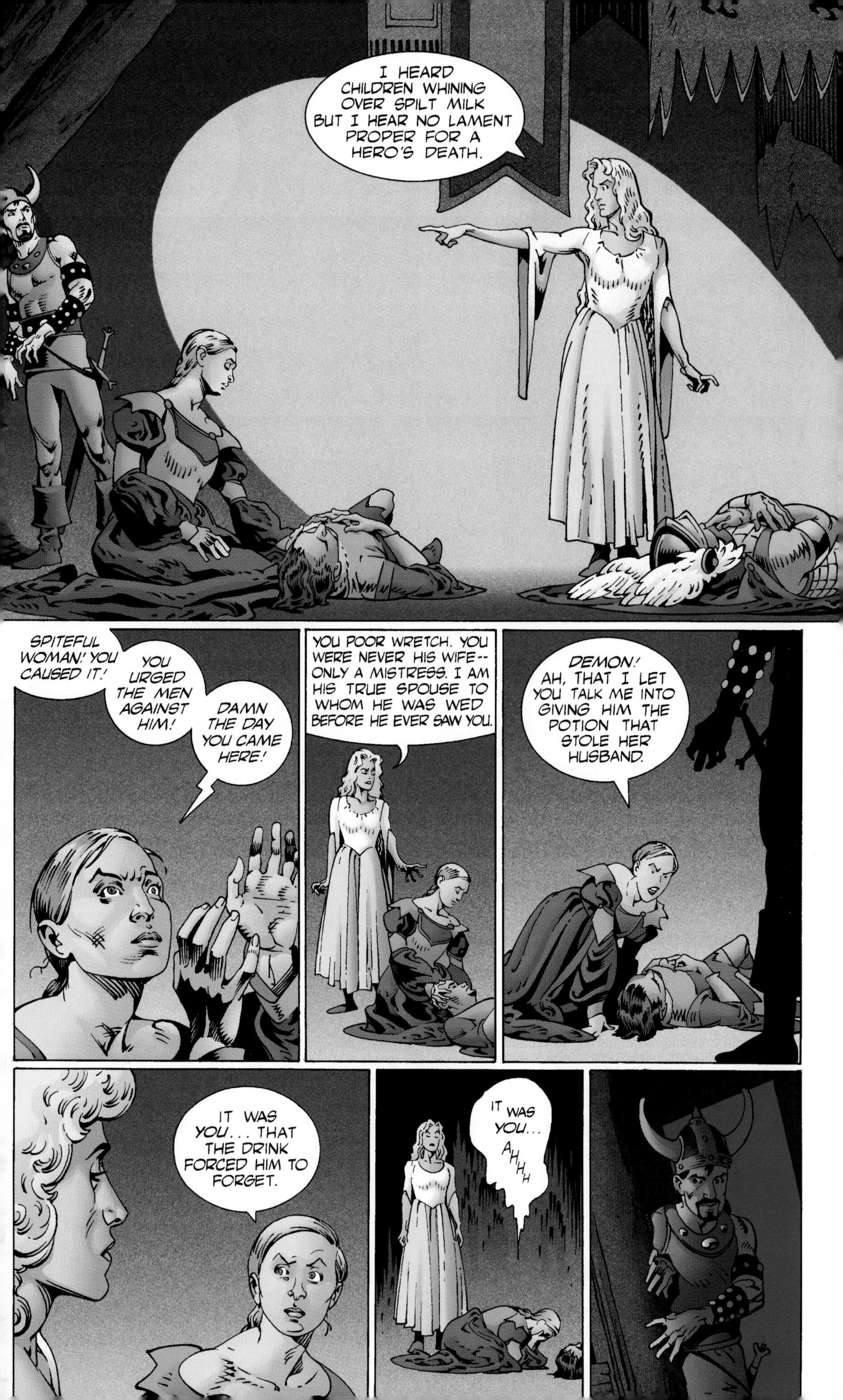
I HEARD CHILDREN WHINING OVER SPILT MILK BUT I HEAR NO LAMENT PROPER FOR A HERO'S DEATH.
SPITEFUL WOMAN! YOU CAUSED IT!
YOU URGED THE MEN AGAINST HIM!
DAMN THE DAY YOU CAME HERE!
YOU POOR WRETCH. YOU WERE NEVER HIS WIFE-- ONLY A MISTRESS. I AM HIS TRUE SPOUSE TO WHOM HE WAS WED BEFORE HE EVER SAW YOU.
DEMON! AH, THAT I LET YOU TALK ME INTO GIVING HIM THE POTION THAT STOLE HER HUSBAND.
IT WAS YOU... THAT THE DRINK FORCED HIM TO FORGET.
IT WAS YOU... AHHH

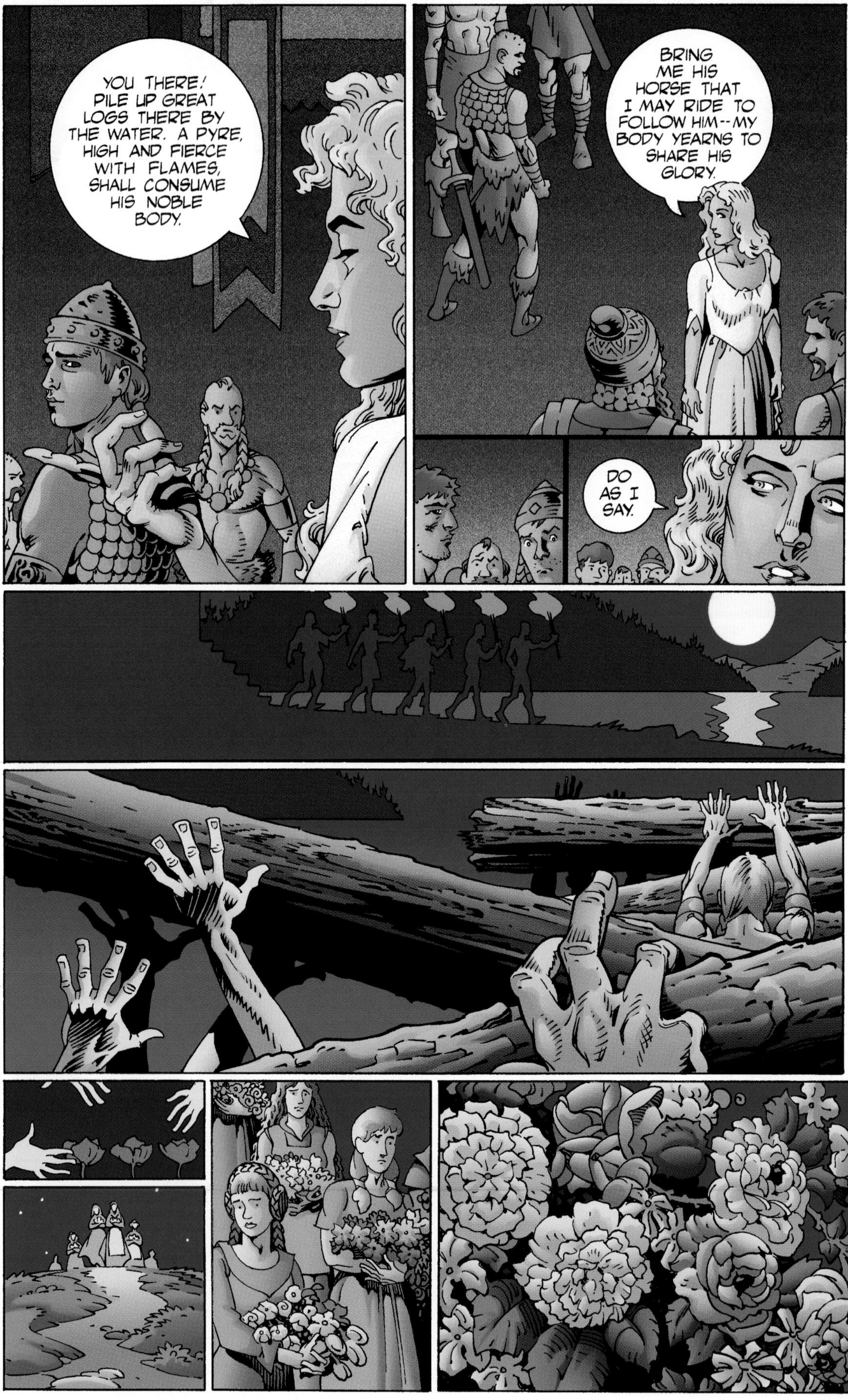
YOU THERE! PILE UP GREAT LOGS THERE BY THE WATER. A PYRE, HIGH AND FIERCE WITH FLAMES, SHALL CONSUME HIS NOBLE BODY.
BRING ME HIS HORSE THAT I MAY RIDE TO FOLLOW HIM--MY BODY YEARNS TO SHARE HIS GLORY.
DO AS I SAY.

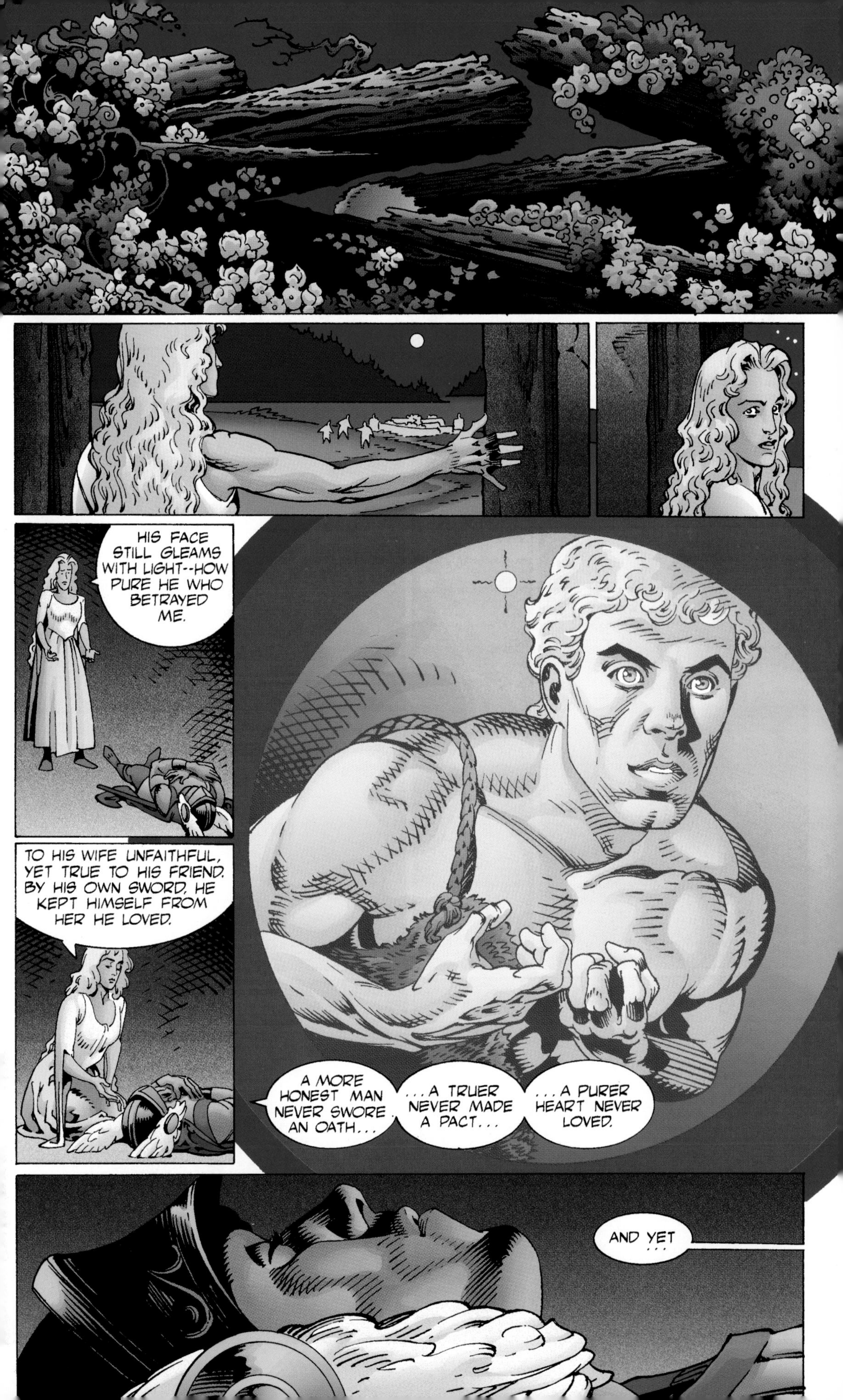
HIS FACE STILL GLEAMS WITH LIGHT--HOW PURE HE WHO BETRAYED ME.
TO HIS WIFE UNFAITHFUL, YET TRUE TO HIS FRIEND. BY HIS OWN SWORD, HE KEPT HIMSELF FROM HER HE LOVED.
A MORE HONEST MAN NEVER SWORE AN OATH...
...A TRUER NEVER MADE A PACT...
...A PURER HEART NEVER LOVED.
AND YET ...

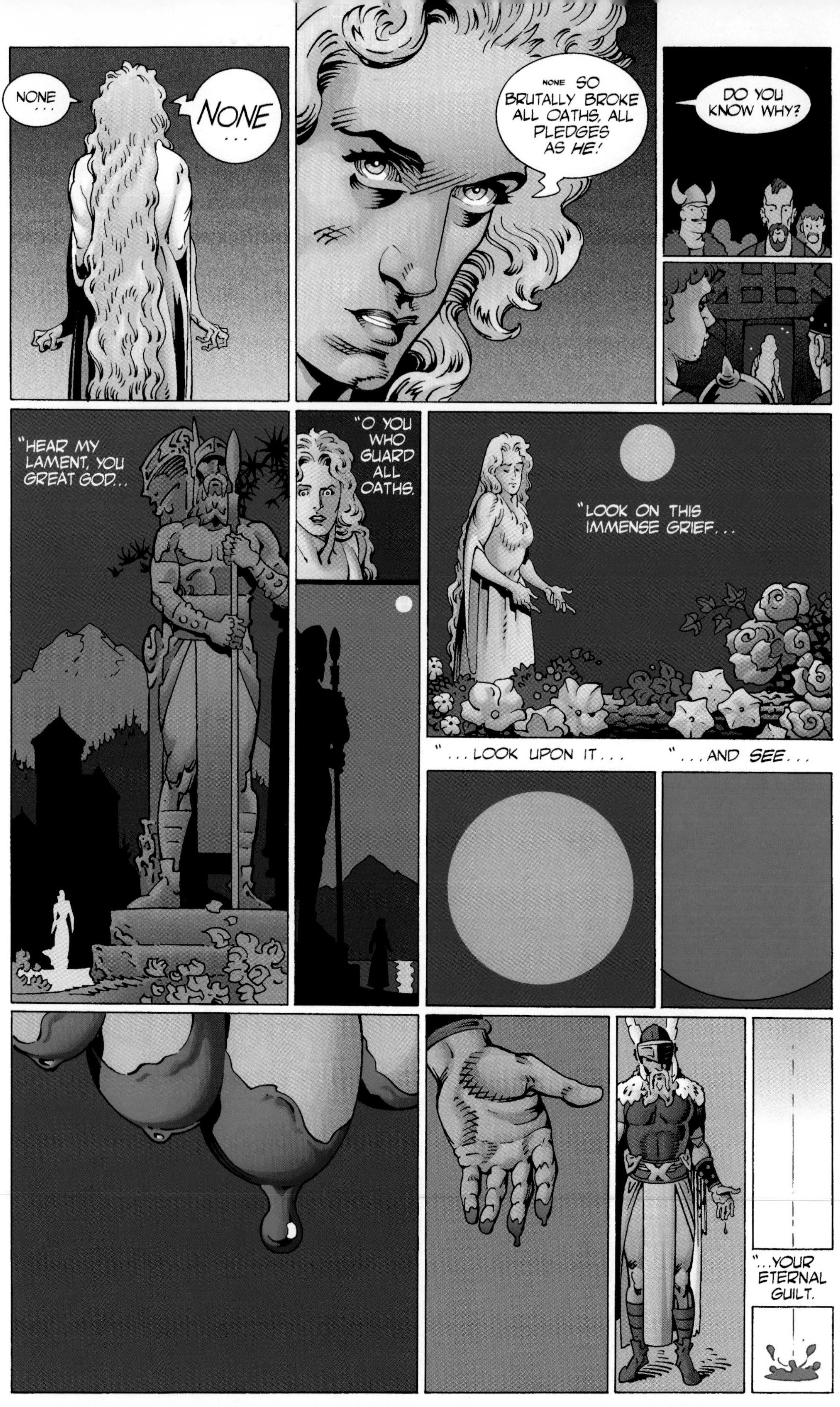

NONE . . .
NONE . . .
NONE SO BRUTALLY BROKE ALL OATHS, ALL PLEDGES AS HE!
DO YOU KNOW WHY?
"HEAR MY LAMENT, YOU GREAT GOD. . .
"O YOU WHO GUARD ALL OATHS.
"LOOK ON THIS IMMENSE GRIEF. . .
". . . LOOK UPON IT . . .
". . . AND SEE . . .
". . . YOUR ETERNAL GUILT.

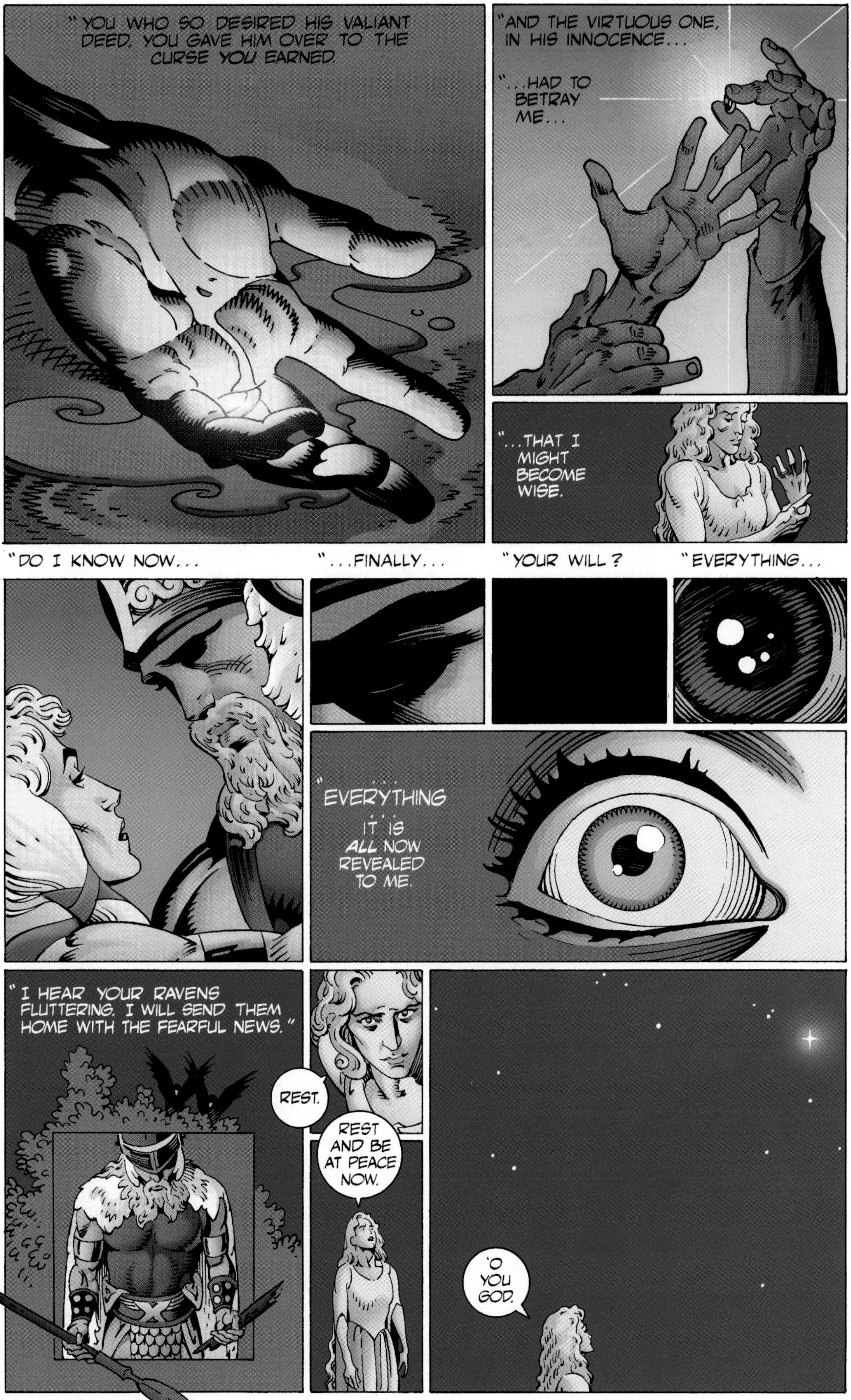

"YOU WHO SO DESIRED HIS VALIANT DEED, YOU GAVE HIM OVER TO THE CURSE *YOU* EARNED.
"AND THE VIRTUOUS ONE, IN HIS INNOCENCE...
"...HAD TO BETRAY ME...
"...THAT I MIGHT BECOME WISE.
"DO I KNOW NOW...
"...FINALLY...
"YOUR WILL?
"EVERYTHING...
"...EVERYTHING
...IT IS *ALL* NOW REVEALED TO ME.
"I HEAR YOUR RAVENS FLUTTERING. I WILL SEND THEM HOME WITH THE FEARFUL NEWS."
REST.
REST AND BE AT PEACE NOW.
'O YOU GOD.

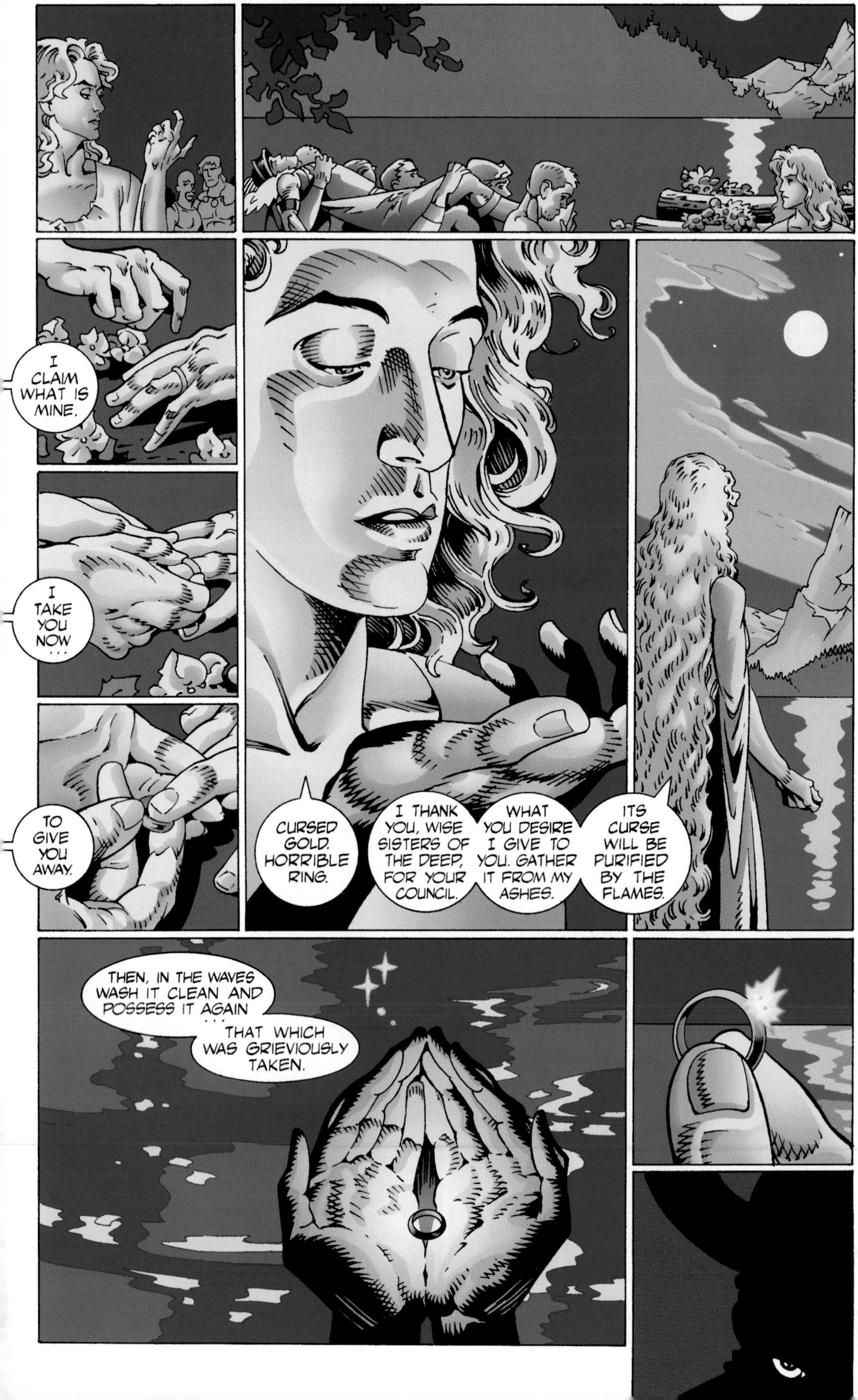

I CLAIM WHAT IS MINE.
I TAKE YOU NOW . . .
TO GIVE YOU AWAY.
CURSED GOLD. HORRIBLE RING.
I THANK YOU, WISE SISTERS OF THE DEEP, FOR YOUR COUNCIL.
WHAT YOU DESIRE I GIVE TO YOU. GATHER IT FROM MY ASHES.
ITS CURSE WILL BE PURIFIED BY THE FLAMES.
THEN, IN THE WAVES WASH IT CLEAN AND POSSESS IT AGAIN . . .
THAT WHICH WAS GRIEVIOUSLY TAKEN.

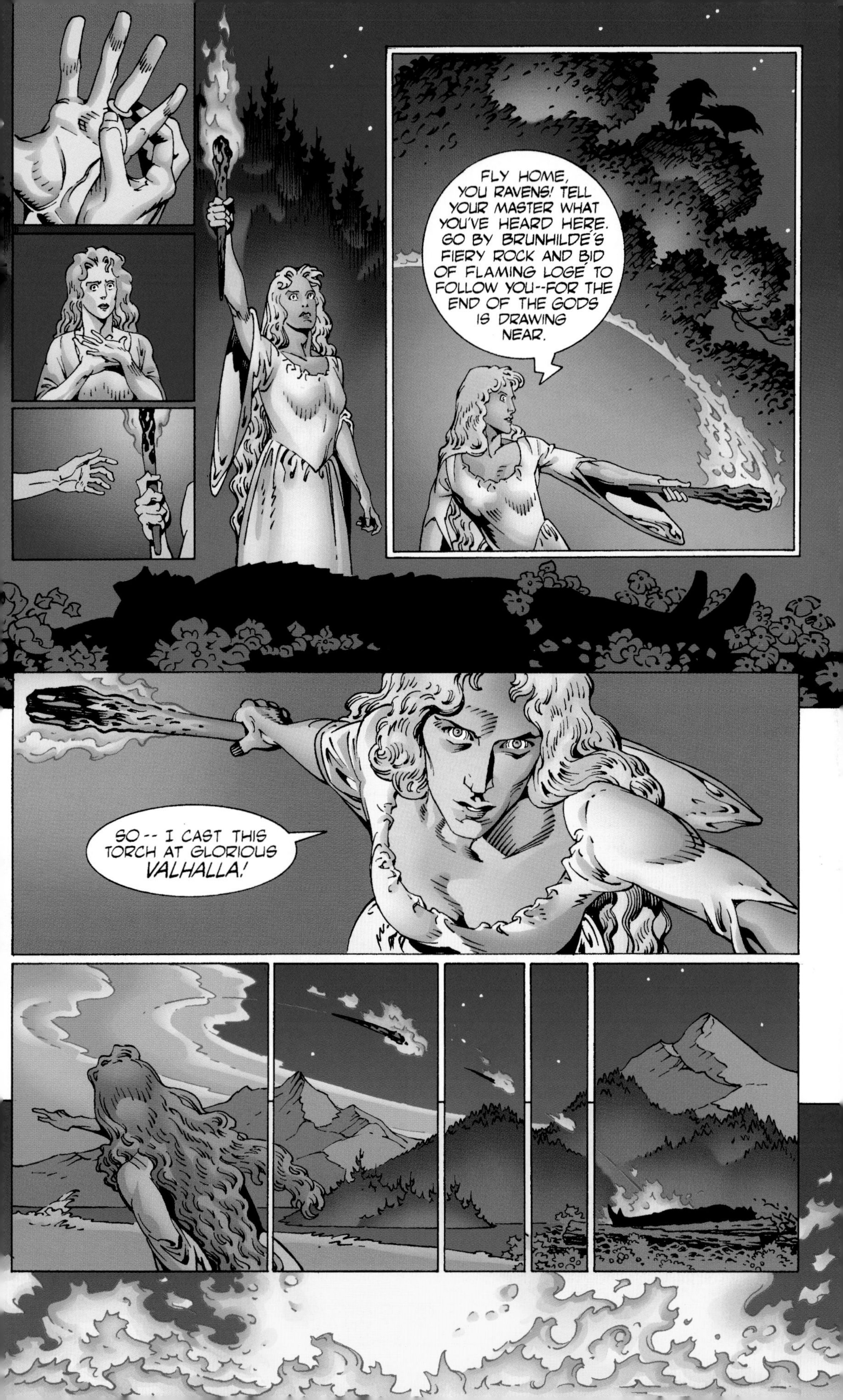
FLY HOME, YOU RAVENS! TELL YOUR MASTER WHAT YOU'VE HEARD HERE. GO BY BRUNHILDE'S FIERY ROCK AND BID OF FLAMING LOGE TO FOLLOW YOU--FOR THE END OF THE GODS IS DRAWING NEAR.
SO -- I CAST THIS TORCH AT GLORIOUS VALHALLA!

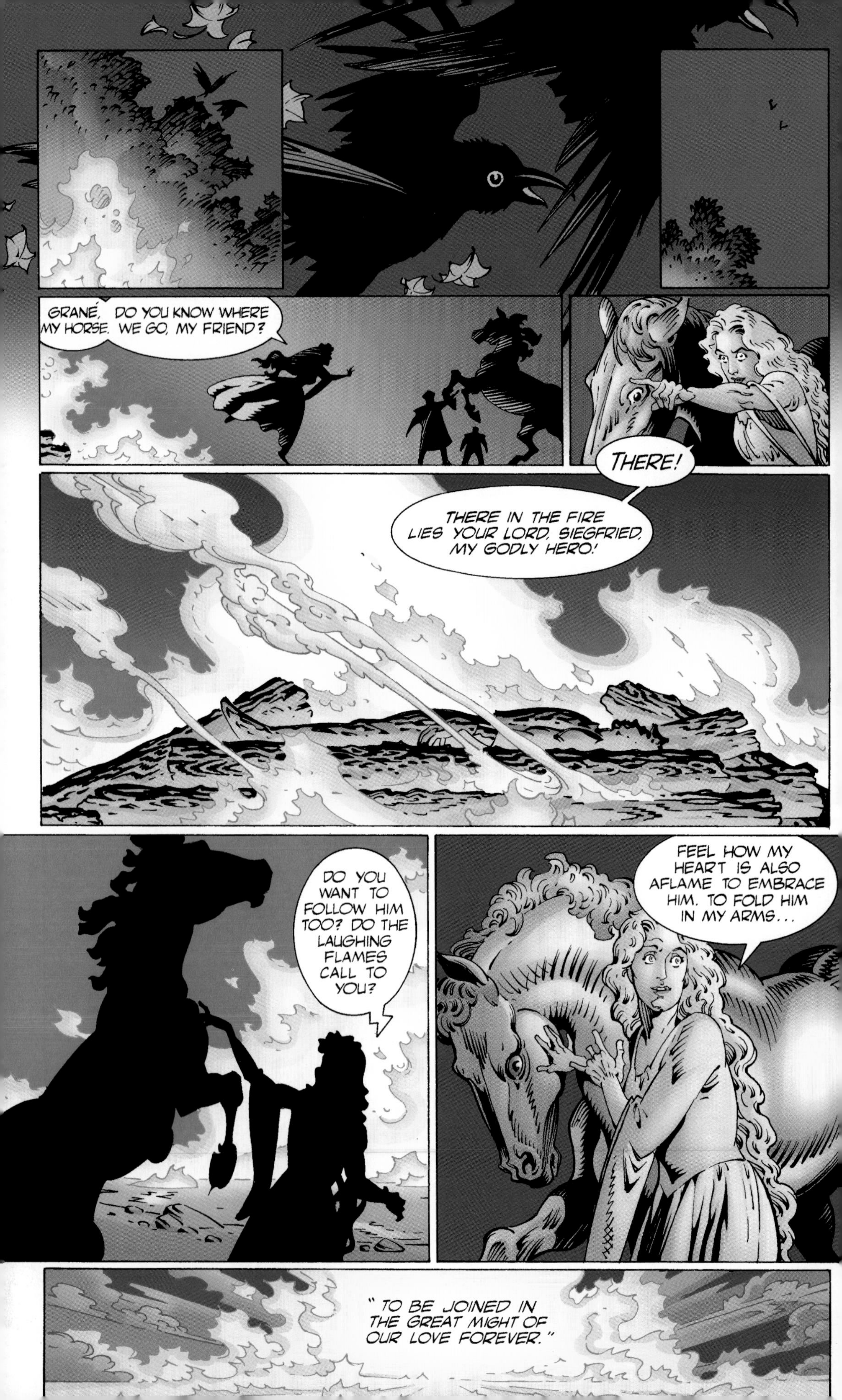
GRANE, MY HORSE. DO YOU KNOW WHERE WE GO, MY FRIEND?
THERE!
THERE IN THE FIRE LIES YOUR LORD, SIEGFRIED, MY GODLY HERO!
DO YOU WANT TO FOLLOW HIM TOO? DO THE LAUGHING FLAMES CALL TO YOU?
FEEL HOW MY HEART IS ALSO AFLAME TO EMBRACE HIM. TO FOLD HIM IN MY ARMS...
"TO BE JOINED IN THE GREAT MIGHT OF OUR LOVE FOREVER."

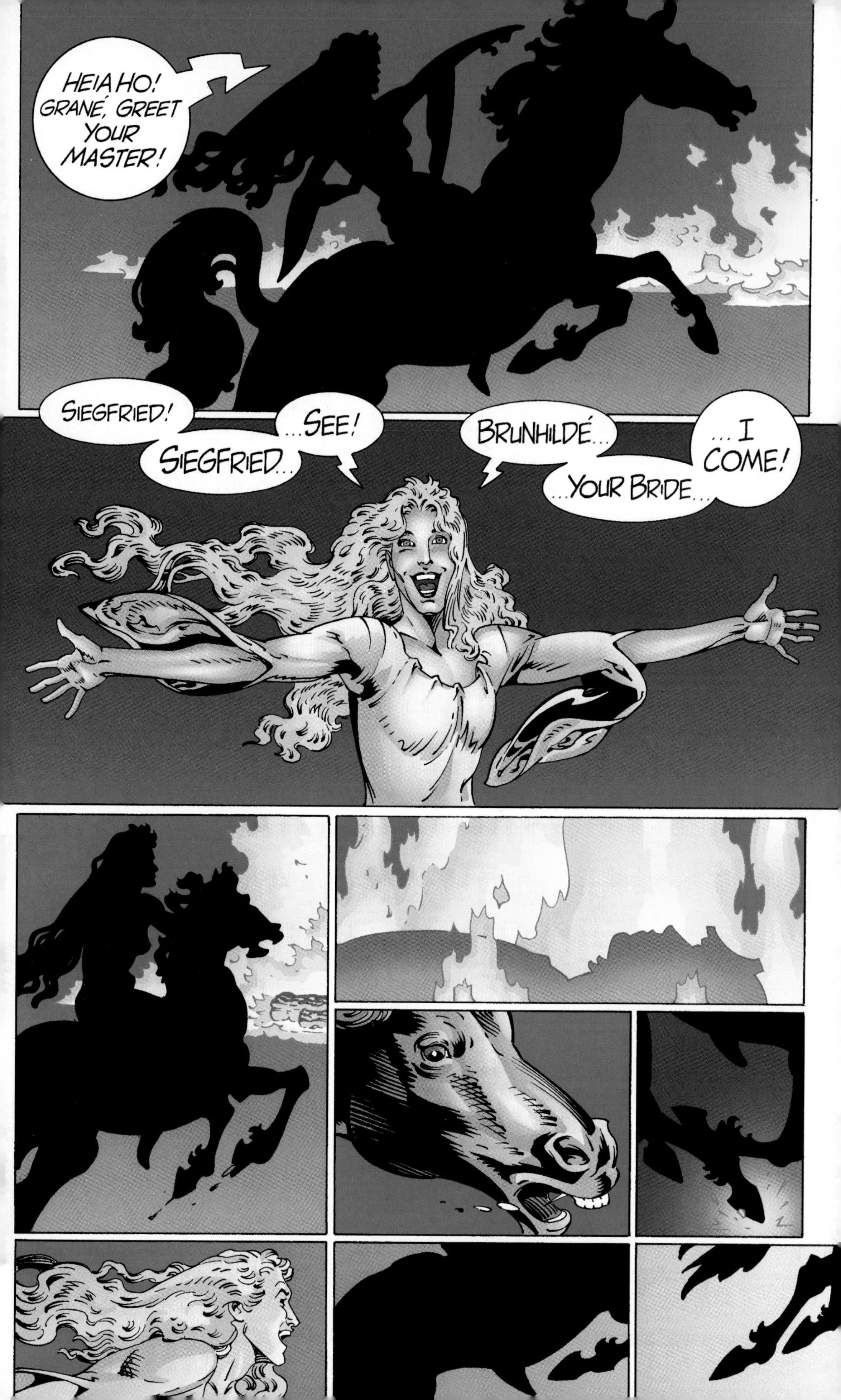

HEIA HO! GRANE, GREET YOUR MASTER!
SIEGFRIED!
SIEGFRIED...
...SEE!
BRUNHILDE...
...YOUR BRIDE...
...I COME!

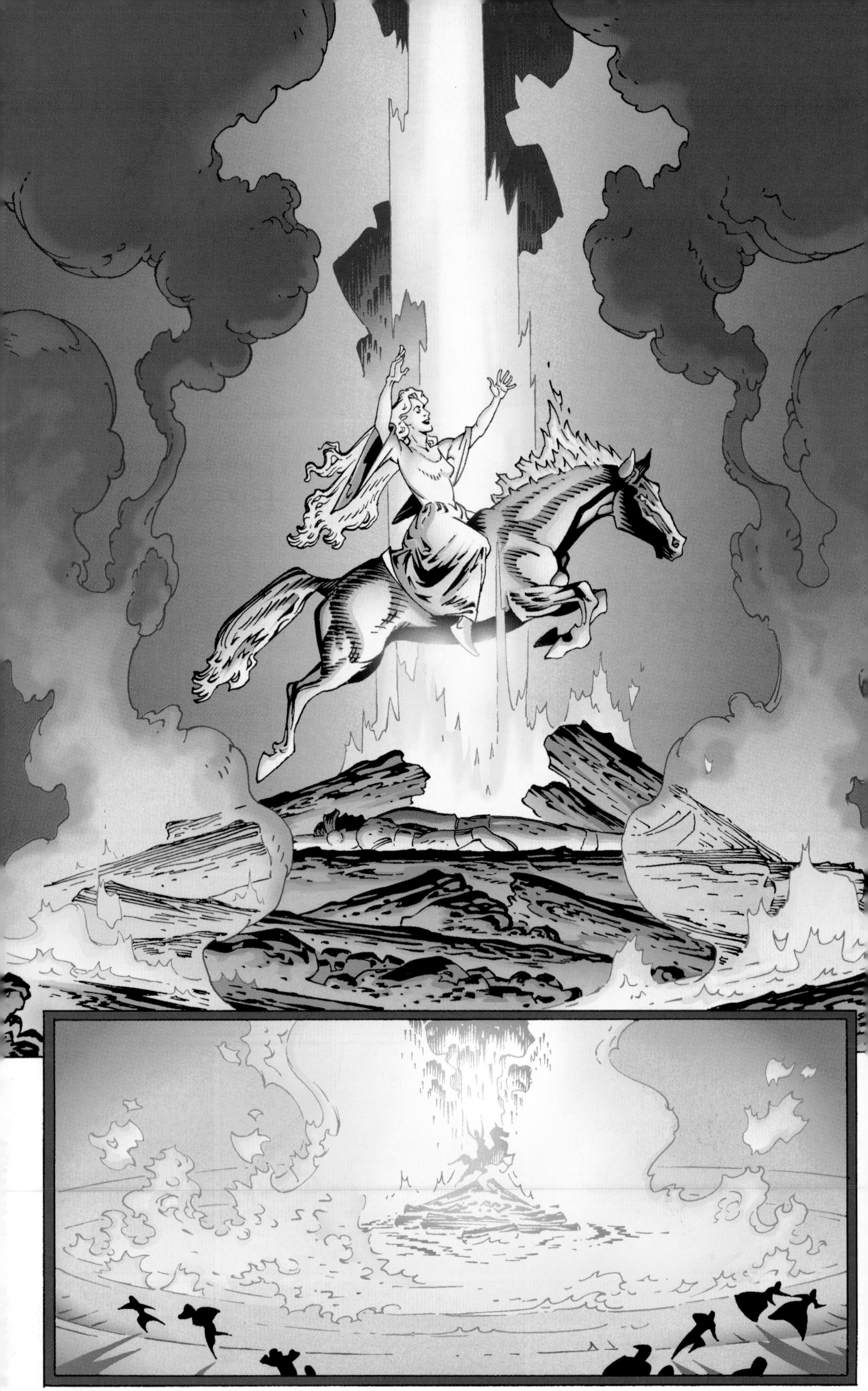

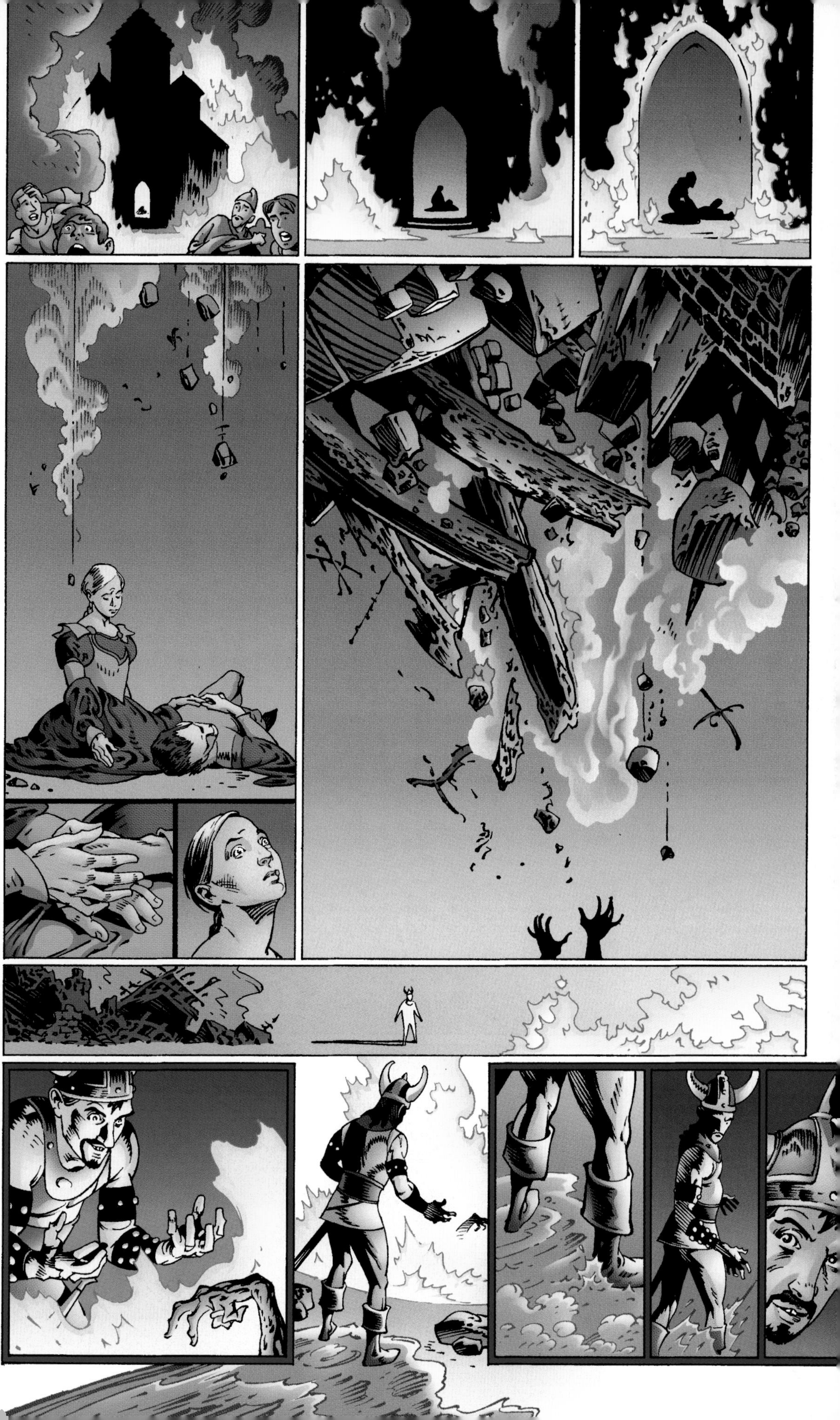

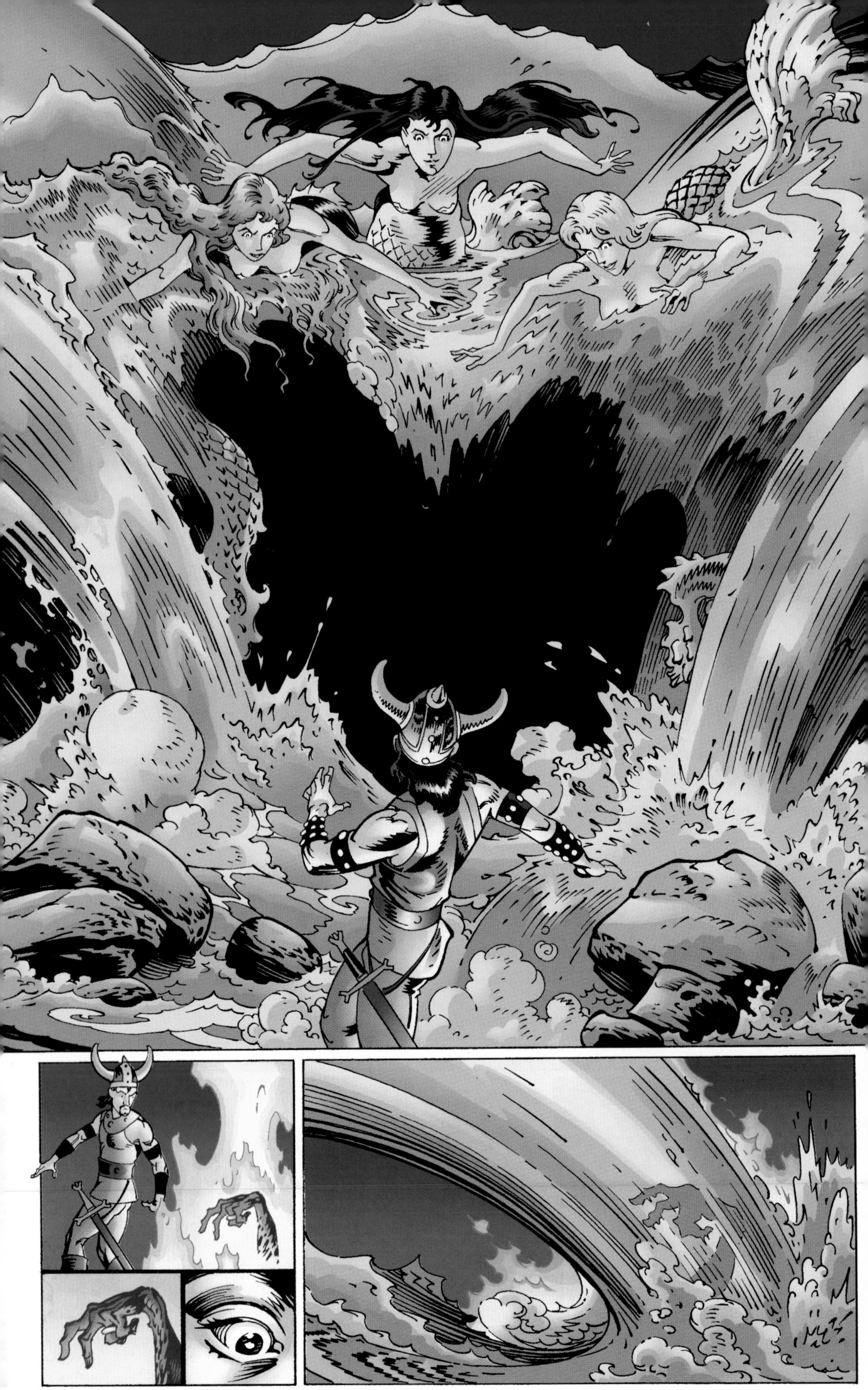

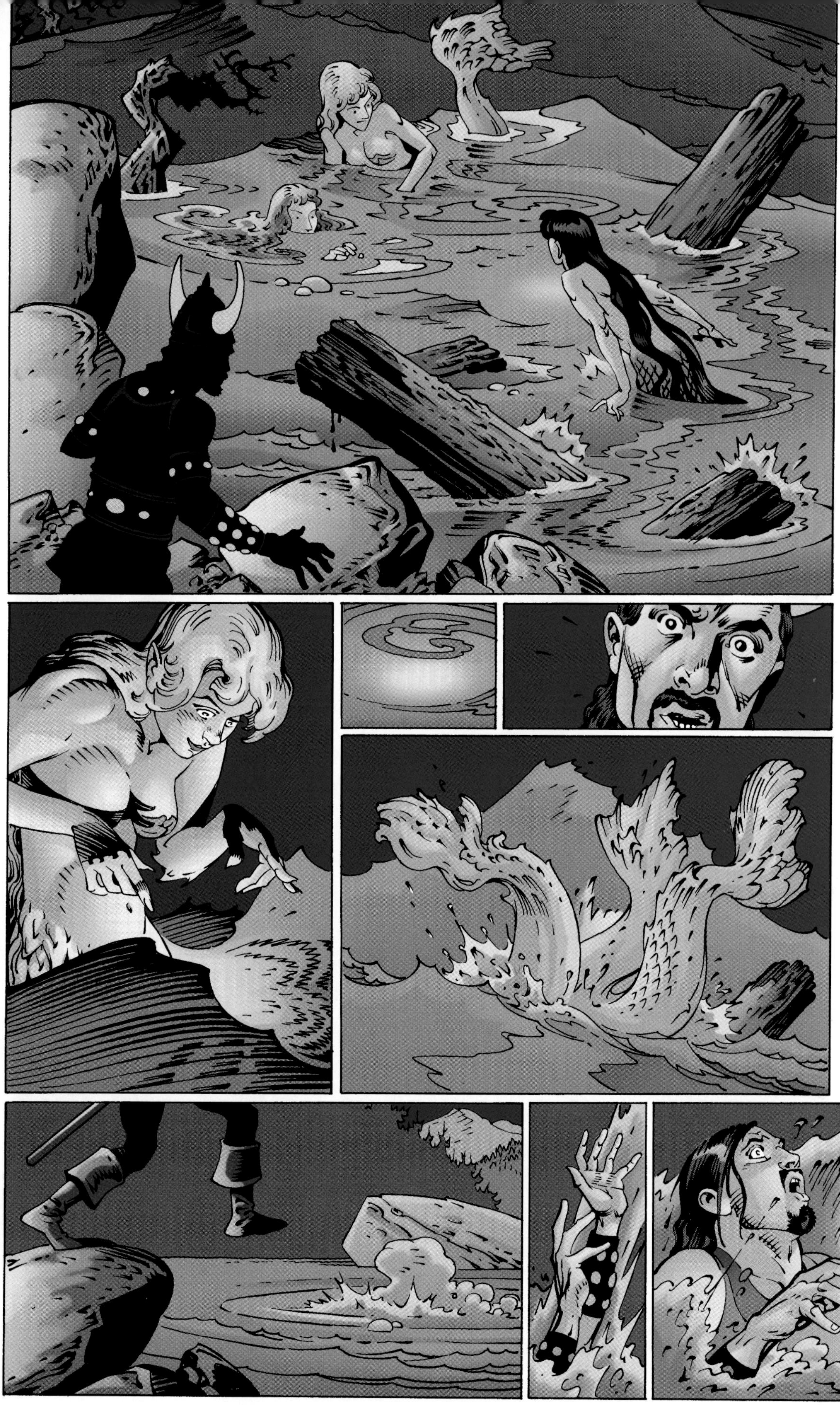

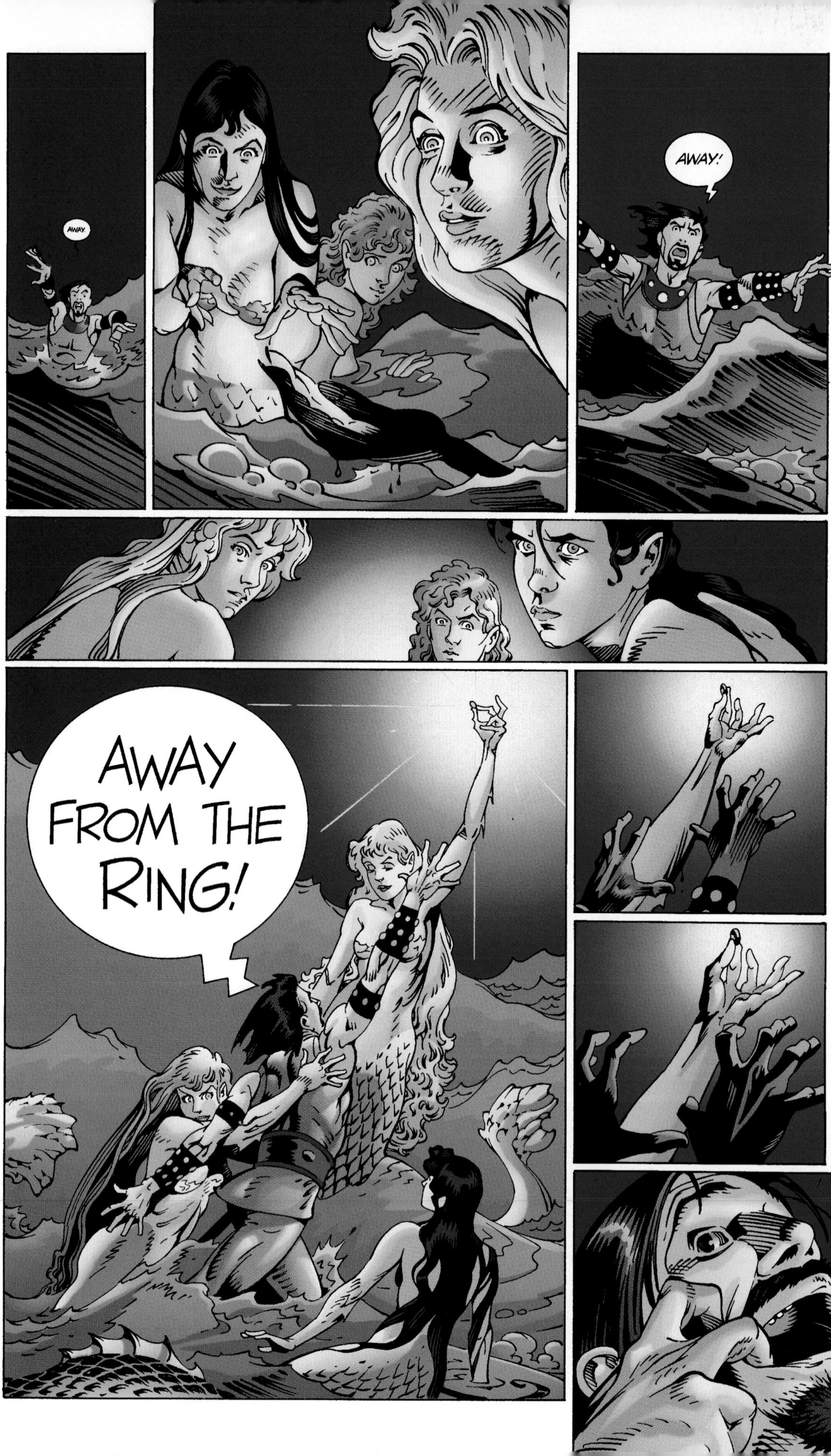
AWAY.
AWAY!
AWAY FROM THE RING!

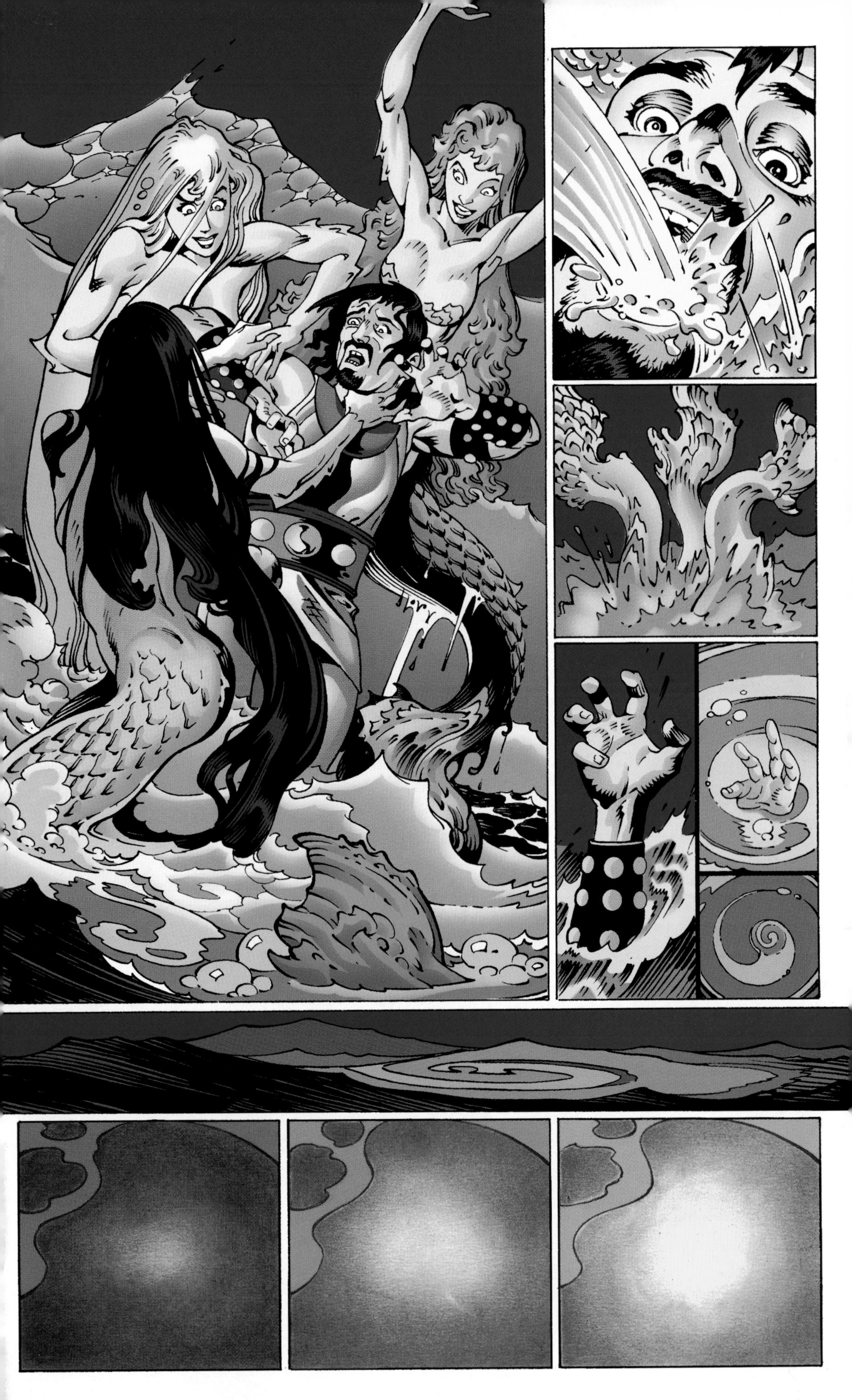

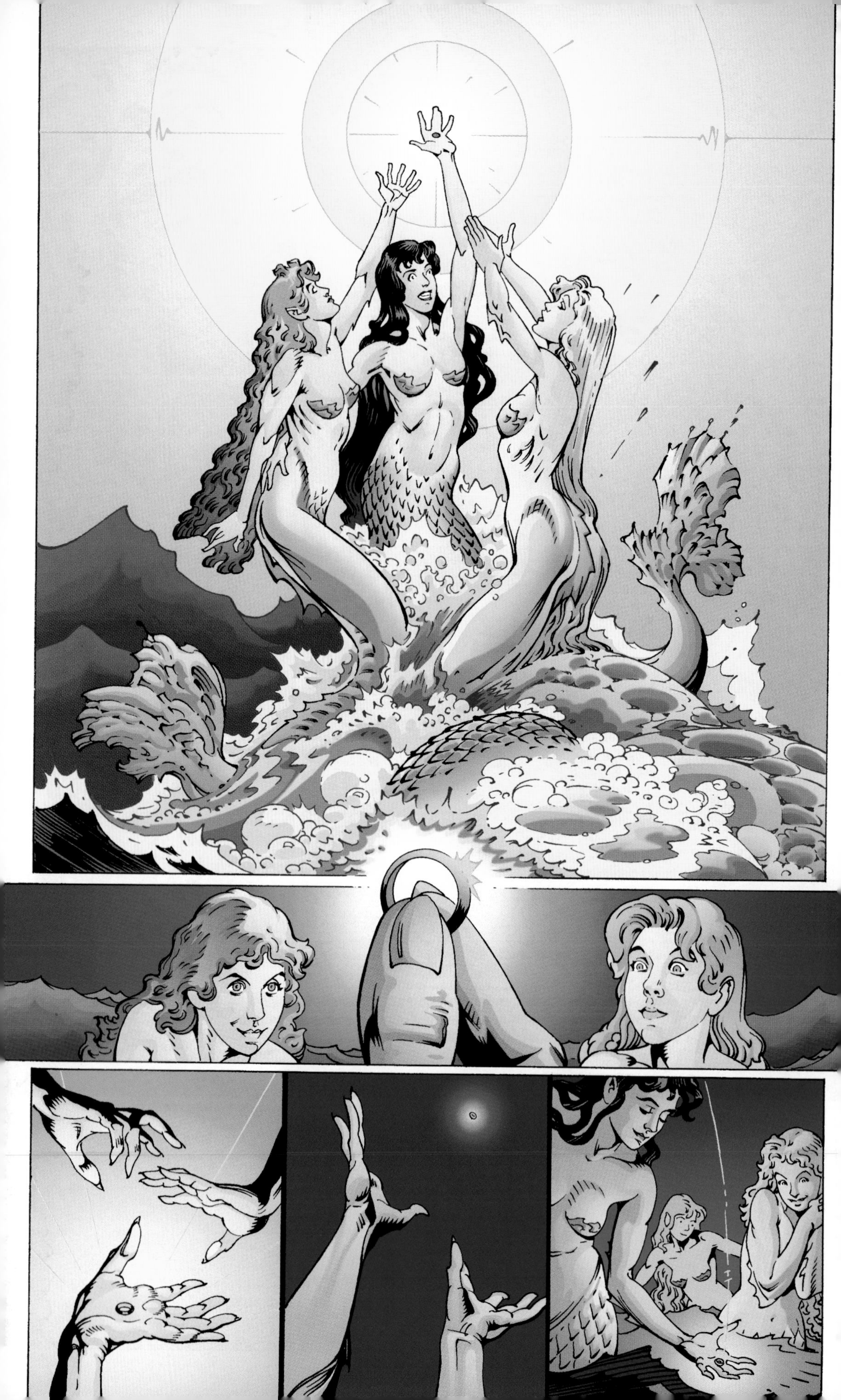

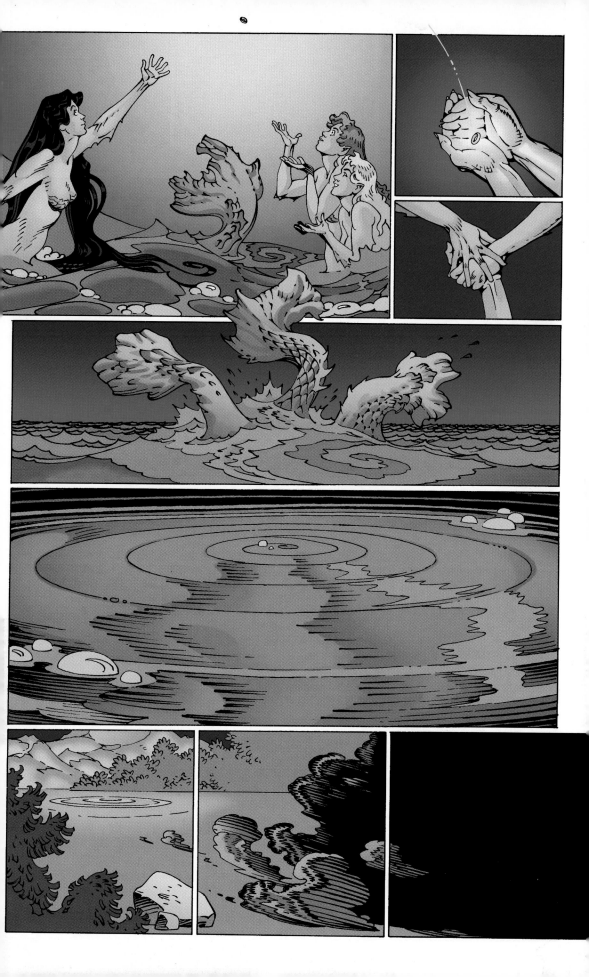

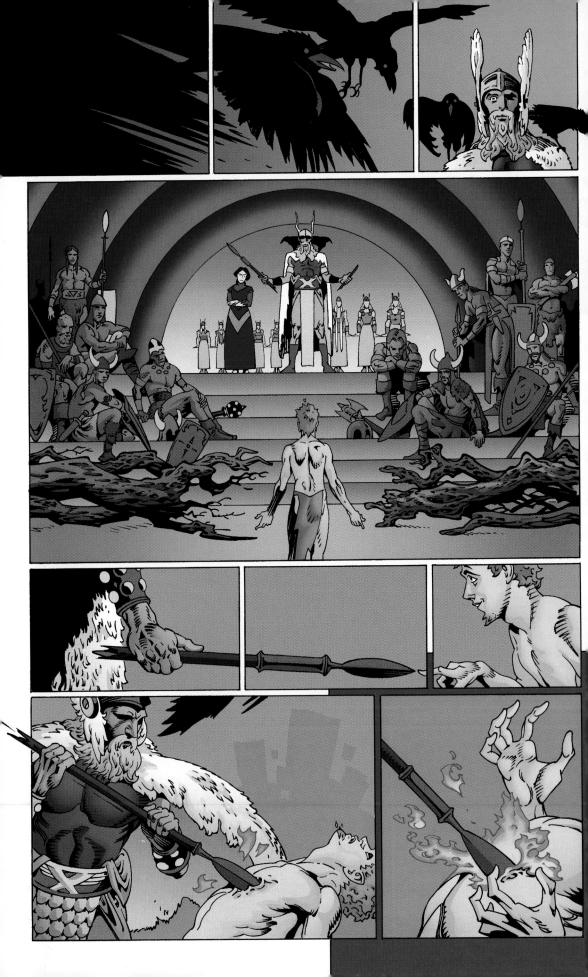

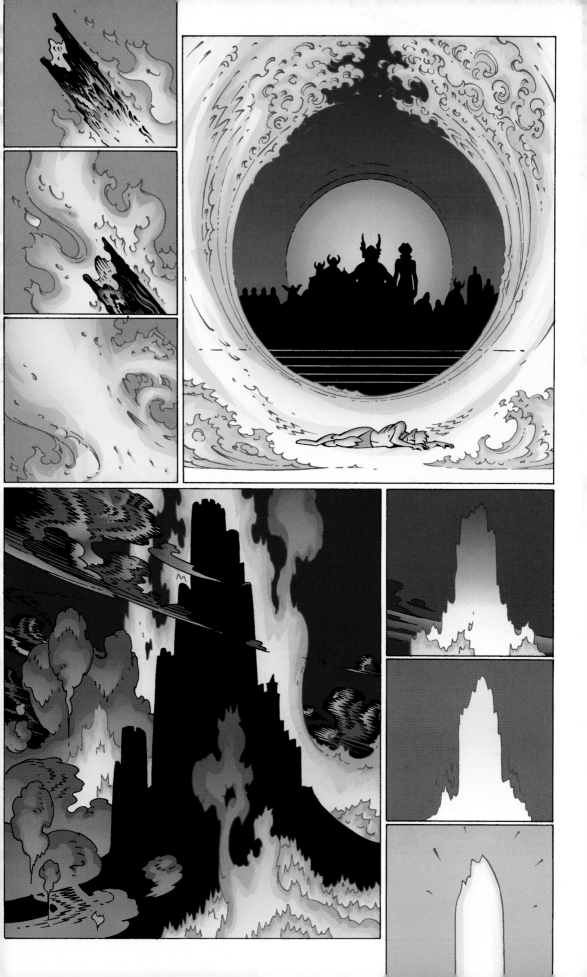

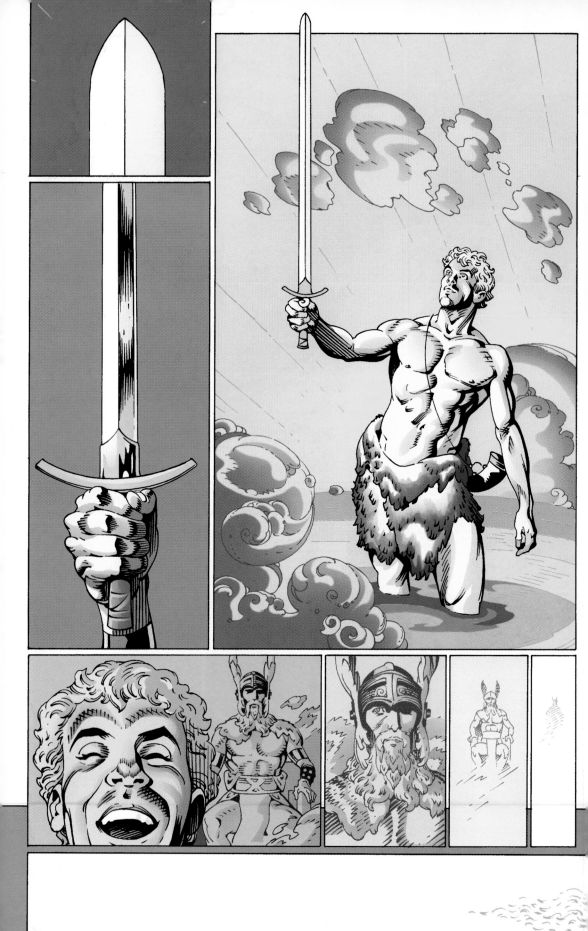

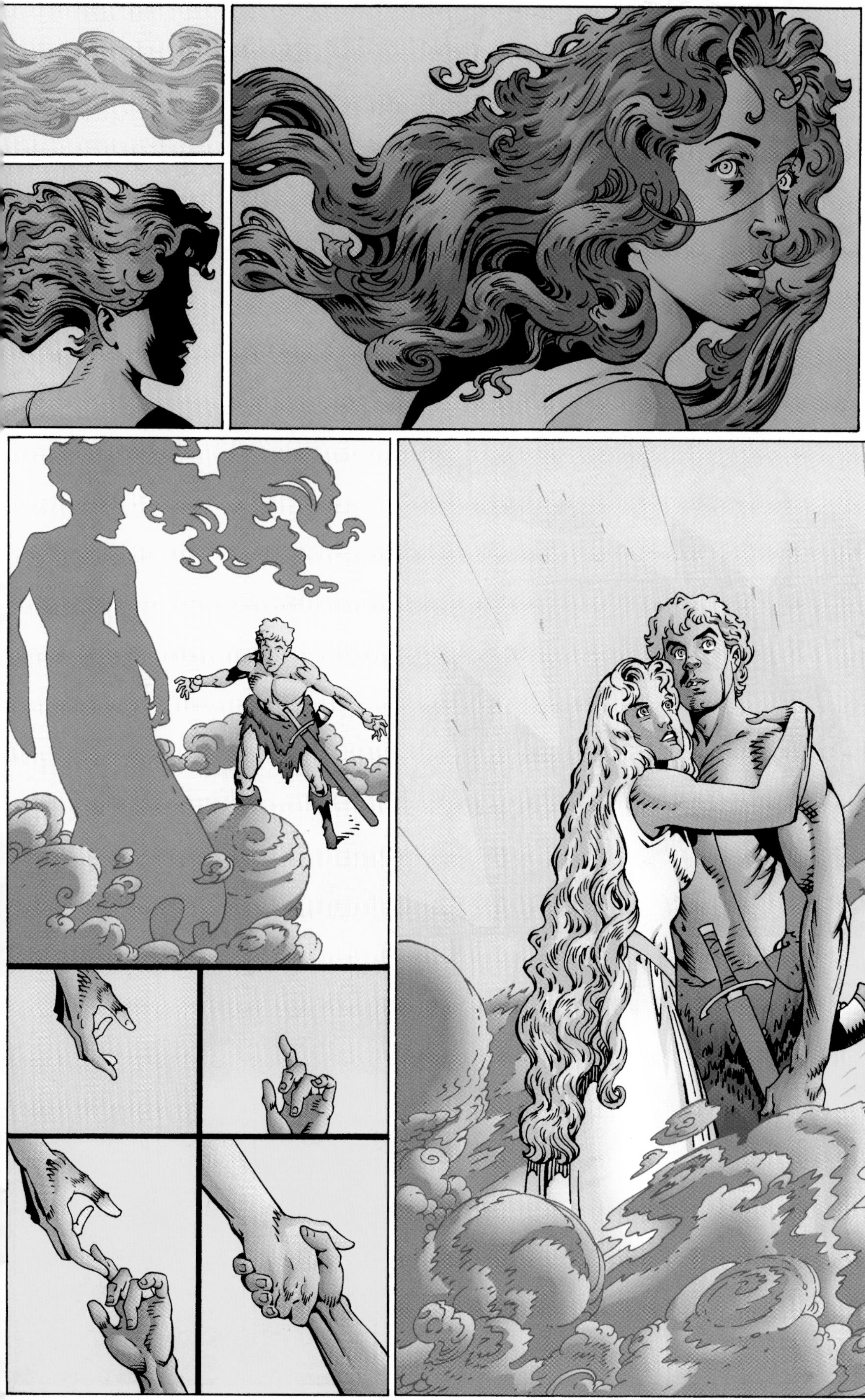

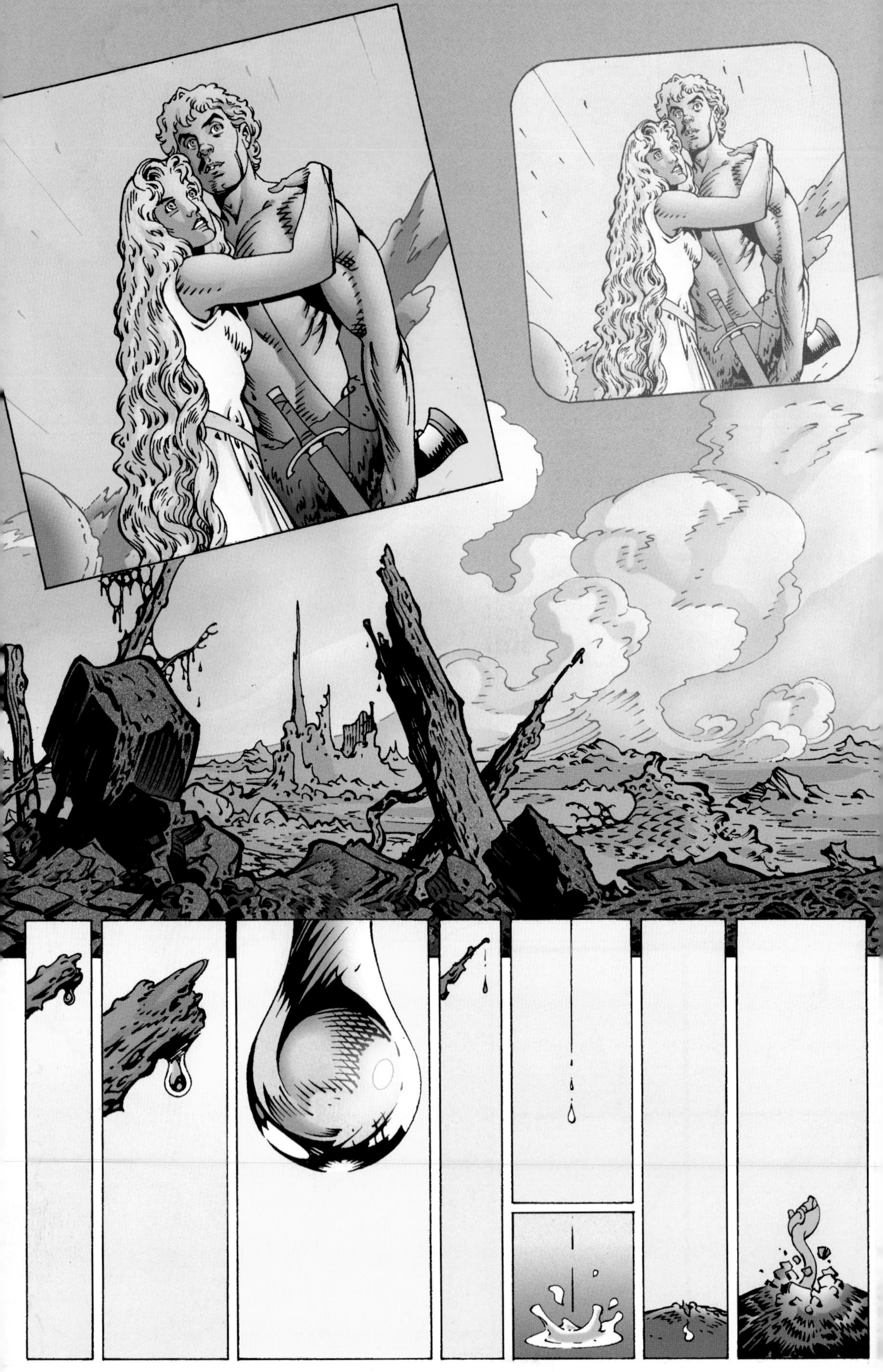

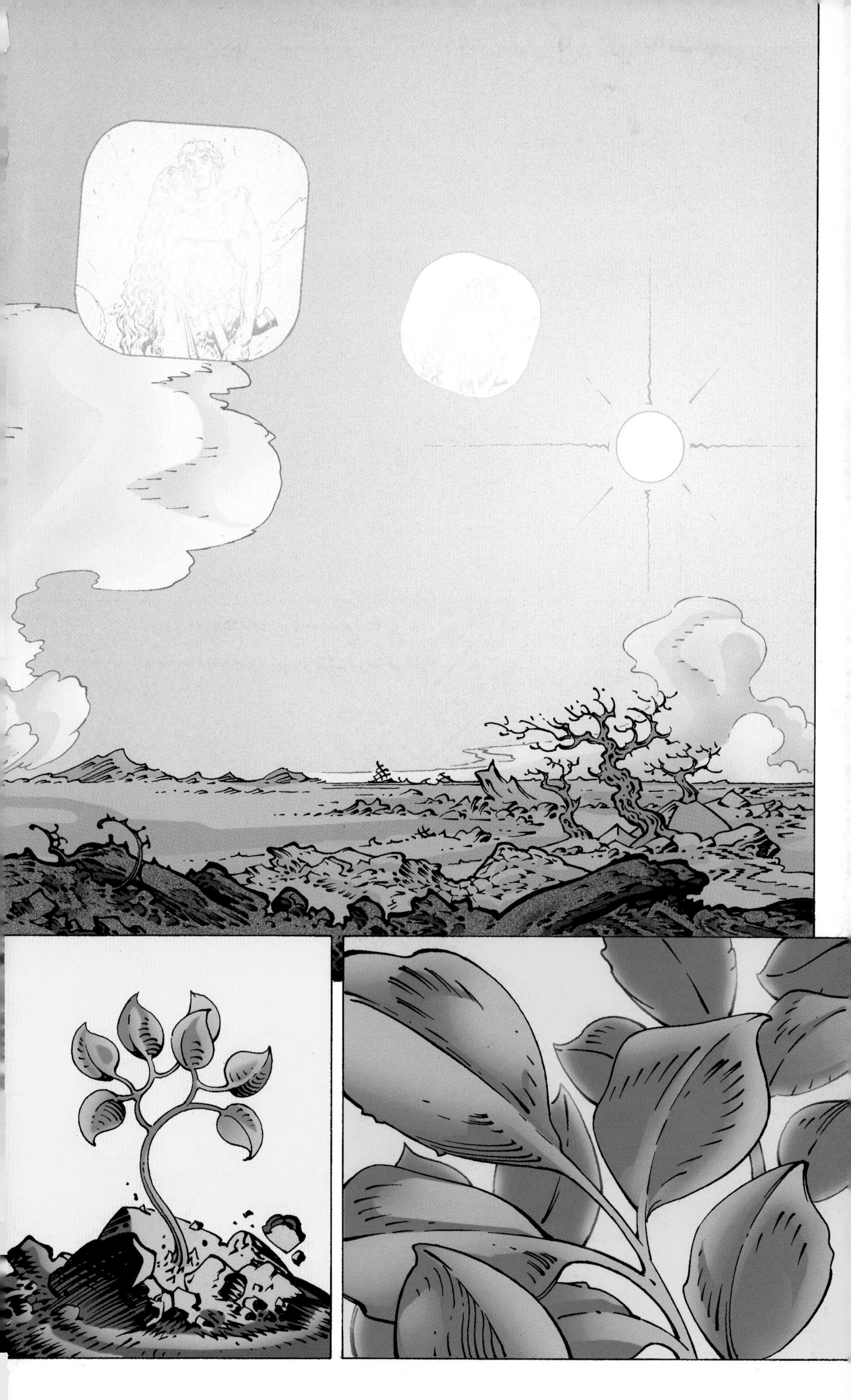

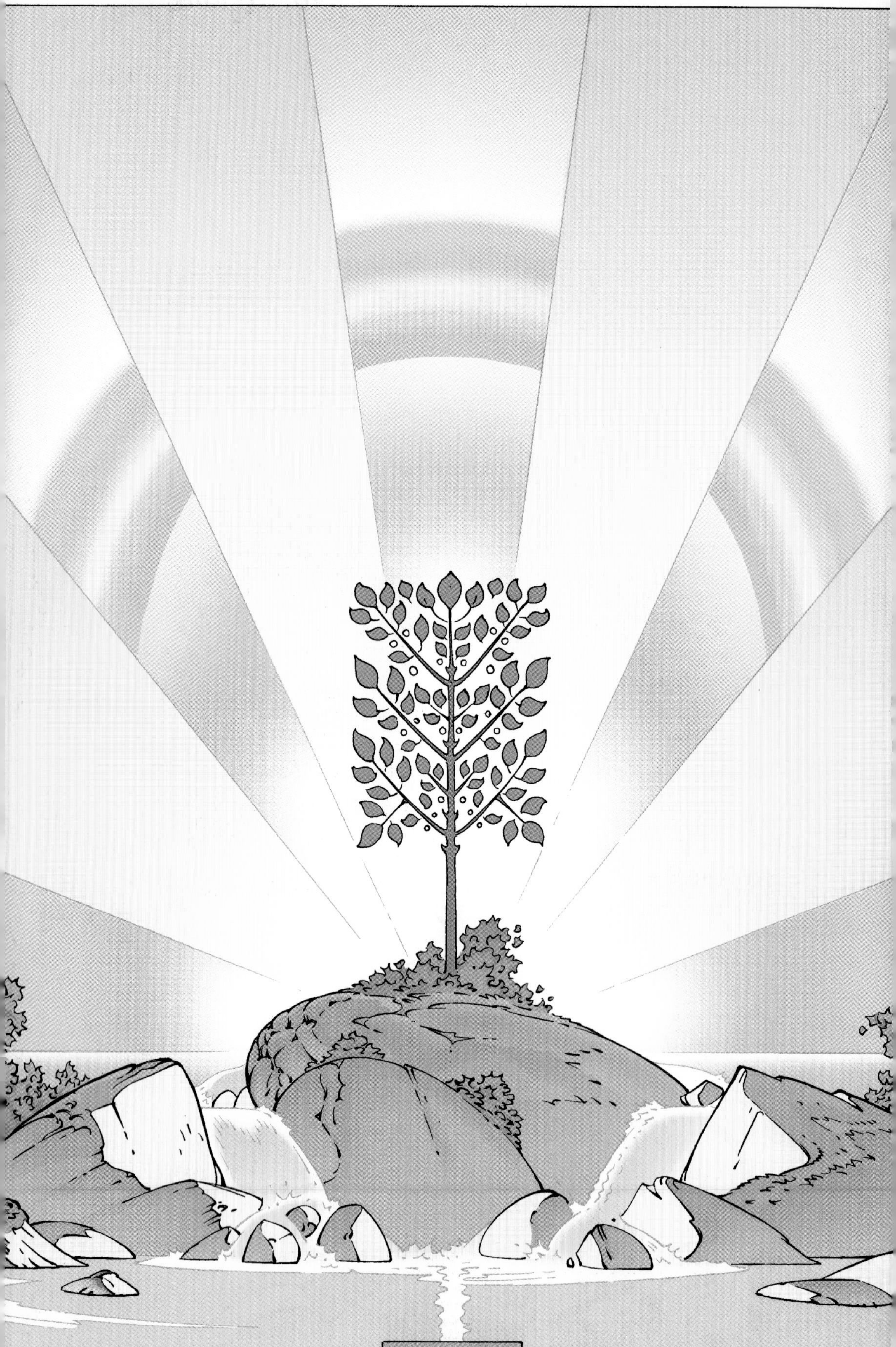
THE END